# Into the Mirror
The Untold Story of Mukhtar Mai

# Into the Mirror
## The Untold Story of Mukhtar Mai

**Bronwyn Curran**

 **UBSPD**®

UBS Publishers' Distributors Pvt. Ltd.

New Delhi • Bangalore • Kolkata • Chennai • Patna • Bhopal
Ernakulam • Mumbai • Lucknow • Pune • Hyderabad

UBS Publishers' Distributors Pvt. Ltd.

5 Ansari Road, New Delhi-110 002
Phones: 011-23273601-4, 23266646-47, 23274846, 23282281, 23273552
Fax: 23276593, 23274261• E-mail: ubspd@ubspd.com

10 First Main Road, Gandhi Nagar, Bangalore-560 009
Phones: 080-22253903, 22263901, 22263902, 22255153 • Fax: 22263904
E-mail: ubspd@bngm.ubspd.com, ubspdbng@airtelbroadband.in

8/1-B Chowringhee Lane, Kolkata-700 016
Phones: 033-22529473, 22521821, 22522910 • Fax: 22523027
E-mail: ubspdcal@cal.ubspd.com

60 Nelson Manickam Road, Aminjikarai, Chennai-600 029
Phones: 044-23746222, 23746351-2 • Fax: 23746287
E-mail: dbs@che.ubspd.com,ubspdche@che.ubspd.com

Ground Floor, Annapurna Complex, Naya Tola, Patna-800 004
Phones: 0612-2672856, 2673973, 2686170 • Fax: 2686169
E-mail: ubspdpat@pat.ubspd.com

Z-18, M.P. Nagar, Zone-I, Bhopal-462 011
Phones: 0755-4203183, 4203193, 2555228 • Fax: 2555285
E-mail: ubspdbhp@bhp.ubspd.com

No. 40/7940-41, Kollemparambil Chambers, Convent Road, Ernakulam-682 035
Phones: 0484-2353901, 2363905 • Fax: 2365511
E-mail: ubspdekm@ekm.ubspd.com

2nd Floor, Apeejay Chambers, 5 Wallace Street, Fort, Mumbai-400 001
Phones: 022-66376922, 66376923, 66102067, 66102069
Fax: 66376921 • E-mail: ubspdmum@mum.ubspd.com

9, Ashok Nagar, Near Pratibha Press, Gautam Buddha Marg, Latouche Road,
Lucknow-226 018 • Phones: 4025124, 4025134, 4025144, 6531753
Fax 4025144 • Email: ubspdlko@lko.ubspd.com

680 Budhwar Peth, 2nd floor, Near Appa Balwant Chowk, Pune-411 002
Phone: 020-24461653 • Fax: 020-24433976 • E-mail: ubspdpune@pun.ubspd.com

NVK Towers, 2nd floor, 3-6-272/B, Himayat Nagar, Hyderabad-500 029
Phones: 040-23262572, 23262573, 23262574
Fax: 040-23262572 • E-mail: ubspdhyd@hyd.ubspd.com

Visit us at www.ubspd.com & www.gobookshopping.com

© Bronwyn Curran

First Published 2008

Bronwyn Curran asserts the moral right to be identified as the author of this work.

Cover photograph by Kate Brooks

Printed at: Rajkamal Electric Press, New Delhi

'What is it I do?' you ask of me
I'll tell you how I toil my days:
I sell mirrors in the city of the blind

— Urdu couplet, on the back of a truck on the
Karakoram Highway

# Acknowledgements

Special thanks to Abdul Sattar Qamar, for plucky research and tireless guidance; to Noor, for her patient translation and endurance of many long journeys to Mirwala; to Iffat Idris for research on *jirga* and *panchayat* systems; to the expert lawyers on both sides of the case, for opening up their files to me; and to the Tatla-Gujjar and Mastoi families of Mirwala, for sharing their stories and hospitality.

# Foreword

As I write, the independence of our country's judiciary is at stake. For Pakistan to move forward and uphold the visions of its founders of a fair and just land for all, the independence of our courts must be fought for.

What follows in Bronwyn Curran's book is an exploration of a bid for justice.

There is more to the Mukhtar Mai case than what has been made public.

I founded my party *Tehreek-e-Insaf* (Movement for Justice) in 1996 to fight for rule of law and human rights through an independent judicial system. Rule of law means human rights; it means everyone equal before the law. Today in the 11th year of our party, finally it has hit everyone in Pakistan that the absence of rule of law is the biggest problem in our country.

When the Chief Justice of the Supreme Court can be shoved into a car by a policeman holding his hair, then that means no one has rights. If the Chief Justice's rights cannot be defended by the state, then no one's rights can be. Mukhtar Mai's case, as with all women's issues in Pakistan, should be looked at from that context.

The Mukhtar Mai case, for me, is a classic case where some innocent people may be implicated. Not for the sake of justice, but for the sake of what is now considered politically correct among the ruling elite of Pakistan, in order to get acceptability in the Western media and from Western governments.

It is also a sad reflection of Pakistani society. Because the rule of law has degenerated and because we do not have justice, we have a classic situation where the NGOs and the media have picked up a case and because it has fitted into a stereotype it has then been catapulted into the international press, where now we find that justice is being distorted in order to please the Western media and Western governments. It is also a classic case of an illegitimate ruler who, in order to get legitimacy, is bending over backwards to portray himself as a so-called "enlightened moderate", as a liberal, as someone who's a bulwark against fundamentalism and extremism and who's trying to reform the society.

But in fact the whole reform process is superficial. It is skin-deep, phoney Westernisation. It is no different to the Westernisation of Kamal Ataturk of Turkey and Raza Shah Pehlavi's father, the Shah of Iran, who in 1935 brought in superficial Westernisation where basically just the appearances were Western. But actually all the reasons why the West left the rest of the world behind, particularly the Muslim world, were not addressed. The reason why the Western countries went ahead of the Muslim world were because a) the Western countries had democracy; and b) they had rule of law, which meant that everyone was equal in front of the law, compared to the third world — especially the Muslim societies, where the kings, the rulers were above the law. The Western societies also went ahead because of their quest for knowledge, freedom of expression, and human rights - better human rights systems. However instead of addressing these issues, General Musharraf has followed Raza Shah Pehlavi and his father Raza Shah, who went for superficial Westernisation. They only aped the superficial aspects but never concentrated on the real reason why the West moved ahead. Instead what all of them did was destroy democracy in their countries, they did not allow democracy to flourish; they destroyed the rule of law by putting themselves above the law; they did not allow human rights to flourish; they did not allow freedom of expression.

Specifically in Pakistan, the money that should be going towards education has been diverted towards defence, non-productive areas, the lavish lifestyle of the ruling elite. Rather than spending money on human development, money is being spent on the ruling elite. Economic policies also are made to benefit the ruling elite.

When we look specifically at what Pakistan's rulers have done for women's development (now this is really the case where Muslim societies get criticized): rather than helping to empower women through rule of law and human rights, they have introduced superficial changes only.

Rule of law is the best way to empower women because the women who are affected in Pakistan are women at the bottom of the social tier. Since the men have no rights, neither the women have any rights, and the only way you can get women's rights is by actually bringing in the rule of law, by protecting the weak from the powerful.

There's an assumption among some NGOs that somehow women's rights can be protected when human beings in general don't have rights. How can only women's rights be protected? Are women an island in this country? Is it possible that a man, a woman's brother, her father, her husband, has no rights but she has rights? How can women be an island in a sea where there are no rights for anyone?

It is rule of law and human rights which should be fought for. Unfortunately certain NGOs have diverted the discourse as if it's only a women's problem, whereas it is in fact a rights problem and a problem of justice and rule of law.

Therefore this window-dressing, where suddenly President Musharraf is trying to appear as if he's some enlightened guy, is only for Western ears. It's only succumbing to pressure from some NGOs who are distorting the discourse in Pakistan for their own agendas and benefit. The discourse should actually be about rights for everyone.

The next most important thing for the empowerment of women is education. I can tell you that in my own constituency of Mianwali I have seen the state of female education. It is truly awful. I approached three federal ministers, telling them about the state of women's education in that part of the country, pointing out that you can't find gynaecologists there, you can't find women teachers, because women have no education there. Hardly any girls' schools are functional, there's no higher education for girls, so how do the authorities expect to empower women by superficial things, like this whole Mukhtar Mai case, or for instance much worse by having these dummy women sit in the National Assembly in reserved seats – unelected women representing no one, except that they happen to be either related to someone, or they are influential enough to have got a ticket. But they do not represent the women of Pakistan because they have not fought elections. They haven't even fought elections within the party. So to say that the President has empowered women through these reserved parliamentary seats for women is again a travesty for women in this country, because those women in parliament do not represent the women in this country. It is another superficial move to please the West.

The three things that, in my opinion, are most important are number one: the rule of law; number two: education and number three: enforcing inheritance laws in Pakistan. Even in the cities women are very poor, but in the rural areas of Pakistan women don't get their property rights, and women are just disempowered by not getting their rights to property. Related to that is the fact that divorced women have no rights at all here. They can't get any property rights, or get their allowances from their husbands, which is another travesty. A husband can go off with another woman and the ex-wife is just left to go back to her parents' place. She is not given her rights. These are the things which really need to be concentrated on if the government is genuine in empowering women.

Instead, here is a classic case in which, under pressure from the press, the government has succumbed and has actually been indulging an injustice in order to please the Western media. It shows the vulnerability the government feels by actually succumbing to this pressure and allowing this injustice to happen.

A case that has spotlighted as much world attention on Pakistan as the so-called "War on Terror" has warrants more scrutiny than it has been given. "Into The Mirror" poses sensitive questions, and dares to delve into both sides of this now-iconic case.

For the first time, Mukhtar Mai's experience in June 2002 is placed into context, with an examination of the surrounding tribal customs and histories, the societal dynamics of her village, and the practice of using women to resolve feuds. This book shows that whatever happened stems not from Islam, but from corruptions of old tribal ways.

Of equal importance, this book exposes for the first time the closed-door trial of the four men accused of gang-rape and the 10 men accused of aiding and abetting. What went on behind the doors of a remote courthouse hearing the trial in August 2002 has never before been made public.

We should be looking under the surface at how much justice has been exercised in the pursuit of justice. Our country's judicial system cannot be taken for granted.

We should also remember that violence against women in Pakistan takes not only the form of rape. It happens countless times each week in the practice of *vani* and *swara*, when families give away their daughters to resolve feuds. The government must fully eliminate the practice of families giving away daughters to settle scores or win land. Our women are not commodities.

Bronwyn Curran's book leaves no doubt that Mukhtar Mai, like too many poor rural women on the subcontinent, was a victim. The questions we should be asking ourselves are: of what precisely was she a victim, and has anyone else become victim along the way?

**Imran Khan**
Member of National Assembly
President, Tehrek-e-Insaf Party
Islamabad, April 2007

# Introduction

There is a theory that the difference between Pakistan and India is primeval, shaped by the cultures that sprang up around the subcontinent's two legendary rivers, the Indus and the Ganges.

The story that follows is from the Indus, from the cotton-growing clans who inhabit the middle reaches of the Indus' left bank as it pounds from the Tibetan plateau to the Arabian Sea. It's a story of the "riverian" people, as a local colleague calls them, living under feudal systems that keep some men in economic bondage, some men in positions of local power and women as pawns.

The Indus has cradled civilizations on present-day Pakistani soil since at least 3,000 B.C. The pre-historic Indus city of Mohenjodaro, with its sister-city Harappa on the nearby Ravi River, traded with ancient Persia, Mesopotamia and Egypt. This tale is set a few hours' drive from the ruins of these bronze-age communities.

When Alexander of Macedonia reached the subcontinent and took control in 327 BC, the first traces of Indus-fed communities were already three millennia old.

Crossing the upper Indus he came across the thriving city of Taxila, a flourishing centre of trade and learning, near present-day Islamabad. It lay hundreds of kilometres north of the remains of Mohenjodaro. Taxila, then, was ruled from present-day Iran under the Aryan Achaemenid Empire.

After a battle further east with a local king named Poros and his elephant cavalry, Alexander led his weary men south to the Arabian Sea shores on their way back to Persia. Along the way he strayed near Multan in present-day southern Punjab. It was near Multan that he was hit by an arrow, suffering a wound that some historians blame for ending his life back in Babylon.

Before and after Alexander led his legions eastwards and wove them around the Indus at the end of the 4$^{th}$ century BC, countless tribes migrated from Central Asia and the Middle East to settle on the subcontinent's fertile river plains.

Among them were the Baloch. Some stopped before the Indus; some only crossed to the river's eastern banks in the last 500 years, encountering other tribes long settled on the left bank, like the Gujjars - herders of water buffalo.

Tribal traditions and tongues blended, dissolved and evolved with each migration, until the wandering clans developed their own area-distinct variations on codes of honour, punishment and pardon.

In Pakistan's dark and treacherously beautiful south, some of these tribes are still wandering, expelled and exiled by tyrannical and revered tribal chiefs.

The story that follows took place between Baloch and Gujjar sub-clans, whose ancestors were rivals for land shrinking in the face of new tribes crossing the Indus and other tribes returning from victorious Mughal battles over Delhi, ready for grants of land as their rewards. The tracts of arable land cease dramatically less than 100 kilometers from the Indus River, meeting without warning the edges of the Cholistan and Rajasthan deserts.

The following story erupted from corrupted codes of honour and retribution, from a place where marriage is a rite of compensation and not love; where 'brides' are commodities for trade in land, cash and arbitrary concepts of honour; where punishment is determined by tribal elders; and rape (of men, women, young, old) is common.

Yet unseen from outside, there is another Pakistan: a land of decadent hospitality; of grace and graciousness, captured in the billowing folds of a gardener's smock and the easy sway of a wide-hipped ayah pushing a pram under a magnolia tree; of azure crystal light from lapis skies on startlingly glorious roses; of peregrines and falcons arcing over sunrise-misted forests cradled in a quiet valley; of pristine alpine meadows carpeted by edelweiss and evening primrose, echoing with shepherds' song and framed by phantomesque Himalayan and Karakoram peaks; of book-stacked parlours of erudite tribal chiefs, barristers, and journalists who call themselves "scribes"; and of night kite-flying from old-city rooftops, above the gaze of 1,001 smouldering eyes, to celebrate a pagan spring festival. A land where poetry is so popular it is recited on mountain treks, in village chats, on the rear-ends of trucks, in political sloganeering, in pop music; where balladeers may still be encountered on a pine forest trail, singing of the eroticism of a beloved's anklet; where wild boars and packs of jackals creep down from the hills and strut the capital's boulevardes on deep winter nights; where the river-fed soil is so fertile it produces carrots red as tomatoes, oranges so blood-red they're called "black", autumn leaves of deeper crimson than rubies, and mangoes of over 100 varieties – including the 'airport-*wallah*' so-named for growing near Multan's airport; where mountain step-eagles run like four-legged beasts to take off; where a labrynthine old city leads to a whispering wall inside a pink-stoned 16th century mosque; where thudding polo horses in winter sun pound a drunken-green field, canopied by banyan and willow trees; and where wild white roses mark a bend in a hill road. A land of time-warped rural villages where time is measured by prayer; of generous-boughed mango orchards and plentiful citrus plantations; of equestrian tent-pegging carnivals on estates of feudal lords; and of paradoxical chivalry, where women are frequently sidelined but rarely allowed to queue, for they are ushered to the front of any counter or line.

It is also the last domain of delicate applications of arcane English: where one does not die but *"expires"* or *"breathes one's last"*; *"peons"* serve tea and clean office toilets; politicians hold "telephonic conversations" and *"air-dash"* when their travel is urgent; the favoured superlative term is *"first-class"*; and *"her modesty was outraged"* is the preferred, gentler description of rape.

# Contents

# Atomic Summer

The white-embroidered goblin sitting before me shifts and jerks, twisting around to her oldest brother Punnu, a short man in prayer-cap and long white smock, then half-jumps back to face me. The muted mid-morning light slides off the cheap copper bangles caking her wrists, bouncing with each excited twist of her robed body.

She appears almost bridal.

Except that in this part of the world, brides wear red.

She is facing me, but I can't see her face. It, all of her, is shrouded in panels of stained white cotton, lace-edged and embroidered. She is swallowed in a dirty white burqa, with a tight-woven grill across the eyes. She looks like a goblin wearing a shuttlecock on top.

The burqa falls to just above her coppery sandled feet, chalky with dust. Frayed blue trousers hang short of her scratched ankles.

I can tell she is short, like her widowed mother who spat curses at me and the entire world's media, before letting me into the courtyard of her poverty-bitten home and weeping her story out.

Like her mother, the girl behind the shroud also seems feisty. That much comes through the cotton.

But right now my time with Salma Mastoi, in a quiet room off these alfresco barristers' 'chambers' opposite a set of hallowed British-era district courts in southern Pakistan tribal territory, is limited.

Officially I shouldn't be in Dera Ghazi Khan, a remote city of tribal chiefs and feudal lords in Pakistan's deep dark south, on the wild 'right bank' of the Indus River. Foreigners are forbidden because of the nearby uranium enrichment plant. The desert hills beyond the city are saturated with uranium. At the plant, the blue mineral is alchemised into nuclear fissure: the guts of the N-bomb.

In fact the Chaghai hills, from where Pakistan burst onto the world stage as the unwelcome first Muslim nuclear power by test-firing its nuclear bomb in 1998, shortly after rival India tested its own atomic cargo — are just a few hundred kilometres away.

"Salma, with your brother's permission, will you show me your face? I've waited so long to meet you."

This is the girl with whom it all began.

Salma's husband is in prison, on charges he has been acquitted of twice, by two separate courts. Her two other brothers are in prison, one of them on charges the High Court acquitted him of a year earlier. Only one is incarcerated on a guilty conviction.

The squat brother in white prayer cap sitting at a distance from us, nods. He walked out of prison two weeks ago, after three years inside for supposedly dragging a teenage boy into the sugarcane and, with two cousins, sodomising him.

"I will show you my face, only if you give me justice first!" Salma snaps.

My translator and I glance at each other.

Who can even pretend to make such a promise, in a land where justice is at best an accident?

\*    \*    \*    \*

It's a disquieting feeling for a reporter to revisit a big story after the dust has settled, when the frenzy has subsided, the deadlines aren't pressing and the competition has gone home... and to discover that so many things are not what they seemed.

To go back with the luxury of the time unafforded when the story was hot.

To sift through documents we never had the time or access to.

To discover another side, of the matter.

To be fair, most of us didn't have the time.

The summer of 2002 in Pakistan was an incendiary season.

## JULY 2002, ISLAMABAD

Nuclear holocaust threatened the subcontinent. The War on Terror rocked the frontier with Afghanistan. In Pakistan's cities, sympathisers of the Taliban and Al-Qaeda executed revenge massacres of Christians and Westerners.

Bunkered in the lush white-walled grounds of the colonial-era Army House, General Pervez Musharraf, the military dictator who had stolen power three years earlier, had prepared to hold elections for the first time since his bloodless coup.

I had just arrived in Islamabad as the new editor for the *Agence France Presse*, in charge of news coverage of Pakistan and Afghanistan for the next three years.

Prophecies of Armageddon erupting in the icy Himalayan heights of Kashmir ran high on the global airwaves. A million Pakistani and Indian troops had been eyeballing each other across their volatile frontier for over six months, poised to strike the holocaust tinderbox.

Diplomats whispered that a hit and run strike into Indian territory by Pakistan's proxy warriors could be the trigger for India to air-blitz a camp on the Pakistani side and set off the world's first post-Hiroshima nuclear attack.

My agency's evacuation plan was 'pack the car and drive to Kabul'. That did little to reassure me. I studied seasonal wind charts and saw that a nuclear cloud would beat us and the other 100 million-plus fleeing Pakistanis to the mountainous Afghan border. There was a deadly war going on at the border anyway.

I worked out my own personal 'red line'—the point at which one ejects. I planned to be disembarking from a military transport plane somewhere in the Middle East by the time my employers considered getting my team out of the shadow of the mushroom cloud.

At a twilight dinner in a friend's midsummer garden, colleagues debated which route to take through the Hindu Kush if we had to flee by road. Miniature lanterns winked from the trees, spices wafted over the lawn, wine spilt on elegant tribal rugs, the scalloped Margalla hills behind grew darker and more alluring, the stars shone deeper in the black-satin sky, while night-birdsong above the chatter and the purr of a homecoming Mercedes made the only sounds in the still, velvet night.

The serenity was irreconcilable with the invisible danger.

That was just the threat from the east.

Another war raged in the west. The War on Terror pounded, screeched, writhed, whined, roared, thudded and shuddered on the border with Afghanistan just 200 kilometres away.

Pakistan had emerged as the frontline of the post 9-11 battle between good Muslim and bad Muslim.

Warriors, skyborne and cave-bound, space-age against stone-age, played out the War on Terror beyond my news bureau's verdant lawn, beyond the trimmed gardens and bucolic hill-station life of Islamabad, tucked into the edge of the Lower Himalaya foothills.

For more than eight months American B-52s, A-10 Warthogs, Apache gunships, and Cobra attack helicopters had been raining down bombs weighing up to 500 pounds each on stone-age villages, raking mountain caves, playing cat and mouse with die-hard zealots in turbans.

The bearded guerrillas fought off hi-tech laser-guided missiles with Kalashnikovs, rockets, landmines, and dreams of martyrdom, killing American soldiers and any Afghan cooperating with them. They took cover in honeycomb-networks of caves and mud-walled fortresses.

The seeds of the cataclysmic 9-11 attacks in the USA had been sown a few hundred kilometres from Islamabad in the biblical-looking borderlands between Pakistan and Afghanistan two decades earlier; and had been germinating for years.

A later breed of Islamic militants, some of whom the CIA had spent billions of dollars arming and training via their Pakistani intelligence proxies to drive Soviet troops from Afghanistan in the 1980s, were turning their weapons on the hand that fed them.

In June 2002 US forces backed by a coalition of international supporters were still strafing Afghanistan's eastern frontier region, trying to drive out Islamic fighters as they kept reappearing.

On the ground, secret American Special Forces units hunted Osama bin Laden and his lieutenants, as the Al-Qaeda figurehead's shadow flickered from cave to mud-brick fortress to mountain crag.

An exodus of expatriate families emptied Islamabad, a sleepy sanguine capital of broad avenues lined with walled villas and startlingly gorgeous gardens, as I began my three-year posting.

The sun-baked city was eerie with abandonment. It burned with the white heat of high summer. Evening's twilight brushed the horizon with a film of faint green. The pre-monsoon oppressiveness, which pulverized the surrounding Potohar plain of the northern Punjab with its heaviness, was so thick one could curl one's hand around it.

The heat silenced what ever little noise remained – except for the relentless caws of South Asia's omnipresent crows.

As they kited slowly above Islamabad's gleaming white trophies of modern Islamic architecture – from the centrepiece Faisal Mosque, with sinister missile-like minarets rising from each corner to give it the look of an Islamic bomb launching pad, to the palatial neo-Mughal prime ministerial secretariat building. I occasionally wondered if this was a foretaste of the aftermath of a nuclear cloud.

Perhaps these crows, like cockroaches, would withstand an atomic blast, long enough to encircle what remained on the capital's scorched lawns.

The vicarious glee of one of my former editors, an excitable Frenchman with electrified silver hair who had brought me into *Agence France Presse* (AFP) two years earlier – at the prospect that I may have the privilege of covering the world's first nuclear conflict danced sickeningly at the back of my mind, taunting with the questions 'what am I doing here?'

I met him a week earlier, in the shiny lobby of a gleaming 24-floor office tower in central Jakarta, my previous posting. Bernarde Estrade, on a return visit to Indonesia from his new post at the United Nations in New York, embraced me with edgy excitement. "*Felicitations* on the Islamabad post! Now you 'ave the chance to report the world's first nuclear war. It will be a first in '*istory!*"

I tried to explain that the prospect of frontline reporting from an atomic war did not thrill me. And for the first time in my career, I was terrified.

The bloody rampage of Islamic militants through Pakistan that year was somehow less frightening. The chances of not being in the sights of a suicide bomber were comfortably large, compared to the chances of escaping tongues of atomic fire. At any rate, I had been a few blocks from fatal bomb attacks more than a few times.

On my first day with AFP in Jakarta, I was taking a phone-call in the garden of our Dutch-era villa-office when the ground warped and nearby tower blocks swayed. The boom followed. A tower of TNT smoke curled above the row of villas across the leafy road. The Philippine ambassador's car had been blown up, a few hundred metres away. He survived, but the old lady selling cigarettes on the kerbside didn't.

During the preceding months in Pakistan, enraged Islamic zealots had injected suicide bombers into a number of Western targets:

**MARCH.** Into a sun-bathed white church in Islamabad's guarded diplomatic quarter on a pristine spring morning, echoing with a chorus of diplomats' families drowsy from an evening of St Patrick's Day carousing, four worshippers were slain mid-prayer by a bomber unleashing grenades as he bolted down the church aisle with a landmine strapped to his chest.

**MAY.** Into a busload of French naval technicians outside the Sheraton hotel in the Arabian Sea port city Karachi, They were waiting to go to work for helping the Pakistani navy in building it's first indigenous submarine. Fourteen French technicians and a Pakistani cigarette vendor lost their lives.

**JUNE.** Into the concrete ramparts barricading the American consulate in Karachi, slaying the guards and a car jammed with a Pakistani mother and her daughters.

In January of the same year, militants in the port metropolis kidnapped US journalist Daniel Pearl, the Wall Street Journal's South Asia correspondent, and beheaded him days later. They filmed his slaughter and released the video.

In the weeks to follow my arrival in Islamabad, the avenging zealots would storm a mountain school for Christian missionaries' children, gunning down six Pakistani Muslim guards but missing the students cowering behind bolted doors, before fleeing into the velvet forest of the Murree hills; and grenade the chapel of a Christian hospital in Taxila, on the site of an ancient Indus civilisation west of Islamabad, killing three Pakistani nurses.

The gold-green of my bureau's walled lawn, the shade of the towering magnolia tree, the gracious strides of gardeners with long smocks billowing behind as they tended the flowerbeds, soothed my spirits each time I glanced up from my computer screen: a glowing white battleground of bombs and body counts, hallowed vows of more death, grieving howls of victims' loved ones, the casual brutality of American soldiers' gung-ho boasts of killings: portraits of hatred and intolerance from both sides of this indefinable war.

Threaded with quiet fears among Islamabad's remaining expats of being the next militant target, were sickening imaginations of Allah's impassioned warriors getting their hands on Pakistan's bristling nuclear arsenal.

Pakistan's President General Musharraf, who had dumped the Taliban, Pakistan's progeny, within hours of the 9-11 Armageddon, preached moderation.

This benign usurper of power, who had metamorphosed overnight from international pariah to the West's new darling thanks to 9-11 and his Taliban back-flip, began outlining his philosophy of 'enlightened moderation' for Islam, early in 2002.

Scanning one of his earliest sermons on enlightened moderation on the plane to Islamabad for an earlier month-long mission, my curiosity in Pakistan felt validated.

From the little I could see then, the Islamic republic, home to the second largest population of Muslims after Indonesia, was emerging as the battleground between 'good' and 'bad' Islam. The coup-leading general was painting himself as the voice of moderate Islam.

Pakistan was then the epicentre of bloody post-9/11 geopolitics, the frontline of the struggle between orthodoxy and modernity, a gruesome new edition of The Great Game—where the enemies this time were divided by faith and confessional fault lines within.

Senators, Defence Secretaries, Secretaries of State from Washington, London, Brussels, Paris and Berlin crisscrossed each other in purring convoys of blacked-out Mercedes and landcruisers along Islamabad's tranquil tree-lined boulevards.

The sterile city was a comfortable dress-circle position for viewing and plotting the war over the mountains in Afghanistan.

In our sun-bathed villa office, where cigar-smoke mingled with heady roses, and the floor-to-ceiling front window gazed onto flowerbeds, my computer screen was awash with death and war, threats and counter-threats in the name of 'Allah' and 'America's freedom', military lies and militant propaganda, and constant premonitions of nuclear attacks.

My focus was jolted on the afternoon of July 1 by a smudged, manually-typed fax.

Typo-ridden and almost-incoherent, it slid on to my desk and swung my attention suddenly from world geopolitics on Pakistan's international frontiers to its interior: its underbelly of illiterate serfs in economic bondage; impoverished cotton and sugarcane farmers; medieval tribal courts; and women treated as commodities for exchange in deals over land and honour.

The scrappy fax came from Multan, 400 kilometers south of Islamabad. Officially named the 'City of Saints' for its gallery of Sufi saints entombed in blue-domed mosques in its old quarter, the city's character is better captured by the wry boast of its residents: 'Welcome to Multan: City of dust, graveyards, beggars and heat.'

One of the oldest cities on the subcontinent, Multan is the gateway to some of the darkest, most impoverished patches of the southern Punjab, Pakistan's most populous province.

This wasn't the first near-illegible fax from our 'man in Multan', local journalist Abdul Sattar Qamar. Qamar had made a name for himself reporting for *The Muslim* newspaper on a group of women apparently forced to parade naked through a southern Punjab village during the reign of Islamist dictator General Zia ul-Haq. I'd become accustomed to Qamar's sometimes baffling South Asian prose, proclaiming with arcanely elegant English the choppings of noses and mouths, acid thrown on women's faces, rapes, and other less grotesque tales of absurdity.

Qamar's fax of July 1 carried the tale of a woman gang-raped on the orders of an informal tribal court, as atonement for her teenage brother's alleged rape of the girl next door.

At first glance it seemed to be another preposterous tale from the deep south. My colleagues and I were close to binning it in disbelief, as we had done with many outlandish stories out of Multan, partly because the process of discerning the truth of what happens in remote villages was too time consuming and complex.

But the tale of July 1 was irresistibly compelling. It fit our perceptions that brutality against women was rampant in rural Pakistan. It confirmed our worst fears of eye-for-an-eye tribal justice.

I asked a local staffer to telephone Qamar and confirm the dumbfounding content.

The barbaric sentence was apparently the outcome of an alleged tribal court convened at dusk to resolve a feud between two neighbouring tribes: the woman's apparently downtrodden caste of buffalo-herders, known as Gujjars, and a reputedly thuggish clan with reputedly powerful connections, the Mastoi Baloch.

The punishment read like a literal invocation of 'eye for an eye' justice enshrined in old tomes of Pakistan's Penal Code, the mainstream British-inherited law.

Although Qamar wrote floral English, he could only reply to my questions or remarks with 'Yes'. An Urdu-speaker had to talk to him.

Qamar got a policeman in the far-away village of Jatoi which is remote even by Multan standards, to confirm the accusations.

A policeman on the record was enough for us to compose a news story, and we published the chilling account on our international wire.

It was the first revelation to the international press. The terrible trial of Mukhtar Mai was made public to the world.

\* \* \* \*

The world erupted in thunderous condemnation

Wilting under the storm of international castigation, President Musharraf took the unprecedented intervention of giving Mukhtar Mai 500,000 rupees (8,300 USD) in compensation within *three* days of the first press report. The funds were 160 times more than the average monthly wage.

The police investigation had barely begun, none of the accused rapists had been questioned, and already the guilt of the accused was assumed. Already Mukhtar Mai was compensated with more money than she or her family could ever have dreamed of.

It was another four years until I met the girl with whom it all began.

The day of the alleged gang-rape of Mukhtar Mai had begun with funeral prayers and another cry of rape – from Salma Mastoi, the girl next door.

I found Salma Mastoi after months of visiting Mukhtar's village years later, and interviewing her extended family to try and piece together what actually happened, and why.

Pivotal to unraveling what exactly happened on the night of June 22, 2002 in the village of Mirwala are the tribal justice codes and the tribal marriage traditions of southern Punjab.

Love doesn't factor. Marriages are contracts, brokered by family elders, with land or honour foremost in the selection of brides and grooms. Women are chattel, especially in resolving feuds between men.

A common marriage solution is the tradition of *watta-satta*, (exchange marriage) whereby family A gives a bride to family B, and in exchange family A receives a bride from family B. The algebraic neatness belies the compromise and heartache for many *watta-satta* brides.

Women, commodified in much of rural Pakistan as pawns for trade in markets of arbitrary honour, are frequently made to bear punishments on behalf of accused male relatives. Under tribal practices of *vani* and *swara*, even baby girls have been betrothed to a relative of the man murdered by their fathers, to save their murderous fathers from prison.

Trying to unearth what happened to Mukhtar Mai on the night of June 22 means deciphering which tribal traditions prevailed when she was brought forth by her men folk and presented before Salma Mastoi's men folk, to win pardon for her brother's alleged rape of Salma.

One thing both sides agree on: it all began in the sugarcane.

# 2

# In the Sugarcane

**JUNE 2002, MIRWALA, SOUTHERN PUNJAB.**

On the lush east bank of the Indus, before the fertile cane and cotton belt gives way to desert, two homesteads face each other across a field. Above the crops the field yields twice a year, two rival tribes watch one another suspiciously. They watch from behind the mud-walled compounds, through gaps in the bricks. However, their women are hidden.

Two teenagers, one from each side of the field, meet in the field's tall sugarcane on a steaming mid-summer noon in Pakistan's furnace. The boy is from the Tatla clan of Gujjars, descendants of buffalo herders from the northern Punjab; the girl is from the Mastoi clan of Baloch, descendants of warriors and cattle-thieves from Central Asia. It is the day after the summer solstice.

Their castes pre-date Pakistan's birth, they pre-date British rule of the subcontinent, yet they flourish today in Pakistan's river-fed centre, where feudal lords still rule over serfs.

She is the most beautiful girl in the village. Her men folk are all away at a mourning ceremony for a kinsman. The boy's father is at his wood stall. His elder brother is tilling a distant field. His sisters are in purdah (seclusion), kneading and frying and scrubbing and sweeping and milking and feeding – hidden behind the walls. Some girls in the village occasionally step from behind the walls to labour in the fields.

The boy likes to watch girls in the fields.

A choir of prophets echoes from minarets across the tapestry of cotton and sugarcane fields, pinned by arcing date palms: zoherwela, the midday call to prayer, reaches crescendo, and fades.

Flies crawl thickly on every pore of exposed flesh. They creep into every orifice—between fingers, under arms, up sleeves. Crows and kites croak overhead. White heat shimmers above the heads of young sugarcane stalks. A plough drones in the distance. A motorbike splutters. The green blades of the stalks are broad and yielding.

The girl carries a sickle. Her black hair is tucked into a head veil, trailing down the long cotton tunic matted against her wet back, past her waist. The boy, tall and gangly, is smothered in a billowing blue smock over loose draw-string trousers. Pubescent whiskers shadow his goofy grin.

Some time after the zoherwela azan (call to prayer) faded, and some time before the aserwela azan (mid-afternoon prayer) rose, something happened between the two teenagers. Several versions exist. The truth hovers under layers of claims and counter-claims.

Salma of the Mastoi Baloch, and Shakoor of the Tatla Gujjars, were seen together. In this ultra-conservative corner of the Indus plains, that is enough for her family to cry rape.

Salma later alleged rape. Raised eyebrows countered that the pair were illicit lovers.

By sunset the pair from the star-crossed tribes were locked up inside four narrow mud walls in the girl's family's bare, dirt-floored home. Their families were locked in feud.

At nightfall Shakoor's eldest sister was delivered by her menfolk to the menfolk of the beautiful Mastoi girl from next door, to atone for her brother's 'disrespect'.

The sister's name was Mukhtar Mai.

Before the night was out, she was sexually assaulted, by at least one man, in revenge. The two tribes have conflicting versions of the context in which Mukhtar Mai was brought before the Mastoi tribe. One version says she was brought to merely beg vicarious pardon for her brother; however, the other version is that her family had agreed to give her away in marriage to Salma's 21 year old brother, to compensate for the alleged violation of Salma by Mukhtar's brother Shakoor.

Witnesses have testified in court to both conflicting versions. Contradictions and inconsistencies surface between every witness.

Since she was sacrificed by her own men folk to atone for her adolescent brother's recklessness, Mukhtar Mai has set up two fledgling schools in this Indus backwater hamlet of illiterates.

She's building a health clinic and welfare centre for rural women, treated as she was, like chattel. She travels the world speaking out in monosyllabic whispers for women subjected to barbarity, and shyly commands audiences of foreign ministers, senators, and international human rights leaders.

She is lionised outside Pakistan as a hero, an icon, a symbol of the downtrodden and abused, fighting back. She is honoured at glittering award ceremonies by Hollywood movie stars.

The woman I began to know during a series of visits to her family's remote village home in 2005, in a bid to piece together what happened on June 22 2002, was quiet and determined. Determined to educate and forge a better life for the little girls of her village, and to have all 14 men accused in her case sent to the gallows.

\* \* \* \*

## AUGUST 2005, MIRWALA

In the steely first cut of dawn, crows descend with slow flaps amid a nursery of shrouded sleeping bodies. Light thuds at my feet pull me from depths of hot sleep, coal wings beating just above consciousness. It is late summer of 2005, in the cotton-growing country of Punjab's far south. The monsoon has refused to break, and the Indus-watered cotton fields are pregnant with humidity. Steam rises from the irrigation canals at night, leaving the night hotter than the day. Sleep is outdoors.

Through the slit of slumber-drunk eyes, black-beaked crows creep into eerie focus, swooping above, between us, settling at our toes. They carouse territorially among the row of white-cocooned sleepers, walled inside a mud-caked courtyard with goats, chickens and water buffalo. Next to me, her fragile frame so tiny and tight-curled that it could be a mere fold in the blanket, lies Mukhtar Mai. On either side of us, pregnant sisters, grandmothers, babies, old men of the village who come to pass the night, slumber on a row of *charpoys* (woven rattan beds on wooden legs), wrapped in white sheets to shield against sticky flies. The ritual dawn invasion of crows brings not a flinch from the shrouded slumberers. I imagine I'm the only one buried alive in a walled graveyard, as the crows circle lower and lower, until hot black sleep engulfs again.

I wake again into sunlight and the bustle of extended family feeding, washing, scrubbing, babies crying, mothers cooing, hens squawking, adolescent girls bending over goats.

Mukhtar's shroud lies abandoned on the charpoy.

From a doorway in the courtyard's mud wall, in a bright yellow tunic already crushed with sweat, she's beaming a warm smile at me, with a new note of playfulness, beckoning.

It's more than three years since a supposed tribal council reportedly sentenced her to gang-rape by four men, to restore the 'honour' of the reportedly higher-caste tribe that dominated the said council.

Each day now the field next door chimes with the recitations of 200 grotty-faced kohl-eyed village girls in the rustic school Mukhtar set up after her apparent rape-by-decree.

Veiled women travel hours on dirt roads to bring to Mukhtar their own tale of rape. She documents their horrors, sends them for medical tests, instructs them in lodging police reports, gives them advice and succour. She's buying an ambulance and making a health clinic for rural women.

The mud-walled courtyard I'd been sleeping in virtually imprisons her other sisters in purdah, the conservative Islamic tradition of shielding women from exposure to outsiders by requiring them to stay inside the family walls, and to cloak their face and bodies. Only on the rare occasions they venture outside. Such traditions, in swathes of rural Pakistan, make little room for young girls to go to school.

I look into the eyes of Mukhtar's illiterate adult sisters. Dim, unlit gazes return my stare. Their lives are a day-in, day-out cycle of washing, kneading, frying, feeding, nursing, sweeping, milking, washing, forever inside these four mud-brick walls... until sleep.

This was Mukhtar's lot, until she was presented by her men folk to the men of the enemy tribe next door.

In a village where no one can read or write, where clans eye each other with suspicion, where rumours fly over who stole the cattle or the crops, and where people live in fear of riverside bandits—hearsay, gossip and perception become truths.

Women who live in purdah have no way of knowing first hand what goes on outside their walls. Even more so if they cannot read or write. In this village, the people don't even speak the same language as the rest of Pakistan. They still have no TV, radio or internet.

Trapped in purdah, they need mirrors on the world outside to see beyond the walls. It's often the local village preacher who holds up the mirror for his illiterate followers, like the mullah of the biggest mosque of Mirwala.

In the two months preceding this visit, Mukhtar has been under house arrest and put on a travel ban list normally reserved for crooks. The government took away her passport and forced her to cancel a planned trip to the US; they moved policewomen into her home who even followed her to the toilet.

Ministers and parliamentarians, men and women alike, have accused her of 'tarnishing Pakistan's image' and 'airing her dirty linen in public', and not behaving in a manner behoving 'eastern women'. The voices of scepticism have had open season. Women parliamentarians have castigated her for talking too much about something most women here keep secret. Doubts about Mukhtar's truthfulness have become public talking points.

The flow of hefty foreign donations to Mukhtar and her women's welfare projects has inspired scorn.

In a shock decision five months earlier, a High Court acquitted most of the men convicted of raping her and of abetting the crime. The freed men returned to a festive homecoming in this village after two and a half years on death row.

"Madam, this is just a business. She was never raped," declared my then-driver after three days in her village. He was espousing popular sentiments. I considered his conclusion outrageous. In his bigoted outlook, the fact that Mukhtar was a divorcee, and had purchased two new motorbikes for her family, was enough to cast doubt. I sacked him immediately.

As Mukhtar's stature has grown abroad, hostility at home has swelled. The whispers that her family cried rape for money have spread beyond the small-minded villagers of Mirwala to the national talk-back radio. One small newspaper has been running a relentless character assassination campaign.

Mukhtar's chain-smoking—which she says only began in the aftermath of her ordeal, and her divorcee status are fodder for aspersions.

While overseas Mukhtar is glorified as an icon for trying to raise third world rural women out of the dimness of illiteracy and brutalisation, and for braving scorn and stigma to speak out against her own abuse, at home she is perceived by many as a blind woman: unwittingly led by a pool of scheming sharks seeking self-aggrandisement, creaming off the river of funds flowing her way.

"Mukhtar Mai is a blind man," once remarked Qamar, my former agency's 'Man in Multan', a local journalist who has followed her story from the beginning.

Despite the shocking popular backlash, on this steamy August morning Mukhtar is somehow managing to grin, broadly.

Steaming sun lighting her buttercup tunic, face framed by matted black curls, she beckons to me from the door in the wall to step out of the courtyard, through the wall, into the dusty yard of the girls' school she's built.

"I want to save the next generation of girls. If they are educated, if they know their rights, they will not let what happened, to me happen to them," she had said on my first visit to her village in 2004.

She has knocked on hundreds of villagers' doors to persuade them to let their girls out to study. She is still knocking.

"If I had been educated, if I knew my rights, that incident would never have happened."

Mukhtar beckons me out of the courtyard of purdah she grew up in, into the pool of light she's woven in the darkness of rural Pakistan, with the determination to save the next generation of girls from her own cataclysmic fate. Now she is holding the mirror for her village's future women.

I am here to look into her mirror, to study what makes her different from other rape victims, to see where she gets her courage from, and to reconstruct what happened on the night she was violated.

Like the rest of the world, I am transfixed by her simplicity and bravery, by her distilled sense of justice and by the nobility of her altruism, but most profoundly by her master act of transforming her own bitter experience into an opportunity to educate the girls of her village and elevate their futures.

This sweating August morning is my third trip down to the deep south of the Punjab to be with Mukhtar in her home environment, to learn her character and interview her family to piece together the genesis of the feud that culminated in Mukhtar's violation.

Her lawyer in Lahore has just thrown open for me the files on Mukhtar's court cases, handing me a three foot high pile of trial testimony transcripts, statements given to police, medical reports, lists of evidence and lengthy judgements from the 2002 trial and the 2005 appeal.

I began with the prosecution witness statements and trial transcripts. I cross-checked their statements with Mukhtar and her family. After sometimes of painful deciphering, I extracted enough points that most of the prosecution side agreed on, to be able to reconstruct the events of June 22, 2002—according to the prosecution version. Reconstructing the defence version of events would come later.

# 3

# In the Name of the Brother

*And we prescribed for them therein (the Torah): The life for the life, and the eye for the eye, and the nose for the nose, and the ear for the ear, and the tooth for the tooth, and for wounds retaliation. But whoso forgoeth (in the way of charity) it shall be expiation for him.*

**Holy Qur'an, 5:45 (M.M. Pickthall Translation)**

## JUNE 22, 2002, MIRWALA

The sugarcane and cotton plants grow thick in this fertile basin of the southern Punjab. Behind their dense curtain, no one can see the village thugs rape girls, boys, women; married and unmarried; the wives, sisters, daughters and sons of fellow villagers. The ripe foliage muffles their grunts and cries.

**DOPEHERWELA** (around the middle of the day)*

Abdul Shakoor, a stooped adolescent somewhere between 12 and 15, lay on a charpoy, a woven rattan bed, under a *shareen* tree by a field of sugarcane. It was summer's zenith. A day earlier the summer solstice had brought the longest day of the year to Mirwala. The village bakes along the eastern bank of the Indus, in Pakistan's remote river-watered centre 500 kilometres south of Islamabad.

The sowing of sugarcane, the winnowing of wheat and maize, the harvest of cotton, prayer times and the path of the sun set the cycles of Mirwala's 1,500 people. The Indus River pounds past Mirwala on its way to union with four other rivers that feed Punjab province. In fact Punjab received its name from these 'five rivers' flowing through it. The Sutlej, Ravi, Chenab and Jhelum rivers pour into the Indus at the mighty Panjnad Canal Headworks, 40 kilometers south of Mirwala, and charge as one river to the Arabian Sea. Rivers Indus feeds Mirwala's crops through a maze of irrigation canals built in the 1930s when the British turned Punjab's southern deserts green, in the twilight years of the Raj. Canals weave through a mosaic of cultivated plains, pinned by clusters of date palms. Heat scales 50 degrees and more in late June.

---

*reconstruction according to prosecution version.

There is no electricity. Generous shareen trees offer the best relief from unforgiving heat. The men of the village sometimes enjoy noonday siesta in their patchy shade. The women almost never step from behind the walls. They live in '*purdah*': by tradition, they cannot be seen by men outside their family, and if they step beyond their own walls they shroud themselves in burqas, voluminous bell-shaped garments cloaking head and body.

While women are made bell-shaped by their burqas, all through the southern Punjab sinewy men with burnished copper limbs are made taller by their high turbans, swathes of white cotton wrapped and knotted flamboyantly around the crowns of their heads, a head-dress that often complements a curled-out black moustache.

On the other side of the sugarcane a palm tree arced skywards, thrusting its fountain of spiky-leafed arms to the harsh high-noon sun. Ghafar Pachaar, a neighbouring farmer, was high up in the tree's nest of ferns, plucking dates. It was the middle of the day: *Dopeherwela*.

Shakoor had been watching three of his sisters, two of them yet to marry, the other long divorced and childless—cook, wash and sweep the earthen-floored courtyard of their mud-walled home. Two other married sisters lived with their husband's families elsewhere. Shakoor wasn't old enough yet to join his big brother in the cotton-sowing routines of June.

White heat shimmered through Shakoor's heavy-lidded gaze as he bobbed in and out of groggy day-sleep. He'd spent most of the morning shadowing his eldest sister Mukhtar, the thin divorcee, as she toiled.

Mukhtar was in her late teens when Shakoor was born, and her arranged marriage was already failing. Her parents had chosen for her a lame man with a club foot, almost twice her age. Umer Wadda was a distant relative from a nearby village. Three months after the wedding, Mukhtar left her marital home and returned to her parents. "He did not understand me, I did not understand him," she said.[1] Three years later he came to her parents' home for the *talaaq*: divorce.

A hand clapped over Shakoor's mouth. Punnu, Shakoor's neighbour, and two others dragged him into the sugarcane.

Mukhtar had always treated Shakoor like her child. She used to watch over him.

Mukhtar looked over the wall to check on her little brother, but only saw an empty charpoy.

From his high palm perch, Ghafar Pachaar could see across the patchwork of heavy-bent sugarcane, ears of flaxen wheat, and newly sowed buds of cotton.

"Mastois took him," he told Shakoor's fretting family.

The Mastois were reputed to have powerful connections in Jatoi, the sub-district surrounding Mirwala, and the sub-district of Rajanpur westwards across the Indus. Local papers portrayed them as violent looters, with a reputation as

---

1.    Interview with Mukhtar Mai in Mirwala, August 2004.

thugs and thieves. The Mastois of Mirwala are a distant offshoot of the Baloch tribes, who settled in southern Pakistan centuries back.

For as long as anyone can remember, the family of Imam Bakhsh Mastoi, a long deceased farmer, have lived next to the family of Ghulam Farid a soft-spoken woodcutter from the *Tatla-Gujjar* caste and the father of Mukhtar and Shakoor. An acre-sized field separates the Mastoi and Gujjar homes; sugarcane and cotton flourish in that field until autumn harvest. Relations are cool, weighted by mutual suspicion typical to families of different tribes.

The Gujjars are descendants of water buffalo herders from northern Punjab. They are a minority in Mirwala — only the families of Ghulam Farid and his wife's two brothers, Sabir Hussain and Ghulam Hussain, hail from buffalo-herder blood. Sabir and Ghulam live one field away from Mukhtar's home, in the opposite direction to the Mastois.

Ghafar Pachaar had lost sight of Shakoor as he and the Mastois melted into the sugarcane, then thick, towering and bent from the weight of its pre-harvest ripeness.

Shakoor claims there were three Mastois—Punnu, the oldest son of the Mastoi family next door, and his cousins Manzoor and Jamil.

Shielded by thick-leafed curtains of sugarcane, as high as a man, Shakoor claims the three men thrashed him and tore his blue *shalwar kameez* (long tunic and trousers). One by one, he alleges, they sodomised him. Shakoor's moans for help were lost in the thicket of leaves and canestalks.

Earth darkening his shalwar (trousers), the tall men hauled him up, dragged him through the sugarcane and emerged before Punnu's home on the other side of the sugarcane.

"You will not speak of this," the men ordered. Shakoor mumbled defiance. Infuriated, the men beat him again and dragged him inside the mud-walled courtyard.

In the courtyard of the Mastoi homestead, Punnu's brothers Abdul Khaliq and Allah Ditta were waiting. They beat Shakoor again. Punnu, Allah Ditta and Abdul Khaliq were the elder sons of the late Imam Baksh Mastoi's five sons. Punnu and Allah Ditta were married with children. Abdul Khaliq was the next in line to marry.

Abdul Khaliq hurled Shakoor into the far room of a three room hut and padlocked it. An hour passed. Dusty sun rays streamed into the dim room and grew longer.

A burst of sunlight fell into the room as the door swung back. Silhouetted against the mid-afternoon sun was a young girl, her hair tucked into a tailing headscarf, shiny bangles caking both forearms. She was Salma, one of the Mastois' six daughters. The girl tripped into the room with a shove from behind as the door was bolted behind her.

Shakoor sweated. In the eyes of the tribe, to be alone with a woman who is not a relative is almost equivalent to rape. It is a violation of the 'honour' of the woman and her family, and common ground for murder of the woman by her family.

The mid-afternoon call to prayer rang high in the sapphire summer sky: *Aserwela*.

In her family's courtyard, Mukhtar heard Shakoor's cry from over the sugarcane. Mukhtar, her mother, and her sister-in-law Shamima rushed out of their compound and squinted towards the Mastoi home. Half-a-dozen Mastois emerged from their behind their own walls.

"Let my son go," Mukhtar's mother, Bachul Khanoum, yelled.

"We caught Shakoor in *ziadti* (fornication) with our girl in the sugarcane," the Mastois shouted back to the Gujjar women.

Mukhtar dashed inside and grabbed her Qur'an. Clutching the holy book, she rejoined her mother outside.

"For the sake of the Holy Qur'an, please let Shakoor go," Mukhtar begged.

"He is locked up, along with Salma," Abdul Khaliq shouted in reply.

Mukhtar and her mother pleaded with their neighbours for another 15 to 20 minutes, then turned back inside their home. They sent for their menfolk.

Hazoor Bakhsh, the eldest of Ghulam Farid's eight children, was sowing cotton in a field about one acre away when he got the urgent message to come home. Ghulam Farid came from his woodstall. Uncles Sabir Hussain and Ghulam Hussain joined them. The four men found the women shrieking: "The Mastois have taken Shakoor. They say he misbehaved with Salma. They won't release him."

Hazoor Bakhsh says he remembered a swaggering threat from some Mastois to Shakoor a week before. "We're going to get you," he claims to recall them saying to his little brother.

ASERWELA (mid-afternoon prayer, around 3pm)

Hazoor Bakhsh mounted his motor scooter and sped to the centre of Mirwala. The nine-kilometre trip took over 10 minutes, weaving through donkey-drawn wooden carts laden with bursting sacks of grain, camel trains, and turbanned men on horseback. Men in white tunics glided through fields of maize along the road; in a drain on the other side, veiled women squatted and scrubbed clothes on a washboard, turning the ditchwater soapy.

At a small bridge over the junction of two canals, Hazoor Bakhsh turned right and coasted along the wall of the Farooqia mosque, the largest of Mirwala's half-a-dozen mosques. It is a 'Jamia mesjid' – a mosque where Friday prayer congregations gather. A madrassa (religious school) is attached.

The residence of the 'imam' or prayer leader of Mirwala, Maulvi Abdul Razzaq, backs on to the swollen canal, where water buffalo wade languorously, bulging eyes skimming the muddy water, unperturbed by whooping boys riding bicycles along the sun-dappled bank.

Hazoor Bakhsh tapped at the imam's door.

"Maulana-sahib, *my* bhai *(brother) has been abducted by Mastoi* biraderi *(tribe),*" he said.

Abdul Razzaq, then 40, had ministered to Mirwala's flock of illiterate cotton, sugarcane and grain farming families for over 10 years.

Large eyes gaze gently from his silver bearded face. He speaks softly with short, firm pronouncements. He quotes easily from the *Haddith* (stories of the life of the Prophet Muhammad PBUH[2]), the *Sunnah* (sayings of the Prophet Muhammad PBUH) and the Qur'an. Students at the Farooqia madrassa revere him.

The only stain in his quarter-century pastoralship of this hot corner of the Indus plains is his rumoured sympathy with the Sipah-e-Sihaba[3] (Army of the Companions of the Prophet), a violent organisation of radicals from the Sunni sect of Islam. Southern Punjab is an epicentre of sectarian radicalism. Sipah-e-Sahaba was banned by the government in 2001, after being linked to hundreds of murders of sectarian rivals over two decades. Some in Maulvi Abdul Razzaq's rural diocese had accused him of harbouring Sipah-e-Sahaba fugitives. There were rumours he'd spent time in militant training camps in Afghanistan, and led protests in support of Osama bin Laden after 9-11.

Maulvi Abdul Razzaq took Hazoor Bakhsh to the nearest police station, a sprawling cream and maroon bungalow in the bustling centre of the nearest township Jatoi, another five kilometres away.

Only the clerk (munshi) was present. The munshi listened sleepily to Hazoor Bakhsh and the Maulvi, and sent them to the residence of the town's chief police officer, Assistant Sub-Inspector Muhammad Iqbal. Office hours finish early for government officers.

The Maulvi and Hazoor Bakhsh told the moustached police inspector that Shakoor had been abducted. Inspector Iqbal agreed to go and see the Mastois. He took Constables Arshad and Majid with him in a police van and headed out to Mirwala. The Maulvi followed on his motor scooter, twisting along the narrow dirt trails between canals and fields.

### Shamwela (late afternoon, just before sunset)

Inspector Iqbal pulled up at the Mastoi home. Abdul Khaliq and Punnu met the inspector and his constables at the entrance. Inspector Iqbal asked them to let Shakoor go.

In a tribal riverine-belt community like Mirwala, Pakistani law and its enforcers hold little sway. They invoke distrust instead of respect. Any authority

---

2.  PBUH — Peace Be Upon Him
3.  Sipah-e-Sahaba: An organization of fanatic Sunni Muslim extremists, blamed for the deaths of thousands of followers of the rival, minority Shia sect of Islam

they have shrinks in the face of tribal elders and clan chiefs. The Mastoi brothers heard out the police order to free Shakoor.

"This boy raped our sister," they responded.

The Mastois refused to do anything until Faiz Muhammad Mastoi, a man in his mid-30s with more land than the rest of the Mastois, showed up.

The Maulvi meanwhile headed to the tiny village mosque, '*Ya Rasul Allah*', a few fields before the Mastoi home. He ran into Khair Muhammad Mastoi, father of Faiz, and another villager Manzoor Ahmad, of the Jatoi clan. The pair were coming from the Mastoi home.

"*Ziadti* (fornication) has been committed with a Mastoi girl. The hand of a Gujjar girl is to be sought in reprisal," the Mastoi elder told the Maulvi.

The Maulvi stopped his scooter at the miniature *Ya Rasul Allah* mosque and went inside to pray.

At the Mastoi home, the police waited an hour until Faiz Muhammad Mastoi showed up. The Mastois had by then convinced the police that Shakoor had been caught 'raping' Salma in the sugarcane field. Iqbal decided to take Shakoor into police custody.

Faiz Muhammad Mastoi ordered Abdul Khaliq and Punnu to release the boy into police hands. The Mastois unlocked the room and handed Shakoor to the police. Inspector Iqbal and his constables bundled the adolescent into their van and drove him to Jatoi police station. Without even a chance of telling his version of what happened in the sugarcane, Shakoor was locked up again, this time in a grimy police cell.

\* \* \* \*

Back in Mirwala, the laws of the tribe took over.

A Mastoi girl's honour was said to be violated. The balance of honour had to be restored.

As tension charged the village, Shakoor's father, the quiet wood-cutter with pointy ears and short white whiskers gloving his leathered brown face, gathered his daughters Mukhtar, Fatima and Tasmiya, his daughter-in-law Shamima, and his own wife Bachul Khanoom.

When tension flares between clans, protection of the women is paramount. The woodcutter tucked his womenfolk into his brother-in-law Sabir's home, a five minute walk from his own home. Two other daughters, Naseem and Rachmat, were safe with their husbands' families.

When honour is out of balance, male elders seek to restore it through the trade-off of women. Elders convene unofficial assemblies and inevitably barter women and girls to bring honour back into balance.

## MAGHREB-ISHARWELA[4] (sunset to the first hours of darkness)

At Maghreb-Isharwela, the clans of Mirwala fell into two gatherings.

Scores of Mastoi clansmen from Mirwala and surrounding villages picked their way along the banks of irrigation channels and gathered beneath the mud walls of the Mastoi home, where Shakoor and Salma had been locked up.

The crowd of Mastois swelled between 70 and 250, according to different witness accounts. A gathering took shape. The gathering did not fit the technical definition of a panchayat: combines the Urdu words 'panj' for five and 'ayat' for verse, to denote a gathering of representatives of all tribes. Some say the 'panj' denotes a gathering of two representatives of each feuding tribe, plus a neutral arbitrator: five in all. The gathering outside late Imam Bakhsh Mastoi's home on June 22 was dominated by Mastois. Token numbers of other clans joined, including Pachaars and Jatois: but Mastois outnumbered all.

There were no Gujjars. Mukhtar and her supporters repeatedly put the number of men present at the gathering at 200 or more.

The Gujjar men gathered elsewhere: at the tiny Ya Rasul Allah mosque, six fields from the Mastoi home. Mukhtar's father Ghulam Farid, her older brother Hazoor Bakhsh, and her uncles Sabir Hussain and Ghulam Hussain huddled with the cleric Maulvi Abdul Razzaq and his brother Haji Altaf Hussain, neighbours Ghulam Nabi, Ghulam Mustafa, and Manzoor Ahmad Hussain, and around a dozen others. The cleric, his brother Haji Altaf Hussain, and Manzoor Ahmad were from the Jatoi clan, the oldest, largest and most influential clan in the sub-district of Jatoi. Together they prayed.

"Auz Billah Mina Shahid Tor Nerah Gim. Bissmillah Rehman Neh Rahim. In the Name of Allah who is merciful and beneficial."

After reciting the namaz (prayer) in Arabic, they fell into their own private prayers, in their native Seraiki tongue.

"We prayed to God to help us and forgive us. We prayed for peace and friendship between our family and the Mastois," Sabir said later.

They were about 20 men in all. Maulvi Abdul Razzaq and Manzoor Ahmad Jatoi were deputed as the Gujjars' 'salis' or 'salisan', the arbitrators for resolving the feud with the Mastois.

The drooping sun streaked the sugarcane rose-gold, as chants swelled in the mournful chorus of the first evening prayer.

Outside the Mastoi home, Faiz Muhammad Mastoi, the head of the clan, assumed the role of head of the gathering. Ramzan Pachaar and Ghulam

---

4.  Maghreb-wela — at the time of sunset prayer.
    Maghreb-Isharwela — the dusk-to-dark hours between Maghreb prayers and Ishar prayers.

Fareed Mastoi were appointed arbitrators for the Mastoi side. Faiz dispatched Ramzan Pachaar and Ghulam Fareed Mastoi to the Gujjar gathering as his messengers.

As they made their way along the dirt paths to the mosque where the Gujjars were gathered, the azan (call to prayer) floated from minarets across the flat Indus plain, collided in their ears, and gently subsided.

The Ya Rasul Allah mosque is small and gaudy. Bold circus stripes of green, red, yellow and blue coat the four roof-top pillars, as though in unconscious homage to the Sikh temples which once dotted the middle Indus plains. The front walls are tiled in white and blue ceramics. Two carved wooden double doors, crowned with elaborate lattice wood screens, flank a grander middle door, normally bolted.

Inside, the last muted light of the vanishing sun drew filigree shadows on the walls.

Straw mats covered the baked earthen floor. Damp stained the peeling white walls. Wooden shutters were flung open in a vain bid to evaporate the stifling heat.

Ramzan Pachaar and Ghulam Fareed Mastoi stepped from the dusk of the fields into the darkening shadows inside.

"Give us one of your daughters," they demanded. It was as Khair Mastoi had hinted earlier.

It was the judgement of Faiz Muhammad Mastoi that a Gujjar girl should be given in marriage to a Mastoi son, in return for the Gujjar boy Shakoor's act of 'ziadti' with the Mastoi girl, Salma. Daughters are a family's highest commodity.

"But the nikah (marriage ceremony) must be performed this very night," the Mastois' negotiators said.

The Gujjar party consulted in murmurs. Manzoor Ahmad Jatoi, representing the Gujjars, turned to Faiz Mastoi's messengers with a counter-proposal.

"Abdul Shakoor is a minor. We believe he is innocent of what you accuse him. But if you suspect illicit liaison between him and the Mastoi girl, let him and Salma be bound in marriage, and the Gujjars will offer their girl in exchange for marriage with the Mastoi son Abdul Khaliq," the Jatoi elder stated. The Gujjar family was conceding to the demand to hand over one of the girls, but only in exchange for a girl from the other family.

The Gujjars' offer was not unusual. Watta-satta, exchange marriage, is a common practice among rural tribes in Punjab and Sindh provinces. In brokering marriage contracts, a family may offer their daughter to a family in return for a bride for their own family. More than 40 percent of marriages in rural Sindh and Punjab are watta-satta arrangements.

Ramzan Pachaar and Ghulam Fareed Mastoi returned to the Mastoi gathering, bearing the Gujjars' offer of watta-satta.

The Mastoi gathering conversed. They rejected the watta-satta proposal, according to the prosecution. The Mastois, the prosecution maintain, wanted badla[5]: revenge. They sent the envoys Ramzan Pachaar and Ghulam Fareed Mastoi back to the Gujjar gathering at the mosque.

Ramzan Pachaar straightened his spine as he delivered the Mastoi gathering's latest pronouncement: 'badla in zina'. In short, rape for rape.

"Your offer of watta-satta is refused," Ramzan Pachaar announced to the Gujjars, according to prosecution testimony.

"We want one of your girls, to rape in revenge. Then compromise will be effected."

Maulvi Abdul Razzaq, Manzoor Ahmad Jatoi and Ghulam Mustafa stepped forth. They refused.

The three representatives of the Gujjars crossed the dusk-shadowed fields to the Mastoi home. They took Faiz Mastoi aside and spoke to him on their own. The Gujjar emissaries renewed their offer of watta-satta, and added an extra sweetener: four kanals of Gujjar land.

Faiz Mastoi agreed.

But the Mastois' arbitrators came forward and protested.

"Zina for zina is the decision," the arbitrators pronounced, according to prosecution testimony. Rape for rape.

The Gujjars' emissaries again refused.

"Seek recourse to the process of the law," Maulvi Abdul Razzaq declared. The mullah insists it was at this point that he turned and left.

The Maulvi mounted his scooter and wound along the dark canal banks back to his residence in in the town. He says it was around 10pm when he reached home.

A waning crescent moon glowed in the eastern night sky. In three days there would be a new moon. The crops were now shrouded in hot darkness.

An oil lamp burned at the entrance to the petite Ya Rasul Allah mosque. The Gujjar men and their neighbours were still huddled in discussion and prayer. The splutter of motor scooters rang from the road. The hum of a plough floated from the fields.

Silhouettes of the Mastoi emissaries took shape, framed by a chalky glow from the horizon.

---

5.   Badla — (Arabic): exchange, lieu, stead, a substitute, recompense, return, compensation, revenge, requittal; in exchange, in return for; to retaliate, take revenge.

"With the consent of Faiz Mastoi, we have come to conclude this matter," declared Ramzan Pachaar and Ghulam Fareed Mastoi.

"Bring us a sister of Abdul Shakoor to seek pardon for his sin, as per Baloch custom. If your girl comes and begs pardon, we will forgive the Gujjar boy and his family. Compromise will be effected." These are their words according to prosecution testimony.

Ghulam Farid Gujjar paled. Mukhtar's father and her uncle Sabir dropped their heads. Daughters are the highest commodity—yet a commodity.

The demand was for 'any' sister. The choice of which sister was left to the Gujjar men.

"Will you harm our sister?" asked Hazoor Bakhsh.

"We give you our promise, here in this mosque: we shall not bring any harm to your sister," the Mastoi messengers replied. "This is the word of Faiz Mastoi."

Their vow was made in the mosque.

Uncle Sabir claims the vow of safety was followed by a threat of attack from the Mastois' envoys. Sabir consulted with his fellow Gujjars.

"It depends on our confidence in their guarantee," Hazoor Bakhsh said.

Ghulam Farid Gujjar had fathered six daughters. He had buried one a year earlier: his third daughter Jawal had died of a cancer-like illness.

Mukhtar was the first-born daughter. She had been divorced for more than seven years, although no-one remembers the exact year she married or divorced. Naseem, the wood-cutters' second daughter, was married with four children. Rachmat, the fourth daughter, was married but childless. Fatima, his fifth daughter, was in her teens. Tasmiya, the youngest, was barely 10. The wood-cutter's choice was bitterly clear.

Tasmiya was still a child. Rachmat and Naseem were already married. Fatima, just out of adolescence, was ripe for marriage. In rural areas, puberty is barely a threshold for marriage. Until the marriage pact is struck and executed, a girl must not be seen outside her immediate family. Married women live with a sliver less invisibility. They are slightly freer to show their faces, although in Mirwala almost all women still wear the burqa when they step outside.

At the other end of the untouchability rankings is the divorcee.

Mukhtar had been wearing the burqa less and less. At home she wore the traditional *shalwar kameez*—long shapeless tunic (kameez) over pantaloon trousers (shalwar), and a dupatta (large shawl) draped over the shoulders and chest. The dupatta is draped over the head in the presence of strangers. To venture outside the home, Mukhtar would wrap herself in a huge black *chador* (cloak).

Since Mukhtar's divorce, no-one had approached her parents to propose a second marriage. Not even the network of relatives, the usual source of grooms and brides in rural Pakistan.

She had etched out a life of activity for herself. She wove beaded headbands and hair extensions and sold them for tiny sums. She mastered needlework embroidery, and gave lessons in embroidery to her girl students. She studied the Qur'an, despite being unable to read or write, and gave lessons on its verses to young girls of the village.

Yet when I asked her a few times to quote her favourite passage, she was dumbstruck. I asked her to guide me to the verses which speak of women. Again, her face went blank. Once she mentioned a chapter she liked, titled 'Al-Yasin'. But she couldn't say what was in the chapter.

Uncle Sabir consulted Hazoor Bakhsh, the oldest of the woodcutter's offspring.

"Take Mukhtar Mai," Hazoor told Sabir. "Fetch her from your place. Bring her to our home. We will meet you there."

Mukhtar was the eldest of the daughters, and "had more understanding than the others," Sabir told me four years later. It was not because she was divorced that we chose her, he insisted.

Sabir trudged through the newly-sowed cotton fields to his house, where the Gujjar women were being kept. The waning moon brightened the banks of irrigation channels as dusk shadows deepened.

Ghulam Farid Gujjar's wife, a round-faced grandmother of 10, with soft cocoa eyes and a spread middle, came towards her youngest brother Sabir, her arms spread wide and palms open in muttered prayer.

Sabir looked past his old sister at her daughters: Mukhtar, Fatima, Tasmiya. Mukhtar in Arabic means "someone invested with power and authority". A lesser known meaning is "the chosen, the selected."

Fatima was the name of the Prophet Muhammad's first daughter. Tasmiya means "a declaration of God's power".

Mukhtar had grown into her name.

"She always spoke like a wise elder," her mother said. She was diligent in her chores. She taught the Qur'an to little veiled girls. Like many illiterate village women, she could read bits of the Qur'an in its original Arabic, without knowing the meaning.

Her father believed she was the one who could handle tough situations.

Uncle Sabir stepped through into the courtyard.

"Mukhtiar," he said, addressing her in the affectionate variation of Mukhtar, "You must go with us to the Mastois. You are to seek pardon for Shakoor."

"Let us ask Shakoor first whether he has committed such a mistake," Mukhtar replied.

"It is not right that I should go there. These are not nice people, she continued."

"The police have taken Shakoor," Sabir replied. "We cannot speak to him."

The mother spoke up.

"Send the men folk to the police station to find Shakoor and get him released."

Uncle Sabir shook his head.

"First the matter must be resolved with the Mastois," he replied.

Mukhtar followed her uncle through the field to her father's home.

Her father and Hazoor Bakhsh were waiting outside the house. With them were Haji Altaf Hussain, the Maulvi's brother, and neighbour Ghulam Nabi.

"It is suggested that you go to the Mastois. I and uncle Sabir will go with you," her father said.

"Their messengers swore in the mosque you will be safe," Hazoor Bakhsh said. "If you go, it will bring pardon. If not, they will kill us."

Mukhtar did not ask why she of the five living daughters was chosen.

# 4

# Save My Honour

"And say to the believing women that they should lower their gaze and guard their modesty; that they should not display their beauty and ornaments except what (must ordinarily) appear thereof; that they should draw their veils over their bosoms and not display their beauty except to their husbands, their fathers, their husband's fathers, their sons, their husbands' sons, their brothers or their brothers' sons, or their sisters' sons, or their women."

*Holy Qur'an 24:31 The Book Of Light*
*(A. Yusufali translation)*

Mukhtar went inside to the room where she slept and took a small Qur'an from near her bed. Sweating, she wound a large black *bochan* (large dupatta) over her head and followed her uncle and father. The *bochan* cascaded over her bright blue kameez, cloaking her upper body. Her matching blue shalwar ballooned until closing tight round her ankles. Only the flesh of her feet, hands and face were visible. She didn't put on a burqa.

"We did not require her to wear burqa while proceeding to the gathering. She was coming to seek pardon," Uncle Sabir explained to the court later.

In the dark, Mukhtar walked behind her father and uncle. The prosecution says that Haji Altaf Hussain, the Maulvi's brother, and Ghulam Nabi came with Uncle Sabir and the woodcutter for support.

Silvery stalks of sugarcane, shining under the thin moon, brushed the four men and the veiled woman as they stepped towards the Mastoi home. The moon was two days off the end of its cycle.

Hazoor Bakhsh stayed behind. Uncle Sabir was worried that Mukhtar's older brother might end up fighting the Mastois.

Unease twisted inside Mukhtar. To bring a woman before a crowd of men from another family and tribe was almost unheard of.

*"Usually women don't appear in front of men, so I was very confused about going in front of so many men. I didn't say anything because my father said Ramzan Pachaar had promised they wouldn't harm me. So I said nothing and just accepted my father's word."*[1]

---

1.  Interview with Mukhtar Mai, Mirwala, 2005-11-30

The shadows of dozens of men flickered in front of the Mastoi home. Not a woman was visible. The Mastoi wives, mothers and children were within the walls.

Mukhtar gripped her Qur'an.

Shrouded in black, she stood silent before the gathering, her gaze lowered. The men of Mastoi family stood a few paces from her.

"Mukhtar Mai, daughter of Ghulam Farid Gujjar, has come and is ready to seek pardon," Uncle Sabir pronounced.

Faiz Mastoi, leader of the gathering, spoke up.

"The Gujjars have brought their girl. She has come to seek pardon. Forgive them."

Mukhtar heard the Mastoi elder's pronouncement.

"But it was '*duniavi siasi taurper* ', delivered in a superficial manner," Mukhtar claimed two months later at the trial.[2]

Uncle Sabir claims to have heard something else from Faiz Mastoi:

"First he said: 'Forgive the girl, as God forgives everyone.' But after this he said: 'Do as you wish, whatever you want'.

They had already decided what they would do. These words of forgiveness were just token words. It is typical for panchayat leaders to say good words to the opposite party, while having already decided something else in their minds."[3]

Before Mukhtar could speak, Abdul Khaliq grabbed her right arm. He had a .30 bore pistol in one hand.[4]

Gasping, Mukhtar wrenched her arm free. She turned to her father, to her uncle, to Faiz. In the layered shadows of Mastoi men she thinks, she glimpsed at over 200 silhouettes.

Three of the shadows materialised against her body. Allah Ditta, an older brother of Abdul Khaliq and Salma; Fayyaz, their cousin; and Ghulam Fareed Mastoi, one of the Mastois' arbitrators. The three men pushed her, shoved her, and dragged her inside the walls of the Mastoi home. Her shoes fell off.

"They didn't give me any time to say anything. They just caught me and took me. Faiz said: 'Do as you wish. Whatever you want, you may do.' When Faiz gave his command, I asked for pardon. They just attacked me. I yelled "Help! Stop!"[5]

Her father and uncle lunged towards her. A crowd of Mastoi men barred their way. They held the Gujjar men in armlock.

---

2. Testimony under cross-examination in Anti-Terrorism Court, Dera Ghazi Khan, August 2002
3. Interview with Sabir Hussain, Mirwala 2005-11-30
4. Added into prosecution witness statements after they were recorded by police are the words "armed with .30 bore pistol" after each mention of Abdul Khaliq's
5 Interview with Mukhtar Mai, Mirwala, 2005-11-30

Mukhtar, thin and slight, begged. "This is not what you promised! You are breaking your word!"

Abdul Khaliq turned to the crowd flashing his pistol.

"*Hashar Kardaingey!* Any among you who follow, will be killed!"

Four men dragged her into Abdul Khaliq's room, next to the room where her teenage brother had been locked up with Salma hours earlier.

"Is there no Muslim here who can save my honour? Is there nobody who can save my respect?" Mukhtar cried. But none came forward.

"*The men took Mukhtar to a room inside. Mukhtar said: 'I'm just like your sister, please have mercy on me, please let me go'. She was looking at everyone's faces, saying: 'Please help me and do something for me.' Nobody responded.*"

Uncle Sabir told me three years later. "*There were only four of us and 200 of them. The Mastois caught all four of us by our arms. They had pistols and rifles. About a dozen of them held us back. How could we break free? We were helpless in front of 200 of their people.*"

"*We heard Mukhtar's screams from inside the room. She was saying: 'Please for God's sake, let me go'. She was crying and shouting:'I have brought the Qur'an with me, so please forgive me'.*"[6]

Several charpoys lay against the walls. The men forced her to the ground. They ripped off her *bochan*. They tore the front and sides of her kameez. They pulled off her shalwar.

They left the door open.

One by one, Mukhtar says, four men forced themselves inside her. Once each.

"*Their faces were like animals. I didn't feel anything. I turned to rock,*" she told me.[7]

Elsewhere in the compound were Allah Ditta's wife and five children; Taj Mai, the mother of Punnu, Allah Ditta, Abdul Khaliq and Salma; and at least three of Taj Mai's six daughters, including Salma.

"*I was made to lie on the ground, not on the cot, without force, mildly. At the time that one out of the four accused committed zina with me, the remaining three remained present there. At the time of zina, my shalwar was not in my legs. At the time that the second person committed zina, he did not clean the smeared place of my private parts. I did not, rather could not, resist with my hands and legs, as I stood overpowered by four persons. The door of the room remained open during the period of zina.*"[8]

---

6.  Interview with Sabir Hussain, Mirwala, Nov. 30, 2005
7.  Interview with Mukhtar Mai, Mirwala, 2005-11-30
8.  Summary of Mukhtar Mai's answers under cross-examination, in Anti-Terrorism Court, Dera Ghazi Khan, August 2002

When the fourth man finished, almost an hour had passed.

Abdul Khaliq, the 21-year-old whom her family had earlier proposed she would marry in a watta-satta exchange marriage contract, pushed her out of his room.

Trouserless, her long tunic ripped, and without her shawl, Mukhtar stumbled towards the doorway of the compound, and fell.

Someone threw her trousers at her as she lay between the room where she'd been attacked and the doorway out of the compound. They landed on her head.

*"My shalwar was thrown on my head while I was two to four paces outside the door of the said room. I had been pushed by Abdul Khaliq and I fell down in front of the galla (open door leading out of the compound). I had called out to my father at the time that I fell down in front of the galla."*[9]

"Abu, (father) Abu," Mukhtar called to her father.

No-one blocked the woodcutter as he went to his semi-naked daughter. He picked her shalwar off her head. In silence, he lifted her from the dust.

*"After one hour Faiz Mastoi said: 'Bring the girl to the Gujjars'. When she came out of the room she was wearing only her kameez. It was torn. Her face was full of anguish. They threw her shalwar outside. Mukhtar's father took the shalwar and we came home,"* Uncle Sabir recalled.[10]

Uncle Sabir picked up her shoes.

Mukhtar wrapped her bochan around her naked legs.

In silence, the father and the uncle took Mukhtar between them and headed into the sugarcane towards home.

*"We didn't ask her what happened and she didn't tell us. We were not game to ask. We were embarrassed and ashamed, so we had no courage to ask her. But we could understand what had happened,"* Sabir told me in November 2005.

The forlorn quiet of the humid night was cut by a final shout from Abdul Khaliq.

"We'll teach you a lesson if you speak of this to anyone. Hashar Kardaingey! Anybody reporting the matter will be dealt with!"

Mukhtar's only memory of emerging from the Mastoi walls is the sight of her father and uncle, being unleashed from the armlock of her attackers' kinsmen. She sensed scores of others were still milling in the shadows.

---

9. All the above sequences and quotes are based on official transcripts of prosecution testimony in the August 2002 trial in Dera Ghazi Khan Anti-Terrorism Court and on interviews with Mukhtar Mai and her family.
10. Interview with Sabir Hussain, Mirwala, 30.11. 2005

She remembers the moonlight. She does not remember how she got from there to her own home on the other side of the field.

\* \* \* \*

In her house the women are howling. The men are silent. Panicked toddlers mimic their mother's crying. The only woman not crying is Mukhtar. She does not speak.

"I did not know anyone. I did not know my family. I was rock."[11]

Bachul Khanoom could not look at her daughter.

*"She was like a madwoman. I just looked at my child and I looked at the sky, I looked back at my daughter and I looked at the sky. How can I describe…? When I remember that moment, I completely forget the present and everything that's happened since, and everything before."*[12]

The shrieking of the women lasted through the night.

"Everyone was weeping. We were not in our senses," Mukhtar told the court later.[13]

In the middle of their wailing, Mukhtar remained rock.

# 5

# A Cow For My Son

*Wishes come to my lips in the shape of prayers:*
*May my life glow like a candle in the dark*
*That the sorrows of the world be banished*
*And with my light*
*May darkness fade*[1]

**Allama Mohammad Iqbal, National Poet**

## MIRWALA, JUNE 23, 2002

In the first frozen moments of Mukhtar's return to home, none came to her.

"All were standing some distance from me. They didn't come to me."

She shut herself in her room. She shut her family out. Numbness fused her limbs. Her body turned to stone. Her eyes paralysed into the stare of a corpse.

"When a woman is raped, she has no feelings. I was like a stone. I felt nothing. I was senseless."

An oblong mirror, edged with scalloped green and blue cloth, hung limp against the wall.

Every morning Mukhtar would gaze into its milky glass while Tasmiya, her youngest sister, knelt behind on the bed and brushed the knots out of her heavy hair, weaving wiry tresses into a plait. Now a dark shape sat motionless in the glass.

Above the howling outside came a knocking on the door. It floated over her.

"I buried my face in my hands and wondered why did God do this to me? What was my sin? Why did God choose me for this?"

The adoring grooming by her little sister was already another life, finished. Mukhtar felt no longer touchable. She didn't want to live any more. The knock kept coming. Now the women wanted to come in.

"Go away. Don't come near me."

Her mother came in.

---

1.

Bachul Khanoum cradled her first-born daughter, still and silent. Slowly she swayed her, and prayed in murmurs.

"*Bismillah* In the Name of Allah, the Beneficient, the Merciful, she cooed. "*Alhumdulli-lah hi rabill-al al amin, ah rahman nerahim maliki yom mehdeen.* Praise be to Allah, lord of the worlds, the Beneficient, the Merciful, owner of the Day of Judgement," she whispered in recital of *Al Fatihah,* the opening verses of the Qur'an.

"*Iya ka na budoo ya ka nestain.* Thee alone we worship, and thee alone we ask for help.

"*Eh dina serat-al Mustaqim serat-al azin.* Show us the straight path, the path of those whom Thou has favoured.

"*An am ta alleihum Rairul maqhubi Aleihhum wallah do alin.* Not the path of those who earn Thine anger, nor of those who go astray. Amin Amen."

Mukhtar was blank.

"My mother was saying something but I don't remember what she was saying."

No prayer came to Mukhtar's lips. The lines of the Qur'an she had taught to little girls vanished from her heart.

"I was unhappy with God for this. I lost hope in Him. I was hopeless, despairing."

Beyond the women's sanctuary, beyond the courtyard, the men still had a deal to make. Shakoor was still in the police lock-up, without charge, and dawn was a few hours off.

The Gujjars sold a cow and a calf to get their boy out of the cell.

The Mastoi elders had demanded 10,000 rupees (160 US dollars) for his freedom. The Gujjars raised 8,000 rupees by selling the cow and calf to a Gopang tribe who lived near the local coal plant. They borrowed the balance. Cash in hand, Faiz Mastoi, Ramzan Pachaar and Uncle Sabir went to the Jatoi police station and told the police to release Shakoor. Uncle Sabir stayed outside the police station while the Mastoi men dealt inside.

Shakoor was brought home around 2 o'clock in the morning. He found his family weeping.

Uncle Sabir told Shakoor his sister had been taken before the Mastoi men to seek pardon for him. To punish Shakoor for violating Salma, the Mastois assaulted his favourite sister.

But Shakoor turned the story upside down. He told his family that Mastois had gang-raped him in the sugarcane hours earlier. He claimed that Salma had never been in the field with him.

Hazoor Bakhsh was sleeping when his sister came home in torn clothes. The family told him what had happened when he woke the next morning.

"I wanted to go the Mastois and beat them. But it was too late."

"I wanted to kill myself. I wanted to drink rat poison. I was ashamed every time I went outside. Everyone asked so many questions about Mukhtar and the incident. I was embarrassed. I had failed to save my sister."

When thoughts came back to Mukhtar's mind, they were of one thing: suicide.

"I thought of drinking insecticides, acid sprays, sprays for the cotton. But my family kept them all away from me. If I had got hold of any I would have drank them."

"I stared at the ceiling fan. I wanted to hang myself from it. But it was too loose. It couldn't hold my weight."

Her step-grandmother came the next day, through the cotton fields. Iqbal Khanoum was the first relative to visit.

On the second day, the relatives began streaming in. Old women with gold nose-rings and dangling bell-shaped earrings, headbands slashed across their foreheads, veils trailing down their backs. Aunts, great aunts, girl-cousins with babies. They gathered in the courtyard.

Mukhtar stayed in her room.

After three or four days the neighbours began coming.

"As people came to know of the incident, they came. Some came to offer sympathies. Some were just curious," Mukhtar recalled.

The women came in to the courtyard. The men stayed outside.

Still Mukhtar did not emerge.

"I sat with her night and day," her mother recalled. "For several weeks I never left her side. She wanted to kill herself, so I didn't leave her alone for one minute. I prayed to God to give her justice."

Bachul Khanoum took the Qur'an from Mukhtar's hands and drew her lifeless gaze to it. "This Qur'an will bring you justice," she whispered to her broken daughter.

"I kept reassuring her: 'God will help you. He will give you bravery and strength. He will give you justice. He will give you a good name. Your name will be respected throughout the world."

Sometimes Mukhtar heard the women talk outside.

"If you take this case to the police the Mastois will kill you," the women said to her mother and sisters.

"I would have been happy to be killed. I thought: 'If they kill me, I will be rid of this situation, this life.' I didn't want to live any more."

Hazoor Bakhsh saw his sister's suicidal state.

"I was scared she would kill herself. She wanted to take rat poison. Everyone in the family was pleading with her not to commit suicide. Our mother, our father, our aunts."

Amid the longings for death rose anger. It planted a seed.

"I felt no shame. I had done nothing wrong. I felt angry."

As the anger grew, defiance began to flicker under the dark moth wings suffocating her heart.

"I want to fight them," Mukhtar declared to her family.

The men folk refused.

"If you go to the police I will commit suicide," said Hazoor Bakhsh, voice high, eyes bulging.

"Go ahead," Mukhtar replied. "It's a pity you didn't kill yourself when they were raping me."

The uncles protested. Her father shook his head. Only her mother supported her.

"If you want to fight the Mastois, if you want to file charges, you should," she whispered to her daughter.

"When she said 'I want to fight', I realised her courage," Bachul Khanoum recalled.

"She is my daughter and she wanted to fight for something right. So I supported her. I knew these men were criminals. They were powerful men doing wrong things."

"I was surprised at her strength and bravery. For one girl to stand on her own and fight for her rights is a very strange thing. She showed courage."

In Mukhtar's recollections, strength was slow in coming.

"For a month I lost hope in God. I kept thinking he would give me strength, but it didn't come.

"After a month I thought, 'I have to make courage in myself first, then God will give me courage to fight'. After that God helped. I felt Him helping me."

# 6

# House of Women

**NOVEMBER 2005, MIRWALA**

"She was his bride!" the old widow hollers in autumn sunshine, surrounded by her rag-clothed grandchildren.

Gold studding her bulbous nose, the matriarch of the house where Mukhtar says she was assaulted, rocks, sobs, and pulls on the tattered corners of a thin purple floral shawl pyramiding her face, and wipes her raging tears.

"We never took their girl! They are telling lies to you and everyone! To take a girl and do such things to her does not exist in Islam. Muslims and Islam know no activity like this."

Taj Mai Mastoi, somewhere in her 60s, cries on a charpoy[1] *in her dust-blown courtyard.*

"No one realises we also are Muslims!"

She clutches her knee to her chin between outbursts of spitting rage.

"There was no rape!" she fires. "There was not even a panchayat! She came as a bride!"

This is a house of women now. All of Taj Mai's menfolk are in jail: two of her sons are accused of raping Mukhtar, another son is convicted of raping Mukhtar's brother. Four of the brothers and two sons-in-law are accused of sanctioning the gang-rape of Mukhtar. Taj Mai's husband Imam Baksh Mastoi passed away before 2002. Aged and small, she has been left in charge of a family of 18 children and women.

The old lady and her two daughters-in-law—their husbands in jail—pick cotton on the fields of landlords, for 15 to 75 cents a day. Sometimes they rope in the older children to work the fields.

In the Mastois' wildly different version of events, Mukhtar Mai and Abdul Khaliq were married by Maulvi Abdul Razzaq in an on-the-spot verbal ceremony at nightfall on 22 June, 2002.

---

1. Sipah-e-Sahaba: An organization of fanatic Sunni Muslim extremists, blamed for the deaths of thousands of followers of the rival, minority Shia sect of Islam

They claim that she had spent three nights in Abdul Khaliq's room as his bride.

"That was their room," yells eight-year-old Tariq Mohammad, Khaliq's youngest brother, pointing to the middle of a three room hut.

The instant marriage, the Mastois say, was to compensate for Mukhtar's brother's 'rape' of their girl Salma. A Gujjar girl's hand was given in exchange for the dishonouring of a Mastoi girl. That's why they never pressed charges for the alleged rape of Salma, the Mastois claim.

On a Sunday visit in November 2005 to the residential compound of the Mastois, only the children are at home. The old lady went to the jail to see her sons. Her daughters-in-law were in the fields picking cotton.

When we returned the following morning, with two armed policemen and a plainclothes officer from Mukhtar's 12-strong permanent police guard as escorts, the old lady and the wife of one of her jailed sons, Maqsooda, were expecting us.

They moved across a barren field to meet us. Accompanying them was a male relative from a neighbouring house, thick lines of kohl under his eyes, his feet bare on the cold cracked earth of the barren field.

Taj Mai explodes in fury. She curses the foreign media for glorifying Mukhtar. She lambasts the publicity surrounding Mukhtar's case as one-sided.

"You come here to talk to me, but I don't want to talk to anyone! There is no justice for me. My conditions are terrible. My sons are in jail," she rants. "No-one wants to hear or tell our reality."

She fires at the police accompanying us. "What kind of police are you? Our little girl went past Mukhtar Mai's house the other day and the police ordered her to get lost. Our little girl is not a terrorist!"

Eventually placated by my translator's insistence that we want to hear her story, the old lady relents and beckons us over the dry field into her dull mud-walled compound.

Poverty stalks this home of no men. It is a stark contrast to the local media portrayal of this family as powerfully-connected wealthy landowners. Only two emaciated goats and two skeletal cows make up their livestock.

Bone-thin dogs and cats saunter through the courtyard. No tea is offered. No food is cooking on any fire. No one is kneading any dough for roti bread, the basic item of village diets.

Unlike Mukhtar's home, no paved road leads to this house, and no electricity lights their nights. Cracked dirt trails run between fields and irrigation ditches to the Mastoi home.

The door to Taj Mai's room sits dislodged inside her room.

"I have no door to my own room. The dogs and cats come in here at night," she says.

Maqsooda, the wife of Taj Mai's second son Allah Ditta, grabs her own little daughter's arm and shoves it at me. It is stick thin and covered in thick protruding lesions.

"Do you have any money for me to fix her arm? I can't afford to take her to a doctor for treatment."

She sticks a thumb through her daughter's worn mud-soaked tunic. "Look at these rags! We can't buy any clothes."

On the night Mukhtar says she was gang-raped in this house, all the Mastoi women – Taj Mai, her six daughters, a daughter-in-law - and an assortment of grandchildren were at home.

The Mastoi women say a *sharai nikah* (verbal marriage) ritual took place between Mukhtar Mai and Abdul Khaliq, witnessed by Mukhtar's father, brother and uncle.

"It was a traditional *nikah*, from the early days of Islam, when nothing was written. There were just witnesses and the Maulvi pronounced them married, without writing any certificate," says Taj Mai.

For the Mastois, 22, June 2002 began with prayers for the dead. A relative in another Mastoi home had passed away. All the adults had gathered at the home of Khair Muhammad Mastoi, several fields away, to offer prayers and condolences. Only Maqsooda stayed at home with the children.

In the middle of the hot mid-summer day, Maqsooda says, she heard Salma, then in her late teens, screaming in the sugarcane crop. She looked over the wall and saw Salma beating Abdul Shakoor with a sickle.

"I ran and grabbed Abdul Shakoor and dragged him back here," she says, pointing to the far corner room of the three-room hut. "I threw him in that room."

A padlock hangs broken above the room's door. Inside rafts of dusted sunlight fall on turquoise-brushed walls and a shelf lined with tin bowls and cups. "That lock was broken when Shakoor tried to escape."

The bricks that once blocked one of the high air vents are still smashed.

"That's where he smashed his way out. He broke these bricks and climbed through the hole and escaped," Maqsooda says.

Maqsooda caught Shakoor again, dragged him back inside and locked him away. She sent for the menfolk to come home from the mourning gathering at Khair Muhammad Mastoi's compound. When they reached home Maqsooda told them she had caught Abdul Shakoor 'raping' Salma and had locked him up.

Shakoor's father and uncles turned up at the Mastoi home and asked them to let Shakoor go. With them were Maulvi Adul Razzaq and the police, Maqsooda recalls. Shakoor's father, brother and uncles persuaded the Mastois not to file charges with the police over Shakoor's alleged actions.

In return, the Mastois demanded the hand of one of Shakoor's sisters.

"Their son raped our daughter, that's why," said Taj Mai. "We were upset because Abdul Shakoor raped Salma."

Shakoor's family offered up Mukhtar Mai. Shakoor was let out of the room and handed over to the police. In the night Mukhtar was brought to the Mastoi home by her menfolk and a *sharai nikah* was performed between her and Abdul Khaliq, some time after Ishar, the last evening prayer, Maqsooda and Taj Mai say.

"No one wrote a nikah certificate. We just collected witnesses. Then the marriage was confirmed. Early Islam required no official statement for a nikah. On that day nothing was written, we just did as they did in early times," Maqsooda says.

Mukhtar stayed in Abdul Khaliq's room for three nights as his bride. According to the Mastoi women.

The floor of the 'bridal' room is hard-baked earth. Like the room next door where Shakoor had been locked up, the walls are painted turquoise. Alcoves and shelves are carved into the mudbrick. Iron bars fill two window holes on either side of the door.

On peeking inside, I find Taj Mai's two unmarried teenage daughters, Parveen and Zarina, huddled in the shadows behind the door. Forbidden to be seen by strange men, they are hiding from the police guards who have accompanied me. They have been watching us through the barred windows.

"With the nikah, our quarrel was resolved," says Taj Mai. "We told them: 'Our families are now joined in marriage. Let there be no more quarrel between us'.

"But after 11 days, Mukhtar went to the hospital for a medical test," Taj Mai said. It was the semen test Mukhtar underwent on the instructions of police after filing gang-rape charges.

"In our minds our families were joined in marriage, but she went and got a medical."

A fresh quarrel had erupted between the neighbouring families after the alleged marriage between Mukhtar and Abdul Khaliq.

"Maulvi Abdul Razzaq, Mukhtar's older brother and her father came and started fighting with us about Abdul Shakoor and Salma," said Maqsooda.

After Mukhtar's medical test, which found positive traces of semen, police swooped on the Mastoi clan.

"The police recorded an FIR (First Investigation Report) from Mukhtar's side and arrested people without any reason," says Taj Mai.

Among the first to be taken in by police were Taj Mai and her daughter Salma.

"They did a medical test on Salma too," Taj Mai said. She doesn't know what the result was.

The mother and daughter were moved on to another, bigger jail, in the district capital Muzaffargarh.

More arrests came in waves until 14 Mastoi men were in shackles, awaiting trial.

"They wrought tyranny on us," Taj Mai spits.

"The real sin was by the other side. Their boy molested our girl. But everyone says it's us who did wrong. The police should start a new inquiry and collect all the neigbours and find out the truth."

"If Mukhtar's family comes here I will tell them what really happened. If Mukhtar thinks something wrong has happened to her, she should just keep quiet. But instead she tells everyone. She even goes to the US."

Taj Mai spends her days now reading the Qur'an, picking cotton and cutting wheat – the crops of other landowners.

"I work daily on the lands of other men. What I earn each day, I spend. I can save nothing. Ask Mukhtiar Mai whether we are wealthy or not. We work on the land of landlords. All our men are in prison."

Taj Mai pulls her knees closer and sobs.

"Mukhtar's family doesn't realise how much I worry about my sons, my grandchildren. We have only children in the house. No young men," she rages.

"I'm the only one earning money for my house. I'm a poor woman."

The embittered Mastoi women's fiercest venom is for the local preacher Maulvi Abdul Razzaq and his role in bringing Mukhtar's case to the police.

They call him the 'architect' of the case.

"The root of all this is Abdul Razzaq," breathes Maqsooda.

"He got involved in this case because of the money he gets from Mukhtar Mai's family, and because of land."

The Mastois told the trial court in August 2002 that Razzaq had grudges against them because they reported him for trying to occupy land they had paid for at a public auction.

They had also accused him of harbouring fanatics from the banned extremist group, Sipah-e-Sahaba.

"He's a Wahhabi, a Deobandi," Taj Mai and Maqsooda charge in chorus, invoking extremist Islamic sects.

From the charpoy where Taj Mai vents her rage, the walls of Mukhtar's home are visible across the field, over the heads of the cotton plants. With a twist of the head one can glimpse the side-wall of Mukhtar's girls' school, shining with a fresh coat of maroon paint.

For the Mastois, the new school is a forbidden world. The little Mastoi girls stay at home.

"Mukhtar Mai doesn't allow our girls to get admission," Taj Mai asserts. "We never tried to send our girls to her school. No-one listens to us, so who would support us in sending our girls to her school? They would never allow it. They didn't even allow our boys."

Taj Mai says her eight-year-old son Tariq joined Mukhtar's boys' school for just a few months, but was driven out. Tariq, the little brother of accused rapists Abdul Khaliq and Allah Ditta, stopped going to the school after one of Mukhtar's nephews threw stones at him and told him to never show his face again.

"None of my children or grandchildren go to her school. No Mastois go to Mukhtar Mai's school," the old lady states.

"All day I just watch and wonder when my sons will come home. No-one takes pity on my grandchildren. There is no justice for us. You can see I have no wealth, no money, no lands. We have gained nothing from this case."

"God does not give us justice."

It wasn't until November of 2005 that I ventured across the sugarcane field to the home of the Mastois, the family whose menfolk are accused of gang-raping Mukhtar. The attack was said to have taken place inside a room in the Mastois' compound.

Mukhtar and her secretary Naseem, the principal of her school, insisted I take some of their police bodyguards with them. Twelve armed policemen are permanently posted next to Mukhtar Mai's home to provide her 24 hour protection. Three policemen were deputed to accompany me and my young lady translator.

The media reports in 2002 had painted the Mastoi family as powerful, politically-connected mini-landlords.

What I found, more than three years after writing about Mukhtar Mai's gang-rape from my newsdesk in Islamabad, was a pit of grinding poverty and disenfranchisement.

The oldest Mastoi son, who was in jail at the time of my visit to his mother and siblings, told me seven months later that on the day I visited, the children had not eaten in three days.

The tale which many had never questioned started to unravel when I met the family of the accused rapists. Salma was their little sister.

Instead of the influential, well-connected, land-owning family they had been portrayed as, they floundered in some of the worst poverty I'd seen.

Mukhtar Mai's family actually had some of the best connections in Mirwala village. They had the backing of the wealthiest, largest and oldest tribe in the tehsil (sub-district): the Jatois. They were also backed by the most powerful figure in the district: the preacher of the biggest mosque in Mirwala, Maulvi Abdul Razzaq, his tribe: Jatoi.

Inconsistencies in both sides' recollections were plenty, but that would happen among any group of people – be they educated Westerners or illiterate villagers - asked to recollect an event three years back.

I sought out the preacher. He had a murky past. He belonged to Pakistan's most murderous gang of Sunni Islamic extremists, the Sipah-e-Sahaba (Army of the Companions of the Prophet)—outlawed in 2001 for its links to the murders of rival Shias.

# 7

# A Crafty Cleric

One person emerges pivotal in bringing to light the gang-rape of Mukhtar Mai: the soft-spoken bearded mullah of Mirwala's biggest mosque.

The Mastoi family harbour their fiercest venom for Maulvi Abdul Razzaq. Without the cleric's June 28, 2002 sermon, and without the cleric by Mukhtar's side, police may never have registered charges of gang-rape.

The cleric was the first to go public with the allegations of gang-rape, in a fiery Friday sermon on June 28, the first Muslim Sabbath after the Mastoi-Gujjar feud.

Over the following two days, the mullah drafted a statement to police in the name of Mukhtar Mai. He was one of the people who persuaded Mukhtar Mai's father to file gang-rape charges.

"I registered the case," he admitted in an interview in 2006.

"I drafted the statement of Mukhtar Mai on her behalf."[1]

One of the police officers who handled the case said that police later summoned the mullah to persuade Mukhtar Mai's reluctant father to file charges.

"Maulvi Abdul Razzaq was called by police to convince the father of Mukhtar Mai to register a case, because the father was not prepared to go ahead with charges," said the police officer, who has asked not to be identified.[2]

The mullah's motivations for publicisng rape claims and then ensuring charges were filed with police became a major source of contention in the trial that convicted six men in August 2002, and in the High Court appeal hearing two and a half years later that acquitted five of them.

In the days following the June 22 Mastoi-Gujjar feud, as anger quietly subsumed Mukhtar's suicidal state, the men of her family tried to douse any will to fight.

"My brother Hazoor Bakhsh said: 'If you go to the police, I will kill myself'," Mukhtar recalled.[3]

---

1. Interview Mirwala, May 2006
2. Interview, Dera Ghazi Khan, May 2006
3. Interview, Mirwala, August 2005

The Mastoi biraderi will kill us, her father and uncles counseled, if you make this public.[4]

Only Mukhtar's mother was on her side.

For six days after the assault Mukhtar stayed in her room, the discomfort of the suffocating 40-plus heat drowned out by her own agony.

For those six days, Maulvi Abdul Razzaq says he tended to his followers, teaching the Qur'an to his students in the Farooqia madrassa (religious school), nine kilometres away in the bustling centre of Mirwala, on the other side of the humid cropfields.

He insists that no one told him for six days that the gathering he had walked away from on the night of June 22 had ended with the alleged eye-for-an-eye gang-rape of the Gujjar woman—despite his key role in trying to broker a compromise between the tribes.

The Maulvi's brother Haji Altaf Hussain testified in the court that he witnessed Mukhtar being dragged into the Mastoi home by four men. He told the court that he heard her frenzied begging to be saved from dishonour. He said under oath that he saw her emerge an hour later in torn clothes.

The brothers Haji Altaf and Maulvi Abdul Razzaq lived in the same house. But Razzaq insists that his brother never told him of the brutal outcome of the feud he himself had tried, and apparently failed, to resolve.

"It is further contended that if such a heinous offence had been committed, Altaf would have narrated it to his brother, who was an arbitrator on behalf of the complainant party and had left the panchayat meeting as the accused party had not acceded to his proposal of exchange marriages between the parties," *the judges of the Lahore High Court noted at an appeal hearing in March 2005.*[5]

Haji Altaf has never explained why he apparently kept from his brother what he allegedly saw on June 22.

\* \* \* \*

I met the mullah of Mirwala's biggest mosque in August 2005.

'He entered an antechamber of the Farooqia mosque compound, facing a swollen canal, flocked by young followers with kohl under their eyes—students of the madrassa. Through the open door one could see water buffalo wading slowly through the canal, their large docile eyes skimming the muddy water's edge. Bicycles glided along the banks.

The mullah spoke softly. His sombre eyes were large and gentle. His beard was long and ashen.

---

4. Testimony under oath, Dera Ghazi Khan Anti Terrorism Court, August 2002
5. Lahore High Court (Multan Bench), March 2005, judgement in Criminal Appeal No. 61 of 2002, Mukhtar Mai versus Faiz Muhammad etc, pg 17

He sat cross-legged on the floor, leant feebly against the wall. His student followers huddled around him, eager to be near.

His expression was deadpan as he recalled the night of the gathering to resolve the feud over Shakoor's alleged rape of the Mastoi girl Salma.

"I went to the Mastoi home after Hazoor Bakhsh came to me and complained that Mastois had kidnapped Shakoor. When I got there the Mastois said to me: 'Shakoor raped our daughter and should be punished'. They asked me, 'What is your decision?'"

"I replied: 'If this is true, Shakoor must marry your daughter. This is the Muslim way.' It was around evening prayer time. When I proposed marriage between Shakoor and Salma, the Mastois refused. They said. 'He has done this to our sister, we must do the same to his sister.'"

"They refused my proposal to marry them, so I left. As I left, the Mastois said, 'We will consider further'."

The mullah says the gathering was a panchayat, an informal village council, attended by 200 to 250 men. He says the panchayat dispersed after he left.

"When I left, the panchayat dissolved and everyone went home," he told me.

"Then the Mastois summoned Mukhtar and her uncle. Mukhtar's uncle brought her to the Mastois' house. When she got there they raped her. I was not present."

I asked him when he was told of the assault.

I heard of it after one week, the Maulvi replied.

According to Razzaq, no-one had rushed any earlier to tell him that his efforts to strike a compromise were shattered, and that a Gujjar woman was violated to avenge her brother's violation of a Mastoi woman. The Maulvi was the man Mukhtar's family had first turned to when Shakoor was locked up for violating Salma Mastoi. Yet according to the Maulvi, none of Mukhtar's family or her supporters sought the mullah's counsel after Mukhtar was attacked. Then an informer came to him on the first Friday following the feud and told him that the feud resulted in an 'eye-for-an-eye' rape. Razzaq says the informer was himself a Mastoi. However, he refuses to give the man's identity.

"A Mastoi man came to me and said: 'Bad things have happened.' It was Friday, before prayers. I replied: 'I shall tell the people in the mosque of this at Friday prayers.'"

The cleric went to his flock.

"There were three or four hundred people gathered for *juma* (Friday) prayers," Razzaq recalled.

Before his congregation, the mullah unleashed one of the fieriest sermons in Mirwala's memory.

One of the worshippers present on that day was Mulazam Hussein, the *'lumberdar'* (unofficial police informer) of Mirwala.

"The Maulvi narrated the story in a very sensational manner," the 75-year old recalled four years later.[6]

"I told them everything. I mentioned the names of everyone involved," Razzaq said.

"I said to my worshippers: 'What shall we do?' The people stood up and said: 'Imam, we are with you'."

"Wrong has been done. Justice must be sought," the mullah declared.

"We are with you," the worshippers murmured in chorus.

* * * *

His flock dispersed, the mullah mounted his motor scooter and wound along the canals between the cotton and sugarcane to the woodstall of Mukhtar's father Ghulam Farid.

"After prayers I took some people to Mukhtar Mai's father and asked him: 'Is this true?' He was afraid. He did not want to talk about it," the mullah recalled.

"He said: 'No. It is false."

"I replied to the father of Mukhtar Mai: 'Ghulam Farid-sahib, do not fear. We are with you. I am with you. Tell us the truth. If there was rape, we are with you and we shall be with you. Do not worry about anything.'"

"'It is not true what you have been told'," Mukhtar's father replied, according to Razzaq.

The mullah left the woodcutter alone.

* * * *

The mullah's sensational Friday sermon had spread through the teastalls and bazaars of Mirwala.

Mureed Abbas, a small-town human rights activist and wannabe freelance journalist, was eating at a shopfront canteen with two other companions, who were aspiring reporters as well, when the tale of a gang-rape by order of a panchayat reached them.

All three were eager to establish themselves as journalists. They had the whiff of a sensational story.

The day after the Friday sermon, Mureed Abbas appeared at Abdul Razzaq's door.

---

6. Interview Mirwala, May 2006

Like the Maulvi, Mureed Abbas was from the Jatoi tribe. But he followed a different strain of Islam to Abdul Razzaq. Abbas was a Shiite. Razzaq was a hardline Sunni.

Abbas wanted to know more about the revelations of Razzaq's Friday sermon.

The mullah invited Abbas and his two companions to come with him on another visit to Mukhtar's father.

Ghulam Farid was chopping wood when the mullah again appeared at his woodstall, this time with some journalists at his side.[7]

"Ghulam Farid-sahib, the people are with you. It is safe to tell us what happened to your daughter," the Maulvi said.

The woodcutter paused.

"Tyranny has been wrought on us once. Let it not be wrought a second time," the woodcutter pleaded.[8]

"I will help you seek justice," the Maulvi replied.

"If we go to the police we will be killed," Ghulam Farid said.

"You have our support. We are with you," the cleric repeated.

"Give me some time."

The cleric returned to his mosque. Ashar prayers rose and fell, the cleric knelt and bent his forehead to the straw mat covering the earth floor in prayer. There was no word from the woodcutter.

The sky flushed apricot and burned in the west. Saturday's Maghreb evening prayers echoed between the minarets of Jatoi. There was still no word from the woodcutter or his daughter.

According to the Maulvi's testimony in the August 2002 trial, Mukhtar and her father came to his residence the next day, Sunday June 30, ready to go to the police.

At dawn on Sunday, Fajjar prayers subsided, the cleric rose from his knees and the first grey light of Sunday, June 30 infused his simple chamber.

The woodcutter stood in his doorway.

"I have brought my daughter."

A ballooning black cloak shifted behind the woodcutter. Mukhtar was veiled. Next to her was Uncle Sabir.

"Let us go to the police," the cleric pronounced.

While retelling the events in August 2005, the cleric said that Mukhtar's father "eventually admitted that the allegation was true."

---

7. Testimony of Abdul Razzaq under oath, Dera Ghazi Khan Anti-Terrorism Court, August 2002
8. " "

"Later I took Mukhtar Mai and her father to the police station to file a First Investigation Report (police report)," he told me.

* * * *

The cleric's role was to be heavily highlighted more than two and half years after bringing Mukhtar's case to the police, when the Lahore High Court met to consider an appeal against the conviction and death-sentences of six Mastoi men over the alleged gang-rape.

"One thing is clear: that in spite of gravity of the alleged offence, if the prosecution story is believed, the complainant party was not ready to report the matter to the police. The matter was reported to the police on the instigation of PW-11 (Maulvi Abdul Razzaq), accompanied by pressmen. As such PW-11 is the mastermind who got this case registered. He appears to have involved them by influencing and pressurizing the complainant and her father Ghulam Farid, who were playing in his hands, according to his own statement," the Lahore High Court stated in its verdict of March 2005.[9]

The prosecution witnesses testifying at the August 2002 trial presented the following account of the registration of gang-rape charges with the local police:

At 7.30 on Sunday morning June 30, Mukhtar, her father, her uncle, the cleric, the cleric's brother and Ghulam Nabi approached a lone police officer stationed in a patrol car at the Jhugiwala chowk (intersection), a few kilometres beyond the outskirts of Mirwala.

Inspector Nazir Babar Ahmad, stationed in the patrol car, was on the lookout for dacoits, bandits who wreaked terror along the Indus banks, kidnapping villagers for ransom and stealing cattle.

The 'Bosun' gang of dacoits had been sowing fear among the riverine villages in recent years. They hid in the foliage along riverbanks, and on islands in the middle of the muddy Indus waters.

"They are very good swimmers," Abdul Sattar Qamar, my fixer in Multan and a constant interpreter of the ways of the southern Punjab, told me.

The gang reputedly could also outwit police trackers when looting cattle.

"When they flee the scene, they put cattle shoes on their feet, so no-one can trace their footprints. Even the expert trackers are lost," Qamar added, giggling.

In the summer of 2002, the Jatoi police had stepped up patrols to thwart the canny Bosun gangsters. The police car now stationed permanently at Jhugiwala chowk was part of the new drive to save the riverine community from kidnapping and theft.

---

9.  Lahore High Court (Multan Bench), March 2005, appeal judgement passed in Criminal Appeal no. 61 of 2002, Mukhtar Mai versus Faiz Muhammad etc pg 24

On June 30, the Inspector says he was confronted with a different cancer plaguing the river people: tribal-administered justice.

It was presented by a cleric.

Without a senior or respected local figure, rural police rarely take any woman's rape complaint seriously.

But Mukhtar Mai had Maulvi Abdul Razzaq on her side.

The cleric had the power of the Sipah-e-Sahaba behind him.

And he was from the largest, oldest and most affluent tribe of Mirwala: the Jatois.

Prosecution witnesses told the court that it was at this point that Inspector Nazir Babar Ahmad wrote up Mukhtar Mai's statement and read it back to her. The witnesses' testimony conflicts with the cleric's own admission in 2005 that it was he who drafted the statement in Mukhtar Mai's name.

According to the prosecution, six men and the cloaked woman followed the Inspector to the Jatoi police station.

When Mukhtar Mai recalls entering the gated garden of the Jatoi police compound on June 30, she remembers a message being brought to them from her older brother Hazoor Bakhsh and Uncle Ghulam.

"If you tell the police of this, we will not be responsible for what the Mastois may do to you in revenge," the pair warned. "We will be helpless in the face of their revenge."[10]

The woodcutter hesitated. His daughter proceeded.

A First Investigation Report was held up to her by the police officer. It carried a statement in her name.

She could not read the statement nor the charges it carried; nor could she sign her own name. She told me later that it hit her hard; she had no idea what the charge-sheet really said. Even if she could read, the language the police used was not her own. She spoke Seraiki, a language peculiar to the southern Punjab. The national language Urdu was foreign to her. Jatoi lay in the heart of Seraiki-speaking country, but all official documents including police materials were in Urdu. And then, an old longing resurfaced. In her youth, Mukhtar says she used to watch some relatives and better-off villagers go off to school. She wanted to learn too. She was eager to read and write. The frustration at her own inability to read her own statement sharpened her long-held desire.

The police gave her an ink-sponge. With the Maulvi's encouragement, she dipped her thumb in it and imprinted her thumb-mark on the police statement in her name. The thumbprint was her signature, on a statement she could not read.

---

10. Interview, Mirwala August 2005

"You must be examined," the police told her. "Go to the lady doctor."

"We left the police station and found a huge crowd gathered," Mukhtar says in recollection.

The Maulvi left the Gujjars' side and melted through the onlookers, she recalls. The Gujjars stood alone before the crowd.

One person came forward to offer help: Rasheed, a relative. Mukhtar says he brought his motor scooter to Mukhtar and offered her the pillion seat. He drove her to the Jatoi Rural Health Centre. Constable Yar Muhammad followed.

On the eighth day after the alleged rape, Doctor Shahida Safdar, the Women's Medical Officer at Jatoi Rural Health Centre, examined Mukhtar. The 'lady doctor' took nine vaginal swabs, sealed them in three phials and gave them to Constable Yar for dispatch to the chemical examiner in Multan, the main city 120 kilometres away.

The timing noted on Dr Safdar's report is 10.30 am Sunday June 30.

Dr Safdar noted in her report:

1.  A healed abrasion 3 x 1 cm on right buttock
2.  Healed abrasion 1.5 x .5cm on perineal area[11]

In Multan, the chemical examiner analysed the nine swabs. Three were from the posterior fornix, three from the vaginal canal and three were from the external vaginal area.

It took a week for the chemical examiner to submit his report to police. The report pronounced: The above swabs are stained with semen.'[12]

The chemical examiner did not differentiate between the three categories of swabs. His report suggested that semen remained in all three areas, including the external region, despite the passage of eight days.

With the finding of semen stains, Dr Safdar concluded rape.

* * * *

Inspector Nazir Babar Ahmed and Deputy Superintendent Muhammad Saeed Awan told the trial court that they drove out to Mirwala on the afternoon of July 30 to inspect the scene of the assault.

At Mukhtar's home, the policemen testified, they recorded more statements from Mukhtar and her family and quizzed the cleric. Inspector Nazir Babar Ahmed says it was on this Sunday that he first asked Mukhtar for her clothes. He knew they would be crucial for semen-testing.

---

11. Medical report tendered as evidence to Dera Ghazi Khan Anti Terrorism Court, August 2002
12. Chemical Examiner's report tendered as evidence to Dera Ghazi Khan Anti Terrorism Court, August 2002

"I have 19 years service in police department. I know that clothes worn by the victim of *zina-bil-jabr* (rape) have strong evidenciary value," he told the trial court.

But Mukhtar declined to hand over her clothes that day. She promised to submit them the following day instead.

It was the Maulvi who collected Mukhtar's dupatta, shalwar, and kameez from her and delivered them to the police, the following day.

But the clothes were never examined for semen stains.

"Those clothes were not sent to the WMO for examination and report, (as to) whether those were smeared with semen," Inspector Nazir Babar Ahmed told the trial court.

He gave no explanation for not testing the clothes for stains, despite having stressed his awareness of the 'strong evidenciary value' of clothes in proving rape charges.

It was during the police investigators' inspection June 30 in Mukhtar Mai's Mirwala home that the first mention was made of Shakoor's claim to have been sodomised in the sugarcane by three Mastoi men—Salma's oldest brother Punnu, and his two cousins Jamil and Manzoor.

The sodomy claim was presented to contest the Mastois' claim that Shakoor raped their girl Salma. Shakoor denied raping Salma. It was he who was raped, Shakoor claimed.

"On 30.6.2002 it came to my notice from the PWs (prosecution witnesses) that Shakoor had been abducted; sodomy had been committed with him on 22.6.2002 and Salma was confined along with Shakoor in one room to save their skin. I recorded statement of Shakoor on 30.6.2002. Maulvi Abdul Razzaq stated to me that the facts of sodomy/confinement were to be confirmed, and thereafter the case would be got registered," Inspector Nazir Babar Ahmad told the trial court.

Inspector Ahmad says he brought the Maulvi over to Deputy Superintendent Saeed Awan to relate the sodomy story.

Awan listened to the cleric. He told the Inspector to register sodomy charges against the three Mastois.

"It came to my notice on 30.6.2002 that Abdul Shakoor had been abducted by Punnu, Jamil and Manzoor, who confined him after committing sodomy. Salma was also confined with Abdul Shakoor to dramatise the event, which facts were stated to me by the complainant party at the spot. I advised the SHO (Inspector Ahmad) to register a case to this effect," Awan told the trial court.

The Maulvi gave the court a different version. He testified that he tried on the day of the police inspection of the crime-scene to register a case of sodomy, but the police "made excuses" to avoid registering the case immediately.

"On 30.6.2002 I had said to police that a case regarding Shakoor should be registered. But police had not registered the same and made excuses...and said that they will verify regarding the said occurrence," Razzaq said under cross-examination.

On July 3 at around 10:00 AM, at the mobile police van parked at Jhugiwala chowk, the Maulvi registered another case against Mastoi clansmen: the sodomisation of Abdul Shakoor.

Police Sub-Inspector Imam Bakhsh recorded Shakoor's statement and read it back to him. The adolescent stuck his thumb in ink and pressed it against the statement in confirmation.

According to a medical report tendered by Dr Fazal Hussain, the Resident Medical Officer at Jatoi Rural Health Centre, Shakoor was examined at 11:15 AM on July 3 for signs of sodomy.

Dr Hussain noted "marks of violence" on the perineal region: he found "the margins of the anus were indurated (callous/hardened)," and noted "a tear on the inner mucosa of the anus."[13]

"The anal examination was painful," Dr Hussain remarked in his July 3 report.

He also noted "two healed abrasions on the left upper chest" and "a stitched incised wound 2.5 cm on the left side of the forehead near the left eyebrow which was oblique in direction."

The doctor gave much more detail about the marks on the chest and forehead than about the anal-region marks. He took two anal swabs from Shakoor and dispatched them to the chemical examiner in Multan to check for semen. And without waiting for the chemical examiner's finding, the doctor delivered a diagnosis of sodomy.

"The signs/symptoms had led to the (conclusion of the) occurrence of sodomy act in my opinion," Dr Fazal Hussain pronounced in writing on July 3.

The chemical examiner issued a report on July 12, eight days later: no traces of semen were found.[14]

Nine months later the men accused of sodomising Shakoor were put on trial for the crime of "unnatural lust" under Pakistan's Islamic '*Hudood*' laws. Dr Hussain was forced to admit under cross-examination at the little-reported sodomy trial that there were no decisive signs of sodomy:

Defence lawyer: "Did you mention seeing any anal fissure or haematoma?"

Dr Hussain: "I did not mention anal fissure or haematoma."

Defence lawyer: "Did you mention the length or width of the tear (on the inner mucosa of anus), or its direction?"

13. Medical report (MLC no. 149 of July 3 2002) tendered as evidence to Dera Ghazi Khan Anti-Terrorism Court, August 2002
14. Chemical examiner's report July 12 2002,, tendered as evidence to Dera Ghazi Khan Anti-Terrorism Court, August 2002

Dr Hussain: "No I did not."

Defence lawyer: "Is it true that induration (hardening) may be the result of some disease or trauma?"

[The doctor's report had cited induration of the margins of the anus.]

Dr Hussain: "It may."

Defence lawyer: "Is it correct that tears disappear in five to seven days?"

Dr Hussain: "It is correct."

[The doctor's report had cited a Tear on the inner mucosa of the anus.]

Defence lawyer: "Is it correct that there can be no symptom (of sodomy) if the examination is conducted after 10 days?"

[The doctor examined Shakoor 11 days after he was allegedly sodomised.]

Dr Hussain: "It is correct."

Defence lawyer: "Who stated that there were pains at the time of (anal) examination?"

Dr Hussain: "The patient himself stated so."

Defence lawyer: "Is it correct to suggest that due to pressure of the government and police, you issued a false MLC (medical report)?"

Dr Hussain: "It is incorrect."[15]

Dr Hussain also tested Shakoor for "potency," to determine whether he was capable of sexual intercourse with Salma, as charged by the Mastois. Through a prostatic massage, the doctor concluded that Shakoor "was fit to perform sexual intercourse."[16]

Dr Hussain subjected the three accused sodomists to the same prostatic massage after their arrests later that month, reaching the same inconclusive diagnosis: "all three were capable to perform act of coitus."[17]

On July 3, having registered two sets of charges – the gang-rape of Mukhtar Mai, and the gang-rape of her adolescent brother – Maulvi Abdul Razzaq of Sipah-e-Sahaba returned to his followers.

\* \* \* \*

The Maulvi's relations with the Mastoi clan came under the spotlight in the Lahore High Court when it met in 2005 to consider the appeal by six men convicted over the assault of Mukhtar Mai.

---

15. Transcript of cross-examination of Dr Fazal Hussain, Additional Sessions Court Alipur, Hudood Case No. 14-2 of 2003, Hudood Trial No. 63-2 of 2003 May 28, 2003
16. Potency Report, tendered as evidence to Dera Ghazi Khan Anti-Terrorism Court, August 2002
17. Potency Reports, tendered as evidence to Additional Sessions Court Alipur, Hudood Case No. 14-2 of 2003, Hudood Trial No. 63-2 of 2003 May 28, 2003

The defence team painted a portrait of pre-existing hostility between the Maulvi and the Mastoi clan.

"It is further contended that Abdul Razzaq has enmity with the Mastoi tribe and there was a motive behind this bitterness… " the Lahore High Court stated in March 2005.[18]

Abdul Razzaq belongs to an orthodox Sunni Muslim organization rooted in the southern Punjab: the Sipah-e-Sahaba, Army of the Companions of the Prophet.

What had essentially been a grassroots organisations linking clerics of the same creed grew over two decades into one of the most violent outfits in Pakistan. Muslims in Pakistan follow one of two sects: Sunni Islam or Shia Islam. However, more than 80 percent are Sunni. Fanatics of both groups began gunning each other down in Karachi in the 1980s. By 2001, Sipah-e-Sahaba had been linked to the murders of several thousand Shi'ites. President Pervez Musharraf outlawed the organisation late that year.

Razzaq, and other known hardline Sunni clerics like him, were routinely locked up by police when Sunni-Shia violence flared and on sensitive Shiite religious festivals.

Abdul Razzaq's brother Haji Altaf Hussain told the trial court that his brother had been part of Sipah-e-Sahaba, but had left its ranks many years earlier.[19] The violence by Sipah-e-Sahaba followers was limited to the organisation's radical fringes. But Abdul Razzaq's links to it were enough to give his opponents ammunition against him.

"Learned counsel for the appellants has contended that…Maulvi Abdul Razzaq belonged to a sectarian group, who is in the habit to create sensation, and he did so in this case due to his personal grudge against Mastoi tribe," the Lahore High Court pointed out.[20]

Maulvi Abdul Razzaq's hatred of the Mastois and their supporter Ramzan Pachaar stemmed from two sources.

Ramzan Pachaar had accused Razzaq of harbouring fugitives from Sipah-e-Sahaba. They had tried to oust him from the Farooqia mosque for giving shelter to Sipah-e-Sahaba militants.

"I have been falsely involved at the instance of Maulvi Abdul Razzaq, as I played role to kick him out from the mosque due to his nefarious designs, harbouring activists of Sipah-e-Sahaba and other indecent activities," Pachaar told the trial court in August 2002.[21]

---

18. Appeal judgement, pg 16, Lahore High Court (Multan Bench) March 2005
19. Testimony of Haji Altaf Hussain under oath, Dera Ghazi Khan Anti-Terrorism Court, August 2002, The State versus Abdul Khaliq etc
20. Appeal judgement, Lahore High Court (Multan Bench) March 2005, pg 18
21. Dera Ghazi Khan Anti-Terrorism Court, The State versus Abdul Khaliq etc, Defence statements August 19, 2002

The second source of enmity was a land dispute in the mid 1990s between Abdul Razzaq and the father-in-law of Ghulam Fareed Mastoi, one of the accused rapists, over a piece of land listed as Lot no. 189 of Sardar Kouray Khan Trust, named after a late clan leader who had bequeathed a massive land holding to the local administration.

Abdul Razzaq told police in a statement in July 2002 that the Muzaffargarh District Council had granted him "two square of land" around 1995.[22]

However Karam Hussein Mastoi, Ghulam Fareed Mastoi's father-in-law, had secured the plot at a public auction and paid a deposit of 16,000 rupees (around 265 dollars).

In his statement to police, the Maulvi accused the Mastois of "illegally occupying different lots."[23]

"It was also stated in his statement... that Mastois had purchased the same and they belonged to the Qabza group. In this way he had shown the enmity between him and the Mastoi tribe," the Lahore High Court judges concluded in March 2005.[24]

However Petition number 2949/1995, lodged in the Lahore High Court in 1995, shows the Maulvi was accused of colluding with two district administrators from the Muzzafargarh District Council to get his name listed as the owner of the plot, despite Karam Hussain Mastoi's purchase of the plot at public auction after making the highest bid. [25]

*     *     *     *

The alleged gang-rape of Mukhtar Mai would not have been made public without the Maulvi's announcement in his Friday sermon to Mirwala's worshippers.

Mukhtar may not have laid charges against the Mastois without the Maulvi's support.

And the Maulvi's motives for persuading Mukhtar, against the will of her menfolk, to lay rape charges against the Mastois became a focus of the defence case.

The prosecution's presentation suggests the Maulvi was acting out of a sense of justice and compassion when he filed the charges – a humble village preacher coming to the help of the oppressed.

In the Mastois' eyes, Abdul Razzaq was a crafty cleric who had seized on a chance to avenge the people who had taken him to court for attempted land-grabbing and tried to expel him from his mosque.

*     *     *     *

22. Appeal judgement, Lahore High Court (Multan Bench) March 2005
23. Abdul Razzaq statement to police, July 2002
24. Appeal judgement, Lahore High Court (Multan Bench) March 2005
25. Haji Karam Hussain v. Maulvi Abdul Razzaq, Writ Petition No. 2949/1995, Lahore High Court

Mureed Abbas, the aspiring reporter, gives a significantly different account of how the case was first brought to the attention of police. He claims that he was the one who brought Mukhtar to the police station on the evening of Sunday, July 30. He says the police report was filed on Sunday evening, not Sunday morning as the prosecution claims.

Abbas says he and the two other small-town reporters went to the police themselves on the weekend following the Maulvi's Friday sermon revelations and hustled them to register a case.

"We told the police: 'If you don't register this case, we will go to your higher-ups and complain about you'," Abbas told me in a meeting in March 2005.[26]

According to Abbas, the police declined to lodge charges without a statement from Mukhtar Mai as the victim.

Abbas says he took the police himself out to Mukhtar's home at the edge of Mirwala late on Sunday afternoon, June 30. The police bundled Mukhtar, her father and younger brother into the back of a police van and drove them in to Jatoi police station.

Abbas remembers a duststorm blowing up behind the police van as he followed on his motorscooter.

"Dust-storms only occur in the late afternoon, that's how I remember what time of day it was," he told me.

It was almost nightfall by the time Mukhtar and her family reached the Jatoi police station, borne in the back of the police van.

Mukhtar Mai and her father also told an investigating magistrate in July 2002 that, contrary to claims in court that they appeared voluntarily at the police station with the Maulvi to register the case, they were in fact picked up by police and brought to the police station. When they got there a statement was waiting, already drafted in Mukhtar's name.[27]

The statement already in police hands had been drafted by the Maulvi, Abbas recalls.

It was so late on Sunday when Abbas and the police got Mukhtar to the Jatoi police station that the Rural Health Centre was closed. The lady doctor, who was needed to conduct a rape examination, was at home in her village, several kilometres away.

Abbas had already filed a news report to three newspapers in Multan, detailing the sensational tale of an eye-for-an-eye gang-rape on the orders of a panchayat. He was not going to let the absence of the lady doctor stop him

26. Interview, Jatoi, March 2006
27. Lahore High Court (Multan Bench), judgement of Criminal Appeal No. 61 of 2002, Mukhtar Mai versus Faiz Muhammad etc, clause 9, page 9

from ensuring the case was registered. He had already filed his story to the Multan newspapers announcing the lodging of charges.

Abbas gave me a detailed account of how he mounted his motorscooter again and drove out to Dr Shahida Safdar's house. It was after 8.00 pm. Abbas brought the doctor back into Jatoi to the locked Rural Health Centre. The lady doctor unlocked the clinic. It was about 10pm on Sunday night by the time she examined Mukhtar Mai.

Meanwhile back at the police station, Abbas recalls seeing Maulvi Abdul Razzaq arrive for the registration of the case.

\* \* \* \*

In my meeting with the Maulvi in August 2005, he made the following observations about the role of the supposed panchayat in the assault on Mukhtar Mai.

"I don't believe the panchayat ordered the rape. Faiz Mastoi ordered the rape, along with Ramazan Pachaar. This order was made by the Mastoi family," the Maulvi told me.

"The panchayat had dissolved after the Mastois refused the proposed marriage (of Shakoor and Salma).

"Then two men, Ramzan Pachaar and Faiz Mastoi, said 'Bring Mukhtar Mai and her uncle, and if the uncle and Mukhtar Mai apologise we will forget everything'. But when Mukhtar Mai and her uncle reached the Mastoi home the Mastois didn't ask for any apology."

The Maulvi had already stressed that he was not present when the direction was given to bring Mukhtar before the gathered Mastoi menfolk, nor was he present when she arrived and when she was allegedly dragged inside the Mastoi home. Therefore, Razzaq's version of events after he left the gathering is at best second-hand.

"This is not a problem of the panchayat system. It has no connection to panchayats. This is a problem of feudal lords. Feudal lords like Ramzan Pachaar and Faiz Mastoi," the Maulvi pronounced.

It was some months later that I saw the land holding records of Faiz Mastoi. A total of 16 acres was listed in his name.

The acreages of feudal lords actually begin in the thousands.

\* \* \* \*

Apart from belonging to the same Jatoi tribe, Mureed Abbas and the Maulvi had something else in common: their loathing of 'feudal lords'.

Abbas spends most of his days gathering data on violence against women and girls and other human rights abuses. He has a portfolio of testimonies and photographs of victims of acid-burns, victims of forced child marriage, victims of nose-chopping, and victims of honour killings. He also gathers data on murders of men. He links most of the crimes to 'feudal lords'.

Abbas showed me a gruesome photograph of a male corpse, covered in large puncture holes. The man had been thrown into a crops thresher, he claimed, on the orders of a feudal lord who was running for election. The victim was an electoral worker. He was being punished for refusing to manipulate polling in favour of the unnamed feudal lord. Abbas did not cite proof for his claims.

Abbas and Razzaq are both campaigners against the scourge of feudalism— ownership of massive swathes of land by a few wealthy families, many of them members of provincial and federal parliaments. In its worst manifestations, feudalism perpetuates a serf-landlord dynamic, whereby villagers live off the land of large landowners and pay dues through a 'tithe' of the crops they cultivate.

Like Razzaq, Abbas sees the alleged crime against Mukhtar Mai as a symptom of feudalism. Both portray the Mastois as a powerful clan backed by feudal lords.

# 8

# Neon Caravans, Tunnels of Love

*I wish I were a flower in your hand*
*So that when you bend your face to smell me*
*I could kiss you*
**Urdu couplet on the back of a Pakistani truck**

Whispers of unrequited love, self-deprecations of abandoned lovers, pining and lovelorn, vows of undying passion in the face of infidelity, sigh and float up and down the highways of Punjab, behind belched diesel fumes and clouds of dust.

*There is no longer my lover, There is no longer my garden*
*There is no longer my flowerbed, Everything is ruined*
*But I'm still longing for you*

Songs of longing, the tender moan of a famished heart, long-distance yearnings, bleat from the most unlikely of places: the back of trucks.

*You came after such a long time*
*And even now you say you have to leave again.*
*Stay a while, so my heart can settle a little,*
*Then I can cheat it by telling it you're still mine*

Pakistani trucks plying the old caravan routes of the Punjab, the fabled Frontier in the northwest, the interior of Sindh, and the ancient Silk Routes of the mountainous north are celebrated for their glossy carnival-esque paintwork, kaleidoscopic portraits, wistful landscapes and elaborate decorations.

Intricate wood carvings in cedar and walnut frame the drivers' cabs. Triangular flags flutter from corner poles. Feathery chains of hammered steel brush the wheels, jangling music to the driver's ears. Koranic calligraphy wraps around cab windows. Faux tiaras crown the drivers' cabs. Towering decorated prows slope two metres above the cabs. Tinsel tumbles down the sides, catching the hot sun. Long-lashed eyes gaze from wheel flaps. Plastic flowers drape the cab doors. Even the wheel hubs are painted, with pointed cones protruding from their centres.

Trucks in Pakistan are canvasses for colourful, exuberant artwork. A plain side, rear or front panel on a truck is a naked canvas. Few owners or drivers leave their panels bare. In fact owners pay up to a million rupees (16,600 USD) to professional truck artists to transform their lumbering lorries into glittering frescoes-in-motion, with larger than life portraits in bold verdant greens, sky blues, hot magentas and buttercup yellows.

Amid the riot of colour and Mughalesque decoration, portraits of raven-haired Bollywood actresses gaze down on rear drivers; a cherubic child, clutching a Kalashnikov and framed by a green valley, smiles Mona Lisa-like through the freight traffic; military dictators and heroes of past display shoulders-full of brass; rare partridges are encircled in light, while depictions of dreamy Kashmiri valleys, peacocks in blue-jewelled splendour, the Prophet Mohammad's winged white stallion in freeze-frame gallop, and dashing cricket heroes criss-cross each other as the trucks meander in death-defying overtakes, hurtling towards oncoming traffic with macroseconds to spare before diving into their home lane.

The trucks are flamboyant murals in motion.

Billboard-sized panels bear giant roses, nuclear missiles, deer, F-16 fighter jets, waterfalls, the Taj Mahal, the capital's gleaming Faisal Mosque, and snow-capped mountains in homage to the giant ranges of the north.

Camel-bone inlay, floral motifs or tiny mirrors edge the borders of painted panels.

Monotonous highways and miserable villages are set aflame with the colour, dreams and patriotism borne by the work-horse trucks.

Less visible to the foreign eye are the romantic Urdu couplets scrawled across the bumper bars.

> *The blisters of my tired feet are asking:*
> *'Why does my beloved live so far away?'*

In the most unexpected of places, the lyrics of Sufi poets and Urdu scholars reach out to drivers stuck behind the diesel-spewing Bedford trucks. The Bedford 'Rockets' flooded Pakistan's market in the 1960s. They remain the most prestigious among the 800,000 trucks plying the highways today.

> *You want another and I want you*
> *You wish for another; I long for you*

It's transportation on a different level, out of the drab landscapes and endless dusty horizons, into an escapist world of heightened colour and romantic love.

> *Please leave the brightness of the glow of your memory in me*
> *You never know in what street the sunset of my life will happen*

Truck poetry is a testament to the pop-culture embrace Pakistanis give to Sufi poetry and classical Urdu couplets. Bumper-bar poetry showcases the romantic longings surging beneath culturally-imposed repression.

Such delicate sentiments also permeate popular rock music, political slogans, school classes and village chatter.

> *The right words must be spoken at the right time,*
> *Fruit is best when it's in season*
> *counsels one driver with simple Sufi logic.*
> *Her walk is essence of intoxication*
> *Her body is sculpted by wine*
> *sighs another*

Beneath the carnival of colour, the cacophony of jingling chains and the craziness of cat-and-mouse highway navigation, a quiet couplet in elegant Urdu script can calm a driver's soaring blood pressure.

> *My body aches after a hard day's labour*
> *O Night embrace me, like my mother's bosom*
> *Come in peace, go in peace*
> *Mother's blessing is breeze from heaven*

Pakistan's long-haul road poets, the modern-day equivalent of the prehistoric Silk Route caravan drivers, wear their hearts on their bumper bars.

> *You should live forever*
> *So I can live in hope of seeing you*

In the days of the camel caravans, traveling merchants would pay coins to hear a professional story-teller. Poets and story-tellers held court in the bazaars lining the old Silk Road caravan routes, spinning lyrics for weary traders for a price. One of the winding bazaars in Peshawar, the dramatic Pakistani frontier city leading to Afghanistan, is still called 'Qisa Khawani', the Street of Storytellers, from the city's days as a merchants' cross-roads.

Today's truckers have taken the tradition of poems-for-a-penny out of the Silk Route-era bazaars and on to the tailplates of their old Bedfords.

A note of almost slapstick self-mocking lies in many couplets' portrayal of the love-sick fool:

> *Came and said the messenger: 'She's coming tonight'*
> *I lit up the house so much, that I burnt it down.*

A distinctly Sufi sentiment celebrates joy over dour faith:

> *Life is with the beloved*
> *Death is with faith*

Portraits of devotion evoke Urdu and Persian masters A. K. Ghalib and

Jalaluddin Rumi.

> *Hold this cup in front of me*
> *That I might see her picture in the cup*
> *I gave my heart to someone who was unfaithful*
> *I will cut out my tongue, If it says anything against her*
> *I've said it: I'm yours*

The highways edging the five rivers of the Punjab near their confluence in the south at the grand Panjnad Head irrigation canal works, carry some of the heaviest cargo traffic in Pakistan. The east-west axis between the Indian and Afghan frontiers criss-cross the north-south axis between the Karachi port and northern Pakistan. Suitably, the trucks down here are among the most dazzling and polished on the country's terrifying roads.

The trucker's life is arduous. Marathon journeys stretch over dun-shaded days, from the teeming Arabian Sea port metropolis of Karachi, through thirsty stretches of Sindh's parched Thar Pakar desert, into the sand dunes of the Upper Indus as they roll into the southern Punjab.

The sand dunes break unexpectedly into flat patchworks of dust-brushed cotton plants in winter, green wheat sprouts in spring, wide-boughed mango trees dripping with their jeweled fruits and the honied gold of harvested wheat bundles as steaming summer sets in, and the thick green stalks of sugarcane at the long end of summer.

Gangs of stone crushers line the strips between the highways and railway tracks, pounding and shoveling stones in Sisyphean labours, evoking prison chain-gangs.

Brick-kilns blight the fields, puffing black smoke above the sweaty backs of bonded labourers, toiling to pay invincible debts to ruthless brick kiln owners who double as money-lenders. In a 12-hour day a man can make 500 bricks and take home 110 rupees (less than two dollars). Labourers who've built up loans of 200,000 rupees (3,330 dollars) have 16 years of work ahead to clear their debt. So they rope their children in to help.

> *Death is better than this miserable life*
> *At least one can have a deep sleep*

Tearing across the southern Punjab bound for the western frontier city of Quetta, the gateway to Central Asian trade routes through the badlands of Afghanistan, the trucks coarse over the flood-prone river flats known as 'katch' to reach the mighty Indus, the mother of all subcontinental rivers. The 'katch' hide the feared dacoits who kidnap for ransom and steal cattle. The river-bank dacoits nail cow-shoes to their flip-flops to disguise their footprints as they spirit their seized quarry across the pounding brown currents of the Indus to the safety of another district.

As drought cracks the earth, villagers pump ever harder at old Persian wheel hand-wells, plumbing the ever-sinking water table.

Truckers' stops lining every highway provide the only interludes: low whitewashed bungalows, arched facades, rank plumbingless washrooms, and some of the best food in Pakistan.: parathas (leavened bread) tandoori-roasted with mouthwatering crispness, tender meat curries, creamy dahl (mashed lentils), chal banna with al-dente chickpeas. Competition for the big market in famished truckers is fierce.

Double-bed sized charpoys lay side-by-side dormitory style. Gypsy women from starving settlements off the road bring the homesick drivers sex at night. The same is provided by the boy 'helpers' attached to each driver.

I found a veteran truck artist in a ramshackle open-air workshop at the edge of the Pir Wadhai bazaar in Rawalpindi, the bustling city next to Islamabad.

He calls himself Tosha Bomb. Like the best artisans in the truck painters' guilds, he learnt the craft from his father as a child apprentice.

Ninety percent of trucks in Pakistan are painted and carry poetry, Tosha Bomb estimates.

"The truck drivers have big hearts. They love each other. They want to entertain everyone," he said on a break between truck makeovers.

"When we see a good verse in front of us, it makes us push our truck harder," said Ashgar, a young trucker's 'helper'who earns 50 dollars a month keeping the truck exterior polished, the engine in order, and the driver happy.

"Every truck should have poetry," he said. "Whoever reads it will become happy."

A full truck art makeover including elaborate ornamentation and painted verse can cost up to one million rupees (16,600 dollars).

"The drivers are not rich. But they will spend huge amounts of money on their truck," Tosha Bomb explained.

"It's like a moving home. I may go hungry, but I'll always keep my truck beautiful. In the same way that Western people treat their pets as more precious than their children, that's how we are with our trucks."

Most of Pakistan's 228,000 kilometre (141,000 mile) road network is potholed and cracked. Ascents up mountains are narrow and skirt hair-raising cliffs. Accidents frequently claim upwards of 40 lives at a time, giving Pakistan the world's third highest road death rate in 2004.

A sense of fatalism pervades the bumper-bar verse:

*The life of a driver is a strange game.*
*If you don't die on the road, you end up in jail*

"The drivers write poetry because it relaxes their nerves," Haji Javed Butt of the All Pakistan Trucks Drivers' Union explained.

"When you're driving under scorching sun for days and weeks with little rest, you can easily go mad.

"When the drivers stop to sleep on the side of the road, exhausted, and they look up and see the colourfulness of their trucks and read the verses on their bumpers, it revives them."

A warning to swooners of their nomadic ways:

*Don't fall in love with us drivers, we are from far away*
*We are not unfaithful, but we always leave*

Light-hearted banter lifts the mood:

*Don't be jealous of my greatness,*
*Just pray for me*

*Shutup, Liar*

*O my beloved, don't get angry with me for nothing*

Then night falls, and the nocturnal driver rolls into another world.

The trucks save their most spectacular secrets for midnight travelers. The glory is no longer the realm of galleries-in-motion on the trucks' side and back panels.

Night is the dance of the trucks' enormous front prows. The high boards above the drivers' cabs are coated in neon lacquers and glazes that glow in the dark, festooned with reflector lights arrayed in geometric patterns.

Suddenly the highways resemble rolling funfairs.

Neon-red tunnels of love plough forward through the fertile lands of the Punjab night, streaking the modern-day trade routes with glow-in-the-dark kaleidoscopes. Some flash, some rotate.

As each towering prow, ablaze in neon oranges, reds and greens, lumbers forward in the queue of decorated Bedfords, more fantastical patterns fan out above the black highway tar.

I woke in the middle of a night road trip through the southern Punjab to find a blaze of neon arches and tunnels bearing down on our car, one blazing lit prow after another. The enchanting displays transport one to the ghost trains and Tunnels of Love in the amusement parks of childhood. I understood the present-day caravan drivers' escape via their frenzied decorations and verse.

Pakistan's national language Urdu was originally the language of poets in India's northern Uttar Pradesh state. Considered one of the most sophisticated languages of the subcontinent, Urdu has been the choice of many of the region's poets and writers.

The verse etched on truck rears is only occasionally original; often it is a variation of the work of 20th century Urdu-language scribe Allama Iqbal, Pakistan's late national poet, or Sufi mystic Baba Buleh Shah.

Their couplets are expressions of Sufism, the liberal artistic Islamic tradition which informs the sensibilities of most Pakistanis, yet is frequently drowned out by headline-grabbing fundamentalists.

*Destroy the mosque, Raze the temple*
*But don't break anyone's heart, Because that's the real house of*
*God*

a driver echoes Baba Buleh Shah

*You should live forever*
*So I can live in hope of seeing you*
entreats another love-struck driver.

On the Great Trunk Road connecting Kabul with Calcutta via Pakistan, the fabled road traveled by Rudyard Kipling's "Kim" in his adventures through British-ruled India, a timber-laden truck ponders the nature of authentic love:

*Love, love is to be spoken only by he who knows what love is,*
*He who can sell even the shirt off his back to please his beloved.*

On a road to Balakot, the northeast valley city buried by the Black Saturday earthquake in October 2005, a truck carries supplies to its shattered people; while its bumper bar verse carries the drivers behind it to a place where people need help to see:

*'What is it I do?' you ask of me.*
*I'll tell you how I toil my days*
*I sell mirrors in the city of the blind.*

In the agrarian villages of rural Pakistan, few read or write and women stay behind their family walls. It's never clear who sees everything. Illiteracy leaves people almost blind, relying on hearsay and rumour, and vulnerable to those with power by virtue of their hierarchy in the mosaic of tribes, or the amount of land they own, or their connections to the large landowners.

The landowners and the 'higher-ups' – police chiefs, prayer leaders, tribal elders—hold the mirrors and wield the power to angle the light, tinker with perceptions, measure illumination, and engage in smoke and mirrors plays of deception.

To delve into the other side of a tale is to step through the smoke and mirrors at play in cities of the blind, pull back the layers of claim and counter-claim, and wade into the other side of the mirror.

# 9

# The Other Side of the Mirror

After reading through the entire transcript of the August 2002 trial of the 14 men accused of either gang-raping or abbeting the gang-rape of Mukhtar Mai, and interviewing members of the Mastoi family and local officials, a new portrait of events on June 22 emerged.

It almost fit the pattern of tribal feuds and resolution processes which commonly employ cruel customs of compensatory marriage to stem feuds and unite warring tribes.

*   *   *   *

## JUNE 22, 2002 MIRWALA

### ** RECONSTRUCTION ACCORDING TO DEFENCE VERSION **

Salma Mastoi, a girl in late teens, strolled into a patch of sugarcane in the field next to the southeast wall of her family's small compound. She carried a sickle.

Her older brothers had left in the morning for another home to mourn a death of a kinsman of the Mastoi clan, a clan descended from the multitude of Baloch tribes. Many Mastoi clansmen had gathered for the funeral prayers. Only the women and children were left in Salma's home—her shrunken widowed mother, her older brothers' wives, her younger sisters and brothers, nieces and nephews.

The heat made the cane steam. With languor, she picked her way along a narrow trail through new cotton plants, and strode into one of the patches of sweet cane crops.

The sugarcane in Mirwala in late July reaches four to five feet—higher than her head. It is high enough to create a small hideaway chamber in the middle. Bend the cane so that it arches in a canopy discreet enough for forbidden lovers.

The cane lay in plot number 38/1/1, 4 kanals (half an acre) in size, owned by Salma's late father. Only one kanal on the plot was under sugarcane cultivation in summer 2002. Two and a half kanals were under cotton cultivation. Salma's family compound sat on the remaining half a kanal. In July that year the cotton was five to six inches high.[1]

Salma tucked her hair into the long shawl over head, tossed its tails over her shoulders and gripped her sickle. She flicked her wrist back and let it swing firmly inwards around a thick canestalk. The blade stuck, encased briefly in the tough outer skin. She yanked it out. The perforated top layer smelt green and young. It wasn't yet harvest time. She flicked and swung her wrist a second time, a third. On the fourth swing she penetrated the wet white flesh under the green skin. Drops of juice seeped through the fibres. The smell was still young; now new notes of sweetness softened the first sour breaths.

Drinking the cane's nectar was a diversion. It was her daily chore to chop the hardy weeds that grow among the canestalks.

She bent over and began hacking at the weeds. She didn't hear the rustle from the parting of the stalks. A shadow crossing the sunlight made her look up.

The goofy fluff-gloved face of the boy next door smiled down on her.

Had she ever spoken to Abdul Shakoor, the Gujjar adolescent almost the same age as her? She insists not.

*"He was not from my tribe. They were below us," she tells me in our meeting three and a half years later. "I never spoke to him in my life."*

*Minutes earlier I was sitting face to face—actually face to veil—with a goblin. A white shuttlecock-topped burqa covered Salma entirely, except for her noisily-bangled wrists and ringed fingers. The bangles rattled with every excited jerk and twist of her body.*

*"Salma, with your brother's permission, will you show me your face? I've waited so long to meet you."*

*The goblin jerks its head around to Punnu, her oldest brother, who walked out of prison two weeks ago after serving three years for supposedly sodomising Mukhtar's brother Shakoor.*

*Punnu nods. The goblin turns back to me.*

*"I will show you my face if you give me justice first!" it sputters through pretty panels of embroidered white cotton.*

*She pauses.*

*With sudden delicateness, Salma Mastoi lifts the veil up over her head, like a bride revealing herself.*

*Here at last is the face of the girl with whom it all began.[2]*

Shakoor lunged towards Salma. She dodged him. Shakoor lunged further.

---

1. Interview with Sawan Razza, patwaari (revenue administrator) of Mirwala, Multan, 06/03/06

2. Interview with Salma Mastoi, sister of Abdul Khaliq,wife of Khalil Ahmed, D.G. Khan, 07/03/06

His hands caught her waist.

"Get away!" she yelled and shoved his hands off.

He grinned. He pulled a small kitchen knife from his pocket.

"Get away Abdul Shakoor or I will shout for my brothers!"

Shakoor seized her hand. Salma shook it free. He grabbed her hand again. She jerked it from him and made to flee, but he caught her long kameez.

The knife scraped against her forearm. She felt it dig into her shoulder. She heard her kameez tear. She fell into the weeds she was supposed to be digging out.

The sight of blood on her arm undid Salma. She raised her sickle and hollered towards home for help. Her sister-in-law heard the cry.

Maqsooda, married to Salma's second eldest brother Allah Ditta, was inside the compound's walls kneading the dough to feed a swarm of babies, children, teenage girls, and her mother-in-law Taj Mai. Four of the children were her own.

Maqsooda heard Salma shouting. She peered over the wall. Salma was raising her sickle against Shakoor, the boy from the house across the field.

The men were all still out. Maqsooda abandoned the half-kneaded dough, threw her veil over her hair as she ran out of compound, swung to the right around the northern mud wall, and right again into the hotch-potch of mid-growth sugarcane and fresh cotton plants.

With the force of a furious mother towards a rebellious child, she grabbed Shakoor by the neck of his kameez and dragged him into the Mastoi home.

Maqsooda was yelling to the rest of the family before she even appeared in the open doorway. "Shakoor was commiting ziadti (rape) with our Salma! I caught him red-handed!"[3]

The sisters sent for the menfolk. A child was dispatched to bolt over the fields to the house of the funeral prayers.

Maqsooda threw Shakoor into a cell-sized room at the end of a row of three. She padlocked the decaying double wooden doors.

Inside sunbeams made shafts of dust grains, striking through a high iron-barred vent. The mud-brick walls were painted bluer than the sky. An inbuilt ledge held shiny tinware—plates, dishes, cups. A poor man's silver armoire.

Outside the women squawked above each other. The emaciated dogs slunked in circles around them, sensing the burden of shame. The women almost didn't hear the rattle of the padlock. The doors were bursting, shaking vertically, and the pathetic padlock split apart. From the dim shadows inside Shakoor burst into the open courtyard.

---

3. Interview with Maqsooda, wife of Allah Ditta Mastoi, Mirwala, 11/05

Maqsooda moved, again with the alacrity of a mother catching a wayward child, and shoved him back inside.

"Where are Allah Ditta and Abdul Khaliq!? We need them now!!" she said of her husband and his brother. The oldest brother Punnu lived 13 kilometres away in the nearest township Jatoi with his wife and three children. He was at his workshop that Saturday, a working day across Pakistan, so he hadn't joined his kinsmen in the funeral prayers.

This time the women held the rotting blue doors shut with charpoys and chairs.

Sensing too much silence Maqsooda pulled the chairs back and peered inside. Shakoor was half-way up the wall, balancing on the ledge for the tin crockery, bending the iron bars in the vent to make a big enough space to jump through.

"You scoundrel I'll have you! We'll fix you so you won't know what hit you!"

Salma's big brothers burst into the compound. Prayer caps stuck to the crowns of their heads. Their chests were thrust forth in the indignation of a family wronged.

"Give us Shakoor," demanded Abdul Khaliq. He was only the third eldest of the sons, but as the oldest unmarried son and the one closest in age to Salma and the other sisters, he shouldered the responsibility for the girls – the vassals of a family's honour.

In the villages of southern Punjab they call women the "mokhadis ghai": sacred cow.[4]

Abdul Khaliq tore the blue doors back. The darkness blinded him momentarily—until sunlight bouncing off the tin revealed the shift of a blue smock shift. Salma's big brothers beat him. This teenager, from another family and another tribe, a tribe they scorned as beneath them even though they had more land, had been caught in the field with their unmarried sister. It's enough for a brother to cry rape.

The interview session with Salma Mastoi continued....

*"Salma, what happened after Shakoor caught your clothes and you fell?" I ask.*

*She drops her eyes. She squeezes the hand of my translator, a city girl her own age.*

*"It's not easy for me to talk about such things." She bites her lip.*

*"Did he kiss you?"*

*"Yes."*

---

4.  Interview with Ashfaq Ahmad Qureshi, Jatoi Tehsildar (sub-district administrator), Jatoi, 05/03/06

*She rolls up the sleeve of her right arm to show a long, faded scar. She says that's where Shakoor scratched her with his small kitchen knife.*

"And more?"

Silence.

"Was that all?"

"No, there was more."

*She is shifting side to side, looking around perhaps for her brother, but we had already asked all the men to leave the room — the high-ceilinged bar-room of the barristers' bazaar of Dera Ghazi Khan. Salma now lives about 2 hours drive from this tribal city, in a village on the west bank of the Indus, across the muddy river from Mirwala where she grew up. She moved here after marrying a cousin, Khalil Ahmed. Khalil, his father and uncles were charged with abetment of the alleged gang-rape of Mukhtar Mai, but were acquitted in the first trial. The government threw him and his relatives back into prison two and half years later—one year before my meeting with Salma—as it sought to show the world its disgust with the High Court's March 2005 acquittal of three alleged rapists and two other alleged abettors.*

Fresh shouts came from across the field. Shakoor's sisters and mother were yelling at the Mastois from their own compound.

"Where is Shakoor? Is it true that you have him? Let him go!" they yelled.

"He is confined. We have locked him up for committing ziadti on our sister," the Mastoi men retorted.

Word spread rapidly at the funeral gathering that a Mastoi girl's honour had been violated. In the throes of mourning, Mastoi emotions were already high.

In small groups the men of the Mastoi extended family broke away from the prayer gathering and made their way across the fields towards the home of Allah Ditta, Abdul Khaliq and Salma.

Since their father Imam Bakhsh had passed away some years earlier, the oldest sons Punnu, Allah Ditta and Abdul Khaliq were left to manage the household of almost 20. Imam Bakhsh's widow Taj Mai was tiny. Her apparent frailty belied a feisty spirit.

The Mastoi Baloch are the fourth largest caste in the sub-districts of Jatoi and Jampur. The Indus River slashes through the two sub-districts. Travelling from Jatoi villages like Mirwala or Ranpur to the villages of Jampur takes 3.5 hours, whether by road or by walking to the banks of the Indus to take a frail wooden boat.

For their numbers, Mastoi elders were courted by local politicians of Jatoi and Jampur courting votes for seats in the Punjab provincial assembly and the National Assembly.

The Mastoi elder with the largest land holding was Faiz Muhammad Mastoi, about 35 years old, son of Khair Muhammad Mastoi. They lived in Ranpur, the village next to Mirwala. Faiz had 16 acres of land in his name: six acres in Mirwala and 10 acres in Ranpur.[5]

But the late Imam Bakhsh Mastoi's family was one of the poorest in the area. Just 2.5 beeghas, the equivalent of 1.25 acres, was left to his five sons and six daughters.[6] It's a paltry plot of land for the subsistence of a farming family.

The sons found other work—Allah Ditta as a tubewell mechanic, Abdul Khaliq as a kharadia (motor and farm machinery mechanic), Punnu at a mechanics workshop based in Jatoi.

On their 1.25 acre plot, which lay between their home and Mukhtar Mai's home, Imam Bakhsh Mastoi's sons grew small patches of sugarcane and carved larger squares for cotton plants.

In May they sow the sugarcane seeds. Cotton seeds follow in June. They harvest the cotton from October to December, when the heat relents and nights are even cool. The season is named after cotton: khasif. The sugarcane harvest follows, lasting sometimes until March. In April they burn the stumps of the canestalks. Wheat is planted in December, replacing the cotton crops. Squares of brilliant green sprouts enrich the southern Punjab plains through spring. In its taller, browner incarnation, the wheat is harvested from March to April. The wheat harvest season is called rabbi.

In 2002, Imam Bakhsh Mastoi's field yielded so little sugarcane that it wasn't worth recording in the khasar girdawari (crop registry) for the khasif cotton-harvest season.

The patwaary, the lowest government official at village level, registers all harvested crops in the khasar girdawari twice a year: during rabbi (wheat harvest) and khasif, cotton harvest.

All that is recorded for the harvest of October-December 2002 on Mirwala plot 38/1/1 is four kanals of cotton.[7]

But there was enough sugarcane in the plot to hide Salma and Abdul Shakoor.

In this part of the world, it is forbidden for males and females from different families to be together, especially alone. It is forbidden for a woman to be seen by a man not from her family.

A family's girls are their wealth, investment, and savings. Girls are traded, in the guise of brides, to gain land or to secure land already within the family; they are traded, in the guise of brides, to save a male relative from jail for murder; they are traded, in the guise of brides, in exchange for a bride from another family for their brother, cousin or uncle, and sometimes for their father.

---

5.  Interview with Sawan Razza, Mirwala Patwaari, Multan, 06/03/06
6.  Lahore High Court (Multan Bench) Multan, Judgement in Criminal Appeals Nos. 60-66 of 2002, HCJDA-38,03/03/05
7.  Khasar Girdawari (Crops Registry), Mirwala, Oct-Dec 2002

A girl seen with a non-relative male is stained. The stain can spread through the family, and dash the investment hopes represented by a daughter.

The rage infused Abdul Khaliq, then 21 or 22, more than any other. His prized sister had been touched by a strange man, moreover from the tribe that lived opposite, the tribe that communicated with no others in the village: the Tatla Gujjars, descendants of buffalo-herders. The Tatla-Gujjars owned two acres of land in July 2002, twice that of Salma and Abdul Khaliq's family.

A police van pulled up before Abdul Khaliq's compound and a trio of constables clambered out.

Shakoor's older brother Hazoor Bakhsh, the oldest of the Tatla Gujjar family opposite, lurked behind them.

"We've received a report that you've kidnapped Abdul Shakoor and tortured him. You must release him," one of the officers spoke.

"That fellow has raped our girl! We'll not let him go," Salma's brothers replied.

It was rare for police to show their faces in a village dispute, especially over women.

The aserwela call to prayer rang out. The crows' squawking grew lazier. By now dozens of Mastoi men had formed flocks in the barren field at the western wall of Abdul Khaliq's compound.

"Let Faiz decide," piped up Ghulam Fareed Mastoi, a relative from neighbouring Ranpur village.

Faiz Mastoi's father Khair Muhammad was already among the crowd, but Faiz had not yet reached.

The police agreed to wait. An hour passed.

Faiz Mastoi, one of the larger landowners of the Mastoi clan, walked hurriedly into the crowd.

"Let the boy go, but only into the hands of the police," Faiz declared. This way Shakoor was freed from the Mastois, but was still in custody pending a decision on his punishment.[8]

Shakoor was dragged from the dark room of his confinement and bundled into the police van. Behind the dust, the dozens of men of the Mastoi tribe were left alone in an akath, a gathering of the members of an extended tribe, to determine how to salvage their honour and amend the violation of Salma.

Some men from the Pachaar tribe fell in among them, including Ramzan Pachaar, about 35 years old, like Faiz. Pachaar was best friends with Hazoor Bakhsh, Shakoor's older brother.

8. Prosecution testimony, State vs Abdul Khaliq etc, FIR 405/2002, Anti-Terrorism Court, Dera Ghazi Khan, 07/2002

The local preacher Abdul Razzaq stood before them. He had come as the representative of the Tatla Gujjars, who had gathered in distress at the tiny Ya Rasul Allah mosque, about two kilometres away across six fields.

"I want revenge for the disrespect of my sister through zina," Abdul Khaliq seethed.[9]

"Wait," the bearded cleric ordered. "The Gujjars propose to marry Shakoor to Salma, and in exchange they offer their eldest daughter Mukhtar Mai to one of Salma's brothers, if you free Shakoor from police custody."

"I will consult with my elders," Abdul Khaliq replied.

He came back to the cleric.

"Our honour is violated by the Gujjar boy. It must be equalized!" Khaliq spat.

"We accept your watta-satta (exchange marriage) offer on this condition only: that a *sharai nikah* (oral marriage, without certificate) and the *rukhsti* must be performed here and now!"

*Rukhsti*: The delivery of a bride by her menfolk to the house of the groom's family. It has evolved to connotate the consummation of a marriage. Varying periods of time may fall between the *Nikah* (marriage ceremony) and the *Rukhsti*.

"Agreed," said the cleric.

"After that, we will get Shakoor freed and you can perform his nikah with Salma in the morning," Abdul Khaliq concluded.

"Agreed," said the cleric.

It was obvious Abdul Khaliq would be the groom. By age, he was the next in line of Salma's brothers to be married.

The divorced 30 year old sister of the teenager who had violated his sister was not Abdul Khaliq's ideal choice of wife. But it would help him equalize the violation of Salma's honour.

The cleric left the Mastois' akath.

Maghrib prayers swelled up around them. Peach dissolved into greys as coloured cloud drifts climbed the sky. The horizon glowered charcoal. Steam began rising from the irrigation canals.

Abdul Khaliq went to fetch Ghulam Hussain from Ranpur village. Hussain was a maternal cousin – technically his first cousin once removed. Khaliq wanted Hussain to attend his nikah.

"I will be married this night," Abdul Khaliq told his cousin. "Come. It is the sulah (compromise agreement to end a quarrel) after Abdul Shakoor of the Tatla Gujjars outraged the modesty of my sister Salma."

---

9.  Prosecution testimony, State vs Abdul Khaliq etc, FIR 405/2002, Anti-Terrorism Court, Dera Ghazi Khan, 07/2002

Ghulam Hussain followed Abdul Khaliq back to Mirwala.

From the trail between the sugarcane patches emerged the men from the house across the field: Ghulam Farid Tatla Gujjar, the father of Shakoor, and Sabir Hussain, Shakoor's uncle. The bearded cleric was with them.

Behind them came a thin woman swamped in a heavy chador. It wrapped over her head, around her neck and shoulders, falling to her knees. Her gaze caught no-one.

The men folk of the Tatla Gujjar clan had brought their eldest daughter to the Mastois.

"The Gujjar girl is here. In the name of Allah the Almighty, let her family be forgiven," Faiz Mastoi pronounced.[10]

From appearances, the *rukhsti* was taking place at once, as Abdul Khaliq had demanded. Shakoor's sister was being delivered by her men folk to the Mastoi men.

The cleric stepped between the Tatla Gujjar men and Abdul Khaliq.

"I marry you, in the name of Allah," he pronounced. Nothing was written, no certificates signed. He used a *sharai nikah* ritual, an oral marriage in accordance with Qur'anic traditions, common in rural areas.

The absence of a certificate has often proved convenient for either side— usually the "oral marriage" groom.

Abdul Khaliq grabbed Mukhtar's right arm and pulled her into his compound. His sisters, nieces, nephews, little brothers, sisters-in-law and mother lay in the inner courtyard, stretched out on rows of rotting charpoys, dozing and half-sleeping.

Ghulam Fareed Mastoi followed behind. Abdul Khaliq's uncle Fayyaz was inside.

Khaliq pulled Mukhtar into his room, the middle of the row of three. Two or three charpoys were inside on the hard-baked earth. Mukhtar found herself next to the room in which her little brother had been locked up hours earlier.

Inside the airless, unlit room she sweltered.

Abdul Khaliq left Mukhtar in his room and joined Faiz Mastoi to head into Jatoi to get Abdul Shakoor released from the police cell.

Shakoor was supposed to undergo exchange nikah in the morning with Salma. It was far from the Mastoi family's first choice to marry their girl to the boy next door of another tribe. But they had verbally agreed to a watta-satta exchange marriage pact.

Shakoor's uncle Sabir came with Faiz and Abdul Khaliq to collect Shakoor

---

10. Lahore High Court (Multan Bench) appeal judgement, pg 38 and testimony by PW 14 Mukhar Mai, State vs Abdul Khaliq etc, FIR 405/2002, Anti-Terrorism Court, Dera Ghazi Khan, 07/2002

from the prison. Sabir waited outside while the Mastoi pair murmured inside with police. They emerged with Shakoor at their sides. The Mastois delivered Shakoor and Sabir at the Tatla Gujjar house around 2 am.

Abdul Khaliq strode through the sugarcane patches back to his own compound. Everyone was sleeping. As dawn grew closer, crows began to swoop above the dozing bodies. Each body had pulled a cloth over themselves head to toe to shield against the adhesive flies. He pulled back the doors of his room and went inside to his "oral marriage" bride.

\* \* \* \*

## FAJJARWELA, JUNE 23

When Salma woke in the morning, Mukhtar was gone. She had seen her come into the Mastoi family compound the night before, and disappear into the middle room with Abdul Khaliq.

"In the morning she wasn't there. She had come in the night. She went into the middle room with Abdul Khaliq. She didn't look happy."[11]

The courtyard was thick with tension and wailing babies and confusion.

All Salma could make out was that she was no longer required to prepare for a nikah with Shakoor from next door.

"I never wanted to marry him. It was my family's decision."

Nor had Mukhtar wanted to marry Abdul Khaliq. But she told the court that she was ready to go through with a watta-satta exchange marriage deal involving her marriage to Abdul Khaliq, for the sake of her little brother Shakoor's freedom and safety.

While the rest of the family was still sleeping, Maulvi Abdul Razzaq and Mukhtar's father had turned up at the Mastoi house as fajjar (dawn) prayers subsided and demanded Abdul Khaliq.

"Shakoor was returned to us last night. He denies raping Salma. He says that on the contrary, your brother Punnu and two cousins raped him in the sugarcane. To balance our shamed honour, the Gujjars now request from you two girls and 10 kanals (1.25 acres) land," the cleric said.

"Go to hell with you. If you accuse us of sodomy, you shall not have our girl Salma for Shakoor, or any of our girls for any of your men," cursed Abdul Khaliq.

"Then give us back Mukhtar Mai," the cleric insisted.

In the coolness of the first pre-sunrise grey light, Mukhtar's father led his daughter home between the sugarcane towards their compound. The smell of the family's goats drifted over the field. The shame of bringing him a daughter

---

11. Interview with Salma, D.G.Khan, 07/03/06

after giving her away as a compensatory bride, and after a night of consummation, was overbearing.

\* \* \* \*

Maulvi Abdul Razzaq negotiated every day with the Mastois, pleading with them to fulfil their end of the watta-satta deal.

He alternated with pleas to the Tatla-Gujjars to drop their demand for a second girl and a parcel of land from the Mastois.

The cleric had struck the watta-satta deal to save Shakoor from jail and Salma from eternal shame. He was the guarantor. He visited the two families each day to save the deal brokered in his name.

A third person's honour had now been added to the stake: Shakoor's sister Mukhtar Mai. She had publicly spent one night with Abdul Khaliq in his room. Now he refused to keep her as his wife. There was no written marriage certificate to prove that she had coupled with him as his bride.

The Tatla-Gujjars were humiliated. They had handed their daughter over to a foe tribe as a compensatory bride, and she had been tossed out like a mistress in disgrace. They had received nothing in return. They had been cheated on the watta-satta deal.

The oldest son Hazoor Bakhsh turned his anger on the cleric.

"You caved in too soon. You made us give Mukhtar Mai to them prematurely! We should have waited. We shouldn't have trusted those Mastois!"

The cleric visited both families on the Sunday, the Monday, the Tuesday, and the Wednesday. By Thursday his irritation was peaking as the stalemate set in. He had a flock to tend; students to teach at the religious school; and a mosque to run.

"Salma has today married Khalil Ahmed Mastoi, our cousin in Jampur across the river," declared Abdul Khaliq.

The pronouncement struck Abdul Razzaq like a spear.

The marriage of Salma to another Mastoi spelt the end of any deal to save the Tatla-Gujjars and uphold the compromise, *sulah* the mullah had brokered.

"You will pay for this betrayal. If you go ahead with this marriage, I'll take you to the police! I'll get an FIR against you for rape!" the cleric threatened.

"Go to hell," Abdul Khaliq replied.

On Thursday June 27 Salma—promised in a compromise marriage just five days earlier to Shakoor—married her Mastoi cousin Khalil Ahmed Mastoi.

The following day was Islam's Sabbath, the day everyone comes to mosque for the Maulvi's sermon.

In Mirwala's Farooqia mosque, Maulvi Abdul Razzaq faced his white-tunic'ed followers. They were on their knees, heads bent to their prayer mats.

The soft-eyed cleric took his microphone. The worshippers lifted their heads to the preacher.

Before hundreds of devotees, Maulvi Abdul Razzaq began his revenge against the Mastois for reneging on the *watta-satta sulah* and humiliating the Tatla Gujjar family by taking their eldest daughter as an oral marriage bride, and throwing her out the next day.

The Mastoi clan had been his foes for seven years, since Karam Hussain Mastoi took him to the High Court on the charge of corruptingly conspiring with district council officials to have his name listed as owner of a plot of land which Karam Hussain Mastoi had won and paid for in public auction.[12]

Karam Hussain was the father of Ghulam Fareed Mastoi's wife.

In front of the Friday prayer congregation, the Sipah-e-Sahaba cleric accused the Mastoi Baloch men of gang-raping the Tatla-Gujjar woman.

The Mastois got wind of the cleric's betrayal when a local welfare activist who occasionally contributed news reports on violent honour crimes to small-time dailies in Multan began sniffing around Mirwala.

Mureed Abbas was also from the same caste as the Maulvi: Jatoi. The Jatois are the largest and wealthiest caste in Mirwala, Ranpur and the rest of Jatoi sub-district. Mirwala was named after one Mir Khan Jatoi, who first settled in the area 150 years ago.[13]

Mureed Abbas turned up at Mirwala on Saturday asking questions about the outcome of the June 22 feud. His questions focused on a said panchayat, on its 'leader' and on its 'verdict' of a gang-rape punishment.

A Mastoi elder wrote to Mureed Abbas asking him to cease his questioning.[14]

It was too late. Abbas had the whiff of a devastating story, which fit the worst perceptions of violence against women by the powerful or powerfully-connected. It fit his campaign against feudal landlords and the violence by some against their serfs. It was easy to paint the Mastois as wealthy landlords, if only because Faiz Mastoi owned 16 acres. He didn't mention that Abdul Khaliq Mastoi and his extended family owned just 1.25 acres, less land than what Mukhtar Mai's family owned.

On the same day Mureed Abbas turned up at Mirwala with his mini tape recorder, the mullah carried out his threat to go to the police and register gang-rape charges against the Mastois.

The mullah's attempts to secure Ghulam Farid Tatla Gujjar's agreement had failed. Twice he approached the father of Mukhtar Mai and Abdul Shakoor at his woodstall, but the woodcutter refused to take the feud to the police.

---

12. Petition 2949/1995 Lahore High Court 1995
13. Interview with Ashfaq Ahmad Qureshi, Jatoi Tehsildar, Jatoi, 05/03/06
14. Interview with Mureed Abbas, Jatoi, 05/03/06

"If you don't lodge a complaint, we will lodge a complaint against you. We already have your statement recorded on the journalists' tape recorder," the cleric warned.[15]

Like many village men the woodcutter didn't want his family's humiliation made any more public. He also feared further revenge.

Police only listen to charges of gang-rape when a respected figure deposes. The Maulvi of the biggest mosque in Mirwala met the grounds of seniority.

*On Saturday night, the Maulvi drafted the FIR.*[16]

Mureed Abbas also failed to win Mukhtar's father's agreement. He and two other freelance reporters had interviewed the woodcutter and urged him to file a police charge, in vain.

But by Sunday Abbas had enough conviction and went to the Jatoi police with the story he had gathered.

The police still had before them the FIR drafted the night before by the Maulvi, but were reluctant to press charges. Mureed Abbas threatened them.

"If you don't lodge this FIR, my two colleagues and I will go to your higher-ups (seniors)," he said.[17]

"We cannot take this any further unless we have Mukhtar Mai's direct statement. She has not come to us," the police replied.

"Then I will take you to her," Mureed Abbas said.

The police gave in. Assistant Sub-Inspector Abdul Ghaffar and two constables climbed into the police van. Abbas led them on his motor-scooter along the winding 13-kilometre unsealed road to the Tatla-Gujjar home on the edge of Mirwala.

They reached the home between aserwela and maghreb prayers.

The policemen put Mukhtar Mai, Shakoor and their bewildered father into the van and drove them back into Jatoi to the police station.

Mureed Abbas followed behind on his motor-scooter. A twilight dust-storm blew up thrusting whirls of dust between the police van and Abbas' scooter, momentarily blinding him. High summer dust-storms in Mirwala happen only in the late afternoons.

Mukhtar Mai's older brother Hazoor Bakhsh and Uncle Sabir reached the police station as she was about to attest a pre-drafted statement held out by the police, purporting to be her own statement.

But they had been beaten by the cleric. Maulvi Abdul Razzaq had already arrived to oversee the lodging of the FIR he had drafted the night before.[18]

---

15. Lahore High Court (Multan Bench) appeal judgement, 03/03/05, pg 9
16. Interview with Mureed Abbas, Jatoi, 05/03/06 and with Maulvi Abdul Razzaq, 05/06
17. Interview with Mureed Abbas, Jatoi, 05/03/06
18. Interview with Mureed Abbas, Jatoi, 05/03/06

Night was beginning to fall.

"You mustn't thumbprint this FIR," Hazoor Bakhsh and Sabir Hussain beseeched.

Mukhtar's father hesitated.

"Just give us your thumb-print," the police officer said to Mukhtar.

Abdul Razzaq pulled Mukhtar aside and whispered. Mukhtar turned back to the police, dipped her thumb in ink and pressed it to the piece of paper covered in scrawls.

She could not read. She did not even know the language the words were written in. Her only tongue was the local dialect, Seraiki. The words were little more than scrawls to her anyway.

"We need a medical exam now," the police said.

It was after 8.00 p.m on a Sunday night and the town's Rural Health Centre was closed.

Again, Mureed Abbas was undeterred. Before the police had even formally lodged the FIR with Mukhtar Mai's thumbprint, Abbas had composed a news story and dictated it to three newspapers in Multan for Monday's edition: the Daily Sang-e-Meel (Milestone), the Daily Bissat (Chess) and the *Daily Khabrain*.[19]

Abbas drove out to the village residence of the local 'lady doctor' Shahida Safdar, the Women's Medical Officer of Jatoi Rural Health Centre. She lived some eight kilometres from Jatoi town.

Abbas picked her up and brought her to the closed health clinic. The lady doctor unlocked the threadbare clinic, turned on the lights in her examination room, and conducted the routine examination for rape victims: three swabs each were taken from the interior canal, exterior genital region, and posterior fornix. The doctor saw no semen in the external region, nor did she expect to eight days after the alleged attack. But she took external swabs anyway as routine.[20]

The nine swabs were given to a police constable for onward dispatch to the Chemical Examiner in Multan for semen detection.

"Where are the clothes you wore at the time of the occurrence?" Dr Safdar asked her dumbstruck patient. "We can test them also."

"They've already been washed. They are in my house," Mukhtar replied.[21]

It was almost 10.00 p.m on Sunday night.

---

19. Interview with Mureed Abbas, Jatoi, 05/03/06
20. Testimony by Dr. Shahida Safdar, WWO Jatoi Rural Health Centre, State vs Abdul Khaliqetc, FIR 405/2002, Anti-Terrorism Court, Dera Ghazi Khan, 07/2002
21. Lahore High Court (Multan Bench) appeal judgement, 03/03/05, p12

The police FIR tendered to the court in the July 2002 trial for the alleged gang-rape of Mukhtar Mai listed 7.45 a.m Sunday as the time of lodging.[22] The medical report tendered to the court listed 10.30 a.m Sunday as the time of examination.[23]

Mureed Abbas was summonoped to testify in the court on his role in registering the charges. But police detained him on the day he was due in court and told the judge he had absconded to the mountains of northern Pakistan.[24]

Mureed Abbas never got the chance to tell the court of his role and the Maulvi's role in lodging the rape charges, nor the chance to tell the court that police and the doctor had listed a false time of report in their documents.

He was also denied the chance to show the court electoral roll records and voter registration cards to show that police had wrongly arrested a Mastoi man with the same name as one of the accused men.

---

22.  FIR 405/2002 Jatoi Police Station (see annex)
23.  Medical report on examination of Mukhtar Mai, Jatoi Rural Health Centre, 30/06/02 (see annex)
24.  Interview with Mureed Abbas, Jatoi, 05/03/06

# 10

# Rough Trade: Vani and Swara
## ونی

### THE CRUEL AND COMMON CUSTOMS
### OF COMPENSATORY MARRIAGE

*"No drums beat for these brides; there is no wedding dress, no mendhi,
no procession, no festivity. For a vani bride, her wedding is a funeral."*
**Pakistani activist**

Atonement. Penance. Reparation. But the tribes call it 'settlement',
'compromise', 'compensation'.

In the name of the father, the brother, the uncle; in the name of 'our
traditions', young girls in Pakistan's rural backwaters are given away as
sacrificial brides to the enemies of their families, to save their own men folk
from jail or the gallows. The marriage is a guise for a lifetime of perpetual
bondage. That is made clear from the first day.

"The girls are given away wearing their ordinary clothes. There is no
bridal makeup, no jewellery. There is no dowry, there is no drumbeating.
There is no festivity," explained a school principal, in the Punjabi district of
Mirwala, who has been campaigning to end the practice since 2002.[1]

The cruel centuries-old custom is known as *vani* or *swara*. Vani loosely
translates as 'blood marriage', from the Pashto word *vannay* for blood, drawing
a vague reference to its hallowed effect of staving off a blood feud down
generations. The custom condemns girls into virtual slavery. Betrothed into a
family wronged by one of their menfolk, they become the vassal of the wronged
family's perpetual revenge.

This custom was only outlawed by Pakistani legislators in January 2005,
through a law that carries no retrospectivity. *Vani* pacts struck before the law
came and are still honoured without punity.

The justifications for the barbaric custom are manifold and coated with a
distorted sense of nobility: it prevents lifelong feuds between families; if the
menfolk went to jail or the gallows, then the whole family would suffer from

---

1.    Interview, Mianwali, April 2006

the loss of the breadwinner, thus by giving away his daughter or sister or niece, the guilty man is still punished but remains able to look after his family.

A principle still enshrined in Pakistan's mainstream law even supports the broad concept of compensation in place of punishment for crimes like murder: the *Qisas* and *Diyat* principle dictates that a murderer convicted by a formal court may buy his way out of his sentenced punishment by handing over cash or property.

In rural Pakistan, a man's women folk are his property.

"The use of women as part of a compensation agreement is based in the notion of women as not independent persons with rights of their own, but as objects owned by men, whether they be fathers, husbands or sons," Amnesty International wrote in a 2002 report on tribal justice in Pakistan.

*Vani* and *swara* are yet another manifestation of women's status as chattel: pawns for trade in markets of arbitrary honour.

In some cases the compensatory brides are paying for their own brothers' elopement in a sinful "love marriage" with a girl from another clan. *Vani* brides are frequently betrothed in childhood, sometimes as babies. Some are already in their teens, the conventional marriage age in rural areas. After puberty they are handed over for consummation of the marriage, the *rukhsti*.

Infact grooms are sometimes boys themselves. Sometimes they are adult men already with one or more wives. Sometimes they can be even old men who are already grandfathers.

Sisters, Naheed Akhtar and Sahib Khatoon, betrothed in atonement for a murder committed by their uncles more than 16 years before they were born are common in Pakistan. By the time the *vani* sisters came of age, their murderous uncles were already dead. Another girl, Wazeeran Khatoon was betrothed to a grandfather more than four times her age.

\* \* \* \*

## MAY 2006

The cultivated Punjab green faded behind as we wound up a lonely pass through the barren Black and White Mountains, on a broken road south from Islamabad.

Skirting suddenly desolate crests and empty gullies, the perfect lair of bandits who rule the empty road at night, I got why my previous drivers had refused to take this back road to Mianwali, one of the grimmest dustbowl districts of the Punjab's remote west. This time I had a woman translator from the city. She thought the chance of bandits in the rocky folds of the barren mountaintop romantic. The landscape was of Cowboy westerns, of Mexico-US border adventures, of American Indians on horseback. The romance halted as the other side came into view.

Below us, plains of cracked earth stretched forever into dirty horizons. Low wind-blown scrub pockmarked the dry fields. There was nothing there. Then there was, somehow: a scattering of dun-walled shanty homes. Afghan refugees' dwellings.

How its occupants could *eke* out a living here was impossible to imagine. As our eyes accustomed to the shades of sand, dun and mud, another settlement came into view: coloured tents. Pink, purple, and green patches on canvas stretched over bamboo, splashes of colour on the arid landscape. Shadows flickered under the canvas shades.

"Gypsies," my translator said.

"They supply the truck stops with sex at night," a local activist elaborated later. "They're thieves and bandits. The men abuse their women."

We were traveling to Mianwali, another wretched Indus backwater. A wheat-growing and cotton-farming district of one million people, it lies five hours south of Islamabad and five hours north of Mukhtar Mai's village in Muzaffargarh. Mianwali is cradled in sandy plains straddling the border between the Punjab and the western frontier tribal lands dominated by ethnic Pashtuns. Afghanistan's border is just 100 kilometres away. Pashtuns far outnumber Punjabis in Mianwali.

The town lies on the heroin smuggling route out of Afghanistan. Heroin addiction is smothering its youth. Stone-crushing gangs line stretches of the potholed road, smashing rocks into smaller and smaller pieces, shifting them from one pile to another, in 40-degree-plus temperatures. It was hard to see the point of moving them from pile to pile. The same stone-crushing gangs line the road to Muzaffargarh in the Punjab's south, along the railway tracks, shifting stones from railway carriages to the road, and back, sometimes into trucks then out.

The stone-crushers earn less than 100 rupees ($1.60) a day. However, they fare better than the brick labourers.

Cigar-shaped brick kilns blot the roadside every few miles, fouling the landscape with their puffing black smoke. The brick factories are notorious for their use of bonded labour, children and adults, heirs to the debts of their forefathers.

Right now it is harvest time. The gathering of the grains brings on an out-of-place sense of well-being and plenty. Bundles of newly-cut wheat lie tied and strewn in the fields. Machines blow out clouds of gold-flecked dust, sifting the chaff from the grain. Camel trains amble on the highway's sides, buckled under bulging sacks of grain. Giant bulging udders ply the roads: trucks bursting at the seams with chaff to be used for animal fodder.

Mianwali in 2005 and 2006 was emerging as the apparent heartland of the trade in child brides between tribes to stem blood feuds and save their menfolk from punishment.

*Vani* is the tribal tradition of handing over a bride to the family of men murdered or wronged by her father, uncle or brother to the family he has wronged. The handover of the girl is a trade-off for waiving the punishment of her wrong-doing male relative. The larger aim is to end a feud which could otherwise span generations with years of deadly consequences. Vani brides have been offered still in diapers. In some cases, they were not even conceived when the crime, for which they are condemned to atone, was committed. In one case, the bride was born 18 years after her father's crime.

An old warplane mounted on a roundabout announced the entrance to Mianwali. We turned left, looking for the lawyers' chambers, and found ourselves instead in the gardens of the district courts. As in other Punjabi towns, the courthouses are painted Mughal red and stand on sweeping manicured lawns. Before us a hundred or more tribesmen in white and blue shalwar kameez, some in turbans, stood clutching floor to ceiling bars. Policemen with rifles stood in front of the open-air cells.

"These are the men on trial today," a rotund policemen volunteered. Other armed police waved their rifles vigorously when I tried to photograph the public display of the day's accused.

Traditionally, for any of these men, a conviction in today's trials could be waived afterwards by giving away their daughter to their victim's family. That is the way of the tribe.

\* \* \* \*

'A wedding party of two grooms came home empty-handed.'

That was the headline of a story in the middle pages of an April 2006 newspaper that brought me to Mianwali.

The sad tale of the fruitless wedding had happened a month earlier in Daud Khel village 20 kilometres south of Mianwali, on a miserable colourless plain in the shadow of the barren Black and White mountains. Daud Khel is known for its cement factory and little else.

Two grooms had set out to marry two sisters on a Saturday in March 2006. The dual match was perfect. The grooms and brides were second cousins. The brides were educated, Kulsoom was in tertiary college and Nusrat was in secondary college. They were handsome Pathan girls, tall and self-possessed, the eldest of 10 siblings. The grooms had respectable jobs, one as a police inspector and the other had his own fertilizer business. Both sets of parents were satisfied.

Around 300 guests had gathered on a hot spring night at the girls' family home for the nikah, the solemnization of the marriage by the local mullah.

Suddenly two local boys, jobless, uneducated, and hooked on the Afghan heroin that is flooding Mianwali, turned up. "Cancel this marriage! These girls are our wives, betrothed to us 18 years ago!" The mullah backed out and refused to perform the nikah. The boys' family went home without their brides.

The fate of the brideless grooms had been set on a stifling April morning 21 years earlier, when Amanullah Khan of the Niazi tribe was walking to work at the Kohat Cement Factory.

"Coward," hissed Amanullah's neighbour Ataullah and his two brothers. "Come and claim the land that you pretend is yours." A scuffle followed the taunts. Someone had a knife. Amanullah grabbed it. With a thrust, Ataullah was dead. Amanullah became one of those men on public display clutching the bars of the district court cells. He was condemned to death for murder and sent to death row in Mianwali jail.

"I killed in self-defence. They were three, I was one. They attacked me. They stabbed me first with a dagger, I snatched it and stabbed them back," he tells me.[2]

Amanullah had two daughters: Kulsoom and Nusrat. Ataullah, the man he murdered, had two sons: Akramullah and Shafaullah.

Amanullah had spent several years on death rown when his tiny daughters were betrothed to Ataullah's sons and a sum of 250,000 rupees (4,166 USD) was paid to Ataullah's family. In exchange, Amanullah walked out of jail and was spared the hanging he had been condemned to.He says the devilish deal was brokered by the village panchayat in his absence. Amanullah's father had represented him at the panchayat.The elders did not bother to decree which boy would marry which girl.

The girls grew up ignorant of their betrothal until high school. Classmates giggled and pointed at them. "You've been 'given'!" the other girls used to whisper and smirk. For the grooms came of age as illiterates, never studying beyond primary school. When the sisters confronted their parents about the rumours that unknown husbands were waiting for them somewhere. Their father confirmed. But he vowed to never hand them over.

\* \* \* \*

I found the girls in their home in May 2006, inside a mud-wall compound with two rooms and a courtyard. It lay at the end of a narrow lane in Daud Khel. In the sauna of a room jammed with nine charpoy beds, the sad-eyed sisters sat beneath a shelf of tiny crockery and recounted the genesis of their childhood blood betrothal.

"Our land was claimed by another man Ataullah, so our father killed him," Kulsoom recounted.

"Nobody liked that man," Nusrat piped up. "My dad was going to the cement factory for work. Ataullah was sitting with his son and brother. Ataullah

---

2.   Interview, Daud Khel, April 2006

provoked my father. He called him a coward and told him to come and claim his land in person. He used bad language with my father. When they insulted my father a third time, he turned around and grabbed their dagger and stabbed them. One man died—*Alaullah*."

"My father was badly injured in the scuffle. He was jailed. Our grandfather was also accused, but he was freed on bail. Later on a panchayat was convened," recalled Nusrat.

It was 1990. Five years had passed since the killing.

"The panchayat decided our father would be freed if he gave 250,000 rupees and the two of us to his victim's two sons."

Prayers were held to solemnize the patch-up between the two families.

"It was a verbal nikah," Amanullah recalled.

"The girls' grandfather — my father — gave them away. I would never have agreed to it. But I was in jail. I had no say. I was 24 years old. I found out about the pact when I got out of jail. I did not like this deal, but it was all over and done by the time I got out. My father was pressured. He was all alone. He had no brothers to back him up. He gave in under fear and pressure," said Amanullah.

The girls' grandmother weighed in: "No-one ever consulted me."

Amanullah ignored her: "It has been my life's quest to save my daughters, ever since I got out of jail."

"We found out about our betrothal at school. The other girls told us," Nusrat said. "They used to talk and point at us, saying 'You girls have been given away."

Amanullah spoke up: "I was not going to give my daughters away, so I had not told them. There was no need to bother."

The girls confronted their father. "It is true," he confirmed. "But rest assured, we will never hand you over."

The grooms lived just half a kilometre away but the girls had never laid eyes on them.

"Not even I have ever seen them," grandma piped up again.

"They are heroin users. They only went to primary school. They have no job. They don't work," moaned Nusrat.

"Why did you refuse?" I asked the girls.

"Because it was over a murder that we were given. Even if those boys were good people, we would still refuse, because the exchange was made in bad blood," Nusrat said.

"Our anger is at the panchayat," Kulsoom said. "They are the ones who made this decision. If they had not, we would not have suffered."

More than 10 years ago Amanullah began sending people to the murdered man's house with a defiant message: 'You shall never get my daughters'.

"The boys' family ignored me. They would respond by threatening 'We shall take them anyway.' About two years back they began demanding one million rupees from me."

Without telling their parents, the girls took their own steps to escape their childhood betrothal. One of their classmates was related to a human rights lawyer who had been fighting the tradition of vani.

"Even I had no idea the girls were making approaches outside the family for help," grandma chimed in.

The would-be grooms signaled a fight: they went to the civil court and filed petitions seeking custody of the girls they claimed as their rightful wives.

"We were married to those girls many years ago in a sharai (marriage) nikah and now the father is refusing to give us our rightful wives," the dead man's sons deposed in their court petition.

Months of court hearings were held. The would-be grooms never came to a hearing. In early 2006 the civil court decided in the girls' favour and dissolved their childhood betrothals. The girls were declared free from the *vani* pact.

Amanullah found new grooms for his daughters. A date was set for the new nikah.

On a hot March night 300 relatives gathered in Amanullah's courtyard for the betrothal ceremony. In the middle of the mullah's prayers, two uninvited guests burst into the gathering: the girls' jilted childhood grooms.

"We shall kill you if you perform this nikah," they threatened the mullah.

The mullah departed. "I do not recognise your daughters' divorce from these men. Civil courts are not empowered to annul a marriage, in the eyes of Islam." The family of the would-be new grooms' departed, with a warning to Amanullah: "Sort out this mess for good, or our boys will never be able to marry your daughters."

The new grooms-to-be went home brideless.

A new panchayat was convened. On April 5 they came up with a compromise. They told Amanullah to give the spurned childhood grooms 175,000 rupees (2,900 USD).

"Then you and your girls will be free."

Amanullah paid the cash. Amanullah showed the new grooms' family the statement from the panchayat: "On behalf of Ikramullah and Shafaullah, sons of murdered Ataullah, we have received 175,000 rupees in payment from Ataullah Khan. The girls are now free from our side," it stated.

It was dated April 9 and signed by the original grooms Ikramullah and Shafaullah, a local council representative, and the sub-district mayor.

"Now the new grooms have seen this paper dated April 9 from the panchayat," Amanullah said. "In two months we will try again to hold the fresh nikah," Nusrat said.

But the girls' dowries were used up in the legal battle for the girls' freedom. All the family furniture was sold off. There is nothing left to pay for the weddings. "We sold off everything. Now a second fresh wedding is ready. But we have nothing to celebrate with. We have no finances," Kulsoom said. "We promised ourselves we would commit suicide before letting ourselves be sacrificed."

There is little lasting peace for Amanullah. He has two sons: Efanullah, 12, and Kamran, 10. "It is worrisome, this murder history and family feud," he muttered. "I have enormous fears for my two sons. I fear for my life and my sons' lives day and night, because of that murder 21 years ago."

Grandma weighed in again: "No matter what, we are enemies."

"Do you mean that the family of the man you killed still want revenge?" I asked Amanullah.

"Yes. One hundred per cent. The money I gave them was just to get my daughters freed. We had a truce in the mosque. We all took oath, we hugged each other. But they didn't do it with their heart. They still have malice."

Throughout our exchange, the girls' mother stayed silent. The stress had damaged both her kidneys, the girls explained.

"What is your goal now?" I asked the sisters.

"We both want to be teachers. Even after getting married we will study," Kulsoom replied.

"I shall make sure of that," said Amanullah. "My daughters will continue their studies after their marriage."

\* \* \* \*

The rough trade in brides to settle feuds in Pakistan's rural backwaters is another variation of the cruel custom of getting women to pay for a sin they have nothing to do with. It's part of the old zar, zamin, zan (gold, land, women) philosophy that disputes arise from, and are solved through money, land, or women. When military dictator General Zia ul Haq changed the law to make murder a pardonable offence in 1980, he sanctioned compensation through land, money and property. The compensation marriages are brokered to evade a death sentence or prison term by the men of the family. Little girls pay for their menfolk's sins. Atonement for someone else's crime.

As each cruel tale of *vani* unfolded in Mianwali, I recognised the same themes that prevailed in Mukhtar Mai's tribulation: *badla*—revenge; *sulah*—settlement or compromise; eye for an eye and 'equalisation' of stained honour.

Mukhtar Mai was offered as a compensatory bride to Abdul Khaliq Mastoi to atone for her brother's misdemeanour. Both sides agree on this. It's on whether the Mastois accepted the offer or not that their versions of events conflict.

\* \* \* \*

*Vani* evolved in the days before courts, police and the writ of a government; when the way of the tribe was the only law. Among the war-ready tribes, a *vani* marriage was the logical way to prevent blood feuds down generations: unite the warring tribes through a marriage union.

"It was part of our culture when there was no awareness, 400 years ago," says Abdur Rashid, a school principal in Mianwali and part-time journalist who put *vani* on the map and into the national consiousness when he exposed a horrifying case in 2002.[3]

"The most horrible aspect of this tradition is the girls are given away in wearing their ordinary clothes. There is no makeup, no jewellery, no dowry, no drumbeating, no festivity. Those girls were betrothed 20 years ago, 10 years ago. Now, fully grown up, some of them are refusing to consummate the marriage because their spouses are not balanced with them. The grooms are unmatched, illiterate. They are heroin addicts. They've adopted social evils. When the girls are highly qualified graduates, do you really think they can go with husbands who are heroin addicts?"

In 2006 laws cover every district, the government's fingers extend into every remote village, courts operate to over-full capacity, and police are on hand—albeit to varying degrees of effectiveness. Yet present-day tribes still feign to stem feuds by giving away their girls as slave-brides, without their consent.

Each *vani* tale of recent years is a portrait of despair:

ABBAKHEL VILLAGE, **15** KILOMETRES NORTH OF MIANWALI, **2002**

Rejoicing and prayers came from the village square, crowded with tribesmen and mullahs.

Village elders offered up prayers, led by preachers with beards. Men in white turbans and tunics handed out halwa sweets.

Five absent girls were being betrothed to five men, to save the girls' four uncles from the gallows. Their unchosen grooms were the relatives of the three men murdered by their uncles in 1988. The betrothals were being blessed just in time to save the murderers. Without the group betrothal, the murderers would be hanged in five days' time. The murders were the latest in a spiral of bloody revenge killings between foe clans stemming back to 1954, when one brother murdered another.

*Walis* (representatives) stood in for the girls as the mullah recited the nikah blessings.

The girls stayed in their homes. The oldest of the five absent brides was 16. Wazeeran Khatoom's unsolicited groom was overjoyed. He was 77. He was still married to his first wife. He had several grandchildren. Wazeeran's

---

3. Interview, Daud Khel, April 2006

14 year old sister Tasleem was betrothed to a 55 year old. The youngest bride was 18 months old.

Among the joyous villagers stood one man weeping. In this unholy communal betrothal, the weeping man was sacrificing his two daughters— aged five and three.

Abdur Rashid, a teacher from a tertiary college back in Mianwali town, watched the sob-wracked man. He was a fellow teacher.

"He was weeping like a woman," Abdur Rashid told me from the office of his new school in Mianwali, four years later. "He knew there was no way out. Only five days remained until the four relatives would be hanged otherwise."

The day of rejoicing in Abbakhel was a turning point for girls sworn against their will, without their knowledge, to the vengeful relatives of men murdered by the girls' menfolk.

"I could not believe my eyes," Abdur Rashid told me. "I had seen this professor crying in the college the day before. He was howling bitterly. 'What is it?' I asked. He replied: 'Tomorrow we are holding a compromise. We have to give away eight girls and 700,000 rupees (11,600 USD).' His own daughters were among the eight vani girls to be handed over."[4]

"Four of this man's uncles were to be hanged. A date was fixed. To save their lives, the family was giving away their girls. I went with him the next day. I was so disturbed. Among them was a 16year old girl betrothed to a 77 year old."

"I witnessed the nikah. I saw a large gathering. The girls were not present. People were offering prayers. Religious scholars were with them. The Nawab (ruler) of Kalabagh district and the head of the Niazi tribe, Malik Assad Khan,

---

4.  Amnesty International 'Tribal Justice System in Pakistan,' 2002: "After exhausting their appeals and request for pardon they were to be executed on 27 July 2002. However on 23 July 2002 a local council of elders brokered a compromise according to which the four convicted men's immediate family were to pay 8 million rupees and hand over eight girls to the relatives of the murder victims. The council comprised local landlords, including the Nawab of Kalabagh, clerics, and former legislators, including two former legislators. More than 4,000 villagers reportedly watched the negotiations and cheered its conclusion, which was celebrated with the distribution of sweets...On 25 July police intervened to cancel the forced marriage of 18 year old Wazeeran Khatoon and 14 year old Tasleem Khatoon, daughters of two of the convicted men, to 77 year old and 55 year old relatives of the murder victims. Police enforced a divorce in both cases before the girls could be handed over to their husbands and the marriage consummated... After police intervention the family formally withdrew their demands for eight girls to be handed over to them and informed the administration and the district and sessions court that they would be ready to accept mere monetary compensation and forgive the convicts. The family of the convicts had reportedly sold their land to raise the required amount."

were among them. The Pirs (living saints) of Blot Sharif and Bohr Sharif towns were there too."

"A journalist came and asked the mullah 'Why are you performing nikah with a baby?' The mullah replied: 'Islam permits us, so we are doing it.' But in fact Islam says the girl must give her consent to a marriage."

"When the 77 year old groom came to lift his girl bride at her home in the evening, she was weeping and clutching the Koran to her chest. She was very handsome, as we Pathan are. She was nice and tall."

Abdur Rashid wrote about the mass vani pact in Abbakhel in national newspapers. The reports shocked city readers. The Supreme Court intervened and ordered police to intervene and save the girls from marriage to the old men. At gunpoint the police ordered a divorce. The grooms refused. The police brought the groom and the teenage bride Wazeeran to a court. She told the court she didn't want to marry the grandfather. The court cancelled the betrothal. To compensate their victims' relatives, the murderers who had been saved from the gallows sold land and gave the money to the victims' instead of child-brides.

Now Abdur Rashid files reports almost weekly on vani cases for Pakistan's biggest-selling English language daily, The News.

### BUNDIAL VILLAGE, QAIDABAD, KHUSHTAB DISTRICT, 40 KILOMETRES FROM MIANWALI, MARCH 2006

In March 2006, a cobbler's son eloped with a blacksmith's daughter against both their parents' wishes. The newly-weds mailed the nikahnama (marriage certificate) to their families. Village elder Malik Yar Bandial convened a tribal council.

"A tooth for a tooth, and an eye for an eye," the council concluded.

At gunpoint, the elders forced the cobbler Ghulam Muhammad to give his two daughters to the blacksmith in compensation, along with 180,000 rupees (3,000 USD). Rehana, 7, would be betrothed to the blacksmith's nephew Ramzan, 8. Amna, 11, was to be betrothed to the blacksmith's son Afzal, 28, already married with two children.

The cobbler refused. Malik, the village elder, pointed a gun at him.

Local mullah Muhammad Eissab of the Zakir Wali mosque solemnized the nikahs. The date for the consummation of 11-year-old Amna's marriage to her 28 year old groom was set for April 20, 2006. Seven-year-old Rehana's consummation would be held off until she reached puberty.

Under the new anti-vani law, the Supreme Court ordered police to intervene. Police helped broker a divorce between the child brides and grooms. Rehana and Amna were saved.

## SULTANWALA VILLAGE, MIANWALI DISTRICT 1992

Sultanwala village gave birth to three girls who grew up to lead a rebellion against *vani*.

The three Khan sisters Amna, Abida, and Sajida were betrothed as girls to men they had no desire to marry – relatives of the man their uncle murdered. The girls grew up, got educated, and got tough. Amna, the eldest, began a masters degree in literature. She's now dubbed the spearhead of the rebellion in Mianwali. The man behind the mutinying sisters is their father: Jehan Khan Niazi.

The sisters and their two cousins were a package of five girls pledged as vani brides in 1992 to free their uncle Iqbal Khan from a death sentence for murdering his cousin Zaman Khan. Zaman and Iqbal Khan had lived across the road from each other.

The girls were betrothed to five male relatives of the dead man. In exchange, Uncle Iqbal was pardoned. Jehan Khan Niazi says he was forced at gunpoint to sacrifice his daughters to save Iqbal. He sent his girls away to the city to get educated and avoid their fate.

The dead man's uncle Muhammad Aslam Khan threatened bloodshed if the *vani* pact was broken. He foretold the deaths of 200 people in fighting between the families, if the betrothals were not honoured.

The Supreme Court intervened in December 2005, ordering police to ensure the girls were not forcibly handed over to their childhood grooms and to give them security.

In January 2006 police arrested the girls' uncle Iqbal and his brother Razzaq. The new laws outlawing vani criminalise both the parents who give their daughters away, and the families who accept the daughters as compensation for a serious crime. Muhammad Aslam Khan, the uncle of the murdered man, was freed on bail.

Amna wailed: "It seems that we are being punished for crying out against the cruelty. Hopes for justice which were kindled with the intervention of the Supreme Court have been snuffed out. The lower courts are constantly denying bails to my uncles, while the people of the rival family have been released after serving only a short stint in the lockups."[5]

## PUCCA GHANJERANWALA VILLAGE

Three brothers from the Malik Tarair clan—Muhammad, Suhalat and Abdur Rehman — killed Muhammad Rafiq of the Malik Sooei clan over a land dispute. The killers were sentenced to death, it was 1960. In 1982 the killers were still on death row. The feuding clans reached a compromise.

Under laws allowing murder to be pardoned through compensation, the

---

5.   Dawn newspaper, May 10 2006

Malik Tarair clan agreed to give 50,000 rupees and three girls as vani brides to the Muhammad Rafiq's family to 'settle' the feud.

Kausar was married immediately. Naheed Akhtar, then 6, and Sahib Khatoon, then 4, were betrothed to Irfan and Ahmed Nawaz. The girls had not even been born when the original crime was committed. Naheed and Sahib are now 20 and 18 and the three killers have passed away. Grooms Irfan and Ahmed are still demanding their childhood brides.

\* \* \* \*

It's usually jirgas and panchayats that broker the cruel *vani* and *swara* pacts.[6]

More often than not, the marriage nikah ceremonies are performed orally, in the 'sharai nikah' tradition. There are no certificates.

"Jirgas have become synonymous with the heinous practice of *swara* to settle debts, in violation of Pakistan's constitution, religious injunctions, and court rulings like that of the Peshawar High Court which in November 2000 declared *swara* unlawful," activist Beena Sarwar wrote in The News.

"These bodies continue to settle disputes arising from murder or runaway marriages; young girls are sacrificed at the altar of family or community 'honour' and packed off to alien households, where they live as virtual slaves."[7]

*Vani* and *swara* are barbaric traditions seeped in tribal concepts of revenge carried down generations, blood feuds, arranged marriage, collective punishment, and the value of women as chattel for enacting transactions in justice.

Brides from the family of the man who murdered the groom's relative are never going to be honoured, beloved wives. The fate of the vani bride is to bear a lifetime of recriminations and abuse from vengeful victim's relatives. A vani bride is betrothed into drudgery and slavery. Yet the cruel custom has its defendants even today.

They are mainly from the Niazi tribe, a Pashtun clan who brought the tradition with them when they migrated from the Afghan frontier over the Indus River and settled in Mianwali.

"The philosophy behind it is to punish murderers," Niazi elder Khurshid Anwar Khan Niazi explained to me.[8]

"When a man murders, he goes behind bars. He is free. He is getting his meals in a timely manner. He is enjoying the jail. The burden is with the family. It is the family who decides to give away their daughters instead. Whenever families kill each other, these feuds go on for generations. For the sake of ending the enmity, they decide on *vani*."

---

6. Amnesty International, 'Child Marriages'report in Stop Violence Against Women campaign: "These decisions are often made by a jirga or panchayat who are a council of elders from the community who convene an informal court to decide methods for resolving disputes."
7. The News, 'Jirga Injustice, Beena Sarwar, November 14, 2004
8. Interview, Mianwali, April 2006

Khurshid Anwar Khan Niazi is a commercial tax lawyer in Mianwali. He holds the title of 'senior decision-maker' within his Niazi clan.

"When you see any custom inherited from your ancestors, you know there must be a good reason behind it. When it was introduced several hundred years ago, it was a good practice, because there were no courts. Family feuds were settled by elders of the tribe.

Basically it was to unite two enemies, to settle disputes, to turn enemies into blood relations. This was the main philosophy behind the tradition.

But now with the passage of time, everything has changed. Now it is misused by some persons who are against our traditions and customs. They are misusing it."

The tax lawyer boasts that no new vani pacts have been struck since 2002 in Mianwali.

"If you look at all the murder cases here in a single year, you will see that *vani* pacts are struck in just a few of the cases. It's only when the murder is within the same clan. *Vani* pacts are never arranged outside the clan."

"Consider why the families are doing it," he pleads. "Consider their sorrow. They are desperate. They are thinking, 'If we don't do this now, we shall always have to carry a gun every time we step outside, we will always live in fear'."

Khurshid Anwar Khan Niazi knows a clan in the village of Chudroom, 25 kilometres east of Mianwali. Rivals within the clan have been spilling each other's blood for years, taking more than a dozen lives between them. The killers were eventually convicted and hanged on court orders. After the executions, the clans began giving their girls away to each other in marriage to stem the feud.

"Now the two clans are living in peace and quiet. All the *vani* weddings were completed within a year. The girls were of marriageable age," the Niazi elder said.

A former Federal Law Minister Khalid Ranjha defended the practice before an Amnesty International delegation:

"At the cost of a single (girl's) life, more killings could be prevented. Moreover. while such women might suffer in their first year of a forced marriage into an antagonistic tribe, the birth of the first child would end all discrimination," the minister was quoted as saying.[9]

---

9. Amnesty International, 'Tribal Justice System in Pakistan', 2002: "Federal Law Minister Khalid Ranjha similarly told an Amnesty International delegation in July 2002 that while there was an 'inhuman aspect of females being made a victim' when handed over by a jirga to a tribe to 'settle' a long-standing dispute, this was a cultural tradition which had its merits; at the cost of a single life, more killings could be prevented. Moreover while such women might suffer in their first year of a forced marriage into an antagonistic tribe, the birth of the first child would end all discrimination.'

An elder of the Jatoi tribe who held a seat in parliament, Sardar Khadim Hussain Jatoi, espoused the supposed benefits of reconciliation which a *vani* pact was meant to bring. He called it, "the best way to cool tempers, to heal the conflict, and to bring families together through the link of marriage."[10]

*The Niazi tax lawyer of Mianwali pleaded the case for vani in a column for the* Dawn *newspaper:*

"The warring tribes in fact introduced the custom of vani for patching long-standing family feuds, particularly those arising out of murder. The custom descended down to the present time, with the philosophy and intention behind it to punish the party committing murder or seriously violating the honour of the other party and to create a blood relationship among inimical parties for doing away with the continuing feuds, as well as mitigating or demolishing altogether the chances of re-emergence of previous enmity among the future generations of the parties, since they would be interrelated by blood through the custom of *vani*."[11]

"It is also misleading to say that the males save their lives at the cost of miseries to the lives of their females. Family feuds do bring more misery to the females of warring tribes."

Families who have sacrificed their daughters and left them to bear the punishment of their male relatives enjoy "benefits", according to Khurshid Anwar Khan Niazi, by reducing tensions between families feuding over a murder.

"What happens when a vani bride backs out of a years-old pact under which her father was pardoned for murder and freed from jail or saved from the gallows? It gives rise to grievance among families who are still mourning the murderous death of their loved one."

"Such ... practice is not only reviving the old enmities among the people, but also giving rise to genuine grievance of the victim parties who are heard asking: 'What about the blood of their dear ones, shed at the hands of accused parties, if they are not going to marry the females given in *vani*?'"

After the publicisation of brutal *vani* cases in Mianwali and tireless lobbying by activists like Abdur Rashid and lawyer Khalilur Rehman, the Human Rights Commission's representative in Mianwali, the government outlawed the practice in January 2005.

---

10. Amnesty International, 'The Tribal Justice System in Pakistan,' 2002: "Many tribal sardars believe that the giving of a woman is, as Sardar Khadim Hussain Jatoi put it 'the best way to cool tempers, to heal the conflict, and to bring families together through the link of marriage.' This view may be unduly sanguine; women handed over in this manner live in hostile environments without their consent and continue often to be ignobly treated.
11. Dawn newspaper, 'Vani in True Perspective', February 21, 2006

Courts had ruled against the practice in earlier years, but with little impact.

In November 2000, the Peshawar High Court in North West Frontier Province ruled that in cases where victims' families had the right to pardon a murderer in exchange for payment of compensation, "the handing over of women shall not be a valid form of compensation and lower courts shall not accept such agreements."[12]

The court described *vani* and *swara* as 'tyrannical', illegal and against Islamic law. It advocated for punishment of anyone practicing the customs. Few clans paid heed.

"(The Peshawar High Court) held that a marriage contract was void if made in the context of *swara*. This judgement has been ignored, as the practice is reported to persist," Amnesty International reported.

Two years later, the Supreme Court added its voice to calls to end the customs, also declaring *vani* and *swara* "un-Islamic". The apex court instructed the four provincial High Courts "to ensure that trial courts do not allow for a woman to be given as compensation."[13]

It took until 2004 for the government to introduce a clause into the Pakistan Penal Code declaring illegal the giving away of girls to settle murders and other crimes. It was part of a package of laws signed off by the President in January 2005. *Vani* and *swara* now carry a penalty of 10 years prison.

The law criminalises those who agree to give away their daughters as *vani* brides, and those who accept the vani brides. But it is not retrospective. The law cannot be applied to *vani* cases that were brokered before the law came into effect. Hence the law cannot intervene when girls who were pledged as vani brides before 2005 come of age and seek release from the vani pact. The severing of such pacts can only be brokered privately by friends and mediators.

"There is no law to settle *vani* cases from years ago. This can only be done by common friends in mediation," Khalilur Rehman laments.

Anti-vani activists see another loophole in the law: the criminalisation of parents who give away their daughters as *vani* brides.

"This discourages girls from going public about their *vani* status, as they fear their parents will be punished," Rehman added.

Khurshid Anwar Khan Niazi advocates against moves to free *vani* brides from old pacts. Backing out of pre-established *vani* pacts, he warns in his column, reignites old feuds.

"The scenario…has the tendency of playing havoc with society by reigniting

---

12. Amnesty International 'Child Marriages' report in Stop Violence Against Women campaign
13. Amnesty International 'Child Marriages' report in Stop Violence Against Women campaign

the flames of family feuds. It will be like choosing a bigger evil at the cost of a lesser one."

Niazi has appealed to lawmakers to preserve past *vani* transactions, "lest the present practice may deteriorate the calm and tranquility among the warring tribal people of this district and elsewhere."

\*   \*   \*   \*

The strangely worded clause of Qisas and Diyat in the Pakistan Penal Code, the country's mainstream law, permits the payment of money or property or "equivalent harm" as compensation for crimes, once a court has recorded a conviction. Qisas allows compensation equivalent to the value of the hurt.

Qisas is defined in the law as "punishment by causing similar hurt to (the) convict at (the) same part of (the) body as (the) victim; or by causing his death if he (the convict) has committed murder."

Diyat allows monetary payments or property handover, in place of prison or death sentences. The law defines diyat as "compensation payable to heirs of a victim."

It is easy for tribes to take Qisas and Diyat as sanction for vani and swara.

# 11

# The Algebra of Watta-Satta
وٹہ سٹہ

## 'GIVE-TAKE' *BRIDE EXCHANGE*

*Dhee Walay Da Ser Ghika Honday:*
*The heads of the bride's family are hung low in submission.*

**Village proverb**

*"It is generally believed that to give the sister or daughter to someone is to give the prestige in the hand of that person. In a patrilineal and patriarchal family, women have to move to the house of the in-laws. People perceive that bride-giving is the submission of the bride family to the groom's family. The concept of Izzat (honour) attached with the female, and her submission under the superior (male authority) is common. Moreover... females are usually treated in a manner that creates the fear in the mind of the bride's family."[1]*

The algebra of *watta-satta* requires a longer equation than the more brutal customs of *vani* and *swara*. Translated literally as 'exchange', the balancing principle is eye for an eye. A bride for a bride, a groom for a groom. It embodies perfectly the principal of reciprocity. It's a neat manifestation of the theme of threatened mutual retaliation.

If Family A gives Bride 1 to Groom 1 of Family B, Family B must give Bride 2 to Groom 2 of Family A. And a divorce between Bride 1 and Groom 1 must be followed by a divorce between Bride 2 and Groom 2. It's a plain and simple equation of reciprocity and mutual guarantee or threat than *vani* and *swara*. Once again, love is not considered as a factor.

---

1.    **AHMED, Jamil,** 1983. "Exchange Marriage System: An Ethnographic Study in a Seraiki Village" Research Report submitted in partial fulfillment M.A. Anthropology at Quaid-e-Azam University, Anthropology Department. pg 133

In rural Pakistan, one third of all marriages are *watta-satta* arrangements.[2] In the Punjab and Sindh, the figure is nearly 50 percent.[3]

When the subcontinent was all part of India, *watta-satta* was practiced by Hindus and Muslims alike. It is still found in southern India. It has also been observed in parts of China and west Africa.

Within the equation are variations. The bride may be bequeathed to the recipient family's son, father or uncle. If she is bequeathed to the father, then the recipient family is usually expected to betrothe its girl to the opposite's father. This equation always requires balance. Like love, the already-married status of the father does not figure in the equation. A direct exchange sees the brother and sister in Family A betrothed to sister and brother in Family B. The exchange underlines many elements of the nature of marriage in rural Pakistan: it is brokered by parents with no say given to the bride; it unites two families or clans, thus ending feuds; it is a financial transaction often involving land; the transaction is two ways, i.e. the groom's family must pay as 'bride price' to contract the marriage, while the bride's family must provide an attractive dowry. The dowry is always larger than the bride price. Often the 'bride price' is used by the bride's family to beef up the dowry.

The beauty of exchange marriage is that the families lose no money. Mutual exchange of dowries means neither family is left wanting. In some exchange marriages the dowries are waived altogether, as they cancel each other out.

The principal of creating alliance between families and keeping their status equal underlines many *watta-satta* arrangements. In rural village perceptions, the giver of the bride falls beneath the recipient of the bride. The bride becomes the property of her husband and his family, and is expected to rarely return to the fold of her birth family.

*"In patriarchal society, when a family gives a girl in marriage, its status and prestige becomes low. The groom's family is considered superior to the bride's family. To avoid this psychological inferiority tension, exchange marriage has been described as a solution."*[4]

Jamil Ahmed made the above observation in his 1983 masters' thesis on *watta-satta* practices in Autterya village in southern Punjab's Multan district, a couple of hours drive from Mukhtar Mai's village Mirwala.

---

2. **Pakistan Rural Household Survey-I, 2001**, surveyed rural households nationwide in all four provinces. Thirty-five percent of women surveyed nationally were in watta-satta marriages. The figure was higher in specific provinces of Punjab and Sindh, where 43 percent of women surveyed were watta-satta brides.
3. **Pakistan Rural Household Survey–II, 2004**, surveyed 1800 randomly-selected households in rural Punjab and Sindh. A total of 1649 women aged 15-40 were interviewed. Almost half of the women surveyed reported they were part of a bride exchange. PG 4 WB
4. AHMED, Jamil pg 11

Ahmed's study of *watta-satta* practices lists four purposes of this marriage tradition:

- to rise in hierarchy
- to put conflicts to an end
- to win the battle of status and power
- to guard against danger from outside[5]

In the village Ahmed studied for his thesis, almost all families were involved in *watta-satta* marriage. He scrutinised 47 exchange marriages during his time of study.

He defines *watta-satta* as: *"Exchange marriage is reciprocal interchange, of sisters and daughters, whereby the men for themselves, for their brothers or sons and for any other close kin, obtain the wives to fulfil further reciprocal obligations and also follow the locally accepted restrictions forwarded and accepted by the parties involved."*

A World Bank study into the tradition defined *watta-satta* as *"a bride exchange between families coupled with a mutual threat of retaliation."*[6]

Like all good algebraic principles, *watta-satta* can follow several variations:

**Straight Sister Exchange** (also known as Brother-Sister Exchange): Two men marry each other's sisters. In this module, marriage takes place within the same generation. Usually the elder brother and younger sister pair is exchanged with the younger brother and elder sister.[7] Ninety-four percent of *watta-satta* brides interviewed for the 2004 Pakistan Rural Household Survey involved at least one brother-sister pair, while 68 percent involved brother-sister pairs on both sides.

**Daughter Exchange:** The reciprocal interchange of daughters: two fathers perform their second marriages with each other's daughters.

**Daughter-Sister Exchange:** Family A father gives his daughter to Family B's son, and gets the groom's sister for himself in exchange. Father A thus enjoys a second marriage with a younger generation bride.

**Direct Exchange (also called Symmetrical Exchange):** Only two parties are involved. Family A exchange daughter or sister for Family B's daughter or sister.

**Indirect Exchange:** More than two parties are involved. Family A gives sister or daughter to Family B. Family B has no sister and daughter to reciprocate, so asks close relatives in Family C to provide a sister or daughter

---

5. AHMED, Jamil pg 10.
6. **JACOBY, Hanan G. & MANSURI Ghazala,** Development Research Group, The World Bank, "Watta-Satta: Bride Exchange and Women's Welfare in Rural Pakistan" March 2006, abstract.
7. **AHMED, Jamil,** pg 66

as exchange bride for Family A. Three families thus jointly complete the circuit. Family B is expected to pay back Family C in another way.

**Pait Likhai:** Family A gives bride to Family B. Family B has no sister or daughter to give in exchange, nor has access to any close kin with sister or daughter to be offered in exchange. Instead, Family B promises that the first daughter of the union between Family A bride and Family B groom will be given as a bride to Family A.

*"In this type of marriage, the bride's family eagerly awaits the birth of the bride's daughter,"* Ahmed remarks.[8]

In Autterya village, Ahmed found more than five families who had given away females through the Pait Likhai system.

＊　＊　＊　＊

There are two Punjabi Sayings. *Sainr Sajan: "We are related through marriage and we cannot stand against our sajan, friends and well-wishers."*

*Asan Ral Mil Pay Hain: "We are intermingled with one another and become one people, how is it possible to hit our own hands?"*[9]

These are common pledges of support between families united through *watta-satta*. The extra solidarity that such an alliance brings is one of its greatest attractions. The potential benefits of a *watta-satta* alliance within the circle of connected families are significant. It means cooperation potentially in economic, socio-cultural and affairs. On the flipside, the breakdown of one marriage automatically requires the severing of the reciprocal exchange marriage.

*"A conflict within one family generates a conflict in another family and consequently the relationships of cooperation are changed into divorce and separation from both sides,"* Ahmed writes.[10]

Cooperation is most immediate in agriculture. At key times of the agricultural cycle—ploughing, sowing, harvesting, threshing—families rely on cooperative labour known as *wingar*. They need to share machinery like tractors and threshers. The use of *gariban*, ox-drawn carts, is cheaper shared. They need to borrow one another's milk-producing cows or goats to feed newborns, or to share their buffaloes for transport and ploughing.

Sharing and borrowing are easier if families are equally allied through *watta-satta*. The extent of *watta-satta* families' cooperation can be measured through their *wingar* cooperation, according to Ahmed's study.

*"In this way the institution of wingar is visualised as the instrument by which the affiliation of related households is measured."*[11]

---

8.  **AHMED, Jamil,** pg 10
9.  **AHMED, Jamil,** pg 110
10.  **AHMED, Jamil,** pg 137
11.  **AHMED, Jamil,** pg 137

The loss of prestige felt by the family who gives away a bride cannot be underestimated. Nor can the fears of the bride's parents as to how she will be treated by her new husband.

*"It is generally believed that to give the sister/daughter to someone is to give the prestige in the hand of that person. In a patrilineal and patriarchal family, women have to move to the house of the in-laws. The people perceive that bride-giving is the submission of the bride family to the groom's family. The concept of Izzat (honour) attached with the female, and her submission under the superior (male authority) is common. Moreover... females are usually treated in a manner that creates the fear in the mind of the bride's family."[12]*

The basic utility of a *watta-satta* arrangement is that it helps to allay the fears parents have about how their daughter is going to be treated by her husband's family.

A woman in Sindh province told researchers from the 2004–2005 Pakistan Rural Household Survey that *watta-satta* *"means that you will give a daughter and receive the same in return. It also implies that if our daughter will be in pain, we will treat your daughter the same way."*

With both families in possession of a bride from the other family, the likelihood of abusive treatment is presumed to be lessened because of the likelihood of reciprocity.

The World Bank study of 2006 concluded that *watta-satta* arrangements protect wives because of the mutual threat of reciprocity. If one wife is treated badly, her husband's sister or daughter will be treated badly in return by the wife's natal family.

*"We have shown that a bride exchange, accompanied by mutual retaliatory threats could be a mechanism to coordinate the actions of two sets of in-laws, each of whom wish to restrain their sons-in-law but who only have the ability to restrain their sons. The likelihood of marital discord is indeed lower in watta-satta arrangements as compared to conventional marriages. This result emerges most strongly in the case of estrangement, the clearest and most publicly observable expression of marital discord. But we also find that watta-satta significantly reduces the possibility of domestic abuse and of major depressive episodes."[13]*

But it cuts both ways.

*"The downside is that if deterrence fails, violence in one marriage may spill over into the counterpart marriage. 'When my husband beats me, I go and tell my mother and sister. My brother feels bad about this and then he beats his wife to take revenge. There are many fights in our family because of this... I do feel that it is the women who are being beaten*

12.  **AHMED, Jamil,** pg 138
13.  **JACOBY, Hanan G. & MANSURI Ghazala** pg 138

*in both families,"* a woman from Mirpurkhas in Sindh province told researchers for the World Bank Study."[14]

Consider, then, the rage and shame when the family receiving the bride for their groom backs out of the *watta-satta* pact, and refuses to balance the exchange by handing over a bride from their side.

*"Not taking a woman in return (after giving away one's daughter or sister as bride) is viewed as giving honour for nothing,"* Ahmed stresses. *"Watta-satta, however, serves as balancing of prestige. In this way, each brother-in-law loses a sister to the other. None is viewed as superior and honourable."*[15]

When watta-satta arrangements are not fulfilled, the disputing party tends to seek out relatives from the farthest branches of the extended clan, Ahmed found. When the groom's family is angered or disappointed, it is the bride who cops the punishment.

*"When the expectations of the groom's family are not fulfilled by the family of the bride, it is usually the bride who faces the consequences. Harsh dealing with the bride ultimately hurts her mother."*[16]

In village wedding ceremonies, the groom's family enjoy most of the ceremonies and the bride's family does not share in the happiness.Watta-satta marriages avert the sense of loss the bride's family would feel, if they were not getting a bride in exchange.

*"Watta-satta* fulfils the function of balancing the prestige and *izzat* between families and no one is lower than the other."[17]

Men seeking a second wife, often because their first wife has failed to produce a male heir, cannot contract a second marriage unless he has a sister or daughter to bargain with and offer in exchange.

*"In this system the person who is rich in daughters can become rich in wives,"* Ahmed noted.[18]

In the village case-studied by Ahmed, four married men had exchanged their daughters to win second and third wives for themselves. It is seen as an alternative to an adulterous affair.

The balance inherent in *watta-satta* also applies to the cost of marriage feasts. The preparations and finances are shared equally. Level of expenditure is mutually agreed on. Families can keep it cheap without risk of disdain from the other side. It's all *'give and take'*.

Perhaps the greatest economic benefit is the curtailment of loss of family land through the departure of the bride to another family. As both families are losing brides to each other, it makes sense to keep the land without giving it to their sister or daughter who is leaving the family.

---

14. **JACOBY, Hanan G. & MANSURI Ghazala** pg 7
15. **AHMED, Jamil,** pg 130
16. " " pg 102
17. " " pg 131
18. " " pg 133

*"Exchanging women from the both families leaves their share from the inter-related property in the favour of their respective brothers."*[19]

\* \* \* \*

At the August 2002 trial of Mukhtar Mai's accused gang-rapists and abettors, the defence testified that Mukhtar Mai was a *watta-satta* bride, betrothed to the Mastoi son Abdul Khaliq, aged around 21 the eldest of the Mastois' unmarried sons, in exchange for the Mastoi's girl Salma, who was supposed to marry Mukhtar's brother Shakoor.

The proposed arrangement fit the most popular watta-satta model of brother-sister exchange—which accounted for 68 percent of watta-satta brides surveyed in the Punjab and Sindh in the 2004 Pakistan Rural Household Survey round II.

The *watta-satta* deal, according to the defence case, was the (*sulah*) compromise to end the feud between Mukhtar Mai's Tatla Gujjar clan and the neighbouring Mastoi Baloch clan over Abdul Shakoor Tatla Gujjar's alleged rape of Salma Mastoi.

The prosecution agrees that *watta-satta* was proposed by Mukhtar's family as a *sulah*, but they say it was rejected by the enraged Mastois. The prosecution allege that the younger males of the Mastois, Salma's brothers, were braying for (*badla*) revenge rape.

The defence maintain that the first part of the *watta-satta* went ahead that night, as requested by the Mastois.

In accordance both the nature of compensation marriages, the Mastois assert, Mukhtar was married off in normal clothes without wedding procession, drums, bridal dress, or festivity. As per with the Mastois' demands, they assert, she was delivered by her menfolk for immediate rukhsti (consummation).

The Mastois say that the local mullah, Maulvi Abdul Razzaq, solemnized the instant compromise marriage between Mukhtar Mai and Abdul Razzaq with a sharai nikah (verbal *nikah*, without the *nikahnama* marriage certificate), as is common in compensation marriages to end inter-clan feuds.

The prosecution, including Maulvi Abdul Razzaq, deny this.

They cite the absence of a *nikahnama* (marriage certificate) as proof that it never took place. When I put the Mastois' story to Mukhtar Mai during a November 2005 stay in her home, she grinned and waved her forefinger, saying: "Where is the *nikahnama* to prove it?"

The Mastoi family maintain that they reneged on their end of the watta-satta deal to hand over their girl Salma to Mukhtar's family as the exchange bride, thereby humiliating and enraging Mukhtar Mai's family and insulting their izzat (honour).

---

19.  " " pg 139

A family giving away a daughter or sister as bride to another family is already in a state of sadness, submission and fear, Ahmed tells us:

To intensify the humiliation of Mukhtar Mai's family and jettison any hopes of reviving the *watta-satta* deal, the Mastoi family married their girl Salma off five days later to a distant relative within the same *biraderi* (clan) who lived in a village more than three hours away. This move thwarted Mukhtar Mai's family's hopes of regaining their honour.

*"If a person loses his prestige of izzat by giving his daughter/sister in marriage to another, he regains prestige or izzat by taking a girl in exchange,"* Ahmed found in his study of Autterya village.[20]

Ahmed also notes that when *watta-satta* arrangements collapse, the disputing party tends to seek out relatives from the farthest branches of the extended clan.

Salma's husband Khalil Ahmed, his father and uncles made up seven of the eight Mastois who were arrested in the village of Jampur, three and a half hour's travel from Mirwala on the other side of the Indus River, exactly two days after charges were lodged with police.

Some police investigators told local reporters the eight men were arrested merely as relatives of other Mastois who were accused of gang-rape. The eight arrested from Jampur ended up being charged as alleged members of an alleged panchayat, and accused of conspiring to order the alleged gang-rape. The judge in the August 2002 trial acquitted these eight Mastoi men on lack of evidence. Police investigators had found no evidence against them.

Two years and seven months after their acquittal, all eight were thrown in jail on the orders of President Pervez Musharraf. He gave the order from his airplane, in response to domestic and international outrage at the High Court's March 2005 acquittal of three of the men convicted of gang-rape, and two other men convicted of abetment.

The defence says that the real crime of these eight men was the fact that they were immediate relatives of the man Salma Mastoi was hurriedly married off to, in violation of the proposed *watta-satta* pact between Salma's family and Mukhtar Mai's family, when Salma should have been given to Mukhtar's brother in exchange for the giving of Mukhtar Mai to Salma's brother.

The defence claim that the fury and shame of Mukhtar Mai's family and Maulvi Abdul Razzaq against the Mastois stems from the family's humiliation at giving Mukhtar away as a bride who spent a night with the groom who treated her brutally, yet failing to receive an expected bride in return.

The prosecution reject this account, claiming no *sharai nikah* (verbal marriage solemnization) took place.

---

20. " " pg 131

# 12

# The Revealing

**1 July 2002, Monday.** Mureed Abbas, the aspiring small-town reporter, published his explosive report in the Urdu-language *Daily Khabrain* newspaper. It was the first press report to claim that a woman had been sentenced by a tribal jury to gang-rape.

In Multan, Abdul Sattar Qamar, my newsagency's bespectacled man in the south, was beginning the week with his routine reading of the morning papers. The southern Punjab press was frequently rife with tales of brutality against women: men chopping off the noses, ears, or legs of their wives, sisters or mothers; men betrothing tiny girls to old grooms to save their own menfolk from prison or the gallows. Qamar picked up the more outstanding tales, checked the facts, and filed the reports to our bureau in Islamabad. The tales sometimes did not stand up, and occasionally did not make sense. My colleagues and I often binned them. But not before appreciating the colourful English prose they were framed in. Qamar had a penchant for delicate and flourishing euphemism ("her modesty was outraged" meant a woman had been raped). Qamar's South Asian English sometimes read like a paperback romance. But if I ever rang him up and asked a question directly in English, his unwavering reply was "Yes."

Rapes and gang-rapes were common tales as Qamar surveyed the local papers. But the gang-rape story carried by the Daily Khabrain on July 1, nearly jumped off the page. This gang-rape was executed as a sentence, a vicarious one at that, on the orders of a tribal council, a panchayat.

Qamar jumped at the story. He called the police in Jatoi, 120 kilometres from Multan. The Jatoi police confirmed the harrowing details of Mureed Abbas' report. On a faulty manual typewriter Qamar punched out the details and faxed it to our bureau in Islamabad on Monday afternoon.

The smudged fax sat on my side-desk as I frantically sub-edited the daily pile of copy submitted from Afghanistan and across Pakistan. The latest inch forward in moves to prize Pakistani and Indian troops back from their perilous standoff on the Kashmir border; the US military's latest announcements of body counts in Afghanistan; President Musharraf's latest bids to promote "moderate Islam" and tame the wild network of violent Islamist organisations on home-turf in the throes of avenging America's ousting of the Taliban eight months earlier.

I glanced at Qamar's fax, yet another tale of brutality and absurdity from the deep south, and nearly binned it. I gave it a second glance, and read the near-incomprehensible prose out to my visiting colleague—a brilliant Sri Lankan editor on secondment from our Colombo bureau.

Amal Jayasinghe was invaluable in translating the arcane South Asian English loved by Qamar. Amal's own flair for sumptuous prose and raconteurism was worthy of literature. One of Qamar's faxed reports described "culprits" fleeing a police raid. The culprits "showed the police a clean pair of heels", according to Qamar's report. Despite several re-readings, I was baffled. I could only conclude that "heels" was a typo for palms, and that the culprits had shown their clean palms to police to prove they were innocent.

"No, no!" Amal squealed in mirth. "They skedaddled! The culprits ran away so fast that there was no chance for any soil to stick to their feet!"

Amal and I re-read Qamar's July 1 fax. There was no mirth in this one. I read over and over the lines: a medieval-style jury of tribal elders had ordered a woman gang-raped to atone for the sins of her little brother. A gang-rape as sentence? Vicarious punishment by gang-rape? At the time the rape victim's age was given as 18, and her philandering brother was said to be 11.

I asked one of my Urdu-speaking colleagues to call Qamar and confirm that he had spoken directly to officials himself.

On the phone to Qamar, Jatoi police had read out Mukhtar's thumb-printed statement and the FIR charge sheet, elucidating the charges and confirming the horrific accusations. Back in Islamabad, where the wall of dry July heat was held at bay by our air-conditioned bureau, Amal and I deciphered Qamar's prose, composed a 239-word dispatch, and published to the world the incredulous tale of the peasant woman sentenced by tribal elders to be gang-raped. Next day the entire world had before their eyes:

## PAKISTAN-RAPE

Gang-rape of teenager ordered as punishment for brother's sins MULTAN, PAKISTAN, JULY 1, 2002 (AFP)—A teenage girl was gang-raped in central Pakistan last month as "punishment" meted out by a tribal jury for her brother's alleged affair with a woman of a higher tribe, police said Monday.

A Panchayat or tribal jury ordered four men, including one of the jurists, to rape the 18-year-old girl on June 22 in the village of Meerwala, 120 kilometres (75 miles) southwest of here, police said.

Meerwala lies 610 kilometers southwest of the capital Islamabad.

District police chief Malik Saeed Awan said authorities were informed of the publicly-ordered gang-rape several days after the incident.

He said four men took turns to sexually assault the girl inside a room. She was then ordered to return home naked before 1,000 onlookers.

The rape was to avenge the "insult" caused to a family of the Mastoi tribe by the girl's brothers' alleged "illicit affair" with a woman of a higher social standing.

The girl and her brother were from the lower Gujjar tribe.

The Panchayat had threatened that all women in the accused's family would be raped unless the 18-year-old submitted herself to the public gang-rape.

Awan said police were taking action against members of the Panchayat.

Lawyers visiting the tribal area on Sunday urged the authorities to prosecute the rapists and the jury.

Revisiting our first story is a confronting reminder of the slowness in reaching the truth, especially of a story founded in a rural third-world village of illiterate farm labourers, where details other than land holdings and clan ties mean very little, where no one knows their own real age; where the language of the village is obviously not the language of the nation and two layers of translation are required; and where police are ill-equipped and confused.

Mukhtar's age turned out to be around 30, not 18. Her brother's age was actually 14 or 15, according to the doctor who examined him 2 weeks after the assault. The 'woman' he was accused of misbehaving with was in her late teens, at the most 20 years old.

Mukhtar never walked home naked, nor were there 1,000 onlookers, nor was the 'gathering' she appeared before anywhere near the village centre. It was in a field on the farthest outskirts.

In the court and police records, in interviews I've conducted with Mukhtar and her family, there is no account of the panchayat threatening to rape all the women in her family.

The social standing of her Gujjar clan against the Mastoi clan is debatable: Mukhtar Mai's family shows far more visible signs of established wealth – livestock, tractors, a barn full of stored grain – than the Mastois, and they had far better connections to the considerably influential local cleric than their Mastoi neighbours had. The Mastoi clan were said to be connected to influential large landholders who had seats in the provincial or national parliaments.

News transmits on the international wires in a matter of milliseconds. The gang-rape of Mukhtar Mai sailed silently into newsroom databases and on to news editors' glowing screens from Sydney to Islamabad, Amman to New York, Paris to Caracas, in English, French, Spanish, Portuguese, German, and Arabic. Domestic newsagency partners often translate the copy into Chinese, Japanese, Russian, Urdu and others. The tale of the gang-rape punishment at the hands of tribal elders to atone for a brother's sin was re-printed and broadcast around the world in multiple tongues.

It was just after 8:00 pm Islamabad time when our editing desk in Hong Kong released the story. That meant plenty of time to make the Pakistani and Indian press and newspapers in any country west of Pakistan, but too late for the big regional newspapers east of India.

The account by Agence France Presse was the first to hit not just the international news screens but also Pakistan's national English-language press, who had a loyal fondness for AFP copy and frequently used it in place of their own reporters. On Tuesday July 2, the AFP story landed in Pakistan's English-language press: The Nation, The Daily Times, Dawn and The News. It hit the top-circulation Urdu newspaper, Jang. Shock gripped the nation. Embarrassment and disbelief choked the national consciousness. Overseas and at home, governments and rights groups erupted in fury.

Pakistan's own response was unprecedented.

The reaction from the top echelons of the government and judiciary towards the apparently panchayat-ordered gang-rape was swifter and harsher than ever recorded for any other rape case, before or since.

The President of Pakistan gave Mukhtar Mai half a million rupees (8,300 US dollars, more than 160 times the average monthly wage). The Supreme Court intervened suo moto - ordering swift police action, setting deadlines for arrests, sacking local police and demanding weekly progress reports from senior police on their investigation. The provincial Punjab government launched its own inquiry. The independent Human Rights Commission of Pakistan condemned the assault and held a separate inquiry. Eight Mastoi men related to the suspects were arrested within 24 hours of the first news report by Daily Khabrain.

## JULY, TUESDAY

On 2 July, the day the story burst out of Pakistan's national newspapers, the Governor of Punjab province, a retired Lieutenant General named Khalid Maqbool, reacted immediately. He ordered an intensive police investigation and demanded "tough action against village officials involved in an apparent cover-up."[1]

The Human Rights Commission of Pakistan snapped out a harsh rebuke. "The increasing incidents of terrible atrocities against women are a terrible reflection on the state of society and the status of women within it," pronounced its chairman Afrasiab Khattak.

The same day, police swooped. Eight men with the name of Mastoi were rounded up from two villages on either side of the Indus: Hairo and Rampur. Whether or not they had been party to the attack or involved in the alleged panchayat was less important than their clan name. None of the accused rapists or alleged panchayat leaders were among them.

It was written in some news reports that the eight were relatives of the accused.[2] Pakistani police often arrest the relatives of wanted people as a pressure tactic to force the accused to hand themselves in.

I had observed the same tactic four months earlier, while on secondment to Islamabad, as police struggled to find the cunning militants who had kidnapped and murdered Wall Street Journal correspondent Daniel Pearl. Investigators had identified a psychopathic mild-mannered British-educated militant whom they believed had set the trap to abduct the American reporter. But the task of locating a seasoned militant who had previously kidnapped a foreign tourist in India, who had been freed from an Indian jail in exchange

---

1. Agence France Presse, July 2 2002
2. Reuters, July 2002

for hostages on a hijacked Indian plane in Afghanistan, who had fought Indian troops in the mountains of Kashmir, and presumably still had allies among his former trainers in Pakistan's Inter Services Intelligence agency (ISI). He used proxy guerilla fighters to "bleed" Indian forces controlling the most prized valleys of the Indian-ruled side of Kashmir – was proving more than difficult. The police arrested the militant's in-laws instead.

It worked. The next day Saeed Ahmed Omar Sheikh turned himself in to one of his old ISI handlers in Lahore, the Punjab capital. The police kept the militant's surrender secret for a week. They announced that they had captured him themselves as President Musharraf was meeting President George W. Bush in the US.

### 3 JULY, WEDNESDAY

On 3 July, local reporters began journeying out to dusty Mirwala. From behind her veiled face, Mukhtar Mai lashed out at the police. She told reporters the police had taken an 11,000 rupee bribe to release her brother Shakoor. It was extra ammunition for national scapegoating of the local police. Punjab Governor Maqbool accused police of a cover-up, suggesting they had known of the alleged gang-rape-by-decree from the beginning. According to police and court records, police were only informed on Sunday June 30.

Eleven days after the alleged gang-rape of Mukhtar Mai, President General Pervez Musharraf, the Supreme Court and the government of the Punjab, Pakistan's power-centre province, stepped in.

In July 2002, General Musharraf was approaching the third anniversary of his unconstitutional seizure of power, when he used the army he commanded to topple the democratically-elected government of Prime Minister Nawaz Sharif and reinsert military rule for the fourth time in Pakistan's then 55-year history. As both Army Chief and unelected President, General Musharraf was balancing near-wars on two borders, managing the fury of his constituency for dumping Afghanistan's Taliban rulers once nurtured by Pakistan, watching the western tribal areas become an escape hatch for Al-Qaeda operatives, surviving assassination attempts, and trying to preach moderation to his 145 million compatriots.

The general was pirouetting as the darling of the West for placing his volatile Muslim land on the frontline of Washington's War on Terror, while appeasing outraged conservatives on the homefront by quietly nodding to the passage of proxy guerrilla fighters into the Indian-controlled valleys of disputed Kashmir.

Even the president-in-uniform had to step back from the helm of the world's toughest tightrope walk as leader of a land then considered the most dangerous place on the planet, and take note of the cry of the peasant woman from the hottest banks of the Indus.

Through the official government newsagency, the Associated Press of Pakistan, Musharraf condemned the alleged gang-rape-on-order. He announced that a school would be built in Mukhtar's village in her name.

The head of the Supreme Court, Chief Justice Sheikh Riaz Ahmed, went on state radio and television to blast the alleged crime.

"This is a shocking incident in the 21st century and a blatant violation of human rights as well as human dignity," read the text of the Chief Justice's dramatic public announcement.[3]

The Supreme Court launched an inquiry into the police handling of the gang-rape charges.

The Chief Justice ordered the chiefs of three levels of police - provincial, district and sub-district - to appear before his court in 2 days' time to present full accounts.[4]

The Governor of the Punjab, Lieutenant-General Khalid Maqbool, launched a parallel inquiry. He removed almost the entire Jatoi police force – transferring some officers, suspending others. The only officer left untouched was Jatoi's deputy superintendent Muhammad Saeed Awan. Awan was given charge of a fresh police investigation. The Governor set a 24-hour deadline for the arrest of all involved: the four accused rapists, the panchayat chief, his arbitrators, and the members of the alleged panchayat for abetting the crime.

Governor Maqbool dispatched two provincial ministers to Mirwala village. From the provincial seat of government in Lahore, Mirwala is a journey of 90 minutes by plane plus a rough four hour drive on unsealed roads. The Punjab Law Minister and the Social Welfare Minister headed to Mirwala. On arrival the provincial Law Minister announced that Mukhtar's gang-rape case would be tried in an Anti-Terrorism Court, special courts set up in Pakistan since 1997 to expedite urgent or high-profile cases. This was despite the crime of rape having been omitted some years earlier from the list of offences under Anti-Terrorism laws.

The Punjab government appointed three investigators to an inquiry panel and sent them to Mirwala. Among them was Asma Jehangir, Pakistan's most high-profile human rights activist. Jehangir had been a UN special rapporteur on human rights and chairperson of the Human Rights Commission of Pakistan. The three-person panel was ordered to inquire into the gang-rape of Mukhtar Mai as well as fresh reports that her brother Shakoor had also been gang-raped.

In Mirwala, the cleric had just registered a case of sodomy against three Mastoi men. Salma's brother Punnu, 32, and his two relatives Muhammad Jamil Mastoi and Manzoor Hussain Mastoi, both 25, were accused of

---

3.   Agence France Presse, July 3 2002

4.   Associated Press of Pakistan, July 3 2002: "The chief justice gave 72 hours for the police to investigate and report back to the court."

sodomising Shakoor on the day he had allegedly raped Salma Mastoi. All three were marched off to Dr Fazal Hussain at the Rural Health Centre to be tested for 'potency' within 24 hours of their respective arrests.

"I did not ask the doctor to obtain semen for matching," Police Sub-Inspector Ghulam Shabbir Khan admitted to the court that later tried the three men for raping Shakoor.[5]

Prostatic massages were performed on all three men. Their resulting "penile erections" were listed as "+ve" (*sic*). In all three tests, Dr Hussain found "nothing to suggest that they were unable to perform the sexual act at the time of examination." In all three reports, the doctor added that "primary and secondary sex characteristics are well-developed."

## 4 JULY, THURSDAY

The money came on the 12th day after the alleged gang-rape.

Within three days of the first press report, before the police inquiry had got seriously under way, before anyone had been tried, before anything was proven in court, the Pakistani government gave Mukhtar Mai half a million rupees (8,330 US dollars) in compensation. The Federal Minister for Women's Development, Attiya Inayatullah, travelled to Mirwala and handed Mukhtar a cheque for half a million rupees.

The minister also bequeathed 'guidance' to Mukhtar to set up a school, in the village, for girls.

"The minister told me I should use the money to build a school. She said I should buy land and begin a government school," Mukhtar told me in an interview in August 2004.

"The Women's Minister told me that's what I should do with the money.".

In Mirwala, Minister Inayatullah held a press conference to announce the handover of the huge compensation cheque. She said the government was already considering expediting the trial of the accused rapists and abettors.[6]

The Punjab Governor's three-person inquiry team summoned Mukhtar and her younger brother Shakoor to the district capital Muzaffargarh for questioning. Salma Mastoi, the girl at the centre of the tribal feud that ended in the gang-rape, was also called for questioning. Shakoor was accused of raping Salma, but he counter-accused that it was Salma's brother and cousins who had raped him.

The panel convened at the Muzzafargarh District Court, a 90-minute drive from Mirwala.

They met reporters afterwards and shared the trio's key claims. Shakoor told the panel that the feud of June 22 had begun with three Mastoi men

---

5. Federal Shariat Court (sodomy trial) ***
6. Associated Press, July 4 2002

sodomising him in the sugarcane field. He said they locked him in a room with Salma in their home after he threatened to tell his family.

For her part, Salma Mastoi insisted to the panel that Shakoor had tried to have sex with her, in the same sugarcane field. Salma challenged a reported doctor's finding that Shakoor was "a minor, and incapable to meet the sexual lust of any opposite sex," one of the panel investigators told my agency's stringer Qamar.

"She (Salma) rejected a doctor's finding that he was a minor and incapable to meet the sexual lust of any opposite sex, and insisted that he is not minor," the investigator said.[7]

Mukhtar Mai retorted that Salma was lying. The girl-next-door, according to Mukhtar, had concocted the rape allegation against Shakoor "to save the skin of her family men."[8]

Another police investigator began interviewing witnesses. Mirza Muhammad Abbas, a superintendent from the Dera Ghazi Khan police headquarters, had been deputed to inquire into the conduct of local police. Superintendent Abbas and his assistant Inspector Riaz interviewed Shakoor, Salma and her mother, Mukhtar's uncles Sabir and Ghulam, the Gujjars' 'salis' Manzoor Hussain and Ghulam Mustafa, and police officers, Assistant Sub-Inspector Iqbal and Inspector Nazir Ahmad. Superintendent Abbas ordered his assistant, Inspector Riaz, to interview Mukthar, her father and the cleric.

The three-day flood of journalists, ministers, and investigators asking Mukhtar Mai to relive her horror took its toll.

"I will be forced to commit suicide if justice is not given in the next few days," she burst out to my colleague Qamar. "There is no point in my living now."

"Everyone tries to console me and express sympathy, but no one can tell me what is in store for me. I know some people secretly dislike me and even my own family looks at me like I am an alien."

Mukhtar claimed the Mastois would use their influence to pressure authorities to "sweep the case under the carpet."

Human rights groups pronounced their disgust. A chorus of condemnations branded the alleged jury-ordered gang-rape a "heinous crime."

Meanwhile the accused rapists and abettors had fled Mirwala.

"We are doing our best and hopefully the accused persons will soon be arrested," said the head of the Dera Ghazi Khan police, Deputy Inspector General Asif Hayat.[9]

---

7.   Agence France Presse, July 5 2002
8.   ""
9.   Associated Press, July 4 2002

## JULY 5, FRIDAY

Friday is Islam's Sabbath.

On the first Friday after the alleged gang-rape, the crime was announced in a preacher's sermon at Mirwala's Farooqia mosque. By the second Friday, July 5, the highest court in the land was unleashing its wrath on three levels of police. The Supreme Court convened a special bench in Lahore, the Punjab capital, to hear directly from the head of the provincial Punjab police, the head of the district Muzzafargarh police, and the head of the Jatoi tehsil (sub-district) police on their actions.

The Supreme Court blasted the police for taking a week to register charges. It accused them of "laxity" for failing to arrest the wanted men.Chief Justice Sheikh Riaz Ahmed ordered police to submit weekly progress reports on their investigations and arrests. Local press accused the police of arresting the first lot of eight Mastoi men at whim, to meet the government's deadline.

By July 5, the Punjab Governor's extraordinary inquiry was wrapping up after interviewing key victims and witnesses and surveying police records of the district.

Amnesty International joined the chorus of local rights groups condemning the gang-rape and tribal justice system that allowed it.

"Tribal councils have no legal standing and the Pakistani authorities have failed to take adequate measures to prevent such bodies from taking the law into their own hands," it pronounced in a statement to the world.[10]

Amnesty also condemned police and village residents for failing to prevent the alleged gang-rape, stating: "Given the wide local participation, it must be assumed that the local police was aware of the event as it unfolded, if not directly present during the incident."

Legal experts howled disgust."It's almost like a lynching. Except in this case there is a rape involved, whereas in the Old West the mob would just lynch the person." Pakistani lawyer Naeem Bokhair told CNN.

Late on July 5, police made their first serious arrest: Abdul Khaliq, one of the four accused rapists, had fled over the border into neighbouring Baluchistan province. He was captured in Lasbala, several hundred kilometres from Mirwala.

Meanwhile, police records of rape reported in Muzaffargarh district in June 2002 painted a picture of rampant sexual violence. In the same month that Mukhtar was allegedly gang-raped, 21 other women were raped by 53 men. Thirteen of them were gang-raped. Of the 53 rapists, 45 had been arrested.[11]

---

10.   Amnesty International statement, July 2002
11.   Muzaffargarh district police superintendent Farman Ali Chaudhry

# 6 JULY, SATURDAY

On July 6 the man described as head of the panchayat and leader of the Mastoi clan, Faiz Muhammad Mastoi, walked into the Multan offices of the Daily Khabrain newspaper. He was ready to hand himself in to police. First however he asked for reporter Zafar Aheer. Faiz Mastoi told Aheer to take down every word of his account. The Mastoi tribesman had come to give his own defence before his inevitable arrest.

Faiz Mastoi told the Daily Khabrain reporter that he had neither ordered nor sanctioned any rape.

"Faiz Mastoi told me that he tried his utmost to convince his clan to avoid harsh action," Mr Aheer said in recalling the Mastoi chief's testimony in the newspaper office.[12]

"Faiz Mastoi said to me: 'I convinced my clansmen on this point, that they should get the hand of a girl from the Gujjars in marriage as compensation'," Zafar Aheer recounted.

Six Mastoi men "endorsed my opinion. However the Gujjar family refused," Faiz Mastoi told reporter Zafar Aheer.

The Gujjar family and its supporters rejected Faiz Mastoi's proposal as "unjudicious" and said it "needed to be relaxed."

"Upon this Ghulam Farid Gujjar (Mukhtar's father) and Ghulam Hussain (Mukhtar's uncle) suggested that they produce their girl before the panchayat and leave her at its mercy. The Mastois however responded by insisting on the hand of the girl in marriage. The Gujjars went home and then came back to the panchayat. When they came back they brought Mukhtar Mai with them," Faiz Mastoi told Zafar Aheer.

Faiz Mastoi said he asked his fellow clansmen to forgive Mukhtar's family, by stating: "'Now that they have brought their daughter to the panchayat, we should forgive them.' But the youths among my biraderi (clansmen) did not accept my proposal. Salma's brother Abdul Khaliq caught hold of Mukhtar Mai and took her into his home."

Faiz Mastoi's assertion that he urged forgiveness of Mukhtar's family accords with prosecution witness accounts.

Mukhtar and her supporting witnesses however allege that Faiz Mastoi's words were "duniavi …", meaning "spoken superficially".

Faiz Mastoi said he did not know what happened inside Abdul Khaliq's compound after Mukhtar had been dragged inside.

"After some time she came back. However I did not see her naked, nor was I aware whether she was raped or not," Faiz Mastoi told Zafar Aheer.

---

12.  Interview, Multan, January 4, 2006

As Faiz Mastoi delivered his newspaper testimony, a squad of uniformed police strode into the Daily Khabrain office. They handcuffed the Mastoi man. Before the flashes of the local newspaper's photographer, they escorted him to a waiting police van.

Meanwhile police had begun interrogating Abdul Khaliq, the first rape suspect to be arrested, on where his co-suspects were hiding.

"We have formed four special teams to track the fleeing accused and we want to catch them soon," Muzaffargarh district police chief Farman Ali told my colleague Qamar.[13]

The first police head to roll was Assistant Sub-Inspector Muhammad Iqbal. He was arrested for accepting an 11,000 rupee (183 US dollars) bribe from Mukhtar's family to free Shakoor after police had taken him from the Mastoi home.

"The police officer is found to have been guilty of accepting an 11,000 rupee bribe to release the boy," a police investigator told Qamar.

Back in Mirwala, Mukhtar's father broke his public silence and talked to reporters.

"No-one helped us. We begged for mercy in the name of God from them, but they held guns on us and so we were helpless."[14]

Two days later, on Monday July 8, two more accused rapists were captured: Fayyaz and Ghulam Fareed Mastoi.

## 9 JULY, TUESDAY

On July 9, five days after receiving half a million rupees from President Musharraf, Mukhtar announced she would set up a school.

"I want to set up a mosque, a seminary and a school for girls here," Mukhtar told Qamar, who was visiting her village home.

She said she had received offers of money also from several non-government organizations.

Mukhtar told Qamar that the Supreme Court's intervention had given her confidence. "I no longer feel threatened, as the Supreme Court has taken it upon itself to pursue the case to ensure that all suspects are being hunted," she stated.

Investigators gathered more witness statements. Police took Mukhtar, her father, her uncle Sabir, her brother Shakoor, the cleric and Ghulam Nabi to the closest magistrate—Rana Muhammad Ishfaq, the civil judge of Alipur, to record more statements.

---

13. Agence France Presse, July 6, 2002
14. Associated Press, July 6, 2002

Doctor Hussain tested Abdul Khaliq, Ghulam Fareed Mastoi and Fayyaz for potency.

All three men were handcuffed as he conducted a prostatic massage on each of them.

## JULY 11, THURSDAY

The Supreme Court held a second weekly hearing into the progress of the police investigation on July 11. Police reported to the top court that they had arrested 13 men in total. Eight Mastoi relatives, three rape suspects and accused panchayat chief Faiz Mastoi. One other rape suspect and one of the Mastois' arbitrators were still on the run.

"The hunt for the remaining two accused is on and we hope to track them down soon," police Deputy Inspector General Asif Nawaz Hayat told the court hearing.

Chief Justice Sheikh Riaz ordered police to bring the case to trial "as soon as possible."

He also ordered police protection for Mukhtar Mai. Her family had complained of threats from the Mastois.

"Police should ensure the safety of the victim and provide her protection against any harassment," the Supreme Court judge said.

The Punjab Governor's inquiry concluded that three Mastoi clansmen had sodomised Abdul Shakoor. The inquiry panel accused the Mastois of concealing the sodomy attack act by locking Shakoor up in their home with Salma and concocting the tale of his "illicit" behaviour with Salma. The panel accused police of conspiring to conceal the sodomy assault by throwing Shakoor in a cell in Jatoi police station.

## JULY 12, FRIDAY

The last of the men wanted for the assault on Mukhtar Mai was arrested on July 12: Allah Ditta Mastoi, Salma's second oldest brother, and Ramzan Pachaar, one of the negotiators for the Mastois. Allah Ditta was sent to the doctor for a potency test.

Police took Abdul Khaliq out of his cell and back to his Mirwala home to locate the pistol he was accused of waving as he dragged Mukhtar into his home. Police claimed they found two live cartridges with a pistol.

The hunt began for three Mastoi men accused of sodomising Shakoor: Salma's brother Punnu and cousins Manzoor and Jamil. Jamil was the first to be picked up. He was sent to the doctor for a potency test the next day.

## JULY 13, SATURDAY

Exactly three weeks after her ordeal Mukhtar inaugurated a boys' school in her village, received a marriage proposal from an army officer, and was honoured with an official visit by the Punjab Governor, former Lieutenant General Khalid Maqbool.

The government boys' primary school, established at Mukhtar Mai's request, was the only school within a 20-kilometre radius, local education official Khurshid Ahmed Siddiqui said. He did not mention, or perhaps was not aware, that a government boys' primary school had operated for many years in the centre of Mirwala, nine kilometres from Mukhtar Mai's home and the new boys' school.

Late in the day, Governor Maqbool and his entourage swept in to the far-away medieval-era village of Mirwala. The General-turned-Governor brought pledges to bring Mirwala into the 21$^{st}$ century: electricity, roads, a police station, and schools would be bequeathed to the community of cotton and sugarcane labourers.

"Two primary schools, one for boys and one for girls, will be opened in this village under the title of Mukhtaran Bibi to pay homage to this brave girl," the Governor declared.

Mukhtar's hand was sought in marriage – this time not as an act of revenge or compensation or 'equalisation of honour', but by an army officer from a nearby cantonment. He took out an advertisement in a local newspaper offering to marry her.

It was the first in what was to become a flood of marriage proposals.

## 18 JULY, MONDAY

On July 18 the Supreme Court ordered the Anti-Terrorism Court to try the Mukhtar Mai gang-rape case and to issue a verdict within three weeks.

Police investigators compiled the potency tests, medical reports, and witness statements into a dossier on July 18 and sent it to the Anti-Terrorism Court in Dera Ghazi Khan, 50 kilometres northwest from Mukhtar's village on the other side of the Indus.

Charges of gang-rape against four men and abetment against 10 men were filed in the Anti-Terrorism Court.

The chief public prosecutor of Punjab province submitted a written opinion that the case fell under Anti-Terrorism laws through a section which lists as an act of terrorism any act that "sows terror" and causes "grievous bodily harm".

The Punjab government assigned three lawyers to represent Mukhtar Mai: two women advocates, and the eminent barrister Ramzan Khalid Joya of the Punjab Bar Council.

Mr Joya vowed to seek death sentences for all 14 defendants.

"All the accused are liable for the death penalty or life imprisonment for either rape or abetment under the Pakistan Criminal Code," Joya told Qamar.

The Anti-Terrorism Court set about determining whether the gang-rape charges fell under its jurisdiction, based on the Anti-Terrorism Act of 1997. One of Pakistan's compulsions for establishing Anti-Terrorism courts was to bypass the heavy backlog of the mainstream court system and expedite the trials of "heinous crimes."

As the prospect of a trial drew closer, threats against Mukhtar and her family grew nastier. She reported receiving death threats from one of the Mastoi clansmen in Mirwala.

Punjab Governor Maqbool ordered a safe house for Mukhtar and her family.

The other two Mastoi men accused of sodomising Shakoor, Salma's oldest brother Punnu and a cousin Manzoor – were tested for potency after being arrested a day earlier.

Over the course of 15 days in July, Dr Fazal Hussain of the Jatoi Rural Health Centre conducted no less than eight 'potency' tests: on the four men accused of raping Mukhtar Mai, on the three men accused of sodomising him, and on Shakoor himself. The potency tests proved only this: that the men were capable of intercourse. The tests were of the most basic nature. They consisted of a prostatic massage, and a broad assessment of size.

All accused rapists and all accused sodomists were pronounced capable of performing sexual intercourse.

But, while DNA testing is available in Pakistan, no DNA tests or semen analyses were carried out to link the 'potent' and 'well-developed' defendants to the semen reportedly found on Mukhtar's swabs.

No semen traces were found on Shakoor.

## 23 JULY, SATURDAY

By July 23, Mukhtar and her family were all living in a designated police 'safe house' in Muzaffargarh, the main city of the district of the same name. It was about 50 kilometres from their village home.

"A well-furnished house is provided for the whole family…as per instructions of the Governor of Punjab, Lieutenant General Khalid Maqbool, to protect the life of Mukhtaran Bibi," the chief administrator of Muzaffargarh told Qamar.

Armed police were already guarding the family home in Mirwala.

## JULY 24, SUNDAY

The head of the Anti-Terrorism Court of Dera Ghazi Khan, Justice Zulfikar

Ali Malik, met the prosecution and defence teams to thrash out whether the case fell under the jurisdiction of his Anti-Terrorism Court. Lawyers defending the 14 Mastoi clansmen argued against it. But Judge Malik deemed the case "not an ordinary run-of-the-mill case". He green-lit the case as a terrorist offence.

The trial of the most notorious alleged gang-rape was set to begin on July 26.

\* \* \* \*

Less than a fortnight after Mukhtar Mai was allegedly gang-raped to atone for her brother's alleged sexual misdemeanour, Pakistan's President, the country's top judge, and the provincial Punjab government had intervened; two separate inquiries and a police investigation were launched; instant deadlines were set for the arrest of 14 accused men; and the President had given direct to the victim half a million rupees—160 times the average Pakistani's monthly wage, or 14 times the average annual salary.

The small fortune was deposited into the joint bank account of Mukhtar and her father, Ghulam Farid Gujjar, on July 10. The illiterate peasant who had never earned more than a few rupees by selling embroidered hair pieces was now the keeper of half a million rupees.

Within a month Mukhtar had a safe house for her family, a police guard contingent for their home in Mirwala, a squad of state-appointed lawyers to represent her for free, a grant of land from the government, and promises from the provincial Governor of paved roads, electricity, schools and a police post for her tiny backwards village.

Through the revelations and responses of July 2002, not only were the lives of Mukhtar Mai's family and their Mastoi neighbours transformed forever, the nation's consciousness and the national conscience were shaken in a way no other rape case had done before.

The medieval panchayats or jirgas at the heart of the tribal justice system were scrutinised with unprecedented intensity. Since before Pakistan's birth, tribal justice practices had conveniently filled the massive holes in the mainstream justice sector.

They provided swift and free settlements, the only alternative for poor villagers to fee-charging lawyers and bribe-hungry police and the lengthy court backlogs of the formal justice system. The tribal courts relieved administrations of the weight of more demands on the overburdened and under-resourced police and judiciary. The tribal courts incorporated local customs, perceptions of honour and revenge, family histories, and land trades. They fit perfectly into the fabric of the feudal societies in rural tracts like the southern Punjab, where large tracts of fertile farming lands are monopolised by a minority who employ villagers living on their lands to cultivate their fields for 50 to 80 cents a day, in the knowledge that most of the produce goes to the feudal lords.

It was long perceived that panchayat leaders collaborated informally with dominant landowners to ensure that decisions never went against their interests. For example, that land stayed within a certain clan's hands, or that influential landholders were not punished, or that women never rose above their status as commodities and domestic workers.

The Human Rights Commission seized on Mukhtar Mai's ordeal to vent its scorn of the panchayats' and jirgas' links to local elites.

"Our concern is the existence of extra-judicial tribunals that dish out sentences under the pressure of local elite," said then chairman, Afrasiab Khattak.[15] "The sense of impunity among the elite" was one of the factors to be blamed for brutality against women, he stressed. He pointed out that there was nothing unprecedented about a gang-rape per se; it was the fact that it was apparently ordered or sanctioned by a tribal council.

"This is the first known case where a (tribal) council has ordered such a thing, although in the past in Punjab feudal lords did this to their opponents' families. The vacuum created by the judicial system and the weakness of governance is filled by the jirgas and the panchayats. We have to address the main issue, that is the need to strengthen our institutions."

Aurat Foundation, a women's rights advocacy group, singled out tribal chiefs and feudal lords for condemnation.

"Mostly, those who commit gang-rapes or kill women in the name of honour are influential tribesmen or feudal, therefore, they escape punishment," Aurat's spokeswoman Naeem Mirza said. "Women are often punished for the crimes committed by male members of their families."

From the first week in July, Pakistani society unleashed its outrage through the national press at tribal councils and the barbaric sentence apparently imposed on Mukhtar Mai.

The alleged gang-rape on the orders of the tribesmen's council was "a blot on the nation's conscience", columnist Zubeida Mustafa wrote in Dawn, an English-language broadsheet. "It..is impossible to express the sense of outrage one feels at something so barbaric which can take place in a country that claims to be civilized."

"It is shocking that social conventions and tribal customs continue to be so strong that people in many parts of the country still turn to a panchayat to seek redress for a perceived wrong. What is worse is that in such cases the jirga manages to convene and overrule the law of the land...Drunk with power and driven by a frenzied desire for vendetta, the Mastois were not deterred from the criminal path they took.... More distressing is the common perception

---

15. Agence France Presse, July 18, 2002

that women are the property of their men, as well as the guardians of the family honour...It reduces women to being treated as chattels, if not vassals, of the male members of their family."

The Nation newspaper pronounced the alleged crime a "crying shame for the nation."

Op-ed pieces in mass-selling daily The News mirrored the national bewilderment:

"How do you label such a happening? Animalism?" asked commentator Nasim Zehra.

"No, surely animals have some rules of interaction. The animal world too must function according to some ethic. Calling it a crime is understating the fact. To say it was a hellish event would also not be correct. Hell too would be hard but not so violative of every particle of decency, rationality and propriety. Let the 'happening' remain unlabelled. Let us ask ourselves what after all was the worldview of this panchayat which issued such a ruling? What is the context in which such a worldview emerges, evolves, survives and also is allowed to become ascendant?...The government has to now demonstrate to the people of Pakistan, through quick and concrete action that those responsible for ordering and implementing evil justice will be accordingly punished."

At no point throughout that stormy July did any rights advocate, official, or columnist acknowledge that the allegations had not been investigated or tried.

# 13

# Tribes on Trial

On the fifth Muslim Sabbath following the feud between the Gujjars and Mastois, on the other side of the Indus, Mukhtar Mai's case went to trial. It ran from July 26 until6 the end of August: the verdict came after the last midnight in August. It was the peak of claustrophobic monsoon heat. Drowning in the black folds of a billowing chador, hooded like a dark prophet, Mukhtar Mai came to prosecute her attackers from the notorious Mastoi clan. The first person in Pakistan to take a tribal tradition of justice to court was a woman. Sometimes light caught parts of her narrow chin and mouth; her eyes stayed hidden in the hood's layered shadows. I glimpsed her on television, during this trial. As editor of all copy incoming from Pakistan and Afghanistan, I could rarely leave Islamabad and relied on local 'stringers' for on-the-spot reporting, gathering quotes and scene descriptions, which we would use after deconstructing and reconstructing the raw copy.

The image of Mukhtar Mai brought to mind a description I'd read long ago of cloaked and hooded women in Saudi Arabia. "Death going out for a walk" was the description given by a journalist living in the Middle East. The image stuck in my head. The woman taking these 14 shackled clansmen to trial looked like she had risen from a gloomy grave.

Their feet bound together in shackles and their hands chained to one another like medieval convicts, the 14 tribesmen on trial shuffled into the tiny courthouse. White tunics were matted against their perspiring bodies, moustaches sagged with sweat, turbans tailed down their dripping necks. Hoardes of reporters elbowed each other outside the courtroom in the sweltering right-bank[1] Indus city of Dera Ghazi Khan. The trial was closed to the press and general public. Journalists were barred from entering.

On paper Dera Ghazi Khan may still be part of the Punjab, theoretically ruled by the provincial administration; but Dera Ghazi Khan is tribal land. Justice is administered by tribal chiefs, known as 'sardars', or by their sons with Western university degrees.

An antipodean-educated son of the head of a major tribe from the Dera Ghazi Khan side of the Indus once whispered to me shyly, in the wood-panelled parlour of his father's city villa near Karachi's affluent beachfront, that he had single-handedly adjudicated on murder cases in his clan's heartland.

---

1. The west bank of the Indus River is called the "right bank"

He was embarrassed.

His Western law education and several years practice as a London barrister were not meant to guild him for playing arbitrary judge in an Indus backwater.

Dera Ghazi Khan is the heart of Baloch territory. The Mastois are a long-forgotten distant branch of the sprawling Baloch diaspora.

Dera Ghazi Khan was settled by Baloch tribes as they migrated north up the Indus from Makran, the southern coastal wasteland to which they had fled between the 10th and 13th centuries. The city was founded in 1484 by Haji Khan, a chief of the Mirrani sub-tribe of the Baloch. He established a dynasty. Haji Khan was at the vanguard of Baloches who began to come down from the hills and move east to settle the 'left' or east bank of the Indus. Haji Khan's descendants ruled until 1769, their names alternating between Haji Khan and Ghazi Khan.[2]

The disconnected sons of the early Baloch wanderer-warriors were now on trial in one of their ancestral heartlands. In the dock on trial for their lives were:

*Abdul Khaliq Mastoi:* 20/22years
*Allah Ditta Mastoi:* 24/25years
*Muhammad Fayyaz Mastoi:* 22/23years, s/o[*] Karim Bakhsh, r/o[**] Rampur
*Ghulam Fareed Mastoi:* 35/36years, s/o Allah Bakhsh, r/o Mirwala)
*(all four of them stood accused of abduction, gang-rape and causing grievous bodily harm)*
*Faiz Muhammad Mastoi:* 34/35years, r/o Rampur
*Ramzan Pachaar:* 35/36years, r/o Rampur
(both stood accused of abetting the gang-rape)

Alleged panchayat members, accused of aiding and abetting the gang-rape by virtue of their membership of the alleged panchayat:

*Muhammad Aslam Mastoi:* 30/31years, s/o Mehmood, r/o Rampur
*Allah Ditta Mastoi:* 22/23years, s/o Jan Muhammad, r/o Rampur
*Khalil Ahmad Mastoi:* 24/25years, s/o Ghulam Hussain (s/o Jind Wada), r/o Hairo
*Ghulam Hussain Mastoi:* 45/46years, s/o JindWada r/o Hairo
*Hazoor Bakhsh Mastoi:* 43/44years, s/o JindWada
*Rasool Bakhsh Mastoi:* 36/37years, s/o JindWada
*Qasim Mastoi:* 28/29years, s/o JindWada
*Nazar Hussain Mastoi:* 32/33years, s/o Allah Bakhsh, r/o Hairo

Apart from Ramzan Pachaar, of the Pachaar caste, all were of the Mastoi clan.

---

2.  Gazetteer of the Muzaffargarh District, 1929, Sang-e-Meel Publications, pg 29
    *s/o = son of **r/o = resident of

The charges against the 14 tribesmen traversed three separate laws:

- The British-inherited Pakistan Penal Code of 1860
- The Hudood Ordinance, a set of Islamic-based laws introduced in 1979 to bring Pakistani law in line with "the injunctions of Islam as set out in the Holy Qur'an and Sunnah"
- the Anti-Terrorism Act 1997.

The charges fell under:

- The Pakistan Penal Code: Section 109 (Abetment), Section 149 (Unlawful Assembly) and Section 354-A (Stripping A Woman in Public)
- The 'Enforcement of Hudood' Ordinance on the Offence of Zina (Fornication): Section 10-4 (Gang-rape) and section 11 (Kidnapping)
- The Anti-Terrorism Act: Section 7-C (Grievous Bodily Harm) read with section 21-I (Aid and Abetment).

All 14 pleaded not guilty. All 14 reserved their defence, in statements recorded in front of the Anti-Terrorism Court of Dera Ghazi Khan.

The charges were:

UNDER THE HUDOOD ORDINANCE:

Section 10 (4): *ZINA or ZINA — BIL JABR LIABLE TO TAZIR* (Read with Pakistan Penal Code Section 149 on Unlawful Assembly)

*1. Subject to the provisions of Section 7, whoever commits zina or zina-bil-jabr which is not liable to hadd, or for which proof in either of the forms mentioned in section 8 is not available and the punishment of "qazf" (slander) liable to hadd has not been awarded to the complainant, or for which hadd may not be enforced under this Ordinance, shall be liable to Tazir. (FN\*This applied in this case because the hadd requirements of four witnesses to rape could not be met.)*

*4. When zina-bil-jabr liable to tazir is committed by two or more persons in furtherance of common intention of all, each of such persons shall be punished with death. (ie gang-rape)* ·

*\*Section 8 of the Hudood Ordnances specifies that proof of fornication (Zina) or rape (Zina-bil-jabr) which is liable to Hadd requires either a) a confession by the accused or b) at least four Muslim adult male witnesses. Sections 9 & 10 both state that if these proofs are not available, then the crime is liable to Tazir, which does not require 4 witnesses.*

*\*\*if there are not four witnesses, the court may award Tazir [under Section 9 (2) and (4)]*

***punishment for Zina-bil-jabr (rape) liable to hadd is public stoning to death, or public whipping with 100 stripes. The Court may add punishment it deems fit including death sentence.*

****punishment for Zina-bil-Jabr (rape) liable to Tazir is 4-25 years prison with 30 lashes; for gang-rape the punishment is death.*

## Section 11: *KIDNAPPING, ABDUCTING OR INDUCING A WOMAN TO COMPEL FOR MARRIAGE*

Whoever kidnaps or abducts any woman with intent that she may be compelled, or knowing it be likely that she will be compelled, to marry any person against her will, or in order that she may be forced or seduced to illicit intercourse or knowing it to be likely that she will be forced or decided to illicit intercourse, shall be punished with imprisonment for life and with whipping not exceeding 30 stripes, and shall also be liable to fine; and whoever by means of criminal intimidation as defined in the Pakistan Penal Code (ACT XLV of 1860) or of abuse of authority or any other method of compulsion induces any woman to go from any place with intent that she may be, or knowing that it is likely that she will be, forced or seduced to illicit intercourse with another person, shall also be punishable as aforesaid.

## UNDER THE ANTI-TERRORISM ACT

### Section 7 (c)(read with S21-I) *GRIEVOUS BODILY HARM*

*Whoever commits an act of terrorism under section 6 whereby grievous bodily harm or injury is caused to any person, shall be punishable, on conviction, with imprisonment of either description for a term not less than ten years and not exceeding fourteen years, and shall also be liable to a fine.*

### Section 6 – (1-B) *COERCE, INTIMIDATE OR OVERAWE*

*In this Act, "terrorism" means the use or threat of action where the use or threat is designed to coerce and intimidate or overawe the Government or the public or a section of the public or community or sect or create a sense of fear or insecurity in society.*

*- (2-B)*

*An "action" shall fall within the meaning of Section 6 sub-section (1) if it involves grievous violence against a person or grievous bodily injury or harm to a person.*

## Section 21 (I) *AID AND ABETMENT*

*Whoever aids or abets any offence under this Act shall be punishable with the maximum term of same imprisonment provided for the offence or the fine provided for such offence or with both.*

### UNDER THE PAKISTAN PENAL CODE

Section 109: Punishment of abetment if the Act abetted is committed in consequence of the abetment, and where no express provision is made for its punishment:

*Whoever abets any offence shall, if the act abetted is committed in consequence of the abetment, and no express provision is made by this Code for the punishment of such abetment, be punished with the punishment provided for the offence.*

This means the abettor is liable to the same punishment as the committer of the Act he/she abetted.[3]

The Pakistan Penal Code defines abetment thus:

*A person abets the doing of a thing who first: instigates any person to do that thing; or engages with one or more other person or persons in any conspiracy for the doing of that thing, if an act or illegal omission takes place in pursuance of that conspiracy, and in order to the doing of that thing; or intentionally aids, by any act or illegal omission, the doing of that thing.*

Section 149: Every member of unlawful assembly (is) guilty of offence committed in prosecution of common object:

*If an offence is committed by any member of an unlawful assembly in prosecution of the common object of that assembly, or such as the members of that assembly knew to be likely to be committed in prosecution of that object, every person who, at the time of the committing of that offence, is a member of the same assembly, is guilty of that offence.*

The Pakistan Penal Code defines "unlawful assembly" thus:

An assembly of five or more persons if the common object of the persons composing that assembly is:

1. to overawe by criminal force, or show of criminal force, the Federal or any Provincial Government or Legislature, or any public servant in the exercise of the lawful power of such public servant; or

---

3. Pakistan Penal Code XLV of 1860 [BareAct], Mansoor Book House, pg 56

2. to resist the execution of any law, or of any legal process; or
3. to commit any mischief or criminal trespass, or other offence; or
4. by means of criminal force, or show of criminal force, to any person to take or obtain possession of any property, or to deprive any person of the enjoyment of a right of way, or of the use of water or other incorporeal right of which he is in possession of enjoyment, or to enforce any right or supposed right; or
5. by means of criminal force, or show of criminal force, to compel any person to do what he is not legally bound to do, or to omit to do what he is legally entitled to do.

It notes that an assembly which was not unlawful when it assembled, may subsequently become an unlawful assembly.

## Section 354 (A):
## *STRIPPING A WOMAN NAKED IN PUBLIC VIEW*

*Assault or use of criminal force to (on) a woman and stripping her of her clothes: Whoever assaults or uses criminal force to (on) any woman and strips her of her clothes and, in that condition, exposes her to the public view, shall be punished with death or with imprisonment for life, and shall also be liable to fine.*

The Jattoi police station's sacked Assistant Sub-Inspector Muhammad Iqbal was originally also charged with causing grievous bodily harm under the Anti–Terrorism Act, but justice authorities decided to try him separately in a court of general jurisdiction under Sections 217 and 119 of the Pakistan Penal Code.

*Section 217:* Public servant disobeying direction of law with intent to save persons from punishment or property from forfeiture

*Persons found guilty under this section shall be punished with imprisonment of either description for a term which may extend to two years, or with fine, or with both.*

## Section 119: *PUBLIC SERVANT CONCEALING DESIGN TO COMMIT OFFENCE WHICH IT IS HIS DUTY TO PREVENT*

\* \* \* \*

The defence called six witnesses, including three police officers:

1. Muhammad Younas, Manager of the National Bank of Pakistan, Alipur branch, where Mukhtar and her father opened accounts and deposited monies received after filing charges against the Mastois, starting with 500,000 rupees from the government

2. Nadeem Saeed, correspondent of *Dawn*, an English-language daily
3. Police Head Constable Akbar Ali
4. Police Sub-Inspector Muhammad Ashraf, Muzaffargarh
5. Ghulam Hussain (cousin of Abdul Khaliq Mastoi's mother)
6. Police Superintendent Mirza Muhammad Abbas, who investigated local police

In the dock for the prosecution were 16 witnesses, including nine police officers & two doctors:

1. Dr Fazal Hussain Senior Medical Officer, Jatoi Rural Health Centre, Jatoi
2. Dr Shahida Safdar Women's Medical Officer, Jatoi Rural Health Centre
3. Police officer Rafique Ahmad, FC Muzaffargarh
4. Police officer Ali Muhammad FC
5. Police Constable Muhammad Yar, Jatoi
6. Police Constable Azhar Abbas, Jatoi
7. Judge Rana Muhammad Ishfaq, Civil Judge/Magistrate, Alipur
8. Police Deputy Superintendent Shaukat Murtaza, Muzzafargarh
9. Police Inspector Abdul Latif Khan, Jatoi
10. Abdul Shakoor (caste Gujjar)
11. Maulvi Abdul Razzaq (caste Jatoi)
12. Haji Altaf Hussain (brother of Razzaq) (caste Jatoi)
13. Sabir Hussain (caste Tatla Gujjar, Mukhtar Mai's uncle)
14. Mukhtar Mai (caste Gujjar)
15. Police Deputy Superintendent Muhammad Saeed Awan, Jatoi
16. Police Inspector Nazir Ahmad, Jatoi

The Court called its own witnesses, essentially to prove the jurisdiction of the Anti-Terrorism Court to hear the case by testifying that the actions of the supposed panchayat and accused rapists were intended "to coerce and intimidate or overawe... a section of the community *or... create a sense of fear or insecurity in society."*

The Court Witnesses were:

1. Malik Sultan Mahmood Hinjra, Nazim (Mayor) of Muzaffargarh District
2. Muhammad Amjad, Mirwala representative on Jhugiwala Local Council
3. Abdul Wahid, member of Rampur Local Council
4. Maulvi Faiz Muhammad, prayer leader/cleric
5. Police Constable Abdul Majeed
6. Police Inspector Abdul Latif Khan
7. Police Sub-Inspector Ghulam Shabbir

Acting for the prosecution were:

- Ashgar Gill, chief public prosecutor;
- Public Prosecutor Iftikhar Qazi
- Senior Prosecutor Khalid Ramzan Joya
- Prosecutors Azra Saeed and Sabina Hassan Randhawa
- Qazi Sadar-ud-Din (who withdrew his power of attorney on August 1 after it was found that he had not been appointed or sanctioned by the government to represent Mukhtar Mai)

Acting for the Defence were:

- Saleem Malik, chief defence advocate
- Azhar Trimizi, Zaffar Ahmad Lund and 13 other assisting advocates.

Presiding over the Anti-Terrorism Court was Justice Zulfikar Ali Malik.

\*    \*    \*    \*

On day one of the trial, the prosecution demanded death for all 14 before even entering the courthouse. Holding his own court with a mob of excited pressmen outside the Dera Ghazi Khan courthouse, chief public prosecutor Ashgar Gill declared:

"We will press for the maximum punishment, the death sentence."

The Mastois' chief defence lawyer responded on the second day of the hearing.

"The prosecution case is built on a sand dune," Saleem Malik told the throng of reporters.

Two of the charges carried death: gang-rape, under the Hudood Ordinance, and the charge of stripping a woman of her clothes and exposing her to the public view, under the Pakistan Penal Code. This is the wording of the 1860 Code's Section 354-A. It is often reported as stripping a woman naked and parading her in public. This is how the crime against Mukhtar was widely reported—with journalists taking the wording of a criminal charge literally.

While Mukhtar, according to herself and witnesses, never appeared fully naked, the ripped state of her long tunic and the absence of trousers underneath her knee-length tunic were enough to meet cultural perceptions of nudity. A woman lacking one piece of clothing, for example her tunic, while still wearing underclothes and trousers, is considered "naked".

Naked or semi-naked, in neither state was Mukhtar paraded in full public view. It was near midnight when she emerged from the room where she was raped. The village had yet to experience electricity. Mukhtar said there was no gaslight or candlelight. The moon was a crescent, three days off finishing its cycle. She was on the outskirts of Mirwala, at least nine kilometres from the village centre.

Mukhtar was still clad in her long tunic when she emerged, allegedly seen by her uncle, her father, the cleric's brother, and their friend Ghulam Nabi.

No one can recall exactly how many spectators or Mastoi supporters, if any, were still there when she emerged. It was too dark to see. Mukhtar's legs were bare; so she wrapped her long shawl, called bochan, around them.

Her father and uncle walked her home along an empty, narrow dirt trail through a night-shrouded field of head-high sugarcane.

"They put me between them," Mukhtar told me. She had wound her bochan around her legs sarong-style, underneath her long, blousey tunic or kameez.

Lawyers in black suits, limp in the July humidity, tailed by clerks bent double with bursting files tied with ribbon, strode past the shackled tribesmen from the other side of the Indus.

A lone woman in black, face and figure shrouded, sat in silence, her veiled face bowed.

Never had any court in Pakistan's 55 years convened to hear allegations that a panchayat had ordered or sanctioned the gang-rape of a woman, to avenge the stained honour of a rival tribe.

While technically without any legal standing, panchayats or jirgas are tolerated by authorities for the useful role they serve in mediating disputes swiftly and without cost, and keeping extra cases out of the heavy backlog of cases burdening the formal justice system. They most commonly mediate in disputes over *zar* (gold/money), *zamin* (land) and *zan* (women). They adjudicate the balance of honour. In their purest form they are based on pluralistic representation of all tribes of the area, and adjudicate according to consensus and conciliation. All members are supposed to agree on the fairest solutions, thereby ensuring universal acceptance throughout the area affected.

On trial in the burning Indus-plains heat of late July were not just the Mastoi tribe and the tribal code of the small world of Mirwala and its mosaic of Mastoi, Baloch, Gujjar and other tribes, but the entire tribal justice system and its centuries of existence that predated British colonists. One justice system was putting another justice system on trial. A new court, for terrorist offences, was trying an ancient court, specializing in honour offences.

The first to testify in this unprecedented trial of the tribal justice system and its ingrained custom of balancing honour through the barter of women, was the medical profession.

In a stroke of irony, the focus of the first day's testimony was the virility of the Mastoi tribesmen: the prostatic massages conducted on the four rape defendants to prove their 'capability.'

Dr Fazal Hussain, the Resident Medical Officer of the Jatoi Rural Health Centre, was first in the dock. Each sub-district in Pakistan has one of these state-run health clinics. Dr Hussain's chief role in his appearance as Prosecution

Witness One was to present his findings that the four accused rapists were 'potent for sexual intercourse'. (He appeared later in the trial to testify on his assessment that Mukhtar's adolescent brother Shakoor had been sodomised.)

Four hand-written "Potency Examination Reports" by the doctor were tendered as evidence. Three of the reports were based on his examinations of Abdul Khaliq Mastoi, Fayyaz Mastoi, and Ghulam Fareed Mastoi on July 9, and his July 13 examination of Allah Ditta Mastoi. Each had been brought to him by police within 24 hours of their arrests. Each man was handcuffed as the doctor tested their "potency".

Aside from the 'Marks of Identification', the wording of each scribbled report by Dr Hussain was nearly identical.

"I observed as follows:

> *He is physically well built*
> *His primary and secondary sex characteristics are well-developed*
> *He is not suffering from any chronic or debilitating disease*
> *Penile erection is positive on prostatic massage*

Therefore, I found nothing to suggest that the accused is unable to perform the sexual act at the time of examination." Dr Hussain told the Anti Terrorism Court that his tests proved the four accused rapists were physically capable of the alleged crime. Dr Hussain had performed four other potency examinations in July: on Shakoor and the three tribesmen accused of sodomising him.

Shakoor was examined at 11.15 am on July 3 on police orders, after Maulvi Abdul Razzaq brought him to register charges of sodomy against three Mastoi tribesmen. Unlike the Mastoi tribesmen, Shakoor was not in handcuffs as his 'potency' was tested.

> Dr Hussain found the teenager potent.
> The report states:
> "On examination I observed as follows:
> *He is physically of age appearing 14/15 years*
> *His primary sex characters are well developed while secondary sex characters are scantly.*
> *He is not suffering from any infections/debilitating disease*
> *Penile erection is present on prostatic massage*

In my opinion, I found nothing to suggest that the person under examination is unable to perform the sexual act at the time of examination."

*On the same day, Dr Hussain had examined Shakoor for signs of the sodomy attack alleged to have occurred 11 days earlier. The doctor's notes under 'External Examination' state that the blue shalwar kameez (trousers and long smock) Shakoor had been wearing when he was attacked was 'not stained with blood'. The adolescent's 'gait was normal'. The doctor* noted two minor marks of 'external violence': a stitched 2.5 cm wound near the left eyebrow, and two healed abrasions on Shakoor's chest.

Perineal and anal examination notes listed two marks of violence:

"The margins of the anus were indurated. A tear on the inner mucus was present. That was about to heal. The anal examination was painful."

Without waiting for chemical examination of the four anal swabs, the doctor concluded:

"The signs/symptoms had led to occurrence of sodomy act in my opinion."

On July 12, the Chemical Examiner issued his report on the testing of the swabs. He pronounced: "The above swabs are not stained with semen."

Under cross-examination at the trial into the sodomy of Shakoor in May 2003, Dr Hussain said that the induration of the margins of the anus "may be a result of some disease or trauma." He replied that "it is correct" that no symptom of sodomy can be visible after 10 days. He agreed that mucus tears resulting from sodomy disappear in "five to seven days."

But the doctor rejected suggestions by defence lawyers cross-examining him that he had issued a false medical report "due to the pressure of the government and police".

Under cross-examination in the gang-rape trial at Dera Ghazi Khan on July 26, Dr Hussain was asked why no analysis was performed of the accused rapists' semen.

"The police did not apply for group semen (analysis of semen)," he replied.[4]

In rural areas, the titles of female professionals are often preceded by with the term 'Lady' – as though it's still a novelty to have a woman in the position of doctor, journalist, tailor.

One of my esteemed Pashtun colleagues in Peshawar, a dramatic frontier city before the wild Afghan border, introduced me with eager pride one morning to his newspaper's 'lady journalist.' Even her business card announced her as a 'Lady Reporter'.

It is essential for all health clinics in rural areas to have a 'Lady Doctor', as conservative communities forbid their women to be examined by men outside of their family.

The 'Lady Doctor' of the Jatoi Rural Health Centre, Shahida Safdar, had examined Mukhtar Mai for signs of rape, straight after Mukhtar filed her complaint with Jatoi police on June 30. The Lady Doctor was the second to take the witness stand in the trial of the tribal justice system.

---

4.    Anti –Terrorism Court D.G. Khan Judgement Case FIR No 405/2002 31.8.2002
      pg 51

Dr Shahida Safdar had produced two medical reports on Mukhtar Mai in the preceding four weeks. On June 30 she filled in a standard form for rape victim examinations titled: *"PARTICULARS INJURIES OR SYMPTOMS IN CASE OF POISONING".*

This is the standard form for noting the results of rape examinations.

The report noted that Mukhtar had arrived for exam at 10.30am on June 30.

The form asks for 'two identification marks'. Dr Safdar filled it in thus:

'A black mole mark on the left cheek. A black mole mark on forehead.'

The body of Dr Safdar's report states:

*"I examined a young married (divorced) lady of age about 30 years…of rape one week back. She was fully conscious and well-oriented in time and space.*

1. *Healed abrasion of size 3 x 5 cm seen on Rt Buttock*
2. *A healed abrasion of size 1-1.5 x 0.5 cm on the perianal area. 9 swabs taken from vaginal canal*

Bottle no 1: 3 swabs taken from post-fornix and sent for C/E (chemical exam)

*Bottle no 2: 3 swabs taken from vaginal canal and sent for C/E*

*Bottle no 3: 3 swabs taken from external vaginal area and sent for C/E*

*Final report… given after receiving the report of C/E Multan."*

*The form asked for "The kind of weapon used or poison suspected in case of poisoning".* Marked in handwriting is: *'Rape'.* It was tendered to the court as Prosecution Exhibit D.

The Chemical Examiner issued his report on the swabs on July 6. *"The swabs are stained with semen,"* it pronounced. It was tendered to the court as Prosecution Exhibit F.

Dr Safdar completed a second and final report dated July 10, after receiving the Chemical Examiner's report on the 9 swabs. It is handwritten on blank paper.

*Subject: Final Opinion*

*"Final opinion of Mukhtar Mai D/O Gulam Fareed ..is given as under vide C/E Multan Letter No s-1313/CE dated 06/7/2002: 'The Swabs are Stained with Semen'*

*In my opinion rape occurred."*

Dr Safdar testified that the swabs she took from Mukhtar tested positive for semen. She repeated to the judge the observations listed on her two reports.

*"All the above swabs were handed over to the police for taking the same to the Chemical Examiner for analysis. All the swabs were sealed into three phials and one sealed envelope along with unsealed envelope. I received the result of the Chemical Examiner, according to which the swabs were stained with semen. Keeping in view the report of the Chemical Examiner, and my own finding, rape was committed with Ms Mukhtiar Mai as per my report,"* she testified.[5] Dr Safdar's 'final opinion' report was submitted as *Prosecution Exhibit E.*[6]

Launching into cross-examination, defence counsel Malik Salim challenged the reliability of a semen test eight days after the alleged intercourse.

Dr Safdar replied that while sperms remained motile in the uterine cavity for three to five days, *non-motile* semen could be detected in the genital tract for up to three weeks after intercourse, i.e. it was possible for the three *internal* swabs to be stained with semen.[7] The defence challenged the Chemical Examiner's failure to note in his report whether the semen found on the swabs was *motile or non-motile.*

The defence also challenged Dr Safdar as to why the clothes which Mukhtar Mai had worn at the time of the attack were not examined. The lady doctor replied that she asked Mukhtar Mai about her clothes – the dupatta (shawl), the shalwar (trousers) and kameez (long tunic). Mukhtar had replied that the clothes had been washed since the attack. The defence lawyers challenged the failure to send Mukhtar's clothes to the Chemical Examiner to be examined for semen. The unexamined clothes were introduced as *Prosecution Exhibit U.*

The defence also raised Mukhtar's status as a divorcee and how that may have impacted on a medical test.

"It was not a case of fresh rape and the hymen was old and torn," the defence team contested.[8] The defence asked why *"no effort was made for DNA testing (of the swabs or clothes) which could have supported the prosecution's case?"*[9]

There was no answer.

* * * *

---

5. " " pg 17
6. " " pg 17
7. Lahore High Court, Multan Bench Cr. A no 61/2002 03.3.2005 Judgement pg 12
8. Lahore High Court, Multan Bench Cr. A no 61/2002 03.3.2005 Judgement pg 12
9. Lahore High Court, Multan Bench Cr. A no 61/2002 03.3.2005 Judgement pg 13

**MONDAY JULY 29**

The trial resumed.

Mukhtar's younger brother Abdul Shakoor, age estimated by Dr Hussain as 14 to 15, took the seat. He was the first of the key prosecution witnesses to testify.

PW 10 ON OATH: ABDUL SHAKOOR, S/O GHULAM FARID Caste: Gujjar, aged 12/13 years, r/o Mirwala, tehsil Jatoi district Muzaffargarh

Under oath on July 31 Shakoor told the court that he was sleeping outside his house on June 22 when Punnu Mastoi, Salma's oldest brother, and cousins Manzoor and Jamil Mastoi abducted him and committed 'ziadti'(rape) with" him in the sugarcane field between the Mastoi and Gujjar homes.

*"They asked whether I would disclose the matter; I answered in the affirmative and was beaten. Thereafter I was taken by them in the house and was confined in a room. To cover up their crime, Naseem alias Salma was also confined in the said room. At Maghrebwela, police got me released and took me to the police station. That is all," Shakoor said in his evidence-in-chief.*

The public prosecutor asked him what time he was released from the police station.

*"Up to two/three am, when Faiz (Mastoi) and Ramzan (Pachaar) took me along and I was released. Reaching home, I came to know about ziadti committed with my sister. I also disclosed about commission of ziadti with me."*

Under cross-examination by defence counsel Malik Saleem, Shakoor repeated that he had been brought home from the police station at between two and three in the morning of June 23, and that on return he told his family that he had been sodomised.

*"I did not disclose the commission of sodomy to Iqbal (Police Assistant Sub-Inspector) due to shame. This fact was disclosed to the magistrate (who recorded prosecution statements on July 9). I disclosed to my family members after my release at 2.00/3.00 am about commission of ziadti with me. Ramzan and Faiz brought me up to my house in the night, but I do not know whether they stated to my family members that I had been got released by them...My father did not quarrel with the accused party regarding the commission of sodomy on me."*

Shakoor was asked when he first informed police of the sodomy story.

*"I was present in my house on 30.6.2002 when the police reached to register case being heard today. I made statement to the police on the said date about the commission of ziadti on me."*

Shakoor confirmed that Maulvi Abdul Razzaq accompanied him to the police station to register sodomy charges against the three Mastoi tribesmen on July 3.

D: "Is it correct that Maulvi Abdul Razzaq was with you when your case of sodomy was registered?" Malik asked.

Shakoor: "It is correct."

D: "Is it correct that you were caught red-handed committing inter-course with the said girl Naseem alias Salma?"

Shakoor: "Incorrect."

*Shakoor said he was confined in the Mastoi home from 2.00 pm on June 22 until* Maghrebwela. *Salma was released from the locked room before the police arrived, he added.*

As the tall teenager left the dock, the bearded cleric stepped up.

# 14

# Mullah in the Dock

PW No. 11 ON OATH: ABDUL RAZZAQ, s/o Bahadar Ali, caste: Jatoi, aged 40 years, r/o Meerwala, tehsil Jattoi, district Muzaffargarh

It was the last day in July when the Maulvi of the biggest mosque in Mirwala gave his evidence.

Abdul Razzaq, of the Jatoi tribe, told the trial court that Mukhtar's older brother Hazoor Bakhsh had turned up at his home on June 22 at *Aserwela* (mid-afternoon) and told him that his younger brother Shakoor "had been abducted by Mastoi *biraderi*."

Razzaq accompanied Hazoor Bakhsh to Jatoi police station to seek help. The pair told Assistant Sub-Inspector Muhammad Iqbal. Iqbal and Hazoor Bakhsh drove out to the Mastoi home while Maulvi Razzaq went on his motor scooter.

On the way Maulvi Razzaq ran into Manzoor Ahmad Jatoi and Khair Muhammad Mastoi, the father of Faiz Mastoi, who were coming from the Mastoi home.

"Khair Muhammad Mastoi stated that Abdul Shakoor had committed *ziadti* with their girl, so he had been confined. In *badla* (revenge), the hand of a (Gujjar) girl was demanded."

The Mastois only released Shakoor from their custody when Faiz Mastoi arrived at the home, he said.

"On his (Faiz') command, the boy was handed over to the police," Razzaq stated in court.

Faiz, according to the cleric Razzaq, then suggested that the Gujjars give one of their girls to the Mastoi family "for *nikah* (marriage) with Abdul Khaliq forthwith and perform *rukhsti* (handover of the bride) there and then."

"We went to convey the message to the Gujjar *biraderi* in the mosque where they were present. The Gujjar biraderi stated that Abdul Shakoor was nabaligh (immature) and was innocent. (They said that) if the Mastois suspect the illicit liaison of Salma and Abdul Shakoor, the pair should be bound in *nikah* and the Gujjars will also give their girl (Mukhtar Mai) to Abdul Khaliq."

In the words of the cleric Razzaq under oath, Mukhtar's family had rejected the proposal to merely give one of their girls in compensatory marriage to the Mastoi family, and had proffered a counter-proposal of "*watta-satta*": exchange marriage. The Gujjars would give a girl to the other tribe in marriage, if the other tribe gave one of their girls to one of their sons in marriage.

According to Razzaq, the Mastois' *salisan* (arbitrators), Ghulam Fareed Mastoi and Ramzan Pachaar, rejected the *watta-satta* proposal.

"(The arbitrators) stated that the Mastois had refused to accede to the offer of the Gujjars and that they would take *badla* of *zina* with *zina* (avenge rape with rape)," Razzaq told the trial court.

Razzaq and two other Jatoi clansmen, Manzoor Ahmad Jatoi and Ghulam Mustafa Jatoi, walked over the fields to the Mastoi home to bargain privately with the chief Mastoi negotiator, Faiz Mastoi.

"He (Faiz Mastoi) agreed to watta-satta and the offer that in case Abdul Shakoor was guilty, the Gujjars were ready to give four *kanals* (half an acre) land," Razzaq told the court.

But Faizs' acceptance, according to the cleric, was over-ruled by the Mastoi arbitrators, Ghulam Fareed Mastoi and Ramzan Pachaar.

"Fareed and Ramzan Pachaar did not agree," Razzaq said. "When our offer was not agreed to and Mastois demanded zina for (badla) zina, we went away, saying to them to resort to the process of law."

Razzaq then insisted that he only came to hear of the violent outcome of the negotiations six days later. This was despite living in the same small community and sharing a home with his brother, who was allegedly present when Mukhtar was dragged into Abdul Khaliq's home and when she emerged an hour later, distraught and in torn clothes.

On Friday June 28, an unnamed person came to the cleric and repeated 'gossip' he had heard in a local canteen by 'aubash' (bad characters) detailing the gang-rape resulting from the panchayat, the cleric testified. Razzaq said he was about to give his Friday sermon when the revelations were made to him.

"I condemned the humiliation and the inhuman conduct during the Jumma (Friday) prayer, and (urged) that legal action be taken and the victim be helped." The cleric told the court that he approached Mukhtar's father at his woodstall after the midday prayers and offered to help seek justice. The father refused to admit anything. The cleric returned to the woodstall the next day with two reporters who had heard the cleric's Friday sermon and its shocking account. The three of them told Ghulam Farid Gujjar that he had the support of the people to lay charges over the rape of his daughter.

"Whereupon he stated zulam (tyranny) had been committed with him, second zulam be not perpetrated, and if he disclosed, he would be murdered. We pacified him that people were with him and he had the legal right, whereupon he sought some time to ponder over," Razzaq told the court.

Their urges worked. According to the prosecution, after dawn prayers the following day Mukhtar, her father and uncle Sabir appeared at the cleric's home and "offered to proceed with the legal formalities."

The cleric called his brother Haji Altaf Hussain and Ghulam Nabi to come with them to the police station, as Mukhtar's father said they had both witnessed the crime.

"We all went to Jatoi police station on bus. We alighted at Jhugiwala Chowk (intersection) bus-stop where the statement of Mukhtar Mai was recorded by the SHO (police officer) who was present there in police van."

Mukhtar was then sent to the doctor for examination.

The following day, the cleric said, he went to Mukhtar's house to retrieve the clothes she had worn to the Mastois' gathering. Later he delivered the clothes to the police.

"The aforesaid delivery of clothes was made on the asking of Mukhtar Mai, who stated that the policemen demanded the said clothes," Razzaq told the court.

Defence counsel Malik Saleem launched into cross-examination. He began gently.

Saleem quizzed the cleric on who first proffered the *watta-satta* proposal; on Faiz Mastoi's role in releasing Shakoor from the Mastoi home and handing him over to the police; and on the distance between key sites (such as between the Gujjars' gathering in the small mosque near the canal, and the Mastoi gathering near Abdul Khaliq Mastoi's home.)

D: "At what point was Mukhtar Mai chosen from among the five Gujjar daughters to be offered in *watta-satta* to the Mastoi son Abdul Khaliq?"

Razzaq: "We talked of *sulah* (settlement of a dispute; end of a quarrel) with (Gujjar) biraderi, and said that Ms Mukhtiar Mai be given in *nikah* to brother of Ms Naseem alias Salma," Razzaq replied.

Asked about Ramzan Pachaar's role, the cleric stated: "Ramzan Pachaar is not Mastoi nor is he related to them. But he belongs to their gang."

The cleric repeated under cross-examination that his final words to the Mastois were: "Take legal proceedings."

"God knows what happened thereafter. I was not present at the spot. I was present in the *madrassa* (religious school)."

The judge interrupted with a question: "Where were you between then and June 28?"

The cleric replied: "I had remained present in the madrassa busy in teaching."

Defence counsel Malik quizzed the cleric as to how he could remain unaware for six days of the outcome of the negotiations after playing such a key role and while sharing a house with his brother who witnessed the crime.

"Altaf is my real brother who lives with me at the same place," Razzaq confirmed.

D: "Is it correct that your brother Altaf did not disclose about the occurrence up to the 28th and not even up to 30.6.2002?"

Razzaq: "It is correct."

The cleric estimated it was between 9 and 9.30 pm when he left the June 22 gathering. He said he could not remember who brought him the gossip overheard in the canteen about the Mastois regaining their honour through gang-rape. He believed it was around 1.00 to 1.30 pm as he was proceeding to the mosque to deliver his sermon.

"Straight away I went to the mosque and delivered the sermon."

The next day around midday two journalists, one of them fellow Jatoi tribesman Mureed Abbas, met the cleric at the Shah Nawaz Jatoi canteen in Mirwala.

"They stated that on hearing my speech, they had come to me," Razzaq testified.

Defence Advocate Saleem Malik suggested to the cleric that he and Mureed Abbas first approached the police independently to lodge a complaint about Mukhtar's gang-rape, before securing her family's consent. The cleric denied their suggestion.

Malik also quizzed Razzaq as to why none of the Gujjar family mentioned Shakoor's sodomy claims when they registered Mukhtar's gang-rape case on the morning of June 30.

"No person talked about the commission of sodomy with Abdul Shakoor at the time that the complaint of this case was lodged with the police," Razzaq said.

The cleric was then quizzed about the reporting to police the names of the members of the supposed panchayat.

Razzaq said Mukhtar had named the "armed persons present in the panchayat" in her first police statement on June 30. Her father and uncle had separately given police the panchayat members' names, he added.

"Till such time I remained present in the panchayat, those persons were armed with weapons," Razzaq stated.

With the cleric in the dock, the defence team unveiled their side of the story to the court for the first time. Defence counsel Salim Malik confronted the cleric with the Mastoi version of events.

The crux of the defence argument was two-fold. Firstly they alleged that a verbal nikah, (on-the-spot marriage ceremony) between Mukhtar Mai and Abdul Khaliq had taken place. Secondly, they alleged historical enmity between the Mastois and Maulvi Razzaq over a charge of corrupt land-grabbing against the cleric, and the cleric's links to the outlawed organization of violent Islamic extremists, Sipah-e-Sahaba.

Saleem Malik outlined the Mastois' perception of events as follows:

Shakoor was "nabbed committing intercourse" with Salma in the sugarcane field behind his home. He was "thrashed" by Salma's brothers and then thrown into a locked room in the Mastoi house. "To suppress true facts," the cleric interrupted.

Malik continued his discourse on the Mastoi version of events: When police came to free Shakoor, Abdul Khaliq told them that the Gujjar adolescent had been caught with Salma. The cleric proposed to Mukhtar's father to resolve the problem by giving Mukhtar Mai to Khaliq in marriage, and by marrying Salma off to Shakoor. The compensatory *watta-satta* proposal was then put to Abdul Khaliq's family. Abdul Khaliq asked for an hour to consult with his elders. At 11pm Abdul Khaliq came back to the cleric and told him the deal would be accepted, provided Mukhtar was given to him that very night in marriage. After the marriage with Mukhtar, Shakoor would be freed from the police station. The *rukhsti*, i.e. the delivery of the bride to the groom, had to be performed there and then.

Listening to this account in court, the cleric denied each step of the Mastoi version.

Saleem Malik resumed: the cleric then asked Abdul Khaliq to give him an hour to consult with the Gujjar family on the Mastois' conditions. If the Gujjars accepted Abdul Khaliq's conditions, the cleric himself would perform the *nikah* that night. At midnight, according to the defence, Mukhtar was brought to Abdul Khaliq's home accompanied by the cleric, her father, her uncle, her elder brother and Ramzan Pachaar. The cleric told Abdul Khaliq that the Gujjars had accepted his conditions for meeting their exchange marriage proposal. The cleric performed a *sharai* (verbal) *nikah* between Mukhtar and Abdul Khaliq, and left Mukhtar in the house of Abdul Khaliq, according to the defence counsel.

The cleric flatly denied the defence account.

Saleem Malik continued:

Abdul Khaliq then had to fulfil his part of the deal to release Shakoor from the police station, so that he could be married to Salma the next morning. Abdul Khaliq and Ramzan Pachaar went to the police station and brought Shakoor home at 2.00am. Abdul Khaliq then went home to his own house, where Mukhtar was waiting. But the next morning Mukhtar's father and uncle Sabir came to the cleric's house and claimed they had been defrauded by the Mastois, as Shakoor was innocent of any misbehaviour with Salma. Shakoor's family claimed that in fact Shakoor was the one who had been pack-raped. The Gujjars complained that the cleric's suggestion to give Mukhtar to the Mastois had been followed "in haste." As a result, the Gujjars wanted to increase their demands. They decided to ask the Mastois to give them, in addition, a parcel of land and a second woman to "equalize" the honour. The cleric then took Mukhtar's father and uncle to Abdul Khaliq's house at around dawn. There the cleric confronted Abdul Khaliq and accused him of deceit in marrying Mukhtar, claiming that Shakoor had been raped and not Salma. The cleric said "the matter could only be resolved if the hands of two girls plus land was given to the complainant (Gujjars') party," according to the defence version.

"It is false suggestion," the cleric replied to each point.

Saleem Malik continued:

Abdul Khaliq, infuriated by the sodomy allegations, retracted his family's offer to give Salma to Shakoor in marriage. But the cleric persisted in his proposal that the Mastois give land plus two of their girls to the Gujjars.

"Abdul Khaliq and his elders did not agree," Malik told the court. When Abdul Khaliq refused to bow to the Gujjars' request, the cleric took Mukhtar from the Mastoi home and brought her to his home "to remain there till the matter was resolved."

On Friday June 28, according to the defence, Mukhtar's father claimed he had been discredited by giving his daughter to the Mastois while failing to receive Salma in return, in violation of the agreed *watta-satta* deal. The cleric then threatened the Mastoi family:

"Since the nikah was un-written, a case will be registered against Abdul Khaliq," Razzaq threatened the Mastois, according to the defence.

"False suggestion," the cleric replied in the courtroom.

Saleem Malik continued:

After Abdul Khaliq failed to meet the Gujjars' demands for land and a second Mastoi woman in marriage, the Gujjars went to the police to file rape charges. The defence claimed that Ramzan Pachaar had witnessed the nikah between Mukhtar and Abdul Khaliq, and refused to support the Gujjars in their approach to the police.

Saleem Malik contested that the story of the gang-rape was released to the press through Mureed Abbas, part of the cleric's Jatoi tribe, "in order to pressurize the police, lest they discharge the case. The police were slow, knowing the falsity of the rape case, yet under pressure of the press, the accused persons were arrested," Saleem Malik declared in court.

"False," the cleric retorted.

Hundreds of thousands of rupees were then doled out to Mukhtar Mai, the defence claimed.

"Road, school and hospital, police post and electricity have been provided by the government, but for the betterment of the public," Razzaq retorted.

"The news was being flashed in order to get money," Malik suggested to the cleric.

"False," Razzaq repeated.

\*  \*  \*  \*

In summary, the Mastois' version was that Abdul Razzaq had persuaded Mukhtar's family to accuse the Mastois of rape in order to avenge past disputes with them.

The Mastois claimed Mukhtar had been married on the spot to Abdul Khaliq in compensation for her brother's alleged rape of Abdul Khaliq's sister. The giving of a Gujjar girl would restore the balance of honour. The deal had a second part: that Shakoor would marry Salma. The first marriage ceremony, the Mastois claimed, was conducted by the cleric. In accordance with common practices in rural areas, no written certificate was issued. Abdul Khaliq alleged he took Mukhtar into his room as his bride. The cleric denied conducting any nikah.

The defence argued that Mukhtar's family pressed gang-rape charges because the Mastois rejected the Gujjars' increased demands after hearing Shakoor's claim of sodomy. In anger at the sodomy claims, the Mastois cancelled their side of the *watta-satta* deal to give any girl at all to the Gujjars.

The Mastois portrayed the cleric as the "architect" of the charges against them, accusing him of pressuring the Gujjar family, against their will, to prosecute. The cleric's motivation, the defence contested, was to avenge the Mastois for accusing him of corrupt land-grabbing in 1995 and for their attempts to oust him from the Farooqia mosque on account of his Sipah-e-Sahaba links.

\* \* \* \*

With the Mastois' version now on court record, second defence counsel Zaffar Ahmed Lund took over the cross-examination. He tackled the cleric on his conservative Islamic leanings.

D: "Is it true that you led processions on the issue of Osama bin Laden and (US military action in) Afghanistan?"

Razzaq: "Incorrect."

D: "Is it correct that you were removed from the mosque by the people of the area for your misdeeds?"

Razzaq: "Incorrect."

D: "Is it correct that Ramzan Pachaar had taken an active part the aforesaid campaign (against you) and that for the same reason you have given false evidence against him?"

Razzaq: "Incorrect."

Third defence counsel Azhar Trimizi took his turn.

D: "Were you aware the Ms Mukhtar Mai was divorced seven years ago?"

Razzaq: "Yes."

D: "Was she divorced for her bad character?"

Razzaq: "I do not know."

D: "I suggest that her younger sisters have not been contracted in marriage due to her bad character."

Razzaq: "That is false."

D: Are you aware of the FIR in 2000 against Ghulam Hussain (Mukhtar's uncle) for rape?

Razzaq: "That was a false case," the cleric replied.

Trimizi raised a landgrabbing claim against the cleric.

D: "You have obtained a plot of land belonging to Ghulam Fareed Mastoi's family through collusion with local officials."

Razzaq: "False."

Trimizi then queried the Maulvi's background connections with Sipah-e-Sahaba militants.

D: "Is it correct that you received five years' training in Afghanistan?"

Razzaq: "Incorrect."

Recalled for further cross-examination on August 21, the cleric alleged that police had fabricated early prosecution statements by asking them to thumb-print blank papers and later filling in those papers themselves. Mukhtar and her family were unable to read. They had no way of knowing what was written either before or after thumb-printing the statements.

"They stated that I should sign the papers, so that my statement is recorded. The policemen got forced signatures (from us)," the cleric testified.

Superintendent Mirza Muhammad Abbas, from the Dera Ghazi Khan police crimes unit, had called Mukhtar Mai, the cleric and other prosecution witnesses for interview on July 5 and 6. He deputed his assistant, Inspector Riaz, to conduct some of the interviews on his behalf in his absence.

A line on the allegedly distorted statement in Razzaq's name said that "Ghulam Farid Gujjar and myself had taken milk of one mother." Razzaq rejected the line as concocted.

"We told our story to the Inspector and he himself fabricated our statement," Razzaq said.

However the cleric upheld the statements recorded on July 9 by Alipur Magistrate, Rana Muhammad Ishfaq.

Razzaq repeated that he had left the Mastoi's gathering at around 10.00 pm.

"We went back to our houses and I do not know about the later events; nor did Ghulam Farid Gujjar (Mukhtar Mai's father) state anything to me in this respect."

The defence suggested that the reporter Mureed Abbas had informed the police himself on June 29 of the supposed panchayat's brutal outcome, and that the cleric himself had directly urged Mukhtar to file rape charges.

The defence team put to Razzaq that Mukhtar's father had exonerated Ghulam Fareed Mastoi, one of the four rape suspects, by telling the police that Ghulam Fareed Mastoi "had not committed zina with Mukhtar Mai." Razzaq denied *the assertion*.

The Mastois' defence produced their final card against the cleric: a High Court petition filed against him in 1995 by Karam Hussain Mastoi, father-in-law of accused rapist Ghulam Fareed Mastoi. Petition number 2949/95 of the Lahore High Court stated that Razzaq had clandestinely conspired with local officials to have a plot of land listed in his name, after Karam Hussain Mastoi had officially won the lot at a public auction with the highest bid and a deposit of 16,000 rupees (260 USD).

Razzaq acknowledged the charges. However, he said, he was unaware that Ghulam Fareed Mastoi was Karam Hussain Mastoi's son-in-law.

D: "Is it correct to suggest that for the same reason you have involved all your opponents in this false case?"

Razzaq: "Incorrect."

The cross-examination of Prosecution Witness 11, the mullah of Mirwala, was complete.

\* \* \* \*

The prosecution produced in court two eyewitnesses only to the attack at the Mastois' gathering: the cleric's brother, Haji Altaf Hussain, 45yo, listed as a zamindar (landowner); and one of Mukhtar's maternal uncles: Sabir Hussain.

PW 12 ON OATH: ALTAF HUSSAIN, S/O BAHADAR ALI, CASTE: JATOI, AGED 45 YEARS, ZAMINDARA (LANDOWNER), R.O MIRWALA TEHSIL JATOI, DISTRICT MUZAFFARGARH

Haji Altaf Hussain followed his brother into the dock. Haji is the title for a Muslim who has made the pilgrimage to the Holy City Mecca in Saudi Arabia.

Altaf first repeated the prosecution version: that the Mastois sought "badla" revenge for "zina" rape against their girl Salma; that the Gujjars in return had proposed *watta-satta*, offering Mukhtar in marriage to a Mastoi man in exchange for Salma Mastoi's marriage to Shakoor. That proposal was rejected, and the cleric gave up and went home, Altaf said.

The landowner who'd been to Mecca filled in the sequence of events after his cleric brother had abandoned the June 22 gathering.

"The Mastois did not agree to this suggestion of *watta-satta*, whereupon the three *salis* of Gujjar *biraderi* left the panchayat," Altaf said, referring to his brother Maulvi Razzaq, Manzoor Ahmad Jatoi and Ghulam Mustafa.

"Thereafter Ramzan Pachaar came and stated that Faiz Mastoi stated that Ms Mukhtar Mai be brought to seek pardon for Abdul Shakoor. Thereupon, Sabir Hussain (uncle), Ghulam Farid Gujjar (father), and Ghulam

Nabi took along Mukhtar Mai to the *akath* (gathering) of Mastois to obtain pardon. As she reached there, Abdul Khaliq, armed with pistol, held Ms Mukhtar Mai by the arm and Ghulam Fareed Mastoi, Allah Ditta and Fayyaz took her in the room with pushes."

The court transcript notes that the witness took 'a minute or so in recollecting one or two names of the accused persons.'

"Ms Mukhtar Mai continued raising alarm," Altaf recounted.

"Is there any Muslim who can save my respect?" he recalled her crying. "Is there any Muslim to save my chastity?" was another of her cries, Altaf recollected.

"The accused persons hurled threats that anybody following them would be murdered. They committed ziadti with Ms Mukhtar Mai. Fayyaz threw out her clothes at her. Her shirt stood torn from the front side, so also from the sides. The shalwar and dupatta were thrown by Fayyaz and were in the hand of Ms Mukhtiar Mai. I, Ghulam Farid Gujjar, Sabir Hussain, and Ghulam Nabi witnessed the occurrence. Ghulam Farid Gujjar put on the clothes to Ms Mukhtar Mai and took her along to his house. The accused persons threatened to teach lesson in case the matter was disclosed to any person. For (due to) the threats of the accused party, case was not got registered (immediately). It got registered on 30.6.2002," Altaf testified.

The Haji said Shakoor was released from the police cell at 3.00 am "at the behest of Ramzan Pachaar and Faiz Mastoi, without taking any legal action against Abdul Shakoor" after the police forced Shakoor's family to pay a bribe.

"The thanedar (police officer) demanded 10,000 rupees (166 USD) for release of Abdul Shakoor. The amount was given through Ramzan Pachaar, after selling cow for 8,000 rupees (133 USD) and borrowing 2,000 rupees (33 USD) from somebody. The police reached the place of the occurrence and my statement was recorded," Altaf testified.

Defence advocate Saleem Malik began his cross-examination of the Haji by quizzing him on which party had offered the watta-satta proposal.

"It was the decision of the *salisan* (representatives) of the Gujjars," the cleric's brother replied.

D: "How long was she inside the room?"

Altaf: "I stated to the investigating officer that Ms Mukhtar Mai was turned out after about one hour."

Altaf said the Gujjars' gathering was inside the mosque in Mirwala. The Mastois' gathering was behind the house of Abdul Khaliq Mastoi, five to six fields away.

"Firstly I joined the *akath* of Gujjars. My brother Abdul Razzaq, along with Manzoor and Mustafa, had gone to the *akath* of Mastois, taking the proposal of *watta-satta* only once and it was night, after maghrebwela.

D: "Did you accompany Sabir Hussain and Ghulam Farid Gujjar when they took along Ms Mukhtar to the akath of Mastois?

Altaf: "Yes."

The defence counsel did not believe that Haji Altaf Hussain had really accompanied Mukhtar Mai and her father. Before the trial, Altaf had told investigators that he had stayed in the Gujjars' home while Mukhtar was taken to the Mastois' gathering.

D: "Is it correct to suggest that you were not present in the occurrence; or that at the behest of your brother you have given false evidence?"

Altaf: "Incorrect."

Third defence counsel Azhar Trimizi took over the cross-examination of the Haji landowner.

Trimizi began his attack with the 1995 Lahore High Court petition, number 2949/95, accusing Maulvi Razzaq of corruptly conspiring with local officials to illegally possess land which had been won at public auction by the father-in-law of one of the accused rapists.

D: "Do you know Karam Hussain, son of Ghulam Muhammad Khan, father-in-law of Ghulam Fareed Mastoi (accused rapist)?"

Altaf: "Yes."

D: "Do you know he was a leasee of government land?"

Altaf: "Yes."

D: "Do you know that the said leased land was got allotted to Maulvi Abdul Razzaq and Faiz Jhangla later on?"

Altaf: "No."

D: "Do you know that Karam Hussain filed a writ petition in the High Court and the land stood re-transferred to him?"

Altaf: "No."

D: "Is it correct to suggest that the police helped Abdul Razzaq and Faiz Jhangla obtain possession of the land?"

Altaf: "No, incorrect."

D: "What is Abdul Razzaq's connection to Sipah-e-Sahaba?"

Altaf: "He had connection to Sipah-e-Sahaba earlier on, but not now."

D: "Do you know that shops were gutted on the murder of Hussnain Shah at Jatoi?"

Altaf: "No."

D: "Do you know that Abdul Razzaq was accused in the said case?"

Altaf: "No."

D: "Is it correct to suggest that Abdul Razzaq has nominated Ghulam Fareed Mastoi accused due to aforesaid land dispute?

Altaf: "Incorrect."

D: "Is it correct to suggest that at the behest of Abdul Razzaq you have given false evidence?"

Altaf: "Incorrect."

The Mecca pilgrim's evidence and cross-examination were over in one day.

# 15

# Uncle Sabir

PW 13 ON OATH: Sabir Hussain, s/o Qadir Bakhsh. CASTE: Tatla Gujjar. AGE: 35 years. OCCUPATION: Agricultural R/o Meerwala. TEHSIL: Jatoi

Prosecution Witness number 13, Mukhtar's maternal uncle Sabir Hussain, slid into the dock. Sabir was tall, lean, wiry, with a mop of black hair and black moustache and only five years older than Mukhtar. He was not one of the original 'salisan' of the Gujjars, but stepped in as a key player after the Maulvi departed, according to the Gujjar version.

Sabir's recollection of the Gujjar version of negotiations between the two families carried more incriminating allegations against the Mastois: that they had stated they desired revenge rape, and that they threatened violence if a Gujjar girl was not brought to them.

Uncle Sabir began by recounting the Gujjar version of events, including their offer of *watta-satta* to the Mastois.

"Faiz Mastoi, Ramzan Pachaar and Ghulam Fareed Mastoi did not agree and demanded that badla (revenge) of ziadti (rape) would be taken with ziadti," Sabir Hussain told the court.

"Abdul Khaliq also stated similarly. Our arbitrators did not concede to the latter demand and left the panchayat. Ghulam Fareed Mastoi and Ramzan Pachaar thereafter came to our panchayat and stated that with the consent of Faiz, they had come with the proposal that a sister of Abdul Shakoor should come to them and seek pardon on his behalf to conclude the matter. Otherwise 200/250 persons would attack our house and would abduct our menfolk."

It was the first time the court heard the Mastois had threatened violence.

According to Sabir, the Gujjar men brought Mukhtar to the Mastois "on their trust", despite the Mastois' naked threat of violence.

"Thereafter, on their trust, Ms Mukhtar Mai was taken to the akath of the accused by me, Haji Altaf Hussain, Ghulam Fareed Mastoi and Ghulam Nabi."

Sabir said "many persons" were present, including Faiz Mastoi, Ramzan Pachaar, Abdul Khaliq, Allah Ditta, Fayyaz and Ghulam Fareed Mastoi.

The following testimony by Sabir is one of only two eyewitness accounts of the Mastois' reaction when Mukhtar was brought to them:

"Faiz and Ghulam Fareed Mastoi commanded that Mukhtar Mai had reached, ziadti be committed with her by taking her by the arm. Thereupon Abdul Khaliq, Allah Ditta, Fayyaz and Ghulam Fareed Mastoi took along Ms Mukhtar Mai in the room," Sabir told the court.

Mukhtar "raised alarm and wept", crying out "Is there anybody to save my honour?", according to Sabir.

"The accused hurled threats that if anybody who followed them would be dealt with. After about one hour, Mukhtar Mai was turned out of the room; Fayyaz threw her clothes; Ms Mukhtar Mai's shirt stood torn from the sides and front as she came out, and she called her father Ghulam Farid (Gujjar). Ghulam Farid caught hold of the clothes and put (them) on Ms Mukhtar Mai," Sabir said.

"Abdul Khaliq hurled threats that if the matter was reported, that person would be murdered and dealt with."

Sabir said Shakoor was released later the same night, at around 3.00 am. Ramzan Pachaar had demanded the bribe for his release, according to Sabir.

"Ramzan Pachaar demanded 10,000 rupees for the release; the arrangement was made by Faiz and amount was to be delivered to Inspector Iqbal. 8,000 rupees was collected by selling a cow and its calf, and 2,000 rupees was borrowed which were given to Ramzan Pachaar for this purpose."

The cross-examination of uncle Sabir ran over three days.

In the first few hours he was challenged on discrepancies between what he told the magistrate at Alipur on July 9, what he told police, and what he said in court as evidence-in-chief regarding the negotiations with the Mastois.

Defence chief Saleem Malik challenged Sabir to repeat exactly what Faiz Mastoi said on Mukhtar's delivery to the Mastois' gathering.

D: "Did you not state to the magistrate (on July 9) that Faiz stated that they (Gujjar family) should be pardoned as their girl had come?"

Sabir: "I did not. He stated that 'duniavi', merely to show to the people. In fact he was at the helm of the affairs."

*Duniavi* translates in English as "superficially or worldly, without sincerity". Mukhtar Mai used the same adverb when describing Faiz's direction to the gathered Mastois to forgive her and her family. But she only introduced the term when she testified in court. She had never used the term in any pre-trial interviews with the investigating magistrate or police.

One of the discrepancies in Sabir's evidence concerned who took Mukhtar to the Mastois' gathering, and who was present when she was allegedly dragged away.

In his July 9 statement to the magistrate, Sabir had said it was only himself and Mukhtar's father who brought her before the Mastois.

Yet, in court Sabir claimed Ghulam Nabi and Haji Altaf Hussain also accompanied them.

Then there was the issue of whether Abdul Khaliq Mastoi was armed or not.

Sabir admitted under cross-examination that, unlike his court testimony, he had not told the investigating magistrate on July 9 that Abdul Khaliq was armed with a pistol, or that Faiz had ordered that Mukhtar "be taken by the arm and raped." He only came up with those key points in the court.

He had also not stated to the Alipur magistrate on July 9 his claim in court that the Mastoi men threatened to kill anyone who followed as they dragged her inside.

Resuming cross-examination on Friday August 2, the defence asked Sabir to recall Mukhtar's emergence from the Mastoi house after the alleged attack.

"I stated to the magistrate that on coming out, Ms Mukhtiar Mai called out to her father and the latter picked up those clothes and put them on her."

He was asked to recall the circumstances surrounding the release of Shakoor from prison.

He said that he himself had accompanied Faiz Mastoi and Ramzan Pachaar to get him released. Sabir "remained present outside the police station" while they went inside.

Sabir said the 10,000 rupee bribe was sought by Ramzan Pachaar.

"Inspector Iqbal had not demanded any amount. Inspector Iqbal was innocent in this respect. I stated to the magistrate that Ramzan Pachaar stated that the thanedar (police inspector) demanded 25,000 rupees (416 USD), to whom I said that I was poor man and some kindness be shown, whereupon Ramzan Pachaar stated to give 10,000 rupees," Sabir testified.

Mukhtar was with the rest of her family's womenfolk in Sabir's house when the decision to bring her before the Mastois was taken by the Gujjar family. Sabir brought her out of his house.

"I stated to the I.O. (Investigating Officer) that she had been brought to seek pardon, per Balochi custom."

Sabir said Mukhtar was not naked when she emerged from the Mastoi home.

"As Mukhtiar Mai came out of the kotha (house), her shirt was torn from the front and sides, though it was on her body."

Sabir clarified that the Gujjars and Mastois held their own separate meetings. He used two different terms for the separate tribes' gatherings: both 'panchayat' and 'akath'.

"Our panchayat was in the mosque, to resolve the demand of the Mastois to give badla for the ziadti committed with them. Ghulam Farid Gujjar had organized the akath. We had gathered in the mosque, about 10/15 people and we specifically called Manzoor Hussain Jatoi, our zamindar (landlord) and Maulvi Abdul Razzaq." Relatives and other unrelated villagers made up the rest of the crowd. Then later in the evening "at 9.00/10.00 pm, we held our formal akath."

Sabir told the defence that only two and a half minutes passed between the departure of the cleric from the Mastois' gathering, and the appearance of the Mastois' negotiators before the Gujjars' gathering. They brought with them what the prosecution claims was the Mastois' final proposal: to bring a Gujjar girl before them to seek pardon.

D: "Did you thereafter contact Manzoor Hussain Jatoi and Abdul Razzaq (to inform) that a proposal of bringing Ms Mukhtiar Mai (to seek pardon) had been made by the accused party?"

Sabir: "We did not."

D: "Did you state to Ramzan Pachaar and Ghulam Fareed Mastoi that Ms Mukhtar Mai was innocent, and why should she be brought to the gathering to seek pardon?"

Sabir: "We did not."

D: "Is it correct that women never seek pardon by going to the gathering?"

Sabir: "Incorrect. We are not Baloch."

D: "Is it correct that there is no custom for women to seek pardon?"

Sabir: "Incorrect."

D: "Were you aware or not at the time of taking Ms Mukhtar Mai that Abdul Khaliq had threatened to take revenge for the disrespect of their girl?"

Sabir: "It was not in my knowledge."

Sabir was then asked to repeat what he had stated the previous day in evidence-in-chief:

"Faiz, Ramzan Pachaar and Ghulam Fareed Mastoi did not agree (to *watta-satta*) and demanded that badla (revenge) of ziadti (rape) would be taken with ziadti. Abdul Khaliq also stated similarly," he repeated.

On Sabir's note of self-contradiction, the defence counsel sought adjournment to the following day.

\*    \*    \*    \*

"Was Ms Salma (Mastoi) a virgin?" the defence cross-examiner began the next day.

Sabir: "I do not know, but they said so."

D: "Was she married or not?"

Sabir: "I do not know."

D: "When was Mukhtar Mai married?"

Sabir: "About 6/7 years ago. I have not much sense about the exact year."

D: "To whom was she married?"

Sabir: "I do not know the name of her husband, although he was Gujjar."

In Sabir's admittedly imprecise recollection, Mukhtar lived with her husband for one year and "was divorced thereafter by her husband."

Sabir: "The reason of divorce was that her husband was poor, lame and was unable to work and he required her father to take her."

D: "Is it correct to suggest that Ms Mukhtar Mai was divorced by her husband due to her bad character?"

Sabir: "Incorrect."

D: "Is it correct that up to now, nobody else demanded the hand of Ms Mukhtiar Mai?"

Sabir: "Incorrect."

On his third day under oath, Uncle Sabir was forced to explain who chose Mukhtar of the Gujjars' five living daughters to be brought before the allegedly vengeful Mastois.

Sabir: "Hazoor Bakhsh (Mukhtar's older brother) stated that Mukhtar be taken, after I consulted him," Sabir recalled. He said Ghulam Farid Gujjar also approved the choice of his eldest daughter.

Sabir: "Both Hazoor Bakhsh and Ghulam Farid Gujjar stated that Mukhtar Mai should accompany them to the gathering and seek pardon on behalf of Abdul Shakoor."

Hazoor Bakhsh told Sabir to fetch Mukhtar from his house and bring her to her own family's home, an acre away.

Sabir: "I stated to Mukhtar Mai that her brother was calling her. She accompanied me to the house of her father, where the latter and her brother Hazoor Bakhsh were present."

D: "Did you state to Mukhtar Mai that the accused party had pronounced to take *badla* of *ziadti* with *ziadti*?"

Sabir: "I did not."

D: "Did Ms Mukhtar Mai say that being a young woman, she would not go to a strangers' gathering?"

Sabir: "She did not."

D: "Did Ms Mukhtar Mai say that being innocent, why should she seek pardon?"

Sabir: "She did not."

The Mastois had not demanded Mukhtar in particular, but any sister of Shakoor's, Sabir said.

The Mastois had demanded that "any daughter of Ghulam Farid Gujjar should seek forgiveness," Sabir said.

Sabir did not ask the other men in the mosque to come with him when he brought Mukhtar Mai before the Mastois.

"Hazoor Bakhsh declined to accompany Mukhtar Mai and allowed her to be taken by me. I did not require Hazoor Bakhsh to come along with us lest there may be any quarrel among the parties. We set out to the gathering. No *dang-sota* (steel-tipped wooden club) or weapon was taken along lest there may be any fight. Ms Mukhtar Mai went to the gathering without any burqa, since she went to seek pardon. She did not say that burqa was unnecessary for the purpose. We did not require Ms Mukhtar Mai to wear burqa while proceeding to the strangers' gathering," Sabir testified.

The distance from Mukhtar's home to the Mastois' gathering was some 60 to 70 paces, he estimated.

"Ms Mukhtar Mai stood quiet before the gathering without expressing plea for forgiveness. I pronounced to the gathering that Ms Mukhtar Mai, daughter of Ghulam Farid Gujjar, had come and was ready to seek pardon from the gathering. At the time that the four accused persons started taking her and dragging, she was standing at a distance of about two *karams* (paces) from me. We did not try to restrain her taking by the accused persons, since Abdul Khaliq threatened with pistol to kill us."

D: "Is it correct that you would have quarrelled/fought with them in case Abdul Khaliq was un-armed?"

Sabir: "Correct."

D: "Is it correct that you saved your life, not your respect?"

Sabir: "Correct."

Sabir continued: "At the time of the dragging, Mr Mukhtar Mai stood at a distance of 3-3.5 karams (paces) from the gathering of the accused persons. Ms Mukhtar Mai did not run away when there was pronouncement that *badla* be taken from for the disrespect (of the Mastois' girl). Abdul Khaliq had held her by going to her. We tried to follow the accused persons but 200/250 persons held us."

Sabir estimated that Mukhtar had been dragged a distance of 18 paces over "plain (fallow) land" to the house.

"Ms Mukhtar Mai was taken by the accused by pushing and dragging her. She had fallen on the ground and was dragged there. It was 11.00/11.30 in the night. After one hour, Ms Mukhtiar Mai called out to her father from the house of Abdul Khaliq. We were released by the accused persons and so went towards the house...After putting on clothes to Mukhtar Mai, we proceeded to our house, having heard *hukle* (threat) 'not to report the matter'."

D: "Did Hazoor Bakhsh require you to get a case of ravishing Mukhtar Mai registered at the police station at that time?"

S: "No."

Nor did Sabir contact Maulvi Razzaq or Manzoor Jatoi about the horrific outcome, Sabir admitted.

"None of them contacted us in the following morning to know about the latter events, nor did I go to them for reporting the matter to the police. Nobody disclosed about the occurrence with Mukhtar Mai up to 30.6.2002. Due to fear."

On June 30, Mukhtar's father told Sabir that journalists had approached him and suggested they register charges with the police.

"The case was registered on 30.6.2002," Sabir said.

Saleem Malik used the rest of the cross-examination to establish that the Mastoi family, contrary to press reports portraying them as wealthy landowners, lived in poverty and owned little land.

D: "Are you aware that Abdul Khaliq and his brothers jointly own 2.5 beeghas (10 kanals/1.25 acres) of land?"

Sabir: "I am not."

D: "Do you know whether any of the accused own property, and if so how much?"

Sabir: "I do not know. I was born and brought up in this village and the accused persons are my neighbours, but are not much known to me."

D: "Are you aware that the accused are in fact poor men?"

Sabir: "I am not."

D: "Are you aware that the accused persons have been wrongly flashed in the press to be jagirdar (landlords)?"

Sabir: "I am not."

D: "Are you aware that no case has ever been registered against any of the accused persons before?"

Sabir: "I am not."

D: "Is it correct that you have not given precise and correct answers because in the newspapers they are depicted as hardened, desperate and dangerous criminals?"

Sabir: "Incorrect."

D: "Is it correct to suggest that you have given false evidence due to enmity of the accused, or have suppressed real facts?"

Sabir: "Incorrect."

D: "Is it correct to suggest that before the police, and the magistrate, and in this court, you made statements on the advice of Maulvi Abdul Razzaq and your lawyers?"

Sabir: "Incorrect."

The two year old rape charge against Sabir's step-brother Ghulam, another maternal uncle of Mukhtar's, was put to Sabir.

D: "Do you know that Ghulam Hussain Tatla committed zina with Ms Jindan Mai Pachaar and FIR (First Investigation Report) 179/2000 was registered under section 10 of the Hudood Ordnance (rape) against him?"

Sabir: "No, I do not know."

D: "Do you know that Ramzan Pachaar and Ghazi Khan Pachaar were witnesses of Ms Jindan Mai Pachaar in the said 2000 rape case?"

Sabir: "No, I do not know."

D: "Is it correct that Ramzan Pachaar was falsely involved on account of the aforesaid rape case of 2000?"

Sabir: "Incorrect."

D: "Do you know that none of the closest neighbours of Abdul Khaliq have corroborated the correctness of the version of the prosecution?"

Sabir: "No, I do not know."

Sabir was recalled for questioning on August 21.

The defence introduced two key statements which Sabir had been recorded as telling police investigator Superintendent Mirza Muhammad Abbas during pre-trial questioning. The first was that Faiz Mastoi had said, according to Sabir, on Mukhtar's arrival:

"It is the decree of Allah Taala (Almighty God) that you people forgive Mukhtar Mai."

The second was that Sabir saw no weapons on the Mastois "with his own eyes" during the gathering.

Under oath, Sabir denied making either remark in pre-trial questioning.

# 16

# The Prosecutrix

Mukhtar Mai entered the dock on Saturday August 3, 2002. Swathed in a black chador, her nose and mouth masked, unlit eyes seen but barely seeing, she sat uneasy in the dock. The court called her the "prosecutrix".

The prosecutrix stepped in after uncle Sabir gave his evidence, presenting himself as the one who received the Mastois' request to bring a Gujjar woman to seek pardon for Shakoor's misbehaviour with their girl; as the one who was told by Mukhtar's older brother to take her from among the five Gujjar girls to beg pardon from the menacing Mastois; and as the one who brought Mukhtar to the Mastois. Sabir had told the court he saw men drag Mukhtar into the Mastoi house and watched her emerge an hour later in torn clothes and distraught.

PW NO 14 ON OATH: Ms Mukhtar Mai, D/o Ghulam Farid. CASTE: Gujjar; Aged 30 years, R/o Meerwala, tehsil (sub-district) Jatoi, district Muzaffargarh.

Mukhtar's evidence-in-chief was identical to the four other prosecution witnesses — up to the point where she arrived at the Mastois' gathering. She had not been privy to the preceding negotiations between the two feuding clans on how to restore the Mastois' honour. But she recounted what she had been told by her family.

*"The Gujjars' akath (gathering) decided that in case Abdul Shakoor had committed ziadti, the hand of Salma should be given to him, and in return my hand should be given to Abdul Khaliq accused. Our two persons went to them. Abdul Khaliq, Ghulam Fareed (Mastoi) and Ramzan Pachaar did not agree to the aforesaid proposal and demanded that a girl should be given to them and after committing ziadti with her, in badla (revenge) compromise would be effected,"* Mukhtar told the trial court. She admitted later under cross-examination that she had not witnessed or heard this directly herself.

*"Our salisan (negotiators) did not agree to the demand of the accused party and left the akath (gathering). Thereafter, Ramzan Pachaar and Ghulam Fareed Mastoi came to us and stated that they had been sent by Faiz Mastoi with the message that a sister of Abdul Shakoor should come to them and seek pardon, so the matter would be forgiven and compromise would be effected. Thereupon, I was taken there, where panchayat of Mastois was held. My maternal uncle Sabir took me along."*

*Haji Altaf Hussain, Ghulam Nabi and her father also came, Mukhtar told the court.*

"On reaching there, Abdul Khaliq held me by the arm, which I got released. Faiz stated politically and worldly (duniavi syasi taur per) that 'the girl had come and (should) be forgiven'," Mukhtar testified.

"Abdul Khaliq was armed with pistol. Abdul Khaliq held me by the arm, whereas Fayyaz, Ghulam Farid Mastoi and Allah Ditta (Abdul Khaliq's brother) gave me pushes and I was dragged and taken into the room of Abdul Khaliq accused, where ziadti (rape) was committed with me. I cried out, made entreaties (warstey) but nobody acceded. All the four said accused persons committed ziadti with me turn-by-turn. After about one hour I was turned out. Abdul Khaliq accused gave me pushes. My shirt was on my body, which was torn from the front and the sides. Fayyaz threw clothes on me. My father Ghulam Farid, Ghulam Nabi and Haji Altaf were present there and saw me in nude condition. I knew the accused persons previously and they are present in court today. They hurled threats to us and for the same reason the case was not registered until 30.6.2002."

Mukhtar told the court she made her first statement to a police officer stationed in a van at Jhugiwala Chowk (intersection) on the morning of June 30. She thumb-printed the statement in a mark of attestation. She was sent to the doctor for examination.

"Thereafter I came to the police station and then to my house in Mirwala. The thanedar (Inspector) was present there, who accompanied me and inspected the spot. The thanedar also recorded my second statement at the place of the occurrence," Mukhtar told the court.

There had been no previous mention of Mukhtar and her family actually entering the house of their enemies and taking police into the room of Abdul Khaliq, where they alleged she had been raped.

Mukhtar stated to the court that while police were taking her statement "at the place of the occurrence," she told them about Shakoor's claim to have been sodomised by three Mastoi tribesmen – in contradiction of the Mastois' claim that he had raped their girl Salma.

"The suspicion about illicit relations of Abdul Shakoor with Salma was wrong, as Abdul Shakoor was minor," Mukhtar contested. But the doctors who examined Shakoor had declared that he was capable of sexual intercourse. They estimated his age at 14 or 15.

The prosecutrix estimated "there were about 200/250 persons present in the panchayat of Mastois, out of whom were Aslam, Allah Ditta, Ghulam Rasool, Hazoor Bakhsh, Qasim, Khalil, Nazar Hussain. Also Ghulam Hussain, which I forgot."

Mukhtar did not say how she was able to identify the faces of eight people in a crowd of some 200 faces in the dark. She said she was only before the crowd momentarily before being dragged into Abdul Khaliq's home.

*"Threats were hurled in case I had not gone to seek pardon. Threats included killing."*

Mukhtar said in her evidence-in-chief that she sent the clothes she was wearing on the night of June 22 to the police via Maulvi Razzaq and Manzoor Hussain, the Gujjars' salisan. The clothes were tendered as Prosecution Exhibit U: the kameez was listed as P1, the shalwar as P2, and the dupatta as P3.

Mukhtar concluded her evidence-in-chief at 2.15 p.m. The defence sought adjournment until the following Monday.

Cross-examination of the prosecutrix began on August 5.

Defence counsel Saleem Malik confronted Mukhtar with omissions and contradictions between her July 9 statement to the Alipur magistrate, and her fresh evidence on oath to the court.

Mukhtar had told the investigating magistrate three weeks before the trial that it was the police who had brought her "to the police station on the information of Abdul Razzaq" on June 30, and that later that night the police registered her case.

Mukhtar had not stated to police during her pre-trial questioning about the gathering of 200/250 people  Nor had she cited the eight names of alleged panchayat members.

MM* : "Before the investigating magistrate, I might have forgotten to mention the names of Aslam, Allah Ditta, Ghulam Rasool, Nazir Hussain and Ghulam Hussain who were present and were identified by me in the said panchayat."

Maulvi Razzaq later claimed that only four people made up the alleged panchayat: himself and Manzoor Hussain Jatoi, alongwith Faiz Mastoi and Ramzan Pachaar.

D: "Are you aware that the aforesaid eight persons have been held innocent by the police?"

MM: "No."

Mukhtar had never used the term "duniavi-siasi" (literal meaning 'worldly, for political effect') in her July 9 statement to the investigating magistrate when she recalled Faiz Mastoi's call for pardon of Mukhtar's family on her arrival before the Mastois.

Nor had she used it in her initial police statement. The first time she used the term was in the court.

"I stated to the thanedar (police inspector) that Abdul Khaliq, Ramzan and Ghulam Fareed Mastoi did not agree and demanded of Ghulam Farid Gujjar to hand over a daughter with whom zina would be committed to equalise, whereafter compromise would be effected," Mukhtar told the courtroom. "I stated to the magistrate that when I reached there (Mastois' gathering), Faiz

---

*MM= Mukhtar Mai

Muhammad Mastoi stated that 'The girl has reached; their respect has reached itself; you people forgive them.' I stated that (Faiz) spoke 'duniavi taursey' (in a wordly, insincere manner)."

D: "Is it correct to suggest that you did not utter the words 'duniavi taursey' before the magistrate when he recorded your statement (on July 9)?"

MM: "Incorrect."

However, the words 'duniavi taursey' are not in the statement recorded by the investigating magistrate.

\* \* \* \*

Two detained suspects, Fayyaz Mastoi and Ghulam Fareed Mastoi, appear to be clear cases of mistaken identities. The detained men bear the same name as two men accused of gang-raping Mukhtar Mai, yet documents show they are not the actual accused men.

The defence counsel put to Mukhtar Mai that her family had complained to police and the provincial governor that the wrong Fayyaz had been arrested. The police had first arrested Fayyaz Mastoi of Rampur village. However, according to the defence team, the Gujjars then complained that Fayyaz Mastoi of Rampur had been wrongly arrested and Fayyaz of Mirwala was the real culprit. But Mukhtar insisted under cross-examination that she had identified Fayyaz Mastoi who resides "beyond the canal", as one of her rapists. Rampur is beyond the canal from Mirwala.

D: "Is it correct to suggest that under pressure from the Supreme Court and Government of Punjab to submit challan (inquiry report) by 18.7.2002.... Fayyaz, resident of Mirwala, was to be produced after the arrest of Fayyaz of Rampur?"

MM: "Incorrect."

D: "Are you aware that the Mastois stated that Fayyaz r/o Mirwala was not available, therefore Fayyaz of Rampur was sent to the jail, to be released after Fayyaz r/o Mirwala was arrested?"

MM: "No."

Mukhtar conceded to the court that she had been kept with police for the 10 days preceding the trial at a house in Muzaffargarh. She confirmed the Punjab Governor had given her and her family a police safe house in the district capital after they complained of threats from the Mastois.

MM: "The police has kept us in a house at Muzaffargarh," Mukhtar stated.

D: "Would it be correct to suggest that the police have tutored (you to say) that Fayyaz r/o Rampur should be stated as the real culprit in this court, else the case would be spoiled?"

MM: "Incorrect."

D: "Would it be correct to say that Fayyaz r/o Rampur is innocent, against whom you have given false evidence?"

MM: "Incorrect."

\* \* \* \*

Mukhtar's character and personal background was put brutally under the spotlight.

The cross-examiners' targeted press claims that Mukhtar was a "Hafiz", a person who knows and recites the Qur'an off by heart.

Hafiz are revered figures in Muslim society. Illiteracy has proven no barrier to such endeavours. Many Hafiz cannot read or write their own language, but they can commit the Arabic verses of the Qur'an to memory.

Mukhtar admitted that in fact she could not recite the Qur'an from memory, and therefore was not a Hafiz.

"I am not Hafiz-Qur'an, but I read Nazira[1] Qur'an (by sight)," she stated.

D: "At what age did you attain puberty?"

MM: "About 15 or 16 years of age."

D: "Do you wear the burqa? Or were you a vagabond?"

MM: "I wear the burqa, but was not a vagabond."

D: "Does your family observe purdah?"

MM: "Yes."

Purdah is the tradition of concealing women from all men except their close relatives. This means women stepping out of the house cover themselves in the burqa, until they return home or reach the home of relatives.

D: "Is your current age 35/36?"

MM: "I am aged 30 years now, not 35/36 years."

At this point in Mukhtar's cross-examination, Judge Zulfikar Ali Malik inserted into the transcript a note on her clothing.

"On request of complainant's learned counsel to make observation that the witness is wearing chadarwala burqa (she is covered in a chador, not a full burqa), I observe that it is correct, although the naqab (face-veil) is over the nose."

Defence counsel returned to quizzing Mukhtar on how she was able to identify the 14 accused men, none of whom were related to her, if she had been living her life in purdah, never leaving her own home or her ex-husband's home except to visit relatives.

D: "Is it correct to suggest that Maulvi Abdul Razzaq nominated all the accused persons in the case?"

MM: "Incorrect."

---

1. Nazira Qur'an: a person who recites the Koran by sight, not by memory as a Hafiz does.

D: "Is it correct that at his behest, you have nominated the said accused persons?"

MM: "Incorrect."

\* \* \* \*

During the August 5 cross-examination, Mukhtar recounted how she discovered Shakoor had been locked up by the Mastois on the afternoon of June 22 2002.

*"At about zohirwela (midday), while I was present in my house along with my mother, sisters and wife of my brother, I came to know that my brother Abdul Shakoor stood confined."*

Mukhtar put Shakoor's age at 11 or 12. The defence put to her that he was actually closer to 15 or 16. She stuck to her estimate of 11 or 12 years. The doctor who examined Shakoor assessed his age as 14 to 15.

*"From the house of Abdul Khaliq emanated the voice of Abdul Shakoor, on hearing which I, my mother and the wife of my brother came out of our home. Five or six persons of the accused party came out from their house....The accused persons alleged that they had nabbed Abdul Shakoor while committing ziadti (rape) with Ms Salma. I stated to the investigating magistrate that thereafter we brought the Holy Qur'an from our house... I stated that he be released. Only I and my mother went with the Holy Qur'an to Abdul Khaliq,"* Mukhtar said.

Abdul Khaliq Mastoi's house lay one acre north of her family's home, she said.

*"We proceeded to the house of the accused, where they were present outside, and requested for the release of Abdul Shakoor, without entirely entering in the house of Abdul Khaliq. About 10 or 12 persons were present there."*

D: "Did the accused persons try to take or drag you from the place inside their house when you requested them to leave Abdul Shakoor for the sake of Holy Qur'an?"

MM: "No."

D: "Did you require the accused to allow you to inquire from Abdul Shakoor about the real matter?"

MM: "No. On inquiry Abdul Khaliq stated that Ms Salma was also confined with Abdul Shakoor."

D: "Did you inquire from where the two had been nabbed?"

MM: "They hurled abuses that in case we went ahead we would be killed. For about 15 to 20 minutes we made the entreaties. From there, we came back to our house and sent for our menfolk. About three or four persons including my brother Hazoor Bakhsh and my maternal uncles Sabir and Ghulam Hussain reached....Our menfolk went towards the house of Abdul Khaliq after we briefed them."

Defence counsel asked Mukhtar whether the feud that followed, and the negotiations between the gatherings of the two families were "in her personal knowledge."

"No," she replied.

"I personally came to know the facts when my maternal uncle Sabir Hussain took me along to the panchayat of the accused....Sabir Hussain stated to me that I was to seek pardon for Abdul Shakoor when I was present in his house, from where he took me to my father's house."

D: "Did you state to Sabir Hussain that being a woman, being innocent, and having no concern with the occurrence, why should you seek pardon from strangers?"

MM: "No."

D: "Did you require from Sabir Hussain to inquire from Abdul Shakoor whether or not the latter had committed any such mistake?"

MM: "Yes. He stated that the police had taken Shakoor to the police station. My mother required the menfolk to go to the police station; contact Abdul Shakoor and get him released, whereupon (Sabir) stated that the matter be first resolved with the accused party."

The day's hearing was adjourned at 2.30 pm until Tuesday August 6.

*   *   *   *

When the trial resumed, the questioning turned to who actually accompanied Mukhtar and her uncle to the Mastois' gathering.

*"I stated to the magistrate and police that when my maternal uncle took me along with him there (to the Mastois), my father Ghulam Nabi and Altaf went there along with us,"* Mukhtar said on her third day of cross-examination.

The defence counsel presented her with her July 9 statement to the magistrate, which contradicted her statement in court.

*"My father came later to the panchayat of Mastois,"* Mukhtar was recorded as saying by the magistrate. She had made no mention to the magistrate of Haji Altaf Hussain or Ghulam Nabi also attending.

*"I stated to the magistrate that Ghulam Nabi and Altaf saw the occurrence with their own eyes,"* Mukhtar insisted in court.

The defence again pointed to Mukhtar's July 9 statement to the investigating magistrate, where no mention was made of Ghulam Nabi or Altaf.

In fact, in her statement to the investigating magistrate, Mukhtar had said that Ghulam Nabi and Altaf were at her own home when she returned from the Mastoi home.

Recounting the sequence of events on the day her family and the cleric went to the police to file charges, Mukhtar also contradicted Maulvi Razzaq.

She said that her uncle Sabir had brought the cleric from his mosque to Mirwala to meet Mukhtar, her father, Haji Altaf Hussain and Ghulam Nabi.

"Abdul Razzaq had been brought by Sabir Hussain from the mosque to Mirwala," she told the court.

Razzaq however had told the court under oath that Mukhtar, her uncle and father had turned up at his mosque residence after the dawn prayers on June 30.

Mukhtar was quizzed on the confusion over the apparently wrongful arrest of another man with the same name of one of the accused rapists: Ghulam Fareed Mastoi.

Mukhtar had initially told police that Ghulam Fareed son of Mehmood Mastoi of Rampur village was one of her rapists, but the other prosecution witnesses had later corrected his identity to Ghulam Fareed son of Allah Bakhsh Mastoi, of Mirwala village.

"*Reaching back home somebody, probably my maternal uncle, stated that name of Ghulam Fareed Mastoi son of Mehmood had been wrongly recorded instead of Ghulam Fareed son of Allah Bakhsh,*" Mukhtar replied to the defence questioning.

D: "Was the said accused related to you, or brought up with you, or did you jointly study the Holy Qur'an, or had he ever called you to his house, or had he ever come to your house?"

MM: "No," Mukhtar replied to all the above.

D: "Is it correct to suggest that the police failed to arrest Ghulam Fareed son of Mehmood Mastoi and in his place Abdul Razzaq got Ghulam Fareed son of Allah Bakhsh Mastoi accused arrested, due to his personal enmity with him, and got corrected his name from the police?"

MM: "It is incorrect."

The personal enmity referred to by the defence counsel was the cleric's 1995 land dispute with Ghulam Fareed Mastoi's father-in-law.

\*　\*　\*　\*

One of the accused rapists was Allah Ditta, aged 24 or 25 according to court documents, an older brother of Abdul Khaliq by 2 to 3 years.

Allah Ditta's wife and four children lived in the same house as Abdul Khaliq, where Mukhtar was allegedly gang-raped, the defence team pointed out.

The brothers also had six younger sisters living in the same house, defence counsel stated to Mukhtar.

"*Abdul Khaliq has mother and sisters living with him but I do not know whether Abdul Khaliq has six sisters. Probably they are five sisters,"* Mukhtar stated.

D: "When you returned home, did you and your family consider reporting the matter to the police?"

MM: "No. We were not in our senses. Everybody was weeping."

D: "Were Ghulam Nabi and Altaf actually weeping while you were inside?"

MM: "I don't know."

D: "Did anyone suggest that Altaf and Ghulam Nabi should contact Maulvi Abdul Razzaq and Manzoor Hussain Jatoi for report to the police?"

M: "I don't know. I came to my senses on the day following the occurrence but I did not sit with the remaining members of my family to suggest that Maulvi Razzaq and Manzoor Hussain Jatoi be approached for reporting the matter to police."

D: "Did Maulvi Abdul Razzaq, Manzoor Hussain Jatoi, Altaf or Ghulam Nabi come to your house on the next day after the occurrence?

MM: "I do not know."

D: "Did you go to any of aforesaid persons for the purpose on the third, fourth, fifth days afterwards, up to 30.6.2002?"

MM: "No."

D: "Did anyone come to your house on those days?"

MM: "Neighbours came to our house from 22nd to 29th to know about the facts from me, but I did not see anybody."

News reporters came too, Mukhtar stated, but only after she and her family registered the rape charges. This time she spoke to the visitors – and nearly all the reporters were men, not related to her.

The defence put to her that Maulvi Razzaq had actually registered the case on June 29 and named names, and that police came to collect her in a police van on the night of June 30.

"Incorrect," Mukhtar replied to both suggestions.

D: "Did the accused persons or Mastois murder or injure you or any of your family after you went to the police?"

MM: "No. They had been hurling threats."

D: "Is it correct to suggest that after the registration of the case, the Governor of Punjab, ministers, dignitaries from in and outside the country contacted you?"

MM: "Correct."

D: "Is it correct that you have received lacs (hundreds of thousands) of rupees?

MM: "Incorrect. Not a penny has been given to me."

D: "Is it correct that the government of Punjab has given you five lacs rupees (500,000 rupees)?"

MM: "Incorrect. Not one rupee has been received by me. Dr Attiya Inayatullah (Minister for Women's Development) stated to me that General Musharraf has given me five lacs rupees. She gave me a cheque of five lacs rupees, which I returned to her for construction of school."

The defence later produced bank records from the National Bank of Pakistan, Alipur branch, showing that on July 5, the day after Minister Inayatullah presented the 500,000 rupee cheque, Mukhtar and her father opened two accounts. A cheque for 500,000 rupees, issued by the President's Secretariat Islamabad on July 4, was deposited into her father's account on July 10. The cash was then transferred to the joint account he holds with Mukhtar.

D: "Is it correct that NGOs and persons from in and outside the country have given you lacs (hundreds of thousands) of rupees?

MM: "No."

D: "Is it correct to suggest that money is being received by you and for that reason you are corroborating the story ... lodged by Maulvi Razzaq?

MM: "Incorrect."

D: "Is it correct to suggest that Maulvi Abdul Razzaq and Mureed Abbas, press reporter, have received money from you?"

MM: "Incorrect. They have not contacted me."

\* \* \* \*

Mukhtar was quizzed on further discrepancies between prosecution witness statements and her own statements to police, the investigating magistrate, the court, and to a reporter for a London paper on her state of dress or undress on emerging from Abdul Khaliq's room.

In her original police complaint Mukhtar said she emerged "nude." She later explained that her shalwar (pantaloon-like trousers) were off, but she was still wearing her torn kameez long knee-length tunic.

MM: "I stated that bochan (large dupatta) was thrown at me by my father, after wearing which I went to my house," she said of her comments to a London news reporter.

D: "Is it correct to suggest that only Abdul Khaliq accused had dragged you inside the room and there was no other person with him at that time?"

MM: "Incorrect."

The defence team quizzed Mukhtar about her clothes. Why had she let them be washed? Why did she not bring her kameez to the police the first time she registered the rape charges and point out the tears, as proof? Why did she not get her clothes examined for traces of semen of the four men she alleged took turns raping her?

D: "Is it correct to suggest that those clothes were not smeared, and for that reason the excuse was made that those clothes were washed?"

MM: "Incorrect."

D: "Was the said torn shirt washed as the (other) clothes were washed by your sisters or your brother's wife, and not by yourself?"

MM: "I don't know exactly."

D: "Is it correct to suggest that the clothes were not torn, nor were smeared, or a story had been concocted?"

MM: "Incorrect."

\* \* \* \*

The inevitable quizzing over Mukhtar's divorce began on August 6. Divorce, while not uncommon, carries a deep stigma in conservative parts of Pakistan.

Mukhtar said in reply to defence questioning that she had married 10 years ago (which, if her memory is accurate, would mean she was around 20 when she married). However there are no written records to ascertain the exact date.

MM: "I lived in the house of my husband for about three years. The talaq (divorce) was given with the consent of both of us. The reason was that there was no understanding among two of us. Umer Wadda was the name of my husband. His sotr (cousin) is Faizullah."

D: "Is it correct to suggest that your husband caught you red-handed with said Faizullah and that is the reason for talaq?"

MM: "Incorrect. Faizullah is the cousin of my father."

D: "Why have you not remarried in the past seven years?"

MM: "During the said seven years I refused to contract marriage offers as I did not like to re-marry. Marriage is performed only once."

Mukhtar confirmed that none of her family had consulted her before they proposed the *watta-satta* deal to marry her to Abdul Khaliq Mastoi, in exchange for Salma Mastoi marrying Mukhtar's brother Shakoor.

D: "I suggest that... Maulvi Razzaq performed your *sharai nikah* (verbal nikah) with Abdul Khaliq at 12.00 in the night.

MM: "Incorrect."

D: "Did your maternal uncle Sabir Hussain state to you while taking you to the panchayat of the Mastois that in case the latter agreed, your hand would be given to Abdul Khaliq?"

MM: "No.

D: "Would you have agreed to marriage with Abdul Khaliq, in case the offer of your (Gujjars') panchayat re–marriage of Salma with Shakoor and in *badla* your marriage with Abdul Khaliq had been accepted by the accused party?

MM: "Probably. I would have sacrificed not only for my brother but for the whole of my family."

D: "Did you or did you not wear burqa while proceeding to the panchayat of Mastois with Sabir Hussain?"

MM: "I did not wear burqa but had taken my bochan (large dupatta)."

D: "Did your maternal uncle Sabir Hussain tell you that Abdul Khaliq had proclaimed to take revenge for dis-respect of his sister with *zina*?"

MM: "No."

D: "Did you hear the aforesaid claim of the accused before proceeding with Sabir Hussain to the akath of the Mastois?"

MM: "No."

D: "How many people were sitting in the mosque before you proceeded to the akath (gathering) of Mastois?"

MM: "About 15 to 20."

The witness weeps, notes the judge at this point in the transcripts.

In another note on the transcript, the judge added: "(Learned counsel objects that the judge has no concern with sympathy or morality and the word "weeping" has prejudiced mind of the judge. Heard. Only the fact has been noted, not my inner views given, nor my mind disclosed.)"

D: "How far is the mosque from your house? Is it on the way from your house to the panchayat?"

MM: "It is not on the way. That mosque is situated towards the canal at a distance of about four acres from my house."

D: "Did your maternal uncle ask the sympathizers of your *biraderi* present in the mosque to come along?"

MM: "No."

D: "Did you seek pardon from the members of the panchayat personally, yourself?"

MM: "No. My father had sought pardon from them on my behalf."

D: "Did your family men bring any weapon or *dang-sota*[2] while going to the panchayat?"

MM: "No. It was not our apprehension."

D: "Is it correct that you were not dragged on the ground?"

MM: "Incorrect. Only my feet touched the ground, not my body. There were only one or two injuries on my feet, those injuries were not shown to the WMO (lady doctor) at the time of my medical examination."

D: "Were your shalwar, kameez or dupatta torn while you were dragged?"

---

2. A long wooden club tipped with steel. A potentially deadly crude weapon common in villages.

MM: "No."

D: "Did your father, maternal uncle, Altaf and Ghulam Nabi try to rescue you?"

MM: "Yes they tried but they were stopped by the Mastois."

D: "How far were you dragged?"

MM: "I was dragged about one or one and a half kanals (35-50 paces) distance....There were shoes on my feet which had fallen off during the said occurrence and were brought back after search by Sabir Hussain when I put clothes back on after the occurrence."

In front of the judge, in front of the phalanx of defence lawyers and public prosecutors, in front of the 14 Mastoi tribesmen on trial for their lives, with hordes of reporters outside, Mukhtar had to relive and recount excruciating details of the gang-rape she alleges followed her appearance before the Mastoi gathering.

She later decribed the rape cross-examination as one of the bitterest experiences of her life.

D: "Which items of your clothing were torn?"

MM: "My (knee-length) shirt was pulled and torn, the shalwar was not torn."

D: "Did you sustain any injuries or scratches on your body?"

MM: "Except for one or two bruises, there were no scratches on my body, while my shirt was torn by the accused. I stated to the WMO about the aforesaid scratches but due to passage of eight days, those had disappeared except for one scratch but the WMO stated that it stood cured and was barely visible."

D: "Inside the room, were you on a cot or the floor?"

MM: "I was made to lie on the ground, not on the cot."

D: "With force, or without?

MM: "Without force. Mildly."

D: "At the time that one of the four committed zina with you, did the other three (defendants) remain present?"

MM: "Yes."

D: "Were you wearing shalwar (pantaloon-trousers)?"

MM: "My shalwar was not on my legs."

D: "As the second person committed *zina*, did he clean the smeared place of your private parts?"

MM: "No."

D: "Did you try to resist?"

MM: "I did not, or could not, resist with my hands and legs, as I stood overpowered by four persons."

D: "Was the door of the room open or closed during the period of zina?"

MM: "It remained open. My shalwar was thrown on my head while I was three or four paces outside the door of the said room. I had been pushed by Abdul Khaliq and I fell down in front of the galla (open door). I had called out my father at the time that I fell down in front of the galla, as they had come near... I had not put on the shalwar as it was without string, nor did I use it to cover my body, as my father had arrived just then."

D: "Is it correct to suggest that you were not nude?"

MM: "Incorrect."

D: "Is it correct to suggest that your clothes were not put off by the accused?"

MM: "Incorrect. My father put on the clothes to me in the galla. It was night-time. I was taken straight-away from that place to my house."

The defence counsel asked the judge to note that in Mukhtar's original complaint and FIR, the words "armed with pistol" were added in later, next to the name of Abdul Khaliq.

D: "Is it correct to suggest that you have made all false statements?"

MM: "Incorrect."

With Mukhtar still spent from reliving her ordeal, the head of the defence team launched into an elaboration of the Mastoi version of the events of the night of June 22.

He began by confronting Mukhtar with the Mastoi defence that she had become Abdul Khaliq's wife.

D: "It is our suggestion that pursuant to the decision of your family members, your *sharai nikah*[3] was performed in the house of Abdul Khaliq by Abdul Razzaq in the presence of Ramzan Pachaar, your father and Sabir. That compromise was reached, and thereafter your maternal uncle Sabir Hussain, Ramzan Pachaar and Abdul Khaliq accused went to the police station and brought Abdul Shakoor back, with whom nikah of Salma was to be performed. That at 3.00/4.00am, Abdul Khaliq came to his room, where you were present as his bride. That he performed conjugal duties as your husband on the said night. That before fajjar azan (dawn prayers), Maulvi Razzaq along with your father and Sabir Hussain came there and stated to Abdul Khaliq that *ziadti* had been committed with them and your hand had been taken fraudulently. That your father stated, and Maulvi Razzaq demanded, the hand of Salma for Abdul Shakoor in your exchange, and demanded another girl to be given in marriage along with some land, being the condition of compromise with him. That Abdul Khaliq stated that as his brother Punnu had been accused of committing sodomy with Abdul Shakoor, therefore he

---

3. Marriage according to Sharia, verbally.

could not give Salma in marriage to Abdul Shakoor. That Abdul Khaliq declined to a give second girl and land as proposed, and required that you be taken away otherwise. That as Abdul Khaliq did not accede to the demand of Maulvi Razzaq and Ghulam Farid Gujjar, you were taken along by them with threats by them to take revenge (against the Mastois). That Maulvi Razzaq took you to his house till the compromise could be reached. That Maulvi Razzaq stated to police that you had lived in his house from where you were brought to the police station. That up to 28.6.2002, Maulvi Razzaq and your father tried to compound the matter in terms of their demands, and for that reason the sodomy case was also not registered (as yet). That on 28.6.2002, Maulvi Razzaq threatened to get a case of *zina* registered against the accused persons, as he had performed the nikah verbally and he would not admit the existence of *sharai nikah*. That Maulvi Razzaq stated that nikah between Abdul Khaliq and yourself was performed on his suggestion, so also the exchange marriage was proposed, and Ghulam Farid Gujjar persisted to get the hands of two girls and land from the accused party. For non-fulfilment of the demand, he was proceeding to get the case registered. That Maulvi Razzaq stated that in case compromise was not effected after registration of zina case, the case of sodomy would be planted against the accused. That Abdul Khaliq stated to Maulvi Razzaq to do whatever was in his power to do. That Maulvi Razzaq got the case registered through complaint and on 30.6.2002 brought the police along with him and took you along from his house in the night. That as the demand was not conceded by the accused persons, therefore sodomy case was registered three days later."

Mukhtar dismissed each suggestion as incorrect.

D: "Is it correct to suggest that you have given false evidence at the insistence of Maulvi Razzaq and your father and on account of enmity with the accused persons?"

MM: "Incorrect."

\* \* \* \*

The chief of the defence team Saleem Malik was about to wrap up his cross-examination, when he fired one final question for Mukhtar:

D: "At what stage after the occurrence did you wash yourself?"

MM: "I took bath nine days after the occurrence. I performed astanja[4] (ablutions) during that (nine-day) period."

Mukhtar's admission of genital ablutions cast doubt on the autheniticy of the Chemical Examiner's finding that semen was found on external vaginal swabs eight days after the alleged rape.

\* \* \* \*

---

4. Astanja: washing of one's genitals during ablutions. A compulsory ritual before prayer.

Defence advocate Zaffar Ahmed Lond took over the questioning. His focus was to probe why Ramzan Pachaar had been included in the list of accused men.

D: *"Did Ramzan Pachaar have any connection with the* nikah?

MM: *"I don't know. There was no nikah."*

D: *"Is it correct that Ramzan Pachaar was not present at the occurrence of* zina?

MM: *"Yes correct. But he was present in the* panchayat.*"*

D: "Is Ramzan Pachaar your family's opponent?"

MM: "No."

D: "Did Ramzan Pachaar have no personal grievance against you?"

MM: "No. But he was with the accused party."

D: "Is it correct to suggest that Ramzan Pachaar had disclosed the matter to Sabir Hussain that the Mastois proclaimed that badla of zina (revenge rape) would be taken with zina?

MM: "Incorrect."

D: "Is it correct that Ramzan Pachaar is a friend of your brother Hazoor Bakhsh?"

MM: "Correct. (immediately corrects herself-sic) I do not know."

Mukhtar confirmed that Ramzan Pachaar had helped bring Shakoor back to the Gujjar home from the police station. She did not know whether he had helped release Shakoor on the Gujjars' request.

She said her family had given Ramzan Pachaar 10,000 rupees to bribe police to release Shakoor from custody.

D: "Did Ramzan Pachaar pass on the 10,000 rupees to Assistant Sub-Inspector Iqbal, or appropriate the amount himself?"

MM: "I do not know."

D: "Is it correct to suggest that Ramzan Pachaar refused to support your case and for that reason you have deposed falsely (against him)?"

MM: "Incorrect."

D: "Is it correct to suggest that Ramzan Pachaar has been made an accused for misappropriating 10,000 rupees?"

MM: "Incorrect."

The three-day cross-examination of Mukhtar Mai concluded on August 6.

\* \* \* \*

Prosecution counsel Qazi Muhammad Iftikhar stepped forward.

"On instructions from client, I give up Manzoor Hussain (Jatoi), Ghulam Nabi and Ghulam Farid (Gujjar) as un-necessary."

Key prosecution witnesses: Mukhtar's father, the Gujjars' second *sali* Manzoor Hussain, and Ghulam Nabi – the only non-relative to have allegedly witnessed her being dragged into alleged rapist Abdul Khaliq's house – were dropped from testifying for the prosecution.

No reason or explanation was offered.

Mukhtar Mai was recalled for further cross-examination on August 21 after the judge heard the defendants.

In her recall appearance, Mukhtar testified for the first time that one of her first statements to police had been distorted by at least one of the police officers who interviewed her.

MM: "I disclosed to the Inspector the heart-rending story, which I stated in this court. The Inspector obtained my thumb-impressions on blank sheets of paper, firstly stating that there was great rush. Thereafter I made statement to the Inspector and the statement was read out. After that, I was produced before (Superintendent Mirza Muhammad Abbas, who had been assigned to probe police investigating the case), when I stated that it was not my statement."

Abbas, from the Dera Ghazi Khan police station's Crimes unit, had deputed another police officer, Inspector Riaz, to assist him in interviewing key witnesses as part of his internal police probe.

For the rest of the cross-examination Mukhtar denied elements of her statement to Inspector Riaz, for example that "Abdul Khaliq accused held me by the arm...and took me to his house two kanals away from the panchayat."

In the courtroom, Mukhtar contradicted that statement, saying:

"I stated to the Inspector and Superintendent Abbas that Fayyaz, Ghulam Fareed Mastoi, Allah Ditta and Abdul Khaliq took me from the panchayat to the house of Abdul Khaliq by dragging."

The defence appeared to be trying to establish that 1) only Abdul Khaliq had forced Mukhtar into his room, and that Mukhtar had added the names of three other men to her accusations more than a week later; and 2) that Ghulam Nabi and Haji Altaf Hussain had not accompanied Mukhtar to the Mastois' gathering, but that Mukhtar had added their names later.

D: "Did you say to the Inspector and Superintendent that as you came out (of Abdul Khaliq's house), your father stood over-powered by the accused persons two kanals away?"

MM: "No."

The court was shown a statement in which Mukhtar is recorded to have said "as I came out, my father stood overpowered by the accused persons two kanals away."

D: "Did you state to the Inspector that 'As I came out, my father and maternal uncle Sabir extended support to me and took me along to the house.'?"

MM: "No."

The court was shown the police statement in which Mukhtar was recorded as saying thus.

D: "Did you state to the Inspector that Ghulam Nabi and Altaf had seen the occurrence?"

MM: "Yes."

The court was shown the police statement where Ghulam Nabi and Altaf are not mentioned by Mukhtar.

D: "Did you say to the Inspector and Superintendent that in (your) house Ghulam Nabi and Altaf Hussain were present?"

MM: "No."

The court was shown a police statement in which Mukhtar was recorded as saying the two men were at her house, not at the Mastois' gathering.

The same police statement recorded Mukhtar as replying to Inspector Riaz and Superintendent Abbas that when she was thrown out of Abdul Khaliq's house, she was "not in quite naked condition."

"No, I had worn shirt (knee-length kamiz) and my private parts were covered with dupatta as the *azarband* (string) of my shalwar had been torn. Shalwar was in my hand," Mukhtar was recorded as saying in the police statement.

Mukhtar was then asked to confirm whether her father, her uncle Sabir, and Maulvi Abdul Razzaq were present when she appeared before the Superintendent Abbas and Inspector Riaz for questioning on July 5.

MM: "That is correct."

D: "Is it correct that your father Ghulam Farid (Gujjar) stated to the Inspector and Superintendent Abbas that Ghulam Fareed Mastoi had not committed *zina* with his daughter?"

MM: "Incorrect."

The defence would never get a chance to quiz Ghulam Farid Gujjar on whether he had in fact exonerated Ghulam Fareed Mastoi. The prosecution had cancelled his appearance as a witness.

Mukhtar's final concession on her last day of cross-examination was significant.

She could not remember whether she told police that she knew, before June 22, all the 14 men she accused by name and face.

Having lived her life in purdah in the seclusion of her family's four walls, like all women in conservative belts of rural Pakistan, it would be odd to know by name and face men from other families, other tribes, and other villages.

# 17

# Eight Innocent Men

The prosecution brought four police investigators and a small-town magistrate into the dock.

### PW 7 ON OATH: Rana Muhammad Ishfaq, Magistrate In Court Alipur, District Muzaffargarh

Civil Judge Rana Muhammad Ishfaq was the magistrate closest to Mirwala, based in Alipur, a town 40 minutes drive southeast from Mukhtar's village.

On Wednesday July 9, Magistrate Ishfaq had interviewed Mukhtar Mai, her father, uncle Sabir, Ghulam Nabi, Shakoor and Maulvi Abdul Razzaq as part of the investigation into her claims of gang-rape.

The magistrate was asleep when Police Sub-Inspector Ghulam Shabir Khitran appeared at his residence at around 5.00 p.m on July 9. With the Sub-Inspector were Mukhtar Mai and five other six prosecution witnesses; and in the officer's hand, an application for the magistrate to interview the witnesses and record their statements, in accordance with the Criminal Procedure Code.

"I was asleep. Coming to know of the matter, I took a bath. I sent the Sub-Inspector to the courtroom, where at about 6.00 p.m I recorded the statements of the (six aforementioned) witnesses," Ishfaq testified. The magistrate's court was not in session, so he used the courtroom to conduct his interviews.

"I sent the police out of the courtroom. I informed the witnesses that I was a magistrate in court and that they were not bound to make any statement (to me). I put questions to them to satisfy myself that they were not under some kind of pressure. I gave Ms Mukhtar Mai one hour's time to think over the matter, and after completing all the legal formalities, she made a voluntary statement. Her entire statement was written down and signed by myself," the investigating magistrate told the trial.

Magistrate Ishfaq did the samething with the other five prosecution witnesses.

After taking down their statements he sealed them in an envelope, sent them to the Sessions Judge of Muzaffargarh, the district capital, and forwarded copies to the police investigators.

\*　　\*　　\*　　\*

Testifying at the trial on August 7, the day after Mukhtar Mai's three-day cross-examination concluded, was the local Jatoi police officer who headed the formal police investigation from July 3 to 10, Deputy Superintendent Muhammad Saeed Awan:

## PW NO 15 ON OATH: Muhammad Saeed Awan, Deputy Superintendent of Police, District Muzaffargarh

Deputy Superindent (DSP) Awan had been placed in charge of the investigation on July 3, 12 days after the alleged gang-rape.

Awan immediately interviewed five of the local Jatoi police on the day he took charge.

Abdul Khaliq and Faiz Mastoi were arrested as rape suspects within days. Awan interviewed the suspects on July 6. It was exactly a fortnight since the alleged gang-rape of Mukhtar Mai.

On July 8 Awan arrested three more suspects: Muhammad Fayyaz Mastoi of Mirwala, Ghulam Fareed Mastoi of Mirwala, and Jatoi Police Sub-Inspector Muhammad Iqbal. He recorded their statements.

On July 9 Awan took the first three arrested rape suspects (Abdul Khaliq, Ghulam Fareed Mastoi and Muhammad Fayyaz Mastoi) to the local health clinic for "potency examinations." He made no request for DNA testing or semen analysis.

Defence counsel Malik Saleem focused his cross-examination on the timing of the Gujjar family's claim that Shakoor had been sodomised by three Mastoi tribesmen.

Awan said he first heard of the gang-rape allegation on June 30. On the same day he visited "the place of the occurrence" where Mukhtar Mai's family told him of Shakoor's sodomy claim. Awan told the court that he instructed the police officer accompanying him, Inspector Nazir Ahmad, to register the sodomy charge. However, according to Awan, no police followed his order to register the sodomy charge either on June 30, nor the following day July 1, nor July 2.

Defence counsel Saleem Malik raised the suggestion that police had destroyed all original statements made on June 30.

D: "Is it correct to suggest that on 3.7.2002 a team of police officers destroyed the police record pertaining to this case whereafter new record of proceedings of the police was prepared by you?"

Awan: "Incorrect."

D: "Is it correct to suggest that in the previous record, no witness stated anything about the sodomy case?

Awan: "Incorrect."

D: "In your view, was such a sodomy case a heinous, cognizable and non-bailable offence?"

Awan: "Yes"

The defence asked Deputy Superintendent Awan to confirm the July 2 arrests of the eight accused panchayat members. They were all Mastois and all residents of two villages: Rampur, near Mirwala, and Hairo, across the Indus River in the neighbouring district of Rajanpur.

"On 3.7.2002, the aforesaid eight persons were sent to the judicial lockup," Awan confirmed.

But, significantly, Awan admitted that none of these eight Mastoi men had been named by Mukhtar in her initial complaint to police on June 30. Nor did she name them when she was interviewed by police a second time on June 30.

Nor had Mukhtar's uncle Sabir named any of the eight men, despite his claim that he witnessed the supposed panchayat where Mukhtar was allegedly dragged off by Abdul Khaliq and his co-accused.

In fact *none of the prosecution's witnesses had named the eight men in their original statements to police,* Awan admitted.

"Sabir was eyewitness of the case in whose statement there is no mention of the aforesaid eight persons, nor in the statements of Altaf, Ghulam Nabi, Ghulam Farid (Gujjar), Maulvi Razzaq, or Manzoor," he told the court.

It was then dramatically revealed that the head of the Muzaffargarh district police noted in his own report that there was no evidence against the eight alleged panchayat members picked up from Hairo and Rampur on July 3.

"I forwarded the said report after reading the said report, which contains report that there was no evidence against the said eight persons," Awan told the court.

Judge Zulfikar Ali Malik noted in his closing summary that there was "no evidence" against the eight Mastois of Hairo and Rampur.

"No solid proof could be collected during the investigation," the judge in his trial notes.

\* \* \* \*

Defence counsel Saleem Malik set about portraying the intense political pressure the investigating police fell under once the gang-rape charges became public.

The Punjab Law Minister had proclaimed as early as July 3 that the case would be tried in a special Anti-Terrorism Court, a move unprecedented since the crime of rape had been omitted from the list of offences that could be considered terrorist offences under Pakistan's Anti-Terrorism laws.

The provincial minister had also ordered the release of the eight Mastois of Hairo and Rampur, according to the defence team.

D: "Is it correct that the Punjab Law Minister raided the Jatoi police station on 3.07.2002 and ordered the release of many persons of Mastoi tribe from the illegal confinement of the police?"

Awan: "Incorrect. The said eight accused persons were not produced before the Law Minister as they had already been sent to the judicial lockup."

\* \* \* \*

It was then Deputy Superintendent Awan's turn to explain how police had wrongfully arrested two men who had the same names as two of the men accused of gang-rape: Muhammad Fayyaz Mastoi and Ghulam Fareed Mastoi.

The defence began with the identity of Muhammad Fayyaz Mastoi. Two men of the same name lived in Jatoi sub-district, one in Mirwala village and one in neighbouring Rampur village.

The defence purported that Muhammad Fayyaz Mastoi of Rampur had been wrongly arrested by the police, in place of Muhammad Fayyaz Mastoi of Mirwala. Awan rejected the contention.

The defence turned to Ghulam Fareed Mastoi's arrest. The defence contested that the Ghulam Fareed Mastoi who was named and accused by Mukhtar Mai had fled the area and escaped arrest. Under pressure to meet the government's deadline for arrests, the police grabbed another man with the same name—the man whose father-in-law had, per chance, feuded with Abdul Razzaq in 1995 over a plot of land and lodged a petition against the cleric in the Lahore High Court.

The two men with the same name had different parentages. Ghulam Fareed Mastoi, whose father was Allah Bakhsh, was charged and put on trial, But Ghulam Fareed. Mastoi, whose father was Mehmood Mastoi, is the one who was named in Mukhtar's original complaint to police (the First Investigation Report).

D: "What parentage is nominated in the First Investigation Report?"

Awan: "Ghulam Fareed son of Mehmood Mastoi is nominated accused of the First Investigation Report, with no address given."

D: "Is it correct to suggest that after Ghulam Fareed son of Mehmood Mastoi could not be arrested by you, that Ghulam Fareed son of Allah Bakhsh Mastoi was arrested instead, at the insistence of Abdul Razzaq PW?"

Awan: "Incorrect."

D: *"Is it correct that the government and Supreme Court gave you a deadline for the arrest of the accused and submission of the* challan *(completed police investigation report)?*

Awan: "Correct."

D: "Is it correct to suggest that in order to comply with the deadline, name-sake Mastois were arrested by you and your officers?"

Awan: "Incorrect."

D: "Is it correct to suggest that Ghulam Fareed Mastoi son of Allah Bakhsh Mastoi and Fayyaz Mastoi (both residents of Rampur) were wrongly involved (named and arrested) in the case to meet the deadline?"

Awan: "Incorrect."

D: "Is it correct to suggest that the real nominated accused, of the same names as the aforesaid, disappeared after the registration of the case?"

Awan: "Incorrect."

At 11.55 a.m the defence counsel sought a five minute break in court proceedings so he could formally apply for a piece of evidence to be tendered as a court exhibit, "and to allow the accused and others to take water." The break was granted.

The trial transcript notes the court resumed at 12.35 p.m.

On resumption, the police questioning of rape suspect Abdul Khaliq and his version of events became the focus of cross-examination.

Awan: "Abdul Khaliq was arrested by Sub-Inspector Sadiq, who produced him before me and recorded his statement."

D: "What did he state?"

Awan: "Abdul Khaliq stated before me that he had taken Ms Mukhtar Mai alone in his room; kissed her; he put off her shalwar, and she was taken out (of his room) without any ziadti having been committed with her.

D: "Were any of the accused persons produced either before the Punjab Governor, or the provincial or central (federal) ministers who visited Mirwala, so that their version (the suspects' version) could also come to their (visiting officials') notice?"

Awan: "No."

D: "Were Abdul Khaliq and Mukhtiar Mai ever brought face to face with one another in a meeting to falsify (compare) the versions of another?"

Awan: "No."

D: "Was there any apprehension that prosecution witnesses would tell lies or might resile at the trial?"

Awan: "No."

D: "Did Abdul Khaliq ever admit possession of pistol with him?"

Awan: "No. Despite my interrogation he did not."

D: "Had Mukhtar Mai mentioned anything about the clothes she wore at the time of the occurrence, or did she mention them in her supplementary statement, or did she mention anything about the tearing of the clothes?"

Awan: "No."

D: "Are you aware of the importance of clothes in (zina-bil-jabr) rape cases?"

Awan: "Yes."

D: "Did you enquire about the clothes from the complainant party?"

Awan: "No."

D: "Is it correct to suggest that the investigation team made up the story of the torn clothes?"

Awan: "Incorrect."

D: "Is it correct to suggest that showing Abdul Khaliq as armed with a pistol is a story later on moved by the special investigation team, of which you were a member, to strengthen the prosecution case?"

Awan: "Incorrect."

Deputy Superintendent Awan admitted that he was not present when the alleged police inspection of the "spot of the occurrence" was made; and that he himself had never visited "the room where the *zina* was allegedly committed with Ms Mukhtar Mai".

D: "Is it correct to suggest that the accused are innocent in this case?"

Awan: "Incorrect."

*     *     *     *

Third defence advocate Azhar Trimizi took over.

Under questioning from Trimizi, Deputy Superintendent Awan admitted that Ghulam Fareed Mastoi's address had not been stated by Mukhtar Mai in either of her two interviews with police on June 30, nor in her July 9 interview with the investigating magistrate.

D: "Is it correct to suggest that Ghulam Fareed Mastoi (son of Allah Baksh) has been introduced instead of the real accused Ghulam Fareed son of Mehmood, at the instance of Abdul Razzaq and under government pressure?"

Awan: "Incorrect."

D: "Is it correct to suggest that Ghulam Fareed Mastoi (son of Allah Bakhsh) did not join either the panchayat, or the (gang-rape) occurrence."

Awan: "Incorrect."

D: "Is it correct to suggest that Abdul Khaliq stated that his nikah was performed with Ms Mukhtar Mai in the night of the occurrence, and that his claim was not brought on the record to strengthen the case, nor was it investigated?"

"Objection!" cried the prosecutor. He appealed to the judge to disallow the question. Judge Zulfikar Ali Malik overruled his objection. The question was allowed.

Awan: "Incorrect."

D: "Is it correct to suggest that Ghulam Fareed Mastoi (son of Allah Bakhsh) is innocent?"

Awan: "Incorrect."

Awan was released from the dock.

*     *     *     *

A suspended police officer stepped up to the dock.

Inspector Nazir Ahmad was one of a raft of Jatoi police officers who were suspended or transferred by the Punjab government within days of the gang-rape story reaching the press.

## PW 16 ON OATH: NAZIR AHMAD INSPECTOR (UNDER SUSPENSION) IN UNIFORM.

Inspector Ahmad told the court that he was the officer posted on duty at Jhugiwala chowk (intersection) on the morning of June 30 when—according to the prosecution account—Mukhtar came to lodge her complaint of gang-rape.

"I recorded her statement, all written and signed in my own hand, and her thumb impression was got affixed. She was sent to the hospital for medical examination. The formal complaint (Prosecution Exhibit I) was sent to the police station for registration of the case, through Constable Ali Muhammad," the suspended inspector testified.

"Statements of the witnesses were recorded at the place of the occurrence."

He did not specify if this meant Abdul Khaliq's room, where Mukhtar said she was gang-raped.

"I inspected the spot of the occurrence and prepared a visual site-plan of the place of occurrence, all written and signed in my own hand with five marginal notes. I investigated the case generally and thereafter left to trace the accused."

Inspector Ahmad also oversaw the taking into police possession of the clothes Mukhtar wore on the night of the feud.

He was on duty on July 2 when eight Mastoi men were rounded up from Hairo and Rampur villages.

"I recorded their statements. On the same day, I was placed under suspension."

Chief defence counsel Malik Saleem began his cross-examination.

"From 22.6.2002 to 30.6.2002 nobody reported nor informed me about the present occurrence, nor of Abdul Shakoor's sodomy case," Ahmad replied to the first question.

D: "Surely people of the area would have come to the police station in connection with other cases as well during the aforesaid nine days?"

Ahmad: "I don't remember."

D: "Was the area visited by police officers during the said period?"

Ahmad: "Yes. The roads were patrolled for dacoity (banditry) etcetera."

D: "Did the Beat-in-Charge (the officer in charge of the Mirwala beat) inform you about the occurrences in the aforesaid period, or any other officer who patrolled the area?"

Ahmad: "No. For the first time, on 30.6.2002 at chowk Jhugiwala at 7.30 a.m, the complainant and prosecution witnesses met me. I was present on the road-side with government vehicle there. Along with the complainant came Ghulam Farid (Mukhtar's father), Ghulam Nabi, Sabir Hussain, Altaf Hussain, Maulvi Abdul Razzaq, but on my advice they were present separately when her statement was recorded. They were sitting on a bench at a distance of about 10 to 15 karams (paces)."

The Inspector insisted that Mukhtar Mai had named the accused men herself, without the assistance of the cleric or her family.

"I read out the statement to the complainant, which she admitted correct, except that the parentage of Ghulam Fareed Mastoi accused was stated to be incorrect, whereupon I said that her statement would be recorded at the place of occurrence on visit immediately," Ahmad testified.

He admitted that Mukhtar's alleged objection to the parentage was not noted in the police diary (the karwai).

"I have recorded in the karwai that the statement was read out to the complainant which she understood and admitted the correctness of her statement and thumb-marked it, and I recorded that I attest her understanding and the correctness of the statement."

Inspector Ahmad said he delayed the recording of statements of other prosecution witnesses until they reached the "place of occurrence."

Ahmad: "I had to inspect the place occurrence first and therefore recording of statements of the PWs was postponed. Nine days had passed, but my importance (priority) was inspection of the place of the occurrence first.

D: "Why?"

Ahmad: "I wanted to collect material proof from the place of the occurrence, if any."

D: "Was any article (clothes, semen-stained earth, hairs of the complainant etc) collected from the place of the occurrence by you?"

Ahmad: "No."

D: "Were any footprints preserved?"

Ahmad: "No. It was pacca (hard-baked) earth floor."

\*    \*    \*    \*

Claims that Abdul Khaliq was armed when he allegedly dragged Mukhtar Mai into his house were then put under the spotlight.

The Inspector was quizzed about the insertion of the words 'armed with pistol' after Abdul Khaliq's name in Mukhtar's original police complaint.

D: "Is it correct to suggest that you inserted the words 'armed with pistol' later on?"

Ahmad: "Incorrect. I had omitted the word 'pistol' in haste, which was written immediately after the word 'armed'.

He admitted that no police had initialed the insertion of 'armed with pistol', nor did he record the insertion in his police diary.

According to Inspector Ahmad, he inspected the "place of the occurrence" in the presence of Mukhtar Mai and the other prosecution witnesses.

On the officer's inspection notes, the words 'armed with pistol' had also been inserted later on into the original text.

D: "Is it correct to suggest that you included the words 'armed with pistol' in your inspection note (tendered as Defence Exhibit H) afterwards?"

Ahmad: "Incorrect.

The defence counsel turned to Judge Zulfikar Ali Malik and sought his opinion on the apparently repeated insertion of the words 'armed with pistol.'

The judge recorded in his notes: "Declined (opinion). Will be given at the proper time, i.e. in judgement."

The defence turned back to Inspector Ahmad.

D: "Please explain to the court where, in your inspection note, the words 'armed with pistol' are inserted."

Ahmad: "Those words are written above the word 'Abdul Khaliq'."

Saleem Malik sought adjournment.

The judge noted: 2.35 p.m. Learned defence counsel seeks adjournment, allegedly due to heat and exhaustion.

\*     \*     \*     \*

Cross-examination of the suspended Inspector Nazir Ahmad resumed on August 8. He was asked to recall Mukhtar Mai's first statements to him about the events preceding the alleged gang-rape.

D: "What did Ms Mukhtar Mai state to you about the suggestions of the *salisan* (negotiators) for *watta-satta* exchange marriage?"

Ahmad: "She stated to me that Abdul Khaliq, Ramzan Pachaar and Ghulam Fareed Mastoi did not agree to the suggestion of the *salisan* of both the parties and demanded that Ghulam Farid (her father) should give a girl with whom *zina* would be committed which would equalize and they would come to terms. But (Mukhtar said) this matter was opposed by the remaining participants of the gathering."

D: "Who took her to the (Mastois') gathering?"

Ahmad: "She stated that Sabir Hussain her maternal uncle had taken her to the panchayat. She stated to me that when Abdul Khaliq accused had held her by the arm, she got it released."

D: "At that point, what did Faiz Mastoi say?"

Ahmad: "Faiz Mastoi stated that Ghulam Farid (Gujjar) should be pardoned. Ghulam Farid (Gujjar) is the father of Ms Mukhtar Mai."

The questioning turned once again to the identity of alleged rapist Ghulam Fareed Mastoi – whether Mukhtar had named Ghulam Fareed son of Mehmood Mastoi, or Ghulam Fareed son of Allah Bakhsh Mastoi, the man police arrested.

Ahmad: "Ms Mukhtar Mai named Ghulam Fareed, s/o Mehmood Mastoi twice in her complaint."

D: "Did she state whether she knew the nominated accused persons?"

Ahmad: "She stated that she knew the nominated accused persons very well."

\* \* \* \*

Defence counsel Saleem Malik turned his questioning to the handover of the clothes Mukhtar Mai wore at the time of the alleged crime.

D: Did she mention anything about her clothes at the time she recorded her first complaint?

Ahmad: "No."

D: "Why were the clothes not available for handover on that day (30.6.2002)?"

Ahmad: "Ms Mukhtar Mai stated that the said clothes would be produced on the next following day. But she did not say that those clothes were not available on that day."

D: "Did you tell the complainant to produce the clothes there and then?"

Ahmad: "No."

D: "Was any reason for the non-production of the clothes given by the complainant?"

Ahmad: "No."

D: "Did you inquire from Ms Mukhtar Mai as to where those clothes were?"

Ahmad: "No."

D: "Were those clothes sent to the lady doctor for examination and report (as to) whether they were smeared with semen?"

Ahmad: "No."

D: "Is it recorded in the fard (standard police form accompanying evidence) that her shirt was torn from the front?"

Ahmad: "No."

\* \* \* \*

Distances and the amount of light on the night of the alleged gang-rape were the next focus of Saleem Malik's cross-examination.

Inspector Ahmad estimated the distance between the site of the supposed panchayat and Abdul Khaliq's house at about 35 paces. Mukhtar had at different times estimated the distance at between 35 and 70 paces.

There was no electricity in the whole of Mirwala village, the Inspector confirmed.

He had not asked Mukhtar whether there was any other form of light in the room where she was allegedly gang-raped.

For the first time, a prosecution witness was quizzed about the "site inspection" allegedly made by police on June 30, after Mukhtar Mai made her first complaint to police and underwent a medical exam.

Hitherto, none of the prosecution witnesses had mentioned whether the 20 residents of the Mastoi home had objected to police entering their house, and entering Abdul Khaliq's room, with Mukhtar, the cleric and her family in tow.

Ahmad: "Residents of the house (place of occurrence) were not present when I visited the spot."

D: "Why did you not call them to come?"

Ahmad. "They were not called as they were not present."

D: "Was there no-one of the Mastoi tribe in the area at the time?"

Ahmad: "No. There are individual houses."

D: "Did you require of anyone to produce Abdul Khaliq's family members for questioning?"

Ahmad: "No."

D: "Is it correct to suggest that you did not record the statement of the family members of Abdul Khaliq as they were not ready to support the complainant's case?"

Ahmad: "Incorrect."

D: "Did you make a search of the said house for the pistol allegedly held by Abdul Khaliq?"

Ahmad: "No."

*　　*　　*　　*

The Inspector said he recorded the following prosecution witness statements on that day: Maulvi Razzaq, Haji Altaf Hussain, Sabir Hussain, and Mukhtar Mai.

Six of the eight Mastoi men rounded up on July 2 and later charged with being members of the panchayat were residents of Hairo village, on the other side of the Indus. Inspector Ahmad was asked to explain the location of Hairo village in relation to Mirwala village.

"Mirwala is situated on the eastern bank of the River Indus, three kilometres from the river-bed, and Hairo is situated on the other western side of the River Indus, at a distance of about seven or eight kilometres from each other," Ahmad replied.

Counsel Malik suggested that Inspector Ahmad initiated "wrong proceedings" in arresting the eight Mastoi men on July 2, "under pressure of Maulvi Razzaq." The police officer rejected the suggestion.

The defence counsel queried the alleged wealthy landlord status of the Mastois, as they had been portrayed in press reports. The Inspector's answers revealed they were in fact poorer than Mukhtar's family, and owned very little land.

D: "Is it correct that accused Abdul Khaliq etcetera are *zamindars* (landowners) of two to two-and-a-half beeghas (1.25 acres/10 kanals) of land?"

Ahmad: "Correct."

D: "How much land do all his brothers have?"

Ahmad: "All the brothers have 10 kanals of land (1.25 acres) between them."

D: "Is the financial position of the complainant party (Mukhtar Mai's family) better or worse than that of the accused Abdul Khaliq's family?"

Ahmad: "The financial position of the complainant party is better than that of Abdul Khaliq's family."

D: "Do you know that Ramzan Pachaar is the owner of one to one-and-a-half beegha (less than one acre) of land?"

Ahmad: "I do not know. I have heard that he cultivates land."

D: "Are the Jatois of Mirwala landlords?" the defence counsel asked, referring to the family of Abdul Razzaq, his brother Haji Altaf Hussain and Manzoor Hussain Ahmad Jatoi, one of the negotiators supporting Mukhtar Mai's family on June 22.

Ahmad: "Yes, they are landlords."

For the first time, it was shown in court that the real large landowners of Mirwala – the Jatois — were on Mukhtar Mai's side, whereas the Mastois were among the poorest families in Mirwala.

\*     \*     \*     \*

Third defence advocate Azhar Trimizi returned to the question of the identity of Ghulam Fareed Mastoi.

D: "Is it correct to suggest that Ghulam Fareed, son of Allah Bakhsh Mastoi, was wrongly recorded in the statements of the prosecution witnesses at the instance of Abdul Razzaq?"

Ahmad: "Incorrect."

D: "Is it correct to suggest that during your investigation, it came to your notice that there was enmity between Ghulam Fareed, son of Allah Bakhsh Mastoi, with Maulvi Abdul Razzaq?"

Ahmad: "Incorrect."

D: "Is it correct to suggest that statements of the witnesses (recorded by the magistrate on July 9) were prepared later on after destroying the earlier statements you recorded?"

Ahmad: "Incorrect."

\* \* \* \*

Before closing the cross-examination of the prosecution witnesses, Saleem Malik drew attention to a key phrase that was repeated, identically, in three police statements by prosecution witnesses: "according to Balochi custom."

The prosecution was suggesting that, in calling forth a woman to beg pardon on behalf of her tribe, the Mastois had invoked an ancient rite of the Baloch tribes.

D: "Is it recorded in the statement (to the Alipur magistrate on July 9) of Ghulam Farid Gujjar that 'on the persistent demand of Mastoi *biradri* (clansmen), my brother-in-law Sabir Hussain had brought Mukhtar Mai from the house to the panchayat for seeking forgiveness according to Balochi custom?'"

Ahmad: "It is."

D: "Is it recorded in the statement of Ms Mukhtar Mai that due to the pressure exerted by the accused party, and on their persistent demand for compromise, Sabir Hussain PW took her to the panchayat to seek pardon according to the Balochi custom?"

Ahmad: "It is."

D: "Is it recorded in the statement of Altaf Hussain (Maulvi Abdul Razzaq's brother) that on the persistent demand of Mastoi biradri, Sabir Hussain brought Ms Mukhtar Mai from the house to the panchayat to seek pardon according to Balochi custom?"

Ahmad: "It is."

# 18

# 'As Per Baloch Custom'

*"We are the servants of Hazrat Ali,*

*The true Imam of the Faith,*

*From Aleppo we came,*

*On account of the struggle with Yazid.*

*There are four and forty tribes.*

*By stages we march. From Kerbala and the cities of Sistan*

*The Hots (Mazaris and Dreshaks) settle in Makran. The Khosas in Kech. Dividing out water and dry land.*

*In Nali the Nohs settle, The Jatois settle in Sibi and Dadur.*

*The Rinds settle in Sarawan. The Lasharis in Gandava.*

*This is our footprint and track. This is the Baloch record."*

**Baloch Nama (Chronicles)** [*A]

A white-smocked tribesman with wide moustache removes his white turban. His head bare, he carries the symbol of his pride in his hands to the chief of a rival clan. At stake is zar, zamin, or zan: gold (money), land or women.

It's like a priest removing his collar; an orthodox Jew his prayer-cap; a nun her habit; a general his stripes; a tribal woman her veil.

Head bowed, the moustached Baloch tribesman, approaches the sardar (tribal chief). He places his turban at the sardar's feet; he stoops; he falls to his knees.

"Sardar-Sahib, pardon my people. We seek your forgiveness. Show compassion, we beseech you."

\* \* \* \*

The Bloody Marys came out just after 11 on a mild Sunday morning in the wood-panelled parlour of revered former Baloch sardar, Sher Baz Khan Mazari: a scion of the legendary Mazari Baloch raiders.

Winters in Karachi's seaside Clifton Gardens are balmy affairs. It's warm enough for hundreds of homeless to sleep on the kerbsides. The drive out to Mazari House from my hotel in Karachi's 'Bloody Radius' (so-named for the deadly bomb attacks that blight the same square mile year after year with bloody frequency) wound through Clifton's palm-fringed boulevardes of shaded villas, homes to Pakistan's business and political elite; and even at 10am the kerbside sleepers were still shaking themselves from their shelterless slumbers.

"It's a family tradition on Sundays," Mazari's New Zealand-schooled son murmured to me aside as the vodka cocktails were served. I was still on coffee and he seemed to be apologizing. "My mother insists," he added.

Through the wooden screen doors the lawn glowed green under the muted late-morning sun and Mazari senior's grandchildren played.

The parlour in Sher Baz Khan Mazari's Karachi home is whispered to be the best private library in Pakistan. Two storeys are lined with floor to ceiling shelves: one stacked with books on rose cultivation, another on eagles, another on guns and the 'art' of war. A staircase sweeps up to the mezannine level. A semi-circular display of the ancestors' muscats and sabres fill an alcove in the shelved walls. Sketched portraits of past Mazari warriors, the sardar's ancestors, are hung high.

Disgusted with medieval traditions of autocratic rule over a tribe of thousands, Sher Baz Khan Mazari left the Mazari Baloch ancestral heartland of Dera Ghazi Khan several decades ago and relocated to this Arabian Sea port megalopolis. A 30-year career criticizing successive regimes as an outspoken federal parliamentarian had kept Mazari Sr. mostly in the big cities anyway.

I had sought out the refined tribal chief after he published his memoirs under the distinctive title: "A Journey to Disillusionment". The front page dedication is equally grim: "To the people of Pakistan—leaderless and betrayed."

A line in the introduction, largely an elucidation of his tribal lineage and a scathing indictment of contemporary 'sardarism', stood out:

"During internecine blood feuds it was often women who would make peace by going bareheaded to their family rivals and plead for reconciliation. According to Baloch custom, no man can refuse a request made by a woman who approaches him with her head uncovered. Once her demand has been met it is incumbent upon the patriarch of the rival faction to 'restore' the woman's dignity by placing a sarri or dupatta over her head before she is returned to her family."

I wanted to ask this Baloch sardar about rites of pardon, and in what circumstances a tribe would resort to sending its women to beg vicarious pardon from a rival tribe's chief—as Mukhtar Mai's family claim they were asked to do by the Mastois.

Prosecution witnesses in the trial of Mukhtar Mai's alleged gang-rapists and their alleged abettors claimed that Mukhtar's menfolk had been ordered to bring her before the Mastoi Baloch tribesmen to seek forgiveness "as per Balochi custom," for her brother's alleged rape of the Mastoi girl Salma.

Among families whose women follow purdah — the tradition of secluding women — it is unheard of to bring a woman before any man who is not of their family, and especially who is not of their own tribe. How then could one family bring their daughter, unprotected and without the burqa, before a crowd of rival tribesmen seething with anger at the alleged rape of one of their girls? Prosecution witnesses' answer to this question, put by defence cross-examiners, was that they had been instructed to do so as a pardon-seeking rite "as per Balochi custom."

But how closely do the Mastois, one of many distant sub-tribes or clans of the scattered Baloch tribes, relate to and follow Baloch custom?

What are Baloch customs of seeking pardon, and in what circumstances are they invoked?

For most of 2005 and 2006, the highest-profile Baloch chief in Pakistan, Nawab Akbar Khan Bugti, was under siege from Pakistani troops. They were sent to quell an uprising by his followers over gas revenue distribution. Driven from his tribal seat of Dera Bugti in a remote desert corner near the intersection of three provinces—Baluchistan, Sindh and Punjab — the Bugti Baloch chief had re-established his throne in a rocky pit in a secret sandy mountain hideout. Photos of the besieged despot's hideout—it looked like a medieval prison pit, but he sat at its bottom as though on a throne — were splashed in newspapers, but the location was never revealed. Journalists venturing to meet this educated and particularly tyrannical Baloch tribal chief in 2006 were undertaking two-week journeys on foot, camel and horse-back, crossing rivers by night to dodge government snipers.

Mazari Senior was much more accessible in his Karachi parlour.

\*   \*   \*   \*

Baloch customs of seeking pardon are excruciating, Mazari's son Shehryar, who co-authored his father's memoirs, tells me in the parlour before the extended family assembled for Sunday brunch.

"It is simply unbearable to be on the receiving end of such an act," Shehryar says.

Mazari Senior sat with a blanket across his lap. That's when he wasn't being frequently called out of the parlour by callers at the gate, Baloch migrants to Karachi, who were being harassed by the Karachi police on suspicion of being militants connected to the rebellion in Balochistan. His son did most of the talking.

Shehryar returned to Pakistan just five years earlier, after practising as a barrister in London. He is being groomed to succeed his father. He often, uncomfortably, finds himself single-handedly mediating disputes within the Mazari tribe and handing out penalties for crimes. In his spare time he's a blogger.

A New Zealand accent peeks through, just discernible to an Antipodean ear. This sardar-in-waiting went to school in Auckland. He's the only one of his six siblings to study so far south. A New Zealander had convinced his father to send at least one child down under for education. A British edge has pushed out most of the Kiwi timbre, but it creeps in when he speaks of New Zealand, perhaps conscious that an Australian is listening.

"It is cringeing. It is emotional blackmail. Can you imagine receiving someone who has removed their pride like that—for the turban is the Baloch man's pride—and placing it in your feet, for God's sake?!"

"I've never been able to bear it. When they've come to me like that I've told them 'Get up man, put your turban back on. What have you done and what do you need?' "

In old Baloch tradition, the act of seeking pardon takes on ritual form. The symbolism is staggeringly powerful. It is weighted with meaning.

Usually, it is during a blood feud, when one side is facing rout by the other. Alternately, it may be when one tribe's member has murdered another tribe's man.

But it is more than a white flag.

"It is a sign of real desperation. It means they are at their wits' end. It means they are near death — or fear they are — or they fear their people are about to be wiped out. It is the last resort. A Baloch man cannot stoop lower than that," explains the 30-something sardar-in-waiting.

"Except, to send their womenfolk. In such cases, the women usually remove their veils and approach the head of the other clan, carrying their veils in their outstretched arms."

Sending a woman to seek pardon is the ultimate act of self-humiliation by a tribe in trouble.

But, Mazari Senior and Junior both stress, it is only in cases of dire emergency, in war-like situations where a tribe faces a routing by its rival.

"It's not something that is done in the case of a woman's violation. Under our tribal code if a woman is violated, the man is killed. There's no stuffing around with pardon."

* * * *

The Mastois of Muzaffargarh are a distant clan of the ancient Baloch nation of wandering tribes. So are the Jatois, whose members include Maulvi Abdul Razzaq and his brother, who helped Mukhtar Mai.

The Baloch wound up in present-day south-west Pakistan after centuries of migration across Arabian deserts and Central Asian steppes, dwelling for some centuries in the hills above Aleppo of Syria and later the Caucasian mountains in northern Persia. A series of expulsions led them to present-day Pakistan.

The Baloch place their first settlements in Aleppo "where they remained until, siding with the sons of Ali and taking part in the Battle of Karbala, they were expelled by Yazid, the second of the Omayyed Caliphs in 680 AD, and fled to Kirman in Persia."[1]

Kirman was a northern province of Persia.

The Baloch were followers of the Prophet's son Ali and Ali's sons Hussein and Hasan. After the pair's defeat in the history-shaping Battle of Karbala of 680 AD, the Baloch were expelled by a ruler known as Yazid the 2nd Caliph. The battle of Karbala, in present-day Iraq, heralded the split between Sunni and Shia Muslims.

There are however earlier historical references to the presence of Baloch in Persia. The poet Firdausi and the Byzantine historian Procopius place the Baloch in mountain strongholds in northern Persia in the 3rd and 6th centuries respectively.[2] Procopius named the Caucasus mountains as the lair of the Baloch.

Around the 13th century the Baloch migrated en masse as 44 united tribes to Makran, the desert tract hugging Pakistan's southern Arabian Sea shore, according to British historian Sir Denzil Ibbetson.[3]

Some historians cite their arrival in Makran several centuries earlier.

The 'Dera Ghazi Khan Settlement Report' place some Baloch tribes in the Makran wasteland as early as the 5th and 7th centuries.[4]

Firdausi records in his Shahnama that the Baloch were nearly annihilated by Persian King Naushirvan in their northern Persian mountain strongholds in the late 6th century.[5]

But they were recorded as still holding sway in Kirman in northern Persia in the 10th century, according to H.A. Rose and Sher Baz Khan Mazari.[6]

In 1041 they were expelled from Kirman by Persia's Seljuk rulers and migrated east to Sistan, another northern Persian province, according to Mazari.[7]

"They were then described as holding the desert plains south of the mountains and towards Makran and the sea, but they appear in reality to have infested the desert now known as the Lut, which lies north and east of Kirman and separates it from Khorasan and Sistan. Thence they crossed the desert into Sistan and Khorasan."[8]

---

1.  ROSE, H.A.: 'A Glossary of the Tribes and Castes of the Punjab and North-West Frontier Province'. Vol II, Aziz Publishers, Lahore.
2.  MAZARI, S.K.: 'Journey to Disillusionment', Oxford University Press, 2004
3.  IBBETSON, Sir Daniel: 'Punjab Castes', from 'The Races, Castes and Tribes of the People from the Punjab Census Report 1881', Lahore, 1882, reprinted Lahore 1974 by SH Mubarak Ali.
4.  "" ""
5.  MAZARI, S.K.
6.  ROSE, H.A. and MAZARI, S.K.
7.  MAZARI, S.K.
8.  ROSE, H.A.

Rose says they were "hospitably received" in Sistan by its ruler Shams–ud–Din.

The trouble came from Shams–ud–Din's successor, according to Rose, when he demanded a bride from each of the 44 Baloch bolaks, the Turkish word for tribes. Affronted at the idea of marrying off their women outside their race, the Baloch sent 44 boys disguised as brides instead. They fled southeast into Makran before their royal deception could be uncovered.[9]

In the early 13th century Mir Jalal Khan led the final mass migration from Sistan into Makran, the barren desert tract bound by the Arabian Sea in the south, present-day Iran in the west, and Afghanistan in the north, according to Mazari. It was in the brittle Makran desert, around 325 BC, that Alexander's Macedonian army floundered as it headed back to Persia from the subcontinent.

Mir Jalal Khan was the last leader of all 44 Baloch tribes as a united force.

In the late 14th century, the Baloch began moving northwards towards the Suleiman mountains and up the west bank of the Indus to its fertile river plains.[10]

Where the Baloch first originated is the subject of theory and speculation.

Most Baloch claim to be Qureshi Arabs by origin. Some theories say they are of Turkoman stock.[11]

The most popular theory is that they originated in the hills of ancient Aleppo, in modern-day Syria, as descendants of Mir Hamza, uncle of the Prophet (PBUH).

Another theory posits their birthplace as Persia near the Caspian Sea, from where they migrated to Makran in present-day Pakistan's barren southwest corner.

Yet another theory postulates that the Baloch are native to southwest Pakistan and southern Afghanistan. This theory competes with the belief that the Brahui race were the indigenous people of southwest Pakistan.

Mazari junior is writing what he hopes will be the definitive account of Baloch origins.

His research found elements of the first two theories correct.

The Baloch came to Makran from the northern Persian provinces of

9. ROSE, H.A.
10. QAISERANI, Sajid Mansur; 'Historical Survey of Dera Ghazi Khan', Dera Ghazi Khan Field Staff Report, Lok Virsa, Islamabad 1985. "After living in Makran for centuries, the nomad Baloch tribes had begun to look forward eagerly to move towards the rich and plentiful lands in the north and west."
11. IBBETSON, Sir Daniel

Sistan and Kirman, Mazari agrees. But he believes they had been there much earlier, before the time of the Prophet (PBUH). War had driven the Baloch from Persia westwards to Aleppo in present-day Syria. The later Battle of Karbala threw them eastwards again back into northern Persia, before their great migration at the end of the first millennium into Makran.

After the final mass migration out of Persia under Mir Jalal Khan, the 44 tribes split into five bands under his five offspring. They took the names of his four sons: Rind, Hot, Lashari, and Korai; and his daughter Jato. From them sprang forth the tribes known still as Rinds, Hots, Lasharis, Korais and Jatois.

The five tribes split, with most migrating up the west bank of the Indus river and into stony mountain ranges like the Suleiman. The Hots stayed behind and settled in Makran.

The southwest flank of Pakistan is today named after the Baloch wanderers: Balochistan. It encompasses the southern seaboard along the Arabian Sea, the Persian and Afghan frontiers in the west, and the Suleiman mountains in the northeast.

It was only a matter of time before they would head east again, down the stony Suleiman slopes to the lower ranges and the fertile plains of the Indus.

War again precipitated Baloch movements east, this time into the Punjab, the fertile land of five rivers east of the Indus. This time however it was not as exiles or expellees, but as victorious recipients.

Sovereigns on the subcontinent were in the habit of granting tracts of land to tribes who helped them in war. The land bequeathals were called "jagirs". Jagirs became the channels for Baloch to acquire rich farming land east of the Indus.

Scatterings of Baloch settled in the Punjab after receiving "jagirs" in recognition of military service.

Baloch are first recorded as settling along the Indus at the end of the 15th century, when Sohrab Khan Dodai came into the service of the Langah Rajput rulers of Multan, the flourishing southern Punjab centre over 100 kilometres east of the Indus.

Ruler Shah Hussain Langah sought protection from wilder Baloch raiders in the west of the Langahs' territory along the Indus banks. He took Sohrab Khan of the Dodai Baloch tribe into their service as a mercenary. The Langahs granted Sohrab Khan a jagir along the west bank of the Indus in 1469.

The Baloch were in great force in the 14th and 15th centuries in southwest Punjab as "mercenaries" of Multan's Langah dynasty and "also as independent freebooters," Rose records.[12]

Around 1480 AD Sohrab Khan's sons Ismael Khan and Fateh Khan

12. ROSE, H.A.

founded two cities on the Indus west bank. They were named Dera Ismail Khan and Dera Fateh Khan.[13]

Another Baloch, Haji Khan founded a city south of Dera Ismail Khan and annexed the region in 1482.[14] He named it after his son Ghazi Khan and it became known as Dera Ghazi Khan. The region surrounding the three cities or "deras" became known collectively as "derajat."

So began the rule of the Baloch Haji Khan dynasty on the stretch of the right bank of the Indus still known today as Dera Ghazi Khan, opposite present-day Muzaffargarh district.

Their rule spanned 15 generations over 300 years, with father and son alternating the names of Haji Khan and Ghazi Khan. During their rule the Haji Khan Baloches built irrigation canals and turned desert plains green, built gardens and cities, and turned Dera Ghazi Khan into a major trade centre.[15]

In the late 18th century a wily man from the Gujjar tribe swindled his way into the Baloches' seat of power.

The last Haji Khan's Pir (spiritual mentor) had recommended Mehmud Gujjar as an advisor. The shrewd Gujjar became such a close advisor and confidante of Haji Khan that on the ruler's death, he became custodian ruler as Haji Khan's heir Ghazi Khan was too young to take the reins.

Mehmud Gujjar invited a neighbouring ruler from Sindh in the south to attack Dera Ghazi Khan. The invaders took the young heir hostage and declared Mehmud Gujjar ruler in 1769.[16]

Mehmud Gujjar was succeeded by his nephew, who died in 1779. The Durrani rulers in Kabul then appointed their own governors after the death of Gujjar's nephew.[17] Since 1740 the region had been under the sovereignty of Kabul-based rulers.

On the fall of their reign in 1779, the Gujjars left Dera Ghazi Khan and traversed the Indus, settling in Muzaffargarh.[18]

The British took control of Dera Ghazi Khan in 1849. General Cortlandt became the first deputy commissioner of Dera Ghazi Khan.

\* \* \* \*

Pakistan's ill-attended libraries abound with encyclopaedic tomes on tribes and castes, authored by turn-of-the-century British colonists who studied their Indian subjects with fastidious detail.

---

13.   IBBETSON, Sir Daniel
14.   QAISERANI, Sajid Mansur
15.   ibid
16.   ibid
17.   ibid
18.   ibid

The tone of many is unconsciously pejorative. Under examination are the physical characteristics, the daily habits, the moral character, of their Indian subjects. Many study the "Indian tribes" in the framework of their suitability for military service, in the British-run Indian Raj army.

The tomes go into vast detail on tribes, sub-tribes, clans within sub-tribes, extended families or 'biraderi' within clans, their migration and settlement histories, their customs, divisions of time, dialects, custodial laws, agriculture, religious practices, superstitions, their women's dress, and more.

Take for example, Sir Denzil Ibbetson's discourse on the appearance of the typical Baloch:

"His frame is shorter and more spare and wiry than that of his (ethnic Pathan) neighbour to the north; though generations of independence have given to him too a bold and manly bearing.

Frank and open in his manners, and without servility, fairly truthful when not corrupted by our courts, faithful to his word, temperate and enduring, and looking upon courage as the highest virtue, the true Biloch of the Derajat frontier is one of the pleasantest men we have to deal with in the Panjab...

He is a thief by tradition and descent, for he says 'God will not favour a Biloch who does not steal and rob' and the Biloch who steals 'secures heaven to seven generations of his ancestors.'

...He wears his hair long and usually in oily curls and lets his beard and whiskers grow, and he is very filthy in person, considering cleanliness as a mark of effeminacy. He usually carries a sword, knife and shield, he wears a smock frock reaching to his heels and pleated about the waist, loose drawers and a long cotton scarf; and all these must be white or as near it as dirt will allow of insomuch that he will not enter our army because he would there be obliged to wear a coloured uniform.

His wife wears a sheet over her head, a long sort of nightgown to her ankles, and wide drawers; her clothes may be red or white; and she plaits her hair in a long queue...

As the true Biloch is nomad in his habits, he does not seclude his women; but he is extremely jealous of female honour. In cases of detected adultery the man is killed; and the woman hangs herself by order.

A tally of lives due is kept between the various tribes or families; but when the account grows complicated it can be settled by betrothals; or even by payment of cattle."[19]

Sir Ibbetson's discourse on moral codes and religion:

Both (Pathan and Biloch) have most of the virtues and many of the vices peculiar to a wild and semi-civilised life. To both hospitality is a sacred duty and the safety of the guest inviolable.

---

19.    IBBETSON, Sir Daniel

Both look upon the exaction of blood for blood as the first duty of man; both follow strictly a code of honour of their own, though one very different from that of modern Europe; both believe in one God whose name is Allah, and whose prophet is Mahomet.

But the one attacks his enemy from in front, the other from behind; the one is bound by his promises, the other by his interests; in short, the Biloch is less turbulent, less treacherous, less blood-thirsty, and less fanatical than the Pathan; he has less of God in his creed and less of the devil in his nature.[20]

Or Edward E. Oliver's assessment:

"Essentially a nomad, good-looking, frank, with well-cut features, black and well-oiled flowing hair and beard, attired in a smock frock, that is theoretically white, but never is washed save on the rare occasions when he goes to durbar—the Bilochi is a general favourite. He is a bit of a buck, and when he finds himself passing into the sere and yellow, dyes his hair. It is not uncommon to find an old gentleman with eyebrows of deep black, and the tip of his beard gradually shading off through purple to red, to the roots of pure white. Both are given to hospitality, both ready to exact an eye for an eye, and a life for a life; but the Biloch prefers to kill his enemy from the front, the Pathan from behind.[21]

Oliver notes that most of the Baloch tribes and clans are "physically powerful, hardy, bold, and manly, naturally warlike, open in manner, as a rule truthful and faithful to trust."

Yet, raiding and plundering is their pride:

"...though the average Bilochi would deem private theft disgraceful in the extreme, plunder and devastation of a country have always been held as honourable deeds deserving the highest commendation...

Both (Pathan and Biloch) have but dim perceptions of the difference between meum et tuum, preferring 'the good old rule, the simple plan, that he shall take who has the power, and he shall keep who can."[22]

Large volumes are devoted to the Baloch, their history and divisions, migration patterns and customs, the scores of sub-tribes and clans.

But the Mastoi Baloch sub-tribe barely rate a mention.

Ibbetson lists the Mastois among nine "important tribes" of the Dera Ghazi Khan lowlands.

But they are absent from his list of the 12 "most numerous Baloch tribes of Muzaffargarh," the district directly across the Indus from Dera Ghazi Khan.

The Jattoi Baloch, however, are mentioned in the 12 most numerous.

---

20. IBBETSON, Sir Daniel
21. OLIVER, Edward E.: 'Across the Border or Pathan and Biloch', Lahore 1977
    Al-Biruni
22. ibid

We next find the Mastois mentioned among the four "most insignificant of the broken tribes."

"The four most insignificant of the broken tribes: Mastoi, Hajani, Sanjrani, Ahmadani appear to have descended from hills eastwards towards the river," Ibbetson writes, whereas the Rind and Jatoi tribes "seem to have come up the river in very great numbers."[23]

H.A. Rose described the Mastois as a "servile tribe":

"The Mastoi, probably a servile tribe, is found principally in Dera Ghazi Khan where it has no social status."[24]

Rose notes that the Mastois and Jatois were "not organised as tumans (political confederacies)" like the original Baloch tribes.

The Jatois maintained a stronger presence in Muzaffargarh. They were "not now an organized tribe, but found wherever Baloches have spread, i.e in all southwest Punjab districts" such as Muzaffargarh.

When Ibbetson wrote his turn-of-the-century diatribes, the Baloch made up 15 percent of the population of Muzaffargarh.

\* \* \* \*

As a "servile", "broken", and "unimportant tribe", how closely do the Mastoi clan follow Baloch traditions and customs, or tribal organisation?

"Ballads and traditions testify to a common origin of tribes now widely separated, and differing greatly; so much so that it is doubtful if a northern Bilochi could make himself intelligible to a Makrani of the south," notes Oliver.

"It's only in Dera Ghazi Khan and its frontier that Biloch tribes have a distinct tribal and political organisation," writes Ibbetson.[25]

"Elsewhere in the Panjab the tribal tie is merely that of common descent, and the tribe possesses no corporate coherence. The Dera Ghazi Khan tribes are in the main of Rind origin: Mazari, Bugti, Marri, Drishak, Gurchani, Tibbi Lund, Laghari, Kehtran, Khosa, Sori Lund, Bozdar, Qasrani, Nutkani.

Only these have regular tribal organization. There are many other Biloch tribes which occupy large areas in southwest Punjab. They no longer hold compact territories exclusively as their own, while to great extent in the Derajat itself, and still more outside it, they have lost their peculiar language and habits and can hardly be distinguished from the Jat population, with whom they are more or less intermixed and from whom they differ in little but race."

---

23.  IBBETSON, Sir Daniel
24.  ROSE, H.A.
25.  IBBETSON, Sir Daniel

Ibbetson notes that in Muzaffargarh, the Baloch tribes "more than anywhere intermingled with Jat population. Tribal name merely denotes common descent. Its common owners possess no sort of tribal coherence."

He lists the most numerous Baloch tribes in Muzaffargarh as: the Gopang, Chandia, Rind, Jatoi, Korai, Laghari, Lashari, Hot, Gurmani, Petagi, Mashori, and Sahrani. Mastois are not included in his list of the most numerous.

"Outside Dera Ghazi Khan and along the greater part of the river of Dera Ghazi Khan district, the Biloch settlers own no allegiance to any tribal chief and are altogether external to the political organization of the (Biloch) nation, and do not hold that domination position among their neighbours which is enjoyed by the organized tribes of Dera Ghazi Khan."

Over four centuries lie between the bequeathal of jagirs in the Punjab to Baloch tribes and the present. Many were granted by the Mughal ruler Humayun to Baloch clans for helping him wrest the throne back from Sher Shah Suri in 1555. Sher Shah, a rebel Pathan warrior, had overthrown the previous Mughal ruler.[26]

The centuries diluted the links of the Baloch Punjab settlers to their early cultural identity:

"Over a period of 400 and more years, all these scattered Baloch settlements gradually lost their language and culture ties, thereby abandoning their tribal identity," Mazari wrote in his introduction.[27]

\* \* \* \*

When one considers the landscape of the Suleiman ranges, it's surprising the Baloch didn't move sooner down to the river-fed valleys.

Edward Oliver notes the bleakness and aridity of the stony mountains and valleys they inhabited:

"The most striking characteristics of almost the whole of this extensive country are a succession of rugged mountains and narrow valleys, for the most part barren or uncultivated, conditions due to a great extent, to the want of water. Of rivers, there can hardly be said to be any; what streams there are, have more of the nature of torrents, filled only at rare intervals, and which frequently disappear in the ground at no great distance from their source."[28]

To understand the aridness of the majority of Balochistan, consider the variant names of its plains:

Bad-i-simum: blast of death

Dasht-i-be-daulat: the plain without wealth

---

26. MAZARI, S.K.
27. ibid
28. OLIVER, Edward E.

Dasht-i-bedar: the uninhabitable waste

Dast-i-Goran: the desert of wild asses

Registan: the country of sand [29]

\* \* \* \*

The Baloch brought with them a language of Old Persian. It had traces of Bactrian and Zend. Their languages never had any written character. Their ballads and poems were oral. Their songs exhorted their wanderings, and romance.[30]

Mazari notes that there is a marked absence of abuse words in Balochi.

"Perhaps the worst insult available in the Baloch language is that of calling someone a coward or threatening to pull his beard off. Naturally these terms only applied to men," he writes in his introduction.[31]

Mazari Sr gives us a glimpse into the reverence women are held by customary Baloch:

"The traditional Baloch attitude towards women is one of great respect. Even in rage, a man could not lay a hand on a woman, while any act of molestation or assault was regarded as the most abhorrent of crimes and punishable by death.

During battle it was customary for the womenfolk to tend to the wounded and offer water to the warring parties without favour. They could wander among the fighting men without fear."[32]

\* \* \* \*

While other tribes of the "frontier", as the British called the western border of their subcontinent colony, looked to 'jirgas' or councils of elders for authority, the Baloch followed a single tribal chief.

"The Biloch is as loyal to his chief as a Highland clansman to a McIvor," wrote Oliver.[33]

While a jirga may be assembled, the decision lay in the hands of the chief.

In the case of murder, the practice of marakka may be invoked. Under marakka, the family of the killer calls on the victim's family.

"If they are received well, and they must be received well, for that is the Baloch code of hospitality—this is usually a signal for hostilities to cease and for negotiations leading to a settlement to begin."[34]

---

29.   ibid
30.   QAISERANI, Sajid Mansur
31.   MAZARI, S.K.
32.   MAZARI, S.K.
33.   OLIVER, Edward E.
34.   QAISERANI, Sajid Mansur

Oliver remarked that British presence from 1849 had restrained Baloch "intertribal wars, their old plan of harrying their neighbours' home and driving off everything possessing four legs."[35]

More than that, he notes, British systems of justice and law enforcement had given the warring tribes an alternative means of wreaking havoc on their neighbours:

"...the provision of many and expensive law courts, and more expensive lawyers, nevertheless provides in a great measure a sufficiently exciting substitute, and it is now possible for two chiefs to ruin themselves, and impoverish their clans more quickly by a suit, than by a whole series of fights; and the Border Bilochi is fast becoming civilized enough to adopt the process."

The cause of killing (among tribes west of Indus) is one, more or all of the three Z:

Zan (woman), Zar (gold), Zamin (land), noted researcher Sajid Mansur Qaiserani.

Elopement, or the suspicion of a love affair, could lead directly to killing.[36]

However reprisal murder could be averted by compromise deals.

"...while elopement or suspicion of a love affairs may lead directly to killing, there is still room for manoeuvre and some form of modus vivendi may be sought by the parties involved."[37]

Note the forms the compromise could take:

"...this may take the form of an exchange of women in marriage among the families, or the payment of a fine as determined by the tribal legal institution, the jirga. If however the lovers are caught in flagrante, killing the man is the logical conclusion."

Ibbetson told us similarly:

"A tally of lives due is kept between the various tribes or families; but when the account grows complicated it can be settled by betrothals; or even by payment of cattle..."[38]

\* \* \* \*

When Mukhtar Mai came before the crowd of Mastoi Baloches, she wore her veil on her head. It was a bochan, the large blanket-sized version of the dupatta.

She described it to me – it was blue. It matched her blue shalwar.

"I didn't wear burqa. I wore bochan. Colour was blue."[39]

---

35.  OLIVER, Edward E.
36.  QAISERANI, Sajid Mansur
37.  ibid
38.  IBBETSON, Sir Daniel
39.  Interview, Mirwala village, Muzaffargarh, 2005

Her garments were discussed in cross-examination at the original August 2002 trial.

Defence counsel questioned why she didn't wear the all-covering burqa, seeing as she was allegedly going before a crowd of angry men from a rival tribe, wanting punishment or compensation for the rape of their girl, in one of the most conservative corners of Pakistan. Most women in this area don the burqa when they step outside the walls of their family compound, shielding face as well as body.

Mukhtar told the court that she had stopped wearing burqa in recent times.[40]

I asked her what she carried in her hands.

"A small Koran," she told me.[41]

There was no veil in her hands, as real traditional Baloch rites of pardon demand.

Nor was she told or asked to bear her veil in her hands.

Mukhtar told me that when she reached the crowd of Mastois, she was given no chance to utter a request for pardon.

In fact, according to her and other prosecution witnesses, pardon was pronounced by Faiz Muhammad Mastoi as soon as she reached the Mastois gathering.[42]

According to Mukhtar's version in court, immediately after Faiz Mastoi pronounced pardon, the four younger Mastoi men dragged her inside the family compound.[43]

She has never mentioned, in police interviews, in court testimonies, or in media interviews that she carried a veil or laid it at the feet of Faiz Mastoi. Repeatedly she has said there was no time for her to seek pardon, as she was dragged off within seconds of arrival at the Mastois' gathering.

Mukhtar's appearance before the Mastoi Baloches did not follow the traditional Baloch rite of pardon.

"Bringing a woman before a rival tribe to seek pardon is extremely rare. It is only done when a tribe is really in dire, desperate straits. By that I mean when death is at hand. When the tribe is about to be slaughtered by the tribe with whom it is in the throes of a feud," Mazari junior said.[44]

"But these traditions have dispersed as the sub-clans and their sub-clans within have dispersed. These Mastois, I doubt they follow or know the original

---

40.  Trial in Dera Ghazi Khan Anti–Terrorism Court, August 2002
41.  Interview, Mirwala village Muzaffargarh, 2005
42.  Trial in Dera Ghazi Khan Anti–Terrorism Court, August 2002 "quote"
43.  ibid
44.  Interview Mazari House, Karachi, January 2006

Baloch traditions anyway. Too many centuries have passed, too many lands and rivers have been crossed, since their forefathers set out from the bosom of their original Baloch forefathers."

"As per Balochi custom/tradition" stated three prosecution witnesses in court: the uncle, the preacher's brother, and Mukhtar herself, justifying why they brought their woman, without protection, before a crowd of rival tribesmen furious at the alleged rape of their girl.[45]

If the defence version is to be believed, Mukhtar's family had another purpose in bringing her, unprotected, before the angry Mastoi men, without burqa.

What shape did the sulah take, the settlement of the quarrel? Was it just a request for pardon by an ill-protected woman, or was she delivered, by the menfolk of her family, as a compensatory bride? Is that why no man from Mukhtar's Gujjar family brought a protective weapon along when they accompanied the delivery of their woman to a furious rival tribe? Is that why she did not don burqa?

Women are never allowed to be seen by men not of their family, even moreso by the men of a rival tribe. What made Mukhtar's father and uncle agree to bring their woman, unprotected, her hair veiled but face uncovered, before a group of angry rival men is key to determining what actually happened on June 22, 2002.

---

45.    Trial in Dera Ghazi Khan Anti–Terrorism Court, August 2002

# 19

# Without Oath

The 14 Mastoi tribesmen did not testify under oath.

Under Pakistani criminal law, defendants are not administered the oath by courts.[1]

Each of the defendants answered a near-identical set of 16 questions before Judge Zulfikar Ali Malik on Friday August 9 and Saturday August 10. The Pakistan Penal Code's Section 342,authorises courts to put questions to the accused after the prosecution witnesses have been examined.[2] The Mastoi tribesmen's answers constituted their statement, without oath, to the Anti-Terrorism Court.

The eight men accused of being members of the supposed panchayat and thereby abetting the gang-rape of Mukhtar Mai, and of sharing the common intention of abducting and stripping her naked in public, gave identical answers to identical questions:

1.   Have you heard and understood the prosecution evidence recorded in your presence?

**A:** YES

2.   Is it correct that you, and all your co-accused and the Mastoi biraderi of villages Mirwala and Rampur etc suspected illicit relations between Ms Salma with Abdul Shakoor, and on 22.6.2002 at about zohirwela (midday) Punnu, Jamil son of Ghulam Hussain and Manzoor son of Allah Bachaya (all Mastois by caste), kidnapped Abdul Shakoor from outside his house in Mirwala; committed sodomy on him one after the other in sugarcane field of Imam Bakhsh (Mastoi), then confined him in the house of Abdul Khaliq in Mirwala, and to save their skin, confined Ms Salma with him from aser to maghrebwela (mid-afternoon to sunset)?

---

1.   Pakistan Criminal Penal Code, Section 342 (4):*Except as provided by sub-section (2) of section 340, no oath shall be administered to the accused.*

2.   Pakistan Criminal Penal Code, Section 342 (1): *For the purpose of enabling the accused to explain any circumstances appearing in the evidence against him, the Court may, at any stage of any inquiry or trial, without previously warning the accused, put such questions to him as the Court considers necessary, and shall for the purpose aforesaid, question him generally on the case after the witnesses for the prosecution have been examined and before he is called on for his defence.*

**A:** IT IS INCORRECT.

3. Is it correct that on 22.6.2002 at about maghrebwela, on the direction of Faiz Mastoi, about 200 persons of Mastoi biraderi permitted Assistant Sub-Inspector Iqbal release of Abdul Shakoor from his confinement in the house of Abdul Khaliq, whereafter Abdul Shakoor was taken and illegally kept by Assistant Sub-Inspector Iqbal at Jatoi Police Station without any legal process, and was brought back from his custody by Ramzan Pachaar and Faiz Mastoi at 2 to 3.00 am on 23.6.2002 with promise to pay 10,000 rupees bribe – to Assistant Sub-Inspector Iqbal, which was later on received by Ramzan Pachaar from the complainant party, who had to sell cow and borrow 2,000 rupees?

**A:** IT IS INCORRECT.

4. Is it correct that on 22.6.2002 at or after isharwela (early nightfall) in the area of Mirwala (under the jurisdiction of) Jatoi Police Station, in furtherance of the common intention, your co-accused Abdul Khaliq (armed with 30 bore pistol and live cartridges), Allah Ditta Mastoi, Muhammad Fayyaz Mastoi and Ghulam Fareed Mastoi (co-accused) abducted Ms Mukhtar Mai from, and at the behest of the panchayat of Mastois etc comprising you and your co-accused and others, with the common object that she may be forced to illicit inter-course (gang-rape)?

**A:** IT IS INCORRECT.

5. Is it correct that after the aforesaid abduction of Ms Mukhtar Mai on the aforesaid date, time, and in the house of Abdul Khaliq, the latter, Allah Ditta Mastoi, Ghulam Fareed Mastoi and Muhammad Fayyaz Mastoi committed on her, one after the other, zina-bil-jabr (gang-rape) on your abetment and that of your co-accused and the said panchayat?

**A:** IT IS INCORRECT.

6. Is it correct that after the aforesaid zina-bil-jabr (gang-rape) on the aforesaid date, time and place, Abdul Khaliq and his said three co-accused, in prosecution of the common object of you all, stripped Mukhtiar Mai of her clothes and in that condition exposed her to public view?

**A:** IT IS INCORRECT.

7) Is it correct that on 22.6.2002 you and your 13 co-accused, in prosecution of the common object, convened panchayat of 200/250 persons of Mastoi tribe and sent Ramzan Pachar and Ghulam Fareed (Mastoi) accused to the panchayat of the complainant party and demanded that sister of Abdul Shakoor PW should come in and seek pardon from your panchayat, else 200/250 Mastois would attack and abduct their menfolk, and thereby, you and your co-accused abetted the offences aforesaid committed by your co-accused Abdul Khaliq, Ghulam Fareed Mastoi, Muhammad Fayyaz and Allah Ditta Mastoi?

**A:** IT IS INCORRECT.

8) Is it correct that on the aforesaid date, time and place you and your 13 co-accused and others, in prosecution of the common design of you all, convened a panchayat to intimidate and overawe the community, and to create a sense of fear and insecurity in society, caused/abetted commission of the aforesaid offences by grievous threats, coercion and intimidation of the prosecution witnesses and other persons of the area?

**A:** IT IS INCORRECT.

9. Is it correct that Ms Mukhtar Mai was wearing clothes (kameez, shalwar, and dupatta, prosecution exhibits 1,2 and3) at the time of the occurrence on 22.6.2002, taken into possession by the police on 01.07.2002?

**A:** IT IS INCORRECT.

10. What have you to say about the following documents?

(23 court exhibits are listed, including the potency reports on the four accused rapists, Mukhtar Mai's medical report, press clippings, Mukhtar Mai's initial complaint and formal statement on June 30, prosecution witness statements to the investigating magistrate on July 9, a visual site plan of the scene of alleged crime, police records regarding the recovery of Mukhtar Mai's clothes and Abdul Khaliq's pistol, and the FIR concerning Shakoor's charge of sodomy)

**A:** THESE ITEMS ARE INADMISSABLE IN EVIDENCE AND HAVE ABSOLUTELY NO CONCERN WITH THE CASE.

*12. Why have the prosecution witnesses deposed against you?

**A:** MY DEFENCE IS THE SAME PUT IN CROSS-EXAMINATION BY MY LEARNED COUNSEL.

13. Why the case against you?

**A:** I HAVE BEEN FALSELY INVOLVED, AS I BELONG TO MASTOI TRIBE.

14. Have you anything else to say?

**A:** I AM INNOCENT.

15) Will you appear as witness under section 340 (2) of the Criminal Penal Code?

**A:** NO SIR.

16. Will you produce defence evidence?

**A:** NO SIR.

The statements of the eight alleged panchayat members, from the villages of Rampur and Hairo, were recorded on August 10.

---

* The numbering of questions omitted number 11.

A day earlier the statements of the four men accused of gang-raping Mukhtar Mai and the two men accused of abetting the gang-rape were recorded. All six pleaded innocent.

The questions to alleged panchayat chief  Faiz Mastoi, aged 34 to 35 according to the court, emphasised that he was head of the Mastoi tribe of Mirwala and Rampur villages, hence the release of Abdul Shakoor to Assistant Sub-Inspector Iqbal  was on Faiz' command only.

Faiz Mastoi gave the same answers as the accused panchayat members. He too alleged that he had been named in the case because he was Mastoi.

Ramzan Pachaar, aged 35/36 according to the court, was described in the questions as "a party-man of all co-accused."

Question 4 contained an extra line for Ramzan Pachaar and Faiz Mastoi:

Is it correct that Ghulam Fareed (Mastoi) and Ramzan Pachaar were sent to the panchayat of the Gujjars, and demanded from the complainant party that sister of Abdul Shakoor should come and seek pardon from their panchayat, else 200/250 Mastois would attack and abduct their menfolk?

'IT IS INCORRECT', both men replied.

Ramzan Pachaar, when asked why he had been named in the case, blamed Maulvi  Razzaq and Mukhtar's uncle Sabir Hussain. Pachaar accused the cleric of naming him because of his past efforts to oust the cleric from the Mirwala mosque. Pachaar accused Sabir of harbouring "personal enmity" towards him.

"I have been falsely involved at the instance of Maulvi Abdul Razzaq, as I played role to kick him out from the mosque due to his nefarious design, harbouring activists of Sipah-e-Sahaba and other indecent activities. Sabir deposed against me due to personal enmity," Pachaar stated. He did not elaborate on the reasons for Sabir Hussain's alleged enmity towards him.

The four accused rapists replied identically to the 16 court questions.

Asked why the prosecution witnesses had deposed against them, they replied:

"My defence is the same put in cross-examination by my learned counsel to the Prosecution Witnesses."

Asked why they had been named in the case, they replied:

"Same as aforesaid."

Asked if they had anything else to say, they replied:

"I am innocent."

Ghulam Fareed Mastoi (son of Allah Bakhsh) elaborated. He repeated his lawyers' assertions that he had been substituted for the man originally named by Mukhtar Mai, Ghulam Fareed son of Mehmood. Again, the cleric was blamed:

"I am innocent. I have been falsely challaned (charged) by the police instead of Ghulam Fareed son of Mahmood by the complainant party and the Prosecution Witnesses have deposed against me on the asking of the police and Maulvi Razzaq, who got me challaned due to personal enmity."

Razzaq was accused of naming Ghulam Fareed Mastoi son of Allah Bakhsh to avenge Ghulam Fareed Mastoi's late father-in-law Haji Karam Hussain for taking the him to court over their 1995 land dispute.[3]

Each question-and-answer statement is thumbprinted by the relevant defendant, and attested by Judge Zulfikar Ali Malik with the following note:

Certified that the statement of accused has been recorded in my presence & hearing; was read out, & explained to the accused, who admitted it correct, and the record contains a true & correct statement made by the accused.

---

3.   Haji Karam Hussain v. Maulvi Abdul Razzaq, Writ Petition No. 2949/1995, Lahore High Court

# 20

# The Marriage Witness

The Mastois produced a witness to the alleged 'verbal marriage' of Abdul Khaliq and Mukhtar Mai: Ghulam Hussain, Defence Witness number 5.

Ghulam Hussain was a mulair (maternal cousin) of Taj Mai, the widowed mother of the Mastoi brothers Punnu, Allah Ditta and Abdul Khaliq. He was also the father of Jamil Mastoi, one of the three men accused of sodomising Abdul Shakoor along with Punnu Mastoi.

Ghulam Hussain told the court that at midnight between June 22 and 23, Abdul Khaliq came to his house in Rampur village, close to Mirwala, and asked him to attend his on-the-spot sharai nikah (verbal marriage) with Mukhtar Mai.

Abdul Khaliq narrated to his mother's cousin the feud that had erupted between his family and the neighbouring Gujjar family, Hussain told the court. Abdul Khaliq told him it had begun with the alleged rape of Abdul Khaliq's sister by Mukhtar Mai's brother, and resulted in a *watta-satta* exchange marriage deal between the Mastoi and Gujjar tribes.

According to Hussain, Khaliq told him that he and his uncle had caught Shakoor in their sugarcane field with their younger sister Salma. After capturing him, they had handed him over to Jatoi police, who now held him in custody.

Khaliq told Hussain that Mukhtar was brought to the Mastoi home by her father and two uncles, along with the cleric Maulvi Razzaq. The Gujjar men had asked the Mastois 'not to quarrel'. They offered Mukhtar Mai's hand in marriage to Abdul Khaliq, some seven years her junior, and suggested that in exchange Salma be married to their boy Shakoor.

"Abdul Khaliq stated that her hand be given right then, without delay, or else there would be no compromise, and Maulvi Abdul Razzaq agreed," Hussain told the court, recounting what Khaliq had told him.

"Abdul Khaliq stated that Abdul Shakoor would be brought back from the police station by him, and in the following morning the hand of Ms Salma would be given to Abdul Shakoor."

Ghulam Hussain followed Abdul Khaliq back to his home for the midnight verbal nikah.

At the Mastoi home, "the aforesaid five persons of the Gujjar party were present," including Mukhtar Mai, Ghulam Hussain told the court. They were

Mukhtar, her father, her two uncles Sabir and Ghulam, and the cleric Maulvi Razzaq.

Present from the Mastoi family were Abdul Khaliq's uncle, Taj Mai the widowed mother of the Mastoi brothers, four of Abdul Khaliq's six sisters, his two little brothers Abdul Malik and Mohammad Tariq, and two sisters-in-law including Allah Ditta's wife Maqsooda.

"DW 5 deposed that in his presence. Maulvi Razzaq performed sharai nikah of Abdul Khaliq with Ms Mukhtar Mai," Judge Zulfikar Ali Malik noted in his summation of evidence.[1]

"After the nikah the complainant party said that Shakoor should be brought back from the police station, taking along Sabir Hussain (Mukhtar's uncle). Ghulam Hussain also deposed that thereafter both (Sabir and Khaliq) went to the police station and the remaining persons of the complainant party also left, except Ms Mukhtar Mai, who remained present there in the house of Khaliq."

Ghulam Hussain testified that Maulvi Razzaq told him to go home and come back in the morning for the follow-up nikah between Shakoor and Salma.

When Ghulam Hussain returned to the Mastoi home at 9.00am the next day, he found the cleric, Mukhtar's father and her uncle "present there, busy in hot talks" with Khaliq and his uncle Fayyaz.

"The complainant party demanded that on account of sodomy committed with Shakoor, the hand of one girl be given in badla (revenge or equalisation); a second girl be given in marriage for badla of Mukhtar Mai, and four kanals (half-acre) of land be also given to the complainant party; whereas Abdul Khaliq accused stated that since there was allegation of sodomy committed on Shakoor by (Khaliq's) brother Punnu, therefore he could not marry his sister Salma to Shakoor, and complainant party may do whatever was in its power."

The Gujjar menfolk had turned up at the Mastoi home with the cleric at "fajjar namazwela (dawn prayer time)," accusing Punnu of sodomising Shakoor, according to Ghulam Hussain's testimony.

They took Mukhtar back from Khaliq and threatened legal action, Ghulam Hussain said. Khaliq retorted that he and Mukhtar had already been married.

"Maulvi Razzaq stated that he would take legal action by getting a case registered and would not admit to performing the nikah of Mukhtar Mai with Khaliq, after the latter stated that sharai nikah (verbal nikah) had already been performed," Ghulam Hussain testified.

Everyone dispersed "with no hope of getting the hands in return."

Four days later, the Mastois married Salma off to one of their kinsmen,

---

1. ATC D.G. Khan Judgement 31.8.2002, pg 352

Khalil Ahmed Mastoi of Hairo village, across the Indus. Salma's nikah on June 27 obliterated any chance of the Gujjars winning their demands for either one or two Mastoi girls in marriage to "equalize" their handover of their daughter Mukhtar in marriage and the alleged sodomy assault on their son Shakoor.

Khalil, aged around 24 or 25 according to court documents, was the son of another Mastoi tribesman by the name of Ghulam of Hairo village.

Khalil's father Ghulam had three brothers: Hazoor Bakhsh, Rasool Bakhsh, and Qasim.

Khalil, his father Ghulam Hussain, and his three uncles Hazoor Bakhsh, Rasool Bakhsh and Qasim were among the six Mastois rounded up from Hairo village the day after Mukhtar's charges of gang-rape burst into the press. With another Mastoi of Hairo, Nazar Hussain, the six ended up being accused of participating in the supposed panchayat of June 22 in Mirwala. They were sent to trial.

Ghulam Hussain said that he had told his story to police on June 30, the day Mukhtar filed her gang-rape charges. But he did not know whether police took note of his statement.

* * * *

Five other defence witnesses completed the defence case.

One was the manager of Alipur branch of the National Bank of Pakistan, Mr Muhammad Younas.

He testified that Mukhtar and her father had both opened accounts two weeks after the alleged gang-rape: one in the name of her father Ghulam Farid Gujjar, account number 12604-1, and a second joint account in both their names, account number 15046-1.

The two accounts were opened on July 5 - one day after the Minister for Women's Development Attiya Inayatullah had presented Mukhtar Mai with a government cheque for 500,000 rupees.

Younas testified that a 500,000 rupee cheque issued by the President's Secretariat, Islamabad and dated July 4, 2002 was deposited into Ghulam Farid Gujjar's account on July 10. The cash was then transferred into the joint father-daughter account.

Transaction statements of the two accounts were tendered as defence exhibits.

Nadeem Saeed, a local correspondent for the English-language broadsheet Dawn, testified as Defence Witness 2. Saeed, as all reporters in the southern Punjab, had been covering Mukhtar Mai's extraordinary case since it broke on July 1.

An article published in Dawn under Saeed's byline on July 12 quoted Mukhtar's older brother Hazoor Bakhsh saying that police had got the wrong

Fayyaz Mastoi when they arrested Fayyaz son of Karim Bakhsh, and that the real rape suspect was another Fayyaz Mastoi.

Saeed told the court that he had interviewed Hazoor Bakhsh during a visit to the Gujjars' Mirwala home on July 11.

His article, titled 'Police, Feudals Trying to Save Chief Juror,' was tendered as a defence exhibit.

The third defence witness was Akbar Ali, a constable from the Jatoi police station.

He had produced a copy of a police report against the cleric Abdul Razzaq on March 26, during Moharram, the emotional month of mourning rituals observed by Muslim Shias.[2]

Police Sub Inspector Muhammad Ashraf of the Muzaffargarh city police station was the fourth witness called by the defence.

He was brought in to testify chiefly about the arrest of Fayyaz Mastoi son of Karim Bakhsh, whom the defence team argued had been picked up as a substitute for another Fayyaz Mastoi who was the real 'accused' and had fled.

Ashraf told the court that Fayyaz son of Karim Bakhsh was in custody in the Muzaffargarh district jail on July 14. He was brought out of the jail around 6.00 p.m on the understanding that he could give information on the whereabouts of a man accused of theft in an unrelated six-month old charge. Fayyaz was given two days' remand. But he was not produced before senior police, Ashraf said.

Sub-Inspector Ashraf was asked by the defence whether he was aware that the Governor of the Punjab had ordered police to inquire into the Gujjars' complaint that Fayyaz son of Karim Bakhsh was the wrong Fayyaz. "I was not aware," Ashraf replied.

D: "Is it correct to suggest that Fayyaz accused stated to police that he was not the real accused of the case?"

Ashraf: "Incorrect."

D: "Is it correct to suggest that the highups (senior police) asked you to produce the actual culprit, and on your expression of your inability to do so, Fayyaz was arrested?"

Ashraf: "Incorrect."

D: "Is it correct to suggest that on the orders of highups, Fayyaz accused was again sent back to Muzaffargarh jail (after two days on remand)?"

Ashraf: "Incorrect."

---

2. Moharram: a month of mourning observed by Shia Muslims to mark the slaughter of Imam Hussain, grandson of the Prophet PBUH, and his followers in the 7th century Battle of Karbala. Shias, a minority in mainly Sunni Pakistan, hold debates, mourning parades and bloody displays of flagellation during Moharram.

The final witness called by the defence was Mirza Muhammad Abbas, superintendent for criminal affairs for Dera Ghazi Khan regional police.

Abbas had been put in charge of investigating local police involved in probing the Mirwala gang-rape case on July 3.

On July 4 at the Muzaffargarh police station, Abbas interviewed Shakoor, Salma Mastoi, her mother Taj Mai, Jatoi police Assistant Sub-Inspector Muhammad Iqbal, and Jatoi police Inspector Nazir Ahmad.

On July 5 he interviewed Mukhtar's two maternal uncles Sabir Hussain and Ghulam, and two of the men who supported the Gujjars during the June 22 feud, Manzoor Hussain Jatoi and Ghulam Mustafa.

As part of his probe into the local police, Abbas had his assistant Inspector Riaz interviewed Mukhtar Mai, her father and the cleric Abdul Razzaq. Abbas admitted he was not present when Inspector Riaz took their statements.

"There was three days' time limit given and when I deputed Inspector Riaz to record the statements of Mukhtiar Mai, Ghulam Farid (Gujjar) and Maulvi Abdul Razzaq, there was great rush of foreign media persons in the room, causing disturbance and to save time, the Inspector was deputed to record the statements," Abbas told the court.

But Mukhtar, her father and Abdul Razzaq told Abbas that their statements, as recorded by Inspector Riaz, varied from what they had actually said.

The three, when summoned for verification, stated that "…those (statements) recorded by Inspector Riaz were not correct, but contained variations," Abbas testified.

However the superintendent was forced to admit that he had attested their statements without noting that the three prosecution witnesses had declared them incorrect.

"I made my own separate notes that the witnesses had discarded/disowned the statements made by Mukhtar Mai, Ghulam Farid (Gujjar) and Maulvi Abdul Razzaq on separate sheets attached," Abbas said under cross-examination.

"I attested the aforesaid three statements in routine, without actually confronting or reading out the said statements to the witnesses by him, as there was rush of media persons."

Abbas told his cross-examiners that he had been tasked with investigating local police for: "corruption, negligence, siding with the accused and delay in the case."

He had interviewed Mukhtar, her father, and the cleric as part of his probe as the four were "star witnesses" and he needed to thrash out the facts of the case.

"I did not record fresh statements of the said witnesses myself. I had read out the statements of the witnesses recorded during the investigation, which they had admitted as correct."

Abbas repeated what Sabir Hussain had told him: that Mukhtar was taken back to her house by Sabir and her father after the alleged gang-rape; that Sabir had not seen any weapons in the hands of the Mastois with his own eyes "as it was dark and the Mastois were too far away to see whether they were armed"; and that Faiz Mastoi had stated "Allah Taala (God Almighty) orders that you people forgive Mukhtar Mai."

Abbas said no evidence was produced to him of any *nikah* between Abdul Khaliq and Mukhtar Mai.

The defence team applied to summons Khaliq's uncle Fayyaz Hussain, who had allegedly witnessed the *nikah* between Abdul Khaliq and Mukhtar Mai. However he could not be located anywhere in Mirwala, "having gone into hiding from the time of the registration of this case," Judge Zulfikar Ali Malik noted in his summary.

Four men appeared as Court Witnesses to testify that the alleged gang-rape of Mukhtar Mai qualified as an act of terrorism under Pakistani law. Under the Anti–Terrorism Act, that meant proving that the alleged crime was designed to coerce and intimidate or overawe the public, or create a sense of fear or insecurity.[3]

The Nazim (Mayor) of Muzaffargarh district, Malik Sultan Mahmood Hinjra, testified that the alleged crime was "an unheard of occurrence, which was reported incessantly in the newspapers and on television, and people of the area were terrified."

"Pakistan, an Islamic state, has been defiled in the media due to the occurrence," the mayor said.

The mayor however admitted under cross-examination that he had not heard the Mastois' version of events.

Muhammad Amjad, a local councillor representing Mirwala on the Jhugiwala Union Council, called the incident "great terrorism."

"It caused fear in the area," Amjad told the court.

"The incident was flashed in the media. It gave a bad name to the country. People got terrified, and started shifting."

Amjad admitted under cross-examination that the Gujjars had voted for him in local government elections, while the Mastois had opposed his candidacy.

The third Court Witness was another local councillor, Abdul Wahid from the Rampur Union Council. He said local people were "terrified" by claims – unproven - that Mukhtar Mai had been dragged through the village and attacked in the presence of hundreds of people.

---

3.   Anti-Terrorism Act Section 6 (1b), Manual of Anti-Terrorism Laws in Pakistan 2003 Civil & Criminal Publications, Law Books Publishers & Sellers, pg 29

"People got terrified as such an incident has never previously taken place. It was zulam (tyranny)," Wahid told the court.

"Evil had taken place between the Mastois and Gujjars. The BBC and newspapers narrated the incident, which was true. People got terrified as gang-rape was committed in the presence of so many persons. Nobody's respect was safe."

The councillor said local villagers told him they were considering leaving the area.

"Fear prevailed in the area," declared Maulvi Faiz Muhammad, another local Muslim prayer leader who appeared as Court Witness number four.

Judge Zulfikar Ali Malik declared the Court Witnesses' depositions proved the case qualified as an act of terrorism.

"In the facts and the circumstances, the evidence of these Court Witnesses with regard to fear and harassment in the area on account of the present occurrence is proved."[4]

---

4. Judgement of Dera Ghazi Khan Anti–Terrorism Court 31.8.2002 pg 48

# 21

# Verdict At Midnight

## AUGUST 31, DERA GHAZI KHAN

Journalists wilted in the pregnant heat. The verdict had been expected for five days. The nation was on edge. It had been an incendiary year. On the steamy left bank of the Indus, Dera Ghazi Khan bristled under the heaviest guard it had ever seen.

On each passing eve of the anticipated verdict, Allah was praised and invoked.

"If they escape in this court, then they will have to face the court of the Almighty, where no lawyer can save them," Mukhtar whispered from the shadows of her *chador.*[1]

In her police safe house in Muzaffargarh town, 40 kilometres from the Dera Ghazi Khan courthouse, the veiled prosecutrix prayed for executions. "I am hoping for the death sentence," she murmured. For all 14 men.

The cleric Maulvi Razzaq addressed reporters. "We expect the court to do justice in the name of Allah."

"Allah has given poor people like us the power to stand up. We are sure, *Insh'Allah* (God willing), that he will give the same strength to the judge and deliver justice."[2]

The prosecution and defence had wrapped up their final submissions on August 24, a Saturday. Judge Zulfikar Ali Malik hinted he could deliver his verdict the following Tuesday.

A squad of black-suited police commandos encircled the courthouse. Police barricades were thrown up.

The Gujjars shuddered at rumoured threats from the Mastois.

"They are threatening that if any of their people are hanged, they will kill two of my tribe's men for each Mastoi man hanged," Mukhtar murmured.[3]

The silver-bearded former *Sipah-e-Sahaba* disciple was unfazed.

"The Mastoi tribesmen are vengeful," Abdul Razzaq said. "But we are

---

1. AFP report, Aug 26
2. AFP Aug 31
3. AFP Aug 31

not afraid of dying. Even if we die, even if they kill us, we will have the satisfaction before Allah that we raised our voice against barbarism."

Twenty-nine witnesses had testified over 29 days: two doctors, 15 police officers, a small-town magistrate, two Muslim clerics, a district mayor, two local councilors, a farmer, an adolescent, one haji-landowner, a bank manager, a tribesman and a prosecutrix.

"It was the bitterest and hardest experience of my life to appear before the court and reply, before men, to questions which I could not even discuss with women," Mukhtar Mai said, as she waited daily for the verdict.[4]

"I felt naked before the dozens of people in the court, and before the 14 accused. But Almighty Allah bestowed courage on me to face the situation. I am optimistic that the culprits and their abettors will not go unpunished."

Sixty-eight exhibits were tendered to the court—35 by the prosecution and 33 by the defence. The judge consulted case 17 precedents, from as early as 1959 to as recent as 2002. Seventeen advocates assisted the chief defence counsel Saleem Malik in representing the 14 defendants. Three advocates assisted the public prosecutor Iftikar Qazi.

\* \* \* \*

There were no direct witnesses to the pack-rape of Mukhtar Mai, other than Mukhtar herself. Only two witnesses testified that they had seen her dragged off by the four accused rapists within seconds of being brought before the supposed panchayat. At the last minute, the prosecution had dropped two others who had purportedly witnessed the same: Mukhtar's father Ghulam Farid Gujjar, and Ghulam Nabi, one of the neighbours who had supported the Gujjars' gathering.

Under Pakistan's Hudood Laws, if the prosecution had sought a "hadd' punishment of stoning to death or public whipping, in accordance with the Sunnah (sayings of the Prophet PBUH), Mukhtar would have needed four witnesses who were "adult, pious, Muslim males".[5]

But in the absence of four such witnesses the crime resorts to a Tazir crime, under which no witnesses are required: hence the prosecution of the rape suspects in Mukhtar Mai's under Section 10 of the Hudood Laws on *Zina* (sex crimes). Section 10 covers rape as a Tazir crime. Tazir is "any punishment other than Hadd."[6]

The Sunnah prescribes public stoning to death, or public lashing of 100 'stripes' for rape. Tazir prescribes the death sentence for gang-rape; or a jail term of between four and 25 years for one-man rape.

---

4.   AFP Aug 26
5.   Offence of Zina (Enforcement of Hudood) Ordinance 1979, Section 8, Manual of Hudood Laws, C.M.Hanif, Nadeem Law Book House, pg 363
6.   Offence of Zina (Enforcement of Hudood) Ordinance 1979, Section 2 (e), Manual of Hudood Laws, C.M.Hanif, Nadeem Law Book House, pg 364

Several precedents exist in Pakistani case law in which the sole testimony of the victim sufficed to warrant prosecution, provided the complainant is of "unimpeachable" character and the rest of the prosecution case is credible.[7]

\* \* \* \*

Judge Zulfikar Ali Malik eschewed motor cars, even as a perk of his civil service position. He traveled only by motorcycle. In this and other ways he had earned a reputation for arrogance in his honesty; disdainful of anyone less spartan or luddite than himself.

General Zia, the army dictator who ruled Pakistan from 1977 until his death in a plane crash in 1988, used to make a show of riding his bicycle, eschewing the trappings of military command and dictatorship. Squadrons of security guards followed the pedaling general nevertheless. Zia was the third in Pakistan's gallery of army rulers. On a late autumn day in 1979, seven months after hanging the prime minister he'd overthrown two years earlier, the police and army were so preoccupied with protecting the General's exposed flanks as he bicycled through Rawalpindi that they were unavailable to extinguish the flames and riot that had engulfed the United States embassy.[8]

For this trial of the tribesmen and their ancestral way of justice, the judge had to accept a state sedan. The police escort assigned to travel in front of and behind the judge, accorded for this high-profile trial, would have been of little use if the judge had stuck to his motorbike.

The Dera Ghazi Khan police chief Asif Hayat attributed the heavy security cordon for the trial to "the overall threat perception" countrywide.[9]

It had been a volatile year. Enraged Islamic fanatics had been exploding their wrath on Westerners and Christians in Pakistan for the United States-led invasion of Afghanistan 10 months earlier. A too-curious Wall Street Journal correspondent; diplomats praying in a church in Islamabad's embassy quarter; a bus full of French navy technicians in Karachi; a school for the children of Christian missionaries, in a Himalayan hill-station near Islamabad; a chapel attached to a hospital in the ancient city of Taxila; and the United States consulate in Karachi: blood had flowed from all these targets, in the months preceding the trial of the tribesmen.

On the last Saturday in August, the judge sat in his simple state-provided home and dictated his summation and decision to the court stenographer.

---

7.   Lahore High Court (Multan Bench) Judgement on appeal 03.03.2005 pg 25 "It is settled principle of law that in Tazir cases, conviction can be based on sole statement of the victim, but it should be of unimpeachable character and corroborated by some independent piece of evidence."

8.   Steve Coll, 'Ghost Wars: The Secret History of the CIA, Afghanistan and Bin Laden, from the Soviet Invasion to September 10, 2001' pg29

9.   AFP Aug 31

He waited until nightfall to venture to the barricaded courthouse, fortified like a military base in a war-zone.

Hundreds of journalists sweltered in the courtyard outside, parched after hours without drinking water. They were forbidden from entering the courthouse, as they had been forbidden throughout the closed-doors trial.

Cameramen, photographers and 'scribes' lay on the ground of the outer courtyard, plagued by thick flies, melting after a long day in the searing August sun. The dark brought no relief from the heat. Along this stretch of the Indus in August, nights are hotter than the days. It's something to do with the ground absorbing the daylight heat, and releasing it when the sun has gone.

It was after midnight when Judge Zulfikar Ali Malik pronounced his verdict.

Six men condemned to death: four for abduction and gang-rape; two for abetment.

Abdul Khaliq Mastoi, Allah Ditta Mastoi, Ghulam Fareed (Mastoi) and Muhammad Fayyaz Mastoi were found guilty of abducting and gang-raping Mukhtar Mai.

Alleged panchayat chief Faiz Mastoi and his chief emissary Ramzan Pachaar were found guilty of abetting the abduction and gang-rape.

"In the facts and the circumstances, the defence has failed to make any dent in the investigation or other material brought on the record against the (aforementioned) six accused," the judge declared.[10]

"Taking into consideration all the aforesaid facts and the circumstances of the case, I find that Abdul Khaliq and Allah Ditta, sons of Imam Bakhsh; Muhammad Fayyaz Mastoi, Ghulam Fareed (Mastoi), Ramzan Pachaar and Faiz Muhammad Mastoi, in prosecution of their common design, convened a panchayat, mostly of their Mastoi Baluch tribe of the area, on 22.6.2002 in Mirwala and coerced, intimidated, overawed the complainant party and the community; created a sense of fear and insecurity in society; and thereby committed the offences under Sections 11 (abduction) and 10-4 (gang-rape) of Ordinance VII of 1979 (Hudood Laws), read with sections 149/109 Pakistan Penal Code (abetment through prosecution of a common design of an unlawful assembly); Sections 6-1a, 1b and 2b (causing grievous bodily harm, designed to coerce and intimidate or overawe) of the Anti-Terrorism Act 1979; and Section 149/109 Pakistan Penal Code (abetment and in prosecution of the common object of an unlawful assembly)."

"Actions of the aforesaid convicts were cruel, which overawed and harassed

---

10. ATC D.G. Khan Judgement 31.8.2002 pg 366

the society at large and therefore, they are not entitled to any leniency," the judge declared

Sentences:

For gang-raping Mukhtar Mai, each of the four convicted rapists was sentenced to death, "subject to confirmation by the Honorable High Court."[11]

For abducting Mukhtar Mai, each convicted rapist was sentenced to life imprisonment, plus "30 stripes" or lashes, and a fine of 20,000 rupees (333 USD/444 AUD).

For abetting the gang-rape of Mukhtar Mai, Faiz Mastoi and Ramzan Pachaar were each sentenced to death "subject to confirmation by the Honorable High Court".

For abetting the abduction of Mukhtar Mai, Faiz Mastoi and Ramzan Pachaar were each sentenced to life imprisonment plus 30 "stripes" and a 20,000 rupees fine.

"From the evidence on record, I find that if Faiz Muhammad Mastoi had commanded that Mukhtar Mai be forgiven, the four rapists would not have dared to commit the offences, and that these were committed with his abetment and that of the persons of his clan gathered there," the judge found.[12]

"The role of Faiz Mastoi and Ramzan Pachaar accused persons is of abettor and they have been assigned the specific roles of participation in the panchayat. Without their abetment, Abdul Khaliq and his three accomplices could not commit the abduction and gang-rape of Ms Mukhtar Mai... so (Faiz and Pachaar) are found liable for their criminal acts, as charged and stated in the authority."[13]

For causing grievous bodily harm, all six men were sentenced to life imprisonment plus another 20,000 rupees fine.

Apart from their death sentences, each of the six convicted men had to pay a total of 40,000 rupees (666USD/900 AUD), undergo 30 lashes of the whip, and a life prison term.

All 14 defendants were acquitted of the charge of stripping a woman naked in public view.

"Learned defence counsel submitted that (the charge of stripping a woman naked) was inapplicable in the case, because the occurrence admittedly took place inside the house of Abdul Khaliq (bounded by four walls) and Mukhtar Mai was not stripped of her clothes, nor was she exposed to public view. The prosecution had not much to say in the aforesaid facts and the position in law. Accordingly, I find that the accused persons are not liable to the offences

---

11. ATC D.G. Khan Judgement 31.8.2002 pg 68
12. ATC D.G. Khan Judgement 31.8.2002 pg 368
13. ATC D.G. Khan Judgement 31.8.2002 pg 368

(of stripping a woman naked in public view) in the facts and circumstances of the case," the judge summarised.[14]

Eight men acquitted of aiding and abetting:

The eight Mastoi men who had been rounded up by police on July 2 from Hairo village and Rampur village and later accused of being members of the supposed panchayat were acquitted of all charges.

Judge Malik noted in his summation that they had not been named in Mukhtar Mai's first complaint or formal statement, nor in her supplementary statements to the police, nor in her deposition to the investigating magistrate of Alipur.

"She was duly confronted with her previous statement where their names are not mentioned. They have been found innocent by all the Inquiry Officers, there is no allegation against them, except their mere participation in the panchayat. Learned defence submitted that six of the said accused persons belong to Jampur (in a neighbouring district) and Rampur (a neighbouring village) so their identification by Mukhtar Mai complainant, a *purdah nashin* woman (a veiled woman living in seclusion) is doubtful," he said.[15]

The judge considered that a woman observing purdah was unlikely to know the identities of men living in another village, let alone another district.

"In the aforesaid facts and the circumstances, the aforesaid eight accused persons are acquitted of the charges, on account of the benefit of doubt. They be released forthwith, if not required in any other case."

The judgement was 69 pages long. For the first time in Pakistan's then 55-year history a tribal jury had been punished.[16]

An illiterate peasant woman and a Muslim preacher had fought back against the tribal tradition of commoditising women as chattel for resolving feuds, and won.

And now six tribesmen stood to be hung for using Mukhtar Mai as a pawn for restoring an insulted tribe's honour.

Whether she was gang-raped by four men, as the prosecution said, or whether she was married off to Abdul Khaliq under a *watta-satta* exchange marriage deal, as the defence said, Mukhtar had been reduced to chattel to settle a dispute between her tribe and another over an act that had nothing to do with her. Mukhtar had refused to accept her gender's status as pawn for barter in an arbitrary market of men's "honour".

An illiterate woman who had passed most of her adult life inside the four walls of her family compound, teaching embroidery and the Qur'an to village girls, had taken a generations-old tribal system to a modern-day court for terrorists, and won.

---

14. ATC D.G. Khan Judgement 31.8.2002 pg 369
15. ATC D.G. Khan Judgement 31.8.2002 pg 369
16. Federal Law Minister Khalid Ranjha AFP Sept 1

For her, it was a collective victory for all women in her region reduced to chattel.

The defence team cried foul, accusing the judge of caving in to pressure.

"This judgement has been delivered under duress," chief defence counsel Saleem Malik told reporters waiting outside. "The judge was clearly under pressure from the media."[17]

Mukhtar stayed at home on the day of the verdict.

From the Gujjar family, only Mukhtar's elder brother Hazoor Bakhsh went to the court to hear the judge's decision.

Stepping outside to the explosion of camera lights, the farm labourer proclaimed victory.

"We are grateful to Allah. The oppressors have met their end. This is truly justice."[18]

But Hazoor Bakhsh castigated the acquittal of the eight accused panchayat members.

"They all should have been punished, as they were part of the panchayat which ordered the gang-rape."

The court had heard during the trial that Hazoor Bakhsh had declined to go to the Mastois' gathering with his sister. He did not say how he knew who was present at the Mastois' gathering.

Back in her unlit village home, Mukhtar had fallen asleep at 1.00 am waiting for word of the verdict.

The Gujjar family had grown frantic as midnight came and went, with no word from the court and no sign of Hazoor Bakhsh.[19]

At 2.30 am her father shook her awake. Mukhtar opened her eyes to a crowd of policemen inside her home. They were congratulating her.

"I threw my hands towards the sky and said 'Shukur Allah, thanks be to God. Justice is delivered'."

Journalists traveled the 50 kilometres through bandit-flushed lands to her village the next day.

"My sacrifice has not been wasted," she told them.

Now Mukhtar sat erect. Her voice was deeper. Peering through a narrow slat in her head veil, her eyes were lit.

"I have been praying to Allah that he would grant me justice. I am elated."

---

17. AFP Sept 1
18. AFP Sept 1
19. AFP Sept 1 "My elder brother had gone to the court, but he had not yet returned and we were very upset."

But Mukhtar did not see her victory as complete. She wanted all 14 accused sent to the gallows.

"I want all of them to die," she told me two years later.

"I will never forgive them. They can cut off my limbs, but I will never compromise."[20]

Her lawyers immediately lodged an appeal against the acquittal of the eight Mastoi men from Hairo and Rampur villages. The appeal sought death sentences.

For Mukhtar, justice would only be hers if all 14 were executed.

\* \* \* \*

I later asked one of Mukhtar's closest confidantes Farzana Bari, a gender studies professor and women's rights activist from the Quaid-e-Azam University in Islamabad, why Mukhtar would not be satisfied with life prison terms for the men convicted of raping her or abetting the gang-rape.

The professor saw it as part of Mukhtar's sense of collective responsibility for all women.

"She feels she would be letting her whole gender down if she was to relent in any way," Farzana Bari said.

"The remarkable thing about Mukhtar is her sense of collective responsibility, for all women in her position. She sees herself as fighting for all women subject to such conditions. If she were to relent in any way, the oppressors would gain."[21]

"Right now, the feudals, the tribal chiefs in her immediate area are thinking twice about using women the way she was used. If they see any sign of softening, they might revert to their old ways and think they can get away with it."

\* \* \* \*

In a faint echo of Mukhtar's fears, the Human Rights Commission of Pakistan warned against complacency.

"This case has raised a very important issue: the role of extra-judicial tribunals taking law into their own hands and handing down barbaric punishments," pronounced the Commission's chairman, Afrasiab Khattak.[22]

---

20. Interview Mirwala, August 2004, published Nov 24 2004 by AFP
21. Interview Islamabad, June 2005
22. AFP Sept 1

"The issue will not be over until the state takes up the larger issue of the role of feudal lords and the treatment of women in society. We should not be complacent, as there are more such cases of many unknown women whose voices have not been heard."

Mukhtar's family had their own questions about their future.

"The police are all around us. They say they will protect us, but we don't know what will happen," said Hazoor Bakhsh.

"We don't want to live the rest of our lives under police escort."

# 22

# Genesis of A Jirga

*Zar, Zamin, Zan*: gold (money), land, women. The source of all conflicts.

"It's an extension of the old feudal tribal system which holds 'zar, zamin, zan', as the sources of all conflict, which effectively reduces women to property."[1] Lahore-based lawyer

In any dusty village, spy the circle of turbanned and bearded men, probably sitting cross-legged in a field, on a hilltop, before a mosque, under a tree, on bare ground; or in a tribal chief's home. You won't see any woman near them. This is the village court of rural Pakistan – a gathering of tribal elders, chiefs, large landowners, their oldest sons. They follow no case law. The justice they issue is arbitrary. They have no training in adjudication. Judgements are summary – generally in favour of the dominant tribe and, critics say, aimed at perpetuating power and privilege. Punishments decree the payment of monies, surrender of lands, and tradeoff of women — as trophies of compensation, for women are the traditional repositories of honour. These unofficial village juries are vested with authority stemming from their inherited rule of a tribe, or the vast tracts of land they own. Accused transgressors have been made to walk on fire to prove their innocence. Scorched soles symbolise guilt.

Conflict resolution in rural Pakistan is a male domain. The role of females is that of pawns for trade in dispute settlement. A woman's opinion is not sought. Her judgement is irrelevant. Her voice is never heard.

Courts, police, lawyers, the hallmarks of Pakistan's official justice system, are expensive, under-resourced, over-burdened, ham-fisted, hard to access for remote villagers, and too often corrupt.

Traditional village juries are far more logical. Fee-free, local, instant justice mediation. No travel involved, no wait required.

In northwest Pakistan, they are called '*jirga*', from the Persian word for 'gathering of elders'. Some say *jirga* has its origins in an old Turkish word for 'circle'.[2] Traditional *jirga* members among the Pashtun tribes of the northwest frontier sat in circles as they mediated.

1. **SAEED, Uzma,** criminal lawyer, cited in 'Legislator Fights Pakistan's Blood Marriage' by Juliette Terzieff, Womens E-News, October 27, 2003
2. **YUSUFZAI, Rahimullah**: 'Circled in Controversy', Newsline Magazine August 2002

In southern Punjab and the southern province of Sindh, the village jury is called *panchayat*. Some interpretations say the '*panch*', the Punjabi and Urdu word for five, refers to the number of tribes which should be represented on the council. Others say it refers to the ideal five-man makeup: 2 representatives from each feuding party and a chairman.

A jirga or panchayat is an informal unelected council of local elders, tribal chiefs, and large landowners. They have no official position, nor accompanying wage, nor authority to jail offenders. They convene when two families are in dispute over the three Zs: *zar*, money; *zamin*, land; or zan, women. They hear disputes, make judgements, enforce decisions, and impose punishments.[3]

The priority of the *jirga* or panchayat is to restore honour (*izzat*) and order. Truth and punishment of the guilty are secondary considerations.

Consider these cases of justice mediation, Pakistani-village style:

In the village of Jano in Shikarpur, a district of southern Sindh province, a *jirga* convened to mediate over the shooting deaths of two teenage girls, Tahmeena and Aabida. The 17 year old and 16 year old were cousins from the Bhutto tribe.

They were shot dead beside the village graveyard at 1.00am on May 4, 2004 on the orders of a Bhutto elder and large landowner, Abdul Rasheed. Their crime: traveling to the nearby city of Sukkur without permission to visit their grandparents. Abdul Rasheed Bhutto decreed their permit-less trip showed loose morals and brought dishonour to the tribe. The Bhutto elder and several men ordered Tahmeena's brothers and uncle to kill the girls. They refused. Abdul Rasheed Bhutto and his partners then produced pistols and shot the girls dead themselves. They threw the girls' bodies in Abdul Rasheed Bhutto's fishpond. The bodies were exhumed from the pond on May 14.

A jirga was convened after the killings to mediate between the girls' families and their killers. It was chaired by none less than a federal minister and veteran parliamentarian, Ghous Bux Khan Mahar. Mahar is a pre-eminent political figure from Shikarpur: he was elected four times to the Sindh parliament, held posts in the Sindh cabinet, acted as provincial governor, won a federal seat in 1997 and has held two federal cabinet posts: Minister for Railways and Minister for Narcotics Control.

---

3. **Human Rights Commission of Pakistan**, Karachi Chapter, 'Jirga System in Sindh', 2004: "In Sindh, the jirga system functions as an alternative judicial setup. The jirga has many names such as faislo or panchayat, but essentially they all refer to a gathering of tribal chiefs or influential persons to resolve a dispute or take a decision on an issue that has arisen between two individuals, factions or tribes. This includes passing judgement on criminal acts and deciding the punishment for them. The jirga is conducted purely according to tribal customs or the will of the tribal chief and it therefore exists completely outside the legal framework in the country."

Minister Mahar's jirga judged that the dead girls were '*kari*'(black women) and that their murders thus constituted honour killings, *i.e.* killing a woman to restore the family honour she stained. The jirga determined a punishment: the killers were ordered to pay 600,000 rupees (10,000 USD) to each dead girl's family.[4]

In March 1999 in the North West Frontier Province town of Parachinar, Lal Jamilla Mandokhel, a mentally disabled 16 year old, was raped repeatedly by a junior clerk. Lal's uncle reported the rape to police. Police handed Lal to the elders of her Pashtun Mazuzai tribe in the tribal district of Khurram. A jirga of Mazuzai elders ruled that Lal had brought dishonour to the tribe by being raped. They ordered her killing to restore the tribe's honour. Lal was shot dead in front of the jirga. The tribal elders asked police to give them the rapist so they could kill him also. The police instead detained the rapist "for his own protection."[5]

In August 1999 in the village of Kot Bugti in Baluchistan province, school teacher Liaqat Tehlani was accused of theft. He was summoned to the home of local tribal sardar and landowner, Saleem Akbar Bugti. Tehlani denied the charge. Bugti ordered him to walk over burning coals to prove his innocence. The teacher's feet were singed in the hot coals. His singed soles were taken as proof of his guilt. The Bugti sardar ordered the teacher to pay a fine of 50,000 rupees (833 USD). Tehlani couldn't afford the fine, so he was detained in the sardar's home for a month.[6]

In 1998 Sindh provincial authorities asked tribal leader Sardar Khadim Hussain Jatoi to hold a *jirga* in the courtroom of the Central Jail of Sukkur, a rural area of northern Sindh where feudal lords hold sway. They wanted the *jirga* to help resolve an eight year feud between clans of the Dhareja tribe in which eight tribesmen had been killed. The *jirga* directed each side to pay 200,000 rupees for each life taken. The settlement was brokered within four hours and murder charges were dropped.[7]

In May 2004 a *jirga* convened in Abdu, another Sindh village, to adjudicate on the killing of Hidayat Mahar by her husband two months earlier. Again federal minister Ghous Bux Khan Mahar, a leader of the Mahar tribe, and landlord Shafi Muhammad Mahar, presided over the *jirga* at Shafi's home. The husband had accused his wife of infidelity. The *jirga* found his dead wife innocent. They punished her husband by ordering him to pay 150,000 rupees to his dead wife's family.[8]

Doctor Shazia Khalid, employed by Pakistan Petroleum Limited at a

---

4. **Asian Human Rights Commission**, November 8 2004, Letter to President Pervez Musharraf
5. **Amnesty International 2002 Report** Pakistan: The Tribal Justice System
6. *ibid*
7. *ibid*
8. **Asian Human Rights Commission**

remote gas field in Baluchistan's Sui district, was raped in the Sui Field Hospital hostel on January 2, 2005. Her husband's grandfather agitated for kinsmen in the couple's native town of Khuhra in Sindh's Khairpur district to declare her '*kari*' (black woman).[9] Her husband Khalid Amanullah denied press claims that a *jirga* ordered her death. The couple left Pakistan two months after the rape and have been seeking asylum in the West.

\* \* \* \*

*Jirgas* and *panchayats* are rooted in tradition.

Payment of compensation, or imposition of a punishment comparable to the original crime, are hallmarks of *jirga* and panchayat rulings. Hence those directly responsible for a crime often go unpunished, while innocents pay the price. This is most visible in *vani* and *swara* deals, where murderers evade jail or execution by giving away small daughters to their victims' menfolk, regardless of the age difference.

No women sit on *jirgas* or *panchayats*. Accused women are given no chance to appear before a *jirga* or *panchayat* to defend themselves or speak for their menfolk. They are exclusively male institutions.

Yet women feature prominently in the honour crimes cases dealt with by jirgas and panchayats and in the rulings they make.In fact, women are by far the greatest victims of injustice inflicted by *jirgas* and *panchayats*.

## GENESIS

*Jirgas and panchayats pre-date Islam.*

The Qur'an lays down a set of punishments known as "*hadd*". *Jirgas* are not part of this system of criminal law. Nor are common *jirga* punishments, like the giving away of small girls as compensation brides, connected to Islam. In fact they are un-Islamic.

The jirga evolved from tribal sardari and feudal land-ownership systems predating both Islam and British colonial rule on the subcontinent. Traditional power structures in rural society revolve around tribal chiefs and powerful landowners. As the most powerful figures in society, tribal heads and landowners play a key role in settling disputes.

In its early form the jirga was a forum for reconciliation and feud settlement.

---

9.   **Khalid Amanullah**, husband of Dr Shazia Khalid, in Dawn newspaper, February 3 2005: "My grandfather lives there and he has been putting pressure to declare Dr Shazia as a '*kari*' and that I should part ways with her. I am with my wife but she was very disturbed after his statements appeared in a section of press and we now feel insecure." Mr Aman denied that a jirga was held at his native town and said there were just some statements from his grandfather that were published in a section of the press.'

Writing in the 1880's, British anthropologist Edward E. Oliver described the functions of *jirgas* among Pathan tribes in the North West Frontier, then under British-ruled India:

"Necessity has forced the Pathans like the rest of the world to recognize the need for some form of government, some system that shall enforce even the rudest customary law, some tribal organization to fall back on at a pinch. And his tribal *jirgah* does all this for him and more.

Composed of Khans, mullahs (religious leaders) and headmen, it combines his House of Lords, bench of Bishops and Legislative Assembly; it discharges the functions of all the divisions of the Queen's Bench, Probate and Divorce, the Board of Trade and the War Office. It is at once his convocation and his county court...it performs for him most offices, from those of the Senate to those of the Vestry."

Tribal customs, parish politics, "furnish a lot of business; so do matters concerning debts, deeds, mortgages and sales. And curiously enough, among the most lawless, as perhaps among the most civilised, the law is much more severe on offences against property than against the person."[10]

The *jirga*, Oliver noted, was a convenient resort for handling burdensome blood feuds between tribes:

"While the legal business of the jirgah is far heaviest on the civil side, it has also considerable criminal jurisdiction. Life, even for an Afridi or a Yusafzai (tribesman), is not always beer and skittles; the luxury of reprisals, and the pleasure of personally killing one's enemies, must perforce be occasionally carried out by deputy, or entrusted to a tribunal. Where blood feuds are so common and so bitter that, though they may be allowed to slumber for years, they still remain a sacred heritage to be eventually taken up and continued as long as possible, many a man, whose ancestors have been violent, may find himself with more legacies on his hands than he can hope to carry out. The constant anxiety and watchfulness entailed by a lot of feuds is an inheritance calculated to make life a burden; and, wearied out, the Pathan's only resource is to leave his country for service in India, or to get the most troublesome of his quarrels patched up by the *jirgah*."

In Baluchistan, early society was organized under tribal chiefs. Each tribe had internal line of authority which peaked with the sardar (chief). *Jirgas* consisted of large landowners and tribal elders.

In Sindh and the Punjab, landlords owned most of the lands and local people worked for them, following either the *mustagiri* or *wand* systems of tenant-landlord relationship.

Under *wand*, tenants and landlords divided the crops yielded by the

---

10. **OLIVER, Edward E.**, Across The Border or Pathan and Biloch, 1890 Chapman and Hall, London; 1977 reprint by Al Biruni, Lahore, pp253-54

landlord's plot evenly. Under *mustagiri*, tenants gave a fixed share of each crop at harvest to the landlord.[11]

Under British encouragement the *jirga* evolved into a source of absolute authority.

British colonists ruling the Indian subcontinent before Pakistan was created did much to bolster the prestige and power of the *jirga*.

To the British, the *jirgas* represented a convenient means of indirectly controlling large sections of the population. By empowering jirgas and ensuring they toed the line, the colonial rulers were able to get their will implemented, without having to establish direct control and enforce their decisions.

Sir Robert Sandeman, a British administrator of Baluchistan in the 1870s, is considered the architect of the replacement of traditional rule by sardar in Baluchistan with the *jirga* system operating in the North West Frontier.

"Mr Sandeman was the first English officer to create a system for resolving disputes more easily. He established a jirga or panchayat of Balochi tribal chiefs so that the people could resolve their local disputes according to their own traditions. All the Balochi tribes accepted this idea unanimously and proceedings began to take place in accordance with this system…the way it worked helped a great deal in the administration of the area."[12]

Baloch historian Shah Mohammad Marri argues that before Sandeman introduced the jirga to Balochistan, the system of direct rule by sardars and tribal elders was effective.

"Disputes within a faction were resolved by the head of the faction. He would call both parties and decide their case using his own discretion in an open court. These decisions were generally fair because he had enough resources to investigate the root causes of the matter. Oaths were sworn on the Koran, kalima, a small mound of earth at the local court, all of which were held in deep respect by ordinary people. The court was held in an informal manner…With the implementation of Sandeman's system, an entire tribe was held responsible for a crime committed by one of its members."[13]

Mir Ahmed Yar Khan, a former ruler of Baluchistan's Kalat state, once the administrative centre of Baloch tribes, lambasted the British introduction of *jirgas* among Baloch tribes:

"On the judicial plane, a ludicrous innovation called the *jirga* system was

11. **AHMED, Jamil,** 1983. "Exchange Marriage System: An Ethnographic Study in a Seraiki Village" Research Report submitted in partial fulfillment M.A. Anthropology at Quaid-e-Azam University, Anthropology Department.

12. **RAM,** Rai Bahadar Hattoo: 'Tareekh-e-Balochistan (The History of Balochistan)', Sang-e-Meel Publications, 2001 pg 239

13. **MARRI, Shah Mohammad:** 'Baloch Qaum: Qadeem Uhad sai Asr-e-Hazir tak (The Baloch Nation: from the Ancient Era to Present Times). Takhleeqat, Lahore 2002.

introduced, supplanting the Islamic system of dispensing justice based on Shariah (Islamic laws) and sound Baloch traditions. What was all the more ridiculous was that all members of this '*jirga system*' were nominated by the (British) political agents in their respective regions. Appeals, if any, against *jirga* decisions were directed to be lodged with the agent to the governor-general of India, who would issue final orders in the name of the Khan-e-Baloch. Thousands of innocent people were harassed and put into jails without any trial. Justice was thus openly denied to the people," Khan wrote in his 1975 autobiography.[14]

The British legalised the equivalent Punjabi 'panchayat' system with the 1935 All Punjab Panchayat Act. They were regulated and accountable as conciliation courts. Panchayats were appointed by district commissioners or magistrates, and in some places elected. Their jurisdiction was defined in the mainstream law. They were given set terms of three years. Panchayat rulings were recorded in written form and furnished to those who requested them. They had a minimum five and maximum seven members. The panchayat chief was elected for one year.[15]

Marri argues the *jirga* once played an effective role, but has lost its effectiveness.

"The *jirga* system was undoubtedly a viable way to handle administrative work in the past, but it has created disputes and ill-feeling among the tribes and slowed down the spread of awareness and educational progress among the people. The chiefs and landlords have to great extent changed their role to become more involved in feudal and political power structures."

The system remains to this day strongest in rural areas still dominated by the tribal sardari (chiefs) system, where traditional sources of authority persist such as southern Punjab, Baluchistan, rural Sindh and the North West Frontier Province hugging Afghanistan.

## PROCESS

*Jirgas* and *panchayats* convene to resolve conflicts over the three 'z's: *zar* (gold/money), *zamin* (land), *zan* (women).

Conflicts over women range from rape, to divorce, honour killings, and 'love marriages' *i.e.* when a couple elopes against their tribes' wishes.

Commonly, *jirgas* and *panchayats* are convened on the request of a

---

14. **KHAN, Mir Ahmed Yar**: 'Inside Balochistan – Political Autobiography of Khan-e-Azam' Royal Book Company Karachi 1974 pg 124
15. **REHMAN, Rashid**, Human Rights Commission of Pakistan, Multan chapter, Interview October 12 2005

complainant to hear a particular case. Jirgas and panchayats may convene over a few hours, or several days. Some meet on a regular schedule.[16]

In theory, both parties should agree to the *jirga* hearing their case. However there are cases of people being 'tried' by *jirgas* without their consent.

*Jirga* hearings involve no lawyers and follow no defined criteria for evidence.

Sardars interviewed by Amnesty International researchers in 2002 said they learned how to conduct jirgas from their fathers.

"One sardar said: 'It's all in my head, there is no need to codify it... I have my own intelligence to tell me what is just.' Others have claimed that while not codified, the principles of tribal justice are well-defined."[17]

By tradition, the decision of the *jirga* or *panchayat* must be accepted by both parties. Until it is, the *jirga* or *panchayat* remains convened.[18]

"You have to convince both parties to agree.,." a sardar in Sindh told Amnesty International.

Yet there are plenty of cases of parties claiming after accepting the decision that they were forced at gunpoint to accept it—especially fathers who've given their daughters away to the male kin of the person their relative killed.

The judgement of the *jirga* and *panchayat* is final. There is no system of appeal against their arbitrary rulings.

Amnesty's study of the *jirga-panchayat* system listed the hallmarks of the process of a *jirga* and *panchayat*:

- Accused parties (so long as they are male) must appear in person to present their case. Some *jirgas* have reportedly been postponed when the accused did not present themselves.
- *Jirga* and *panchayat* members stay at the place of the trial as guests of the jury chief.

---

16. **Amnesty International:** 'Pakistan: The Tribal Justice System' 2002 "Tribal jirgas (literally: meeting; faislo, a Sindhi term for both the meeting and the decision; panchayat, council of elders) consisting of elders of the tribe and headed by the sardar (head of a tribe) or, if the dispute is of less importance, local heads of the tribe, can either be called on an ad hoc basis or take place regularly...Many sardars or lower tribal leaders hold regular adjudication days which are widely known and attended by people with a variety of complaints."
17. *ibid*
18. **Amnesty International** "Both the complainant and the accused have to agree to appear before the jirga and to submit to their decision. Proponents of the system have described it as democratic: 'A democratic system prevails among the tribes. People only come to the sardar if both parties agree... if the sardar is a respected person, people will come to him for resolution of conflicts,' a sardar told Amnesty International.

- If doubt hangs over statements made before the *jirga* or *panchayat*, an 'ameen' *i.e.* a reliable person may be asked to "vouch for the truthfulness of the statement by taking an oath on the Qur'an."
- Participants may nominate renowned members of other tribes as arbiters.
- Tribal elders or learned people may function as advisors known as *musheers*.
- Proceedings continue until a solution mutually agreeable to both parties is found, which could take several days in complicated cases.
- The presumption of innocence, access to a lawyer, questions of appeal and review are considered irrelevant to tribal judicial proceedings.

There is no limit to the seriousness of crimes brought before a jirga or *panchayat* for adjudication. In the first half of 2004 alone, at least 85 murder cases came before panchayats in Sindh province.[19]

## WOMEN

Women do not participate in *jirgas* and *panchayats*. Nor may they appear to give evidence, even when they are the victims or the accused.

"The participants of *jirgas* are exclusively male; women do not appear before tribal courts either as accused, complainants or witnesses, or even watch as mere spectators. Some sardars have stated that they have taken up women's cases, for instance when the custody of children is at stake. Women may then approach the sardar with the request to plead their cases against their husbands."[20]

Runaway brides, rape victims, 'black women' (called *kari*) who have stained a family's honour by being seen with the wrong man—or even just accused of such - are the subjects of most cases concerning women brought before a *jirga* or *panchayat*.

They will never be given the chance to explain or defend themselves, nor will a voice be given to any women plaintiffs, witnesses or character referees.[21]

---

19. **Human Rights Commission of Pakistan**, Annual Report, 2004
20. **Amnesty International**
21. *ibid:* "Women are not consulted when important decisions affecting their lives are made; even when they are handed over as part of a compensation agreement to settle a revenge killing or an 'honour' crime. The treatment they can expect in the family to which they are given cannot be thought to be sympathetic. Tribal leaders and others supporting this practice betray a high level of disregard for women's rights when they argue that the handing over of women to settle a dispute produces blood bonds which make for lasting peace and are therefore desirable."

When a woman is involved in the case, her father or brother appear before the jirga-panchayat to speak on her behalf.[22]

The male family members are left to pledge their agreement to the jirga or *panchayat verdict*. Women are not consulted on whether the *jirga*'s decision is acceptable.[23]

Honour killings have been ordered by jirgas.

When an honour killing has already occurred, *jirgas* convene to determine whether the crime was justified and adjudicate accordingly on compensation for the victim's family.

The burden of proof required to prove a woman's violation of honour (for example, illicit relations with a man from outside the family) is extremely low. The mere allegation of wrongdoing is often considered enough to justify honour killing.[24]

Pakistan's legal system, with in-built allowances for victims' families to pardon murderers in exchange for compensation in cash or in kind, makes it far easier to escape punishment for honour killings, than to escape punishment for murders over land or property.

In cases where women have been raped, a jirga has been known to rule that the rape victim has brought shame on her entire tribe and should therefore be killed to save her tribe's honour, as in the case of mentally disabled 16 year old rape victim Lal Jamilla Mandokhel.

In May 2006, two *jirgas* in Upper Dir district of North West Frontier Province issued veritable licences to kill. They vowed to punish or kill anyone caught reporting honour-related crimes to police.

---

22. **MUSTAFA, Zubeida:** 'Jirgas:Defying the Court' October 4, 2004. "Moreover, seeped as they are in patriarchal traditions, the jirgas do not acknowledge the woman's identity, let alone her rights. If she is involved in a case, her father or brother will speak on her behalf. A woman is not allowed to defend herself, especially is she is accused of being a kari and is presumed to be guilty." Pakistanlink.com

23. **Amnesty International:** "Women do not as a rule have access to the tribal justice system. If issues including inheritance or custody of children affecting women arise, they are usually settled in the family with women's interests represented – or misrepresented – by male relatives. Senator Jatoi summarized the situation: "In our system, we cannot call a woman to the jirga." Only in rare cases will jirgas deal with civil issues affecting women, for instance property disputes or inheritance or custody matters; in such forums, it has so far been inevitably men who represent women's interests there. Amnesty International was told that women's testimony would not be accepted in murder cases."

24. **Amnesty International:** "It is the rumour about a woman's inappropriate behaviour that damages the 'honour' of her family or community and the truth of such allegation is not sought to be established. Hence a woman's testimony on her own behalf is not heard at a jirga."

Anyone who reports an honour crime to authorities would be put to death by *jirga*, the *jirga* of Dogram Nihag Wari decreed. The *jirga* of neighbouring Nihag Darra decreed that local people would "take action" against anyone who files police charges against an 'honour killer'. The rulings effectively legitimize honour killings, in an area more adherent to the law of the *jirga* than the state of Pakistan.[25]

"The only victims of all this indifference and community cruelty would be women," Raza Rahman Khan, an analyst based in North West Frontier Province, wrote in The News.

While women do not feature in person in *jirgas* and *panchayats*, they play a star role in the punishments. As vassals of honour, they are given and taken as trophies of compensation.

*Vani* and *swara* compensation marriage pacts are the ultimate manifestation of the concept of woman as vassal of the family honour. A two-fold theory underscores *vani* and *swara* practices: that marriage between hostile tribes generates goodwill and stems further violence, and that women are the custodians of honour. The culprit is punished by having to send his girls to the 'enemy'.

*Vani* and *swara* brides are treated ignobly by the families they are sent to: as unpaid labour, mistresses, and oppressed wives.

The common *panchayat*-decreed punishment for rape in southern Punjab is the handover of a woman, in the guise of a compensatory marriage, according to Rashid Rehman, the chief human rights monitor in the southern Punjab.

"It's very usual in this part of the region—the giving of women in return for honour," he told me in an interview in his suffocating office in downtown Multan, as ineffectual ceiling fans scattered overflowing piles of documents and legal tomes over his crowded desk.

"In rape cases, the first attempt by the panchayat is to console the victim party. While trying to console the victim party, they are trying to treat the accused in the same way, because panchayats have no authority to imprison people or sentence them to torture, as the state has. To equalise the honour of both the victim and accused parties, the panchayats are normally using this method. To avoid criminal liability, they force the accused to give the hand of a lady from his family to the victim's family, to give a female in compensation. They may call it compromise or arranged marriage, but this is the situation."[26]

25. **KHAN, Raza Rahman,'Shrinking Living Space for Dir Women,'** The News, May 23 2006
26. **REHMAN, Rashid,** Human Rights Commission of Pakistan, Head of Multan Chapter, Interview, October 12, 2005

## JUDGEMENTS

The raison d'etre of *jirgas* and *panchayats* is to maintain the balance of 'honour' and end feuds by restoring harmony.

Adjudicating to restore violated honour takes precedence over establishing guilt or innocence, or sifting truth from rumour.[27]

Judgements often entail reversal of the wrong committed against the complainant party, for example in cases of robbery, return of stolen goods; or payment of compensation to the wronged party, in the form of money, property or women.[28]

*Jirgas* have a marked tendency to pass judgements in favour of the more influential and powerful party.

"Not a single *panchayat* will convene against a landlord or powerful person," Rashid Rehman said in our October 2005 interview.

"Normally a *panchayat* is convened against the weak party. But sometimes it depends upon the approach of victim. If the accused and the victim have the same weightage, the *panchayat* analyses the benefits of favouring each side."

In the case of 'love marriages', considered sinful because it involves couples choosing each other for spouses in defiance of their elders, errant couples have been killed as declared "adulterers". The errant groom often finds himself charged with abduction.

"*Jirgas* often rule that a woman marrying of her own choice must be 'returned' to her family, as if she were property. Worse, she may be declared a '*kari*' and thus liable to be killed as an adulteress along with her '*karo*' husband," according to activist Beena Sarwar.[29]

Of the 287 Pakistani women recorded as victims of honour killings in 2005, 20 were for 'love marriages', according to the Human Rights Commission of Pakistan's data.

A dead man in 2002 warranted compensation monies of 200,000 rupees, while a dead woman warranted twice the amount. The murder of a member of a tribal leader's family warranted 1.6 million rupees compensation.[30]

---

27. **Amnesty International**: "The purpose is to make peace, not to punish, the aim is not truth but reconciliation," Amnesty International was told repeatedly... . Justice is understood not in terms of punishment of the guilty leading to a process of remorse and eventual rehabilitation, but strictly in terms of conciliation brought about by restoring a balance disturbed by an offence."
28. **'Primitive Jirga Justice'**: Editorial, Dawn, October 13 2003 "These edicts are generally arbitrary and invariably discriminate against women, treating them as mere chattel to be exchanged to settle tribal disputes."
29. **SARWAR, Beena, "Jirga Injustice,"** The News, November 14 2004.
30. **Amnesty International** report on Tribal Justice System

## LEGAL FRAMEWORK

*Jirgas* and *panchayats* flourish with neither sanction nor explicit ban in Pakistani law. The exception are the regions officially zoned tribal areas: the "Federally-Administered Tribal Areas" (FATA) and "Provincially Administered Tribal Areas (PATA)".

The 1901 Frontier Crimes Regulation governing FATA and PATA sanctions *jirgas*.

FATA is the notorious northwest strip hugging the Afghan frontier. Its rocky moonscapes, Mars-like mountains and occasional forested slopes are the hideout of Al-Qaeda fugitives and probably, at times, Osama bin Laden. PATA covers tribal hinterlands further south, like Dera Ghazi Khan, which nominally fall under the Punjab provincial administration.

The closest they came to official recognition under national laws was 1963, under the West Pakistan Criminal Law (Amendment) Act 1963. At the time Pakistan was divided into East and West, East Pakistan later becoming Bangladesh. *Jirgas* and *panchayats* were approved to adjudicate on civil matters. But the 1963 law was later repealed.

The Constitution of Pakistan forbids courts other than state judiciary.

"No court shall have any jurisdiction save as is or may be conferred on it by the constitution or by or under any law," states Article 175 (1 and 2) of Part VII.

The tribal system of 'sardari rule' was explicity outlawed in 1976, under the System of Sardari (Abolition) Act of 1976. The act states in its preamble:

"The system of Sardari, prevalent in certain parts of Pakistan, is the worst remnant of the oppressive feudal and tribal system which, being derogatory to human dignity and freedom, is repugnant to the spirit of democracy and equality as enunciated by Islam and enshrined in the Constitution of the Islamic Republic of Pakistan and opposed to the economic advancement of the people."

But the only law or ruling expressly banning *jirgas* and *panchayats* is a breakthrough judgement by the Sindh High Court in 2004. The southern province of Sindh is one of the cradles of rule-by-panchayat. Sindh High Court Judge Rehmat Hussain Jafri banned tribal juries in a landmark ruling on April 24 2004, in response to a couple who sought the court's help to save them from murder by their tribe for marrying against the will of their elders.

The bride's father had threatened to kill her and declared her and her new husband "*kari*" and "*karo*": black woman and black man. A *jirga* nine days after their wedding ordered that the the bride be handed over for killing.

Justice Jafri declared trials by *jirga* in breach of the constitution and the law. He exhorted police to prevent *jirgas*.

"The private persons have no authority to execute the decision of *jirgas* nor the *jirgas* have the authority to execute their own decisions through their own sources. If such decisions are carried out and executed by killing persons, then the offence of murder will be committed and they will be liable for action as per the law... the *jirgas* have also usurped the powers of the executing authorities which is not permissible under the Constituion or the law," the 48-page judgement stated.

"It thus appears that jirgas are undermining or attempting to undermine the provisions of the Constitution...the purpose for which they assemble is unlawful."

"It is pertinent to point out that under the West Pakistan Criminal Law (Amendment) Act 1963, trials, which were commonly known as jirga trials, were permissible, but the said law has been repealed. As such the jirga system is unlawful and illegal which is against the provisions of the Constitution and the law of the land."

In a blatant snub to the judiciary, the Sindh government promptly legislated its way around the Sindh High Court ruling.

It drafted a bill, backdated to take effect from April 25 2004, one day after the High Court ban, called the "Sindh Amicable Settlement of Disputes Ordinance 2004". The bill proposed investing sweeping powers in a *jirga* chief appointed by disputing parties.

The Sindh government need not have bothered legislating to save the *jirga*. Their own Chief Minister went and sat on a panchayat within months of the High Court ban. So did Federal Minister Ghous Bux Khan Mahar, according to the Asian Human Rights Commission. Local Sindhi press reported that 25 *jirgas* – many of them peopled by government officials - took place in the six months immediately following the ban.[31]

The principal of buying one's way out of a jail or death sentence is not confined to the medieval tribal juries.

Incredulously, it is enshrined in Pakistan's very own mainstream law, the Pakistan Penal Code.

A sinister and creepy law called *Qisas* and *Diyat* was added to the Pakistan

---

31. **MUSTAFA, Zubeida,** The News, October 2004: "Since April 2004 when Justice Rehman Hussain Jafri of the Sindh High Court (Sukkur Bench) imposed a ban on the holding of jirgas in the province, the Sindhi press has reported 25 jirgas that have been held. What is worse, in many of these, members of political parties and local administration have taken part."
   **SARWAR, Beena,** "Jirga Injustice", The News, November 15 2004: ".. government
   a. functionaries ranging from chief ministers to union council nazims, continue to participate in
   b. these meetings, according to the list compiled from newspaper reports by the HRCP."

Penal Code by secular prime minister Nawaz Sharif in 1997. It legalizes the payment of money or property by a convicted murderer to his victim's family so he can dodge jail or execution.

*Qisas* essentially stands for eye-for-an-eye.

It is defined in the law as "punishment by causing similar hurt to convict at same part of body as victim; or by causing his death if he (the convict) has committed murder."

*Diyat* is defined as "compensation payable to heirs of a victim."

The *Qisas* and *Diyat* law gives the victim's family a huge say in determining the punishment of the person convicted by a court. In short, a murdered man's family may waive the convicted murderer's jail or death sentence in return for money or property. Under tribal law, girls are normally thrown in to the compensation package. While *Qisas* and *Diyat* does not list women as a permitted form of compensation, it does not explicity disallow it.[32]

The *Qisas* and *Diyat* principle can be taken as indirect legal sanction, by those who wish, of eye-for-an-eye justice.

"The attitude to take revenge is drawn from this particular law," Rashid Rehman told me.

"When the state has such laws, people get inspiration from that law, or that principle of law. It's very easy for people to have their own understanding that if the government is inflicting such punishments on people, why not give the same treatment as the government?"

*Qisas* and *Diyat* is tied in with one of the most damaging loopholes in Pakistani criminal law. The victim's family, and not the state, is the plaintiff. Murder is prosecuted as a crime against individuals, not against the state. Consequently, murder victims' relatives get more say in the punishment of the convicted murderer than the state does. It is a literal licence to kill in the name of honour.

Almost 100 percent of honour killings are committed within the family. Hence the victim's relatives and the murderer's relatives are usually the same. If a son kills his mother for even a rumour of illicit relations with another man, the murderous son's father or siblings are unlikely to enforce a jail sentence, because in tribal eyes the son's act of matricide 'restores honour' to their family.

Between 1998 and 2002, 1,464 honour killings were reported. According to Human Rights Commission of Pakistan (HRCP) data, 462 of the women were murdered by their brothers, 395 by their husbands, 103 by their fathers,

---

32. **Amnesty International**: "The amount of compensation is negotiable; the law stipulates that the giving of a woman in compensation is not a valid form of badal-i-sulah but does not explicitly prohibit the practice. In practice, courts repeatedly continue to accept women being handed over as part of a compensation settlement for murder."

58 by their sons, 60 by their in-laws, and 217 by other relatives. That accounts for 1,295 or 88.5 percent of cases. Arrests were made in around 15 percent of cases. The Interior Ministry estimates 4,100 women were murdered in honour killings in the four years from 2002 to 2005.

In 2005, 287 honour killings were documented by the HRCP. The women were shot, stabbed, strangled, axed, beaten with sharp objects, electrocuted, hung, poisoned, clubbed or set ablaze. Close male relatives were the killers of 222 (77 percent) of the 287 reported victims. Eighty-one accused killers were apprehended.

"*Qisas and Diyat* law regards the offences of physical injury, manslaughter and murder not as directed against the order of the state, but against the person of the victim... Under the *Qisas and Diyat* law, the punishment for murder may be either in the form of *qisas*, *i.e.* a punishment equal to the offence committed, or in the form of *tazir*, *i.e.* discretionary punishment. The concept of *qisas* is defined as "punishment by causing similar hurt at the same part of the body of the convict as he has caused to the victim, or by causing his death is he has committed *qatl-i-amd* (intentional killing), in exercise of the right of the victim or a *wali* (heir of the victim, or provincial government if there is no heir). In the case of murder this means that if the relevant rules of evidence are fulfilled, the heirs of the victim have the right to have *qisas* inflicted on the offender. The heirs may waive this right however at any stage, in which case the death penalty cannot be imposed as a *qisas* punishment. The evidentiary requirements for the imposition of the death penalty as a qisas punishment are the confession of the accused before a competent court of the fulfillment of rules of evidence laid down in the *Qanun-e-Shahadat* [law of evidence] of 1984. If these standards are not fulfilled, the court can impose punishments, including the death penalty, as *tazir* punishments, *i.e.* discretionary punishment, if it finds the offender guilty of murder."[33]

The role of the court is virtually reduced to acting as go-between and validating any compensation pact between heirs and killer—essentially, deals of blood justice.

"In *qisas* cases, the law changes the role of the court in the prosecution of murder from the role played by a court before the *Law of Qisas and Diyat* was introduced: its role is merely to ensure fair passage of the case, but the victim's heirs have the right to decide whether or not prosecution is to continue and the punishment be inflicted. Death sentences can only be carried out once confirmed by the appropriate High Court, but even once so confirmed, the heirs of the victim can still pardon the convict and accept compensation, *badal-i-sulha*. An execution can be halted by the heirs 'even at the last moment before the execution of the sentence'. The execution must be carried out in the presence of the heirs, and courts have debated whether the mode of carrying it out as *qisas* may or must involve the heirs actually carrying it out."[34]

33. *ibid*
34. *ibid*

In late 2004 the parliament approved revolutionary laws outlawing honour killings and the practices of *vani* and *swara*. The laws were signed off by President Musharraf in January 2005.

The new laws classify honour killings as premeditated murder with the maximum sentence of death. Parents who give away their daughters as *vani* or *swara* brides, along with the parties who receive *vani* or *swara* brides, are liable to 10 years jail.

However there is no federal law or Supreme Court ruling against *jirgas* and *panchayats*, and the law of *Qisas and Diyat* remains. Under mainstream law, families of murder victims may still pardon murderers, after a court conviction, in return for compensation in money or property. In the ways of the tribe, the most prized piece of property is woman.

## Popular and Official Attitudes

While the tribal justice system is a source of injustice, particularly for women, the poor and the disenfranchised, popular opinion is generally in favour of *jirgas* and *panchayats* over the mainstream justice system.

Courts and police flounder under delays, corruption, bribe demands, and poor resources. Official channels of justice are seen in rural areas as the source of even less justice than what tribal juries mete out.

In official circles, *jirgas* and *panchayats* are tolerated and in many cases condoned.

Government members concede the mainstream justice system is floundering and overburdened. It suits the government to have an alternative system to prevent further overburdening of the courts.

Critics say large landowners perpetuate the *jirga* system as it maintains their status quo by affirming their power and prestige.

Villagers in the southern Punjab believe *panchayats* never rule against large landowners.

Several grand feudal lords and tribal chiefs who sit in the parliament also sit occasionally on *jirgas* and *panchayats* and help to shape judgements and punishments.

"These feudal lords are highly influential and control decision-making processes, parliament and determine societal norms whether good or bad...The feudal mentality has pervaded the modern urban life. MNAs, senators and ministers have supported *jirga* and *panchayat* systems as it helps them perpetuate their authority in their areas... *Jirga* and *panchayat* systems will remain in place as long as feudal and tribal systems continue to exist despite being declared unlawful by a high court," according to constitution expert Abdi Hassan Minto.[35]

---

35. **'Call to Abolish Jirga, Panchayat Systems'**, Dawn, September 25 2004

*Panchayats* and feudal landowners in southern Punjab are incestuously connected.

"*Panchayats* are not only connected to but also supported by feudals. In some cases they are chiefs of the *panchayat*," Rashid Rehman told me.

"It suits feudals because they don't want the people to approach state institutions. To shorten people's exposure to legal institutions, as the feudals don't want people to be acquainted with legal institutions, they're trying to maintain the role of agents between the people and the institutions. So they do not tolerate people themselves approaching or having access to the institutions."

The scions of feudal land-owning families wind up in the parliaments or the federal cabinet with ease, by virtue of their family names, especially in rural Sindh or southern Punjab. The cycle of feudal landowner protecting the *panchayat* protecting the feudal landowner is perpetuated.

Rarely if ever do police or local administrators prevent the holding of *jirgas* or *panchayats* in their areas; rare also are the occasions when police prevent the enforcement of *jirga* or *panchayat* judgements. It usually takes a *suo moto* intervention by the Supreme Court to do so, as the apex court has done in several well-reported *vani* cases.

In 2001, the Dera Ghazi Khan district administration convened a large *jirga* of elders from Punjab and Baluchistan provinces to settle a feud between the Buzdar and Jafar clans, both Baloch tribes.

The Sindh provincial administration once took a tribal chief out of prison so he could chair a *jirga*, according to I.A. Rehman, former chair of the Human Rights Commission of Pakistan.[36]

In fact, the tribal jury system has virtually put the official justice system on trial in several cases documented in Sindh.

A *jirga* in the Sindh district of Nawabshah in 1999 tried a police officer for torturing a detainee to death. The *jirga* convicted the police officer and fined him 300,000 rupees. In November 1998 in Khairpur district, also in Sindh, a former police officer was convicted by a *jirga* made up of Odho tribal elders of killing a landowner from their tribe. He was made to pay 400,000 rupees to the murdered landowner's family. In 2001, another Sindh tribal *jirga* in Rohri district convicted three police officers of killing a woman extra-judicially during a raid. The jirga ordered the three policemen to pay 1.2 million rupees to the families of the dead woman and several people injured in the raid.[37]

---

36. 'Dark Justice' Newsline Magazine, August 2002: "Quite often jirgas are held at official premises and attended by district officials including police officers. … Nazims (mayors) too have attended jirga proceedings. The jirga system has also been strengthened by official sanction."

37. **Amnesty International**

At least one *jirga* was even held in a jailhouse.

In 1998 Sindh provincial authorities asked tribal leader Sardar Khadim Hussain Jatoi to hold a *jirga* in the courtroom of the Central Jail of Sukkur, a rural area of northern Sindh where feudal lords hold sway. He was asked to help resolve an eight year feud between clans of the Dhareja tribe in which eight tribesmen had been killed. The jailhouse *jirga* directed each side to pay 200,000 rupees for each life taken. The settlement was brokered within four hours and murder charges were dropped.[38]

Ruling figures' support of the *jirga* and *panchayat* system was boldly lambasted by the Asian Human Rights Commission.

"Many tribal leaders themselves are parliamentarians, members of the civil administration or men with family links to the authorities. The AHRC criticizes these leaders for being hypocritical as they talk about human rights for all in their official capacities, yet take part in tribal courts in their constituencies.

Even judges and lawyers favour the use of feudal methods to resolve disputes, despairing that the judicial system and the courts are not up to the task.

It has even been openly admitted and used as an argument in the courts that it is the usual practice for feudal lords to put pressure upon the parties in a criminal case to surrender and reach a negotiated settlement to avoid criminal punishment."[39]

Proponents of *jirgas* and *panchayats* argue that people in remote areas can seek mediation without paying lawyers, bribing police and traveling long distances. But just as compelling is the appeal of one's own immediate peers knuckling out resolutions according to one's tribal values:

"Matters are adjudicated upon by the peers of the persons involved, cases remain within the community and the shame generated by wider publicity is avoided. All issues are promptly settled. The norms of settlement enjoy the sanction of tradition and are accepted more willingly than state laws that ordinary villagers cannot comprehend," according to former Human Rights Commission of Pakistan chairman I.A. Rehman.[40]

At the end of the day, the instant free justice of the *jirga* and the *panchayat* suits poor villagers almost as much as they suit the influential landowners and tribal chiefs.

"The weak are trying to get their issues resolved through *sardars*, and *panchayats*.They have no money to satisfy the demands of police officers," said Rashid Rehman.

---

38. **ibid.**
39. **Asian Human Rights Commission**
40. **'Dark Justice'** Newsline Magazine, August 2002

"Those who have (unofficial) authority don't want to involve law-enforcing agencies, because if they involve law-enforcing agencies and institutions, the game will slip out of their hands. Although law-enforcing agents are doing whatever the influential agents (*i.e.* powerful figures) are demanding, in some cases the powerful have apprehensions that the police may not accept their demands. This is why they are maintaining the panchayat system, even though it's not supported by law."

*    *    *    *

In 2002 it was charged and widely reported that Mukhtar Mai was gang-raped on the orders of a 14-member *panchayat* which had convened to adjudicate the alleged rape of Salma Mastoi by Mukhtar's teenage brother Abdul Shakoor. The prosecution charge was that two of Salma's older brothers and two cousins executed an allegedly *panchayat*-ordered punishment of gang-rape. It charged that Faiz Muhammad Mastoi, described as a landlord and tribal chief, chaired the supposed *panchayat* which gave the bestial order.

The Mastoi family however, say there was no *panchayat*. A few dozen, perhaps 30, Mastoi men had gathered outside the home of Salma Mastoi when word spread that she had been raped in the sugarcane by the boy from another tribe, Mukhtar Mai's brother Shakoor.

A number of Mastois had earlier assembled at a nearby Mastoi home to pray for a recently deceased kinsman.

The Mastois say their gathering was an *'akath'*—a gathering of one tribe. An *akath* is not a tribal jury which mediates between two disputing parties and issues punishments.

Unlike standard *panchayats* described by researchers and analysts, the Mastois gathering on June 22 did not take place at the home of a tribal chief or local landlord. It took place outside the home of Salma Mastoi's family, one of the poorest in the village of Mirwala.

The agreement of both sides to the 'punishment' (*i.e.* the punishment of gang-rape alleged by the prosecution) was not sought. The accused person in this case, Mukhtar Mai's brother Abdul Shakoor, did not appear in person. His family was not asked to speak on his behalf. The supposed *panchayat* did not include any feudal lords, large landowners, or tribal chiefs. Faiz Muhammad Mastoi, described by the prosecution as the panchayat chief, was 35 years old at the time. The 15 to 16 acres of land he owned at the time is a fraction of what large landowners possess. Feudal lords' estates are in the range of thousands or tens of thousands of acres. The largest landowning clan in Mirwala is the Jatois. Three Jatoi men represented not the Mastoi family, but Mukhtar Mai's family: Maulvi Abdul Razzaq, his brother Haji Altaf Hussain, and Manzoor Ahmad Khan Jatoi.

Six of the 14 Mastoi men accused of being members of the *panchayat* were poor villagers from Jampur district, on the other side of the Indus River from Mirwala—a journey of three and a half hours by road, and the same traveling time by foot and boat. They included Khalil Mastoi, the man Salma Mastoi was married off to five days after the incident, plus his father, three uncles, and a brother-in-law.

Two other men accused of being members of the *panchayat* and convicted—then later acquitted by the High Court—of abetting the gang-rape were Faiz Muhammad Mastoi and Ramzan Pachaar, both around 35 years old. Pachaar was a close friend of Mukhtar's older brother Hazoor Bakhsh. He lived in the neighbouring village of Rampur and was neither a landowner of any note (he owned a paltry half-acre of land), nor a tribal elder.

The four men convicted of gang-rape—of whom three were later acquitted by the High Court—and accused of sitting on the alleged *panchayat* were:

Allah Ditta Mastoi, the second oldest of Salma's brothers, married with children, aged 24 or 25.

Abdul Khaliq Mastoi, Salma's third oldest brother, unmarried, aged 20 to 22.

Ghulam Fareed Mastoi, then 35 or 36 (allegedly wrongfully arrested as substitute for suspect of same name)

Muhammad Fayyaz Mastoi, aged 22 to 23 (allegedly wrongfully arrested as substitute for suspect of same name).

The original trial judge threw out allegations that the six men from Jampur district and two others from Rampur village were part of the *panchayat*.

Judge Zulfikar Ali Malik stated in his August 2002 summation that the eight men he acquitted had not been named in Mukhtar Mai's first complaint to the police, nor in her supplementary statements to the police, nor in her deposition to the investigating magistrate.

"She was duly confronted with her previous statement where their names are not mentioned. They have been found innocent by all the Inquiry Officers, there is no allegation against them, except their mere participation in the *panchayat*. Learned defence submitted that six of the said accused persons belong to Jampur (in a neighbouring district) and Rampur (a neighbouring village) so their identification by Mukhtiar Mai complainant, a *purda nashin* woman (a veiled woman observing *purdah*, living in seclusion) is doubtful."[41]

The judge considered that a woman observing *purdah* was unlikely to know the identities of men living in another house, another village, let alone another district.

"In the aforesaid facts and the circumstances, the aforesaid eight accused persons are acquitted of the charges, on account of the benefit of doubt. They be released forthwith, if not required in any other case."

---

41. **Dera Ghazi Khan Anti Terrorism Court,** Judgement of Justice Zulfikar Ali Malik, August 31 2002

Judge Zulfikar Ali Malik however concluded that six men—the four alleged rapists plus Faiz Muhammad Mastoi and Ramzan *Pachaar*—had "*convened a panchayat.*"

"I find that Abdul Khaliq and Allah Ditta, sons of Imam Bakhsh; Muhammad Fayyaz, Ghulam Fareed (Mastoi), Ramzan Pachar and Faiz Muhammad, in prosecution of their common design, convened a *panchayat*, mostly of their Mastoi Baluch tribe of the area."

He uses the term 'mostly' to describe the Mastoi-dominated makeup of the alleged six-man panchayat. Other than the presence of Ramzan Pachaar, the men accused of taking part in the alleged panchayat were exclusively Mastoi.

I met the chief prosecutor from the August 2002 trial, Khalid Ramzan Joya, almost four years later. He is an eminent barrister of Multan, who was asked by the Punjab government to head the prosecution team in the trial of Mukhtar Mai's alleged attackers.

I asked him whether the gathering of Mastoi men actually constituted a *panchayat* or an *akath*. If there really was a *panchayat*, I wanted to know how many people were on it. The prosecution had said in court that up to 200 people were present. It had never been made clear why only 14 men were identified and charged, if 14 times that number were present.

The barrister gave seemingly contradictory replies.

"The *panchayat* was made up of Tatla Gujjars and Mastois," Joya replied at first. Tatla-Gujjar is the tribe to which Mukhtar Mai belongs.

I asked how many people in total sat on the supposed panchayat.

"Only two people," he said this time.

"From the Tatla Gujjar side there were none, because they were not in a position to give anyone. In this case, only Ramzan Pachaar and Faiz Mastoi were on the panchayat."

That's not what the trial court was told. The prosecution said 14 men sat on the supposed panchayat. In his conclusion the trial judge named six men as participators in the supposed panchayat.

"Normally, you have two people from one side, and two from the other side, and one is selected as the 'panch', the head. But even one person on his own can be a panchayat," barrister Joya elaborated.

"So, apart from Ramzan Pachaar, Faiz Mastoi and the four accused rapists, why were eight other men brought to court accused of sitting on the supposed panchayat?" I asked.

"They were present. The other eight joined in the proceedings by showing their presence, signaling 'don't worry, we are behind you.' They were not regular members of the panchayat. They facilitated the panchayat, they aided members of the panchayat," the barrister replied.

"But if close to 200 people were present, as Mukhtar Mai and Maulvi Abdul Razzaq said, why were only eight of the 200 brought to court for 'being present'?" I asked.

"These eight were nominated by Mukhtar Mai as active members of the *akath*," he replied.

I didn't ask the barrister why he was now speaking of an *akath*.

He seemed unaware that the judge had clearly pointed out stating himself, that Mukhtar Mai had not named the eight men herself in her statements to police after police investigators declared it same in court.

The trial court judge himself had stated that Mukhtar Mai had never named the eight men in her statements to police or the investigating magistrate.

I asked the barrister why a 35 year old man would be made head of the supposed panchayat.

"Faiz Mastoi was indeed young, but due to his monetary situation, and his involvement with the local council, he used to decide the matters relating to his tribe, feuds between the tribes, and matters relating to the police," the barrister explained.[42]

One of the main investigating police officers in the Mukhtar Mai case resurfaced a few years later in one of the Indus River districts in southern Punjab.

*"This was not a formal panchayat, it was an akath," he said in a private interview in May 2006, at home in his new posting.*[43]

He would only discuss the case on condition of anonymity.

Police arrested the eight Mastois accused of participation in the panchayat and charged with abetment because police were told they had returned to Jampur district across the Indus after the "akath".

However, the investigating police were not "confident that they were actually culprits" in the alleged gang-rape of Mukhtar Mai, the officer said.

For his part, Maulvi Razzaq maintains that 200 to 250 people were present at the gathering.

"It was not an akath, it was a formal panchayat," he said in a private interview at his mosque after evening prayers on a summer evening in May 2006.[44]

The cleric put the number of people on the supposed panchayat at four.

"Faiz Mastoi, Ramzan Pachaar, Manzoor Khan Jatoi, and myself," he stated.

---

42. Interview, Multan, April 28 2006
43. Interview, Dera Ghazi Khan, May 12, 2006
44. Interview, Mirwala Village, May 16, 2006

Every village in the Punjab has a police informer, known as the 'lumberdar.'

The lumberdar of Mirwala village, Mulazim Hussain Jatoi, says he did not witness the gathering. But he says villagers described the gathering as an "akath of a large number of people."[45]

The head of the Multan chapter of the Human Rights Commission of Pakistan, Rashid Rehman—who has spent years documenting rights abuses in the southern Punjab—called the gathering an "illegal assembly."

"This was not a formal panchayat," he told me in our first interview in his office in 2004.[46]

The gathering in Mirwala village on the day into the night of June 22, 2002 differed most strikingly from panchayats and jirgas documented in studies and newspaper reports in a key feature: the appearance of a woman. The alleged summonsing of a woman to seek pardon on behalf of a male relative – in this case Mukhtar Mai appearing on behalf of her accused teenage brother – is in reverse to the norms, under which men appear on behalf of women, while women are kept invisible.

"The participants of *jirgas* are exclusively male; women do not appear before tribal courts either as accused, complainants or witnesses, or even watch as mere spectators," according to Amnesty International's study of the tribal justice system.

In cases of alleged rape, says Rashid Rehman, it is customary for a panchayat to order the hand over of a woman from the accused party to the victim party, in the guise of compensatory marriage.

"It's very usual in this part of the region—the giving of women in return for honour," he said.

"In rape cases, the first attempt by the panchayat is to console the victim party. While trying to console the victim party, they are trying to treat the accused in the same way. To equalise the honour of both the victim and accused parties, the *panchayats* are normally using this method. To avoid criminal liability, they force the accused to give the hand of a lady from his family to the victim's family, to give a female in compensation. They may call it compromise or arranged marriage, but this is the situation."[47]

45. Interview, Farooqia Mosque, Mirwala, May 16, 2006
46. Interview, Multan, August 2004
47. **REHMAN, Rashid,** Human Rights Commission of Pakistan, Head of Multan Chapter, Interview, October 12 2005

# 23

# Custodian of the Cotton Map

*"Son, may God make you a Patwaari."*

*Blessing from unnamed village woman to senior administrator.*

**Disputes over land ownership are the most common cause of litigation in Pakistan. A staggering 82% of all litigation concerns land ownership disputes, mainly due to fraudulent dealings.*[1]

Every village has one, but in Mirwala his name means 'monsoon.'

The *patwaari* makes every villager tremble slightly. He is the lowest in the centralized hierarchy of government revenue officials, his ranking a grade 5—the pay scale of a junior clerk; yet as the keeper of land records and collector of taxes, he wields the most power in every Pakistani village.

So much so that many economic reform organisations are campaigning to dilute his inordinate tax-collecting powers and custodianship of property deeds.

But even recent sweeping devolution reforms of 2001 failed to touch the *patwaari*. As for the 1973 Land Reform attempts to redistribute feudal estates to workers, many a patwaari has colluded with feudal landlords to resist registering land as they were supposed to do in the names of workers and serfs.[2]

"Son, may God make you a *patwaari*," is the oft-repeated benediction of a village woman to a Deputy Commissioner, the highest civil service ranking in the districts.

*Patwaaris* are at the bottom end of a land and revenue administrative system that was conceived by 16th century ruler of the Indian subcontinent, Sher Shah Suri. But they are the custodians of all land records, and the lynchpin of crops revenue collection across Pakistan's four provinces.

Five centuries on, the system is still in use: land title registers across Pakistan have managed to resist computerisation and are maintained manually, in

1. Blue Chip: "Many have seen to it that the 1973 Land Reforms that re-distributed land from the large landowners to long-term occupiers or workers on the land are not implemented.
2. Blue Chip: This has created a situation whereby people continue to work on the land of their 'landlord' without knowing that they are actually the official owners."

hand-scribbled ledgers decipherable only by the most junior clerk of the Board of Revenue: the *patwaari*.

The implications for doctoring, manipulation, fraud, tax evasion, bank loans, sales and investment are staggering. The archaic system is estimated to cost Pakistan billions of dollars in lost investment potential.

The system was the brainchild of Sher Shah Suri, a rebel Pashthun warrior who had interrupted the reign of the Mughal emperors and ruled for five years in the early 1500s. His more famous legacy is the Great Trunk Road, which still runs from Kabul to Calcutta.

Sher Shah commissioned the first map of the subcontinent, to initiate a system of land revenue collection. He created *qanoongos* and *patwaaris* to collect tax on the produce of owners' land: a quarter to a third to be paid to the state in cash or kind.[3]

Sher Shah Suri's administration gave each owner of land a patta or title deed. From this originates the term '*patwaari*'.

The system was refined by Raja Todar Mal, finance minister in Mughal Emperor Akbar's cabinet of "nohdakh" (nine jewels).

British colonists later adopted it during the 19th and 20th century Raj.

It was further consolidated in land legislation as recent as the 1967 Land Record Act and the 1968 Land Revenue Rules, under military ruler General Ayub Khan.

In the *patwaaris*' hands are no less than 17 ledgers – two of them particularly critical: the crops registry or '*Khasar Girdawari*'; and land ownership records. They are kept in a cloth bag called the basta.

By law, the patwaari may never let the ledgers out of his sight.

He also maintains the Lal Kitaab: the 'Red Book.' In this he records extraordinary events on a particular property. Another register records the family tree of a landowner.

"All these registers are cross-linked and are quite scientific in theory. In practice, however, the system is a mess,"[4] the business magazine BLUE CHIP wrote in 2004.

"They are written by hand in the Urdu Nastaleekh script and are full of strange squiggles, crossings out and, to most people, look like gibberish. It is very likely that this is done deliberately by the patwaari to increase his own power and make the record look even more confusing than it actually is. It also makes it easier to tamper with the records and indulge in fraud."

\* \* \* \*

3. Blue Chip: "Collection of revenue was conducted by officers called Qanoongos and Patwaaris, who were instructed to show leniency at the time of assessment and strictness at the time of collection."
4. Blue Chip

"You must meet the *patwaari*," an anthropologist at the Folklore Heritage Institute advised me one autumn morning in Islamabad. It was the first I'd heard of such a position.

"He is usually a very nasty little man. He holds all the records, and all the gossip of the village."

It was spring by the time I found the *patwaari* of Mirwala.

## March 2006 Multan

Spring wheat shoots have turned the southern Punjab radiant green. Towering sugarcane is under late harvest all along the highways.

Sawan "Monsoon" Razza, the *patwaari* of Mirwala, removes the *Khasar Girdawari* and property-deeds register from a stained cream cloth in which they have been wrapped for his journey into the City of Saints from the crop-rich Indus plains. The cloth is tied and knotted like a swag around the ribbon-bound ledgers.

He stands and unfurls the discoloured cloth. Suddenly it is no longer a swag, but a giant faded cotton map.

I behold the *Aks Shajra*.

On the huge cotton cloth is etched every single plot of the *mauza* (village) of Mirwala. The crooked south-west border is the River Indus. Each plot is outlined and numbered.

*"Why not use paper?"* I ask.

*"Paper rips and tears,"* Monsoon Raza replies matter-of-factly. *"And cotton cloth is easier to wrap and carry around."*

About two square metres in size, the *Aks Shajra* is the "reflection of the pedigree of land located in the village," explains the *tehsildar* of Jatoi sub-district, three rungs up the hierarchy from the *patwaari*. Its origins date back to the Mughal era.

The *tehsildar* (sub-district administrator) Ashfaq Ahmad Qureshi has accompanied his *patwaari* for this meeting. So has the deputy *patwaari*. "Monsoon" Raza is largely silent and seemingly respectful as the *tehsildar* does all the talking. In this context at least the hierarchy is respected.

The cotton map system dates back to the Mughals. When the cloth starts to disintegrate, the map is redrawn on a fresh square of cotton.

"Monsoon" Raza points to one of the small squares, labelled 38/1/1.

"This is the field where the incident began," tehsildar explains. It is the sugarcane field between Mukhtar Mai's house and the Mastois' house, the field where Abdul Shakoor allegedly raped Salma Mastoi under the cover of the cane crops.

The *tehsildar* puts out his hand and the *patwaari* hands him the *Khasar Ghirdawari*. The crops ledger is open at the page where the amount of crops collected from each plot during the *khasif* season of October-December 2002 is recorded.

They point to a column marked 38/1/1.

"In this year madam, four kanals of cotton crops were recorded. The record is silent on sugarcane. This means not enough sugarcane was harvested to warrant recording. This means the sugarcane in that field in that year only grew in small patches. In late June-early July the sugarcane is four to five feet high."

\* \* \* \*

Each *patwaari* rules over a *patwaari* circle. The present-day electoral commission uses the *patwaari* circle to delimit the provincial and national assembly seats.

"The *Patwaari* cannot be a good man," Qamar, my erstwhile fixer and guide to Multan, declares sardonically on our way to meet the keeper of the key records and the cotton map.

"Why not?"

"He is the collector of taxes and bribes," Qamar replies. He pauses, and breaks into customary giggles.

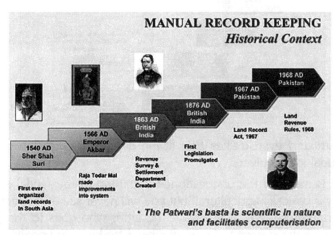

**MANUAL RECORD KEEPING**
*Historical Context*

* *The Patwari's basta is scientific in nature and facilitates computerisation*

Countless columnists and letters to newspaper editors have railed against the persistent stranglehold of the *patwaari* on rural life, 500 years on from Emperor Akbar's reign, bemoaning the failure of the recent devolution program and campaigns for administrative reforms to knock him off his lucrative throne.

"None of them, so far as my information goes, bothered to cut the *patwaari* down to size, something inconceivable nowadays when the federal and provincial governments claim that everything is being computerised," wrote Hafizur Rahman in *The News English-language daily*. (25/02/06).

"The power of the *patwaari* lies in the fact that he is the custodian of the revenue record of his circle...not only is he the keeper of the record but also the only one who fully comprehends it. Highly talented is the *tehsildar* or *naib tehsildar* who can beat the *patwaari* at this comprehension, while the deputy commissioner (or whoever has replaced him) who could do so is still to be born. So they used to say in the Punjab."

Rahman calls the *patwaari* "the most powerful official in the villages where his writ runs."

Qualification requires matriculation. Aspiring *patwaaris* attend a *patwaar* school for two years.

The *patwaari* "has almost life-and-death control over variations in the record that he can manipulate, to the advantage or loss of the landowner or tenant. Both are at his mercy.

Everything revolves around him and this is where corruption starts—the tremendous authority and meagre salary."

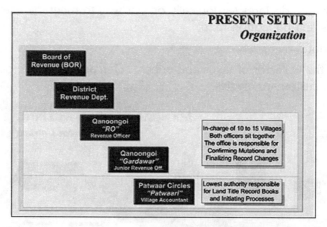

The *patwaari* even makes *Pirs* (living descendants of Sufi saints) and Punjabi feudal lords quiver:

"Much is made of the unquestioned dominion of the feudal lord in the system that is basically agricultural, but you will never see a *patwaari* bowing and scraping before him. It is always the latter who goes to the *patwaari* when he wants the system to be manipulated for his own benefit," Rahman railed.

"*Pirs* have a great hold over the mass of our people—even over those who are highly educated and otherwise enlightened. But in the people's book the *patwaari* takes precedence over the spiritual mentor. It is an apt illustration of the Punjabi adage: '*The fist is nearer than God.*'

"The case of his powers is unique. They may not find a match anywhere else in the world—a small official exercising enormous authority by virtue of his specialised knowledge of an intricate system of land revenue. I don't think routine reforms can find a replacement for him...I am sure the great experts of the (World) Bank would go into a spin if they were ever confronted by the *patwaari's* books and ledgers. It's a different language altogether."

The notorious *Nawab* (ruler) of Kalabagh district—on the remote northwest bank of the Indus 300 kilometres north of Mirwala—monstrous in his reputed treatment of serfs and foes, petted his *patwaari*. Rumour has it that the Nawab fed his *patwaari* and his family from his feudal kitchen three times a day.[5]

"He is truly the one man around whom the rural economy revolves," Rahman concluded.

\*   \*   \*   \*

Nearly 14,000 *patwaaris* operate in Pakistan, handling approximately 190 million land records containing the details of 150 million landowners – all in manual form.[6]

Each *patwaari* is assigned responsibility for the original records of two to eight revenue estates. One revenue estate may cover one large village or two to three small villages.

"Inexplicably, the original land records of a particular area are in the custody of the patwaaris, who are also the sole custodians of the records of government lands," Blue Chip wrote.

"A *patwaari* is required to keep the original land records with him at all times and has the authority to make changes relating to ownership, use and taxation in the original record. The *patwaari* is entitled to make changes in the original record books and is also the issuing authority of evidence of title or *fard*. A *patwaari* can easily issue a title in the wrong name and thereby create a bogus sale transaction. Large landowners have also been in the habit of bribing *patwaaris* to tamper with land records and adjust them in their favour."

No centralised record of land ownership between different areas exists. To determine one person's property across country means checking the land registers of different *patwaaris* for different areas. As land records are the basis for calculating income tax, the *patwaari* system.

Recording "mutations" or transfers of land ownership through sale or inheritance provides a further window for abuse by the *patwaari*. It is a laborious and time-consuming process of cross-indexing all the *patwaari's* 17 registers.

Details of mutations are updated every four years. Amendments are made in red ink. A completely new book is prepared each four years.

"Therefore, at any given time, a register of landowning is a historical record, not a current record. To further complicate the matter, some *patwaaris* have used the whole amendment procedure to make the land records yet more indecipherable," Blue *Chip wrote.*

---

5.   The News, February 25, 2006
6.   Blue Chip

"Large landowners have the financial resources to ensure that the records are adjusted in their favour."

\* \* \* \*

Hard statistics can be hard to come by in Pakistan, outside of sport. In three years reporting on Pakistan, one of my almost daily frustrations was the difficulty in obtaining solid statistics to give a story backbone.

I soon realized I couldn't blame my team of reporters. The officials they were contacting simply didn't have many statistics to hand, or none that were updated or relevant. Sometimes principles of state secrecy overruled. Getting hold of estimates of the number of Pakistani soldiers killed in the 1971 war with Bangladesh was impossible. A report exists but it is confidential.

I eventually found that the disregard for preciseness was part of village life.

"How far to the shrine of your ancestors' *pir* (spiritual guide)?" I asked Mukhtar Mai's kind-faced mother, who had just finished recounting to me the doomed prophecy the family pir (spiritual mentor) had foretold for her daughter 10 years earlier.

"If you leave in the night, you reach in the day. If you leave in the day, you reach in the night," she replied.

Naseem, Mukhtar's city-educated 'secretary', piped up: "It's about three and a half hours."

"How much water courses through this stream in summer?" an engineer asked the chief of a village where a new reservoir was to be built. "A lot, sahib. A lot of water."

Assessing how many women die in honour crimes in a certain year is an art of estimation. The Human Rights Commission's annual report is a collation of local newspaper reports.

So meeting the *patwaari* of Mirwala and his supervising *tehsildar* was an encounter of joyous statistical discovery. The two ledgers he brought wrapped in the cloth map contained facts and statistics that were beautiful in their coldness and hardness. It was a quenching of statistical thirst.

The *tehsildar* pronounces the facts with the overly-slow clarity of a schoolmaster, and the occasional dramatic flourish of a stage performer, as he delivers the key statistics of Mirwala:

• The Mastois are the fourth largest caste among Mirwala's 3,360 residents.

• The largest caste are the Jatois – also a sub-tribe of the Baloch.

• The largest landowners in Mirwala village are the Jatois, possessing 600 acres of the total 1,536 acres that make up Mirwala (more than one-third of Mirwala's total area).

Mir Khan Jatoi was the first to settle the village of Mirwala, around 1860. As he cultivated the land the area became known as Mir-Wala. Tribes of Pachaars, Ghazlianis, Lasharis and Mastois were the first to follow.

Maulvi Razzaq, the Mirwala cleric who supported Mukhtar Mai's family in the alleged gang-rape case, belongs to the Jatois.

Second in size after the Jatois are the Bokharis, followed by the Rajputs. After the Mastois in fourth place are the Khokars, Patavys, Ghazlianis, Bunds, Lagharis, Chijerahs and Koolungs. Gujjars, including the Tatla Gujjar clan of Mukhtar Mai, are among the smaller sized tribes.

The lowest and poorest caste in Mirwala are the Mauchis (cobblers), with a total of five acres between them.

On June 22, 2002, the total amount of land registered in the name of Ghulam Farid Tatla Gujjar, father of Mukhtar Mai and Abdul Shakoor, was 15 kanals, or 2 acres.

On June 22, 2002 the total amount of land registered in the name of Mukhtar Mai's five uncles was four acres.

On June 22, 2002 the total amount of land registered in the name of the Mastoi family next door was 1 to 1.25 acres.

"The Mastois are not a rich family. They are poor. One to two acres means nothing in agriculture," the tehsildar remarked.

On June 22, 2002 their clan-fellow Faiz Muhammad Mastoi, convicted of abetting the gang-rape of Mukhtar Mai despite Mukhtar Mai's own statement that he commanded his relatives to "forgive the lady and her family," owned 6 acres in Mirwala and 10 acres in Rampur.

Since 2002, the total amount of land now registered in Mukhtar Mai's name is 25 kanals, just over 3 acres.

Four kanals (half-acre) have been purchased in her older brother Hazoor Bakhsh's name since 2002.

Four kanals (half-acre) have been purchased in her younger brother Abdul Shakoor's name since 2002.

Another 15 acres have been acquired in the names of Mukhtar Mai's uncles since 2002 – the five uncles together owned 19 acres as of March 2006.

Mukhtar Mai's extended family has multiplied its landholdings since the 2002 case from six acres to 25 acres – some 400 per cent.

They have also purchased a tractor, four motorbikes, and a car. The tractor is parked in the joint compound of three of the uncles, along with large livestock holdings of water buffalo, cattle and goats; and a huge barn spilling over with sacks of grain.

"This is the record," the *tehsildar* Ashfaq Ahmad Qureshi declares after the *patwaari* Sawan Raza deciphered the ledgers.

"After 2002, the living standard of Mukhtar Mai's family has increased upwards *("By leaps and bounds," Qamar intervenes)* while the living standard of the Mastois has gone down, and down, and down."

"Below poverty level," adds Qamar.

"Now the Mastoi family in Mirwala has the lowest living standard," said the tehsildar.

The governor of the Punjab granted electricity to Mirwala to compensate Mukhtar Mai. He paved the road to her house.

Still, no road leads to the Mastoi house. Nor has their house been connected to the electricity grid. Every home in Mirwala is now connected to the electricity grid, except for the families of two castes: the Pachaars, and the Mastois.

"There is no man in the house of the Mastois," concludes the *tehsildar*, as the *patwaari* wraps his ledgers again in the faded cotton map.

"Only women and children are living there. There is no earning hand."

The map once again a swag for the ledgers, they turn to head into the night and back to their agrarian Indus flatlands.

"One final thing Madam. About this area: this is a loving area. This is the truth. The love is from the heart."

# 24

# The Evidence

*"The principle of innocent until proven guilty has vanished since 9-11. Everything is upside down. Now they are guilty until proven innocent."*

**Criminal lawyer hired privately by Mukhtar Mai for two days**

The trial of Mukhtar Mai's alleged gang-rape may never have stood up in a Western court.

In fact, it may never even have made it to court in the West, the evidence is so weak.

It shouldn't have stood up in the Pakistani anti-terrorism court which heard the trial in July-August 2002.

But the judiciary, police force and the government were under excruciating, furious domestic and international pressure to present heads on platters, for a crime most people watching failed to question.

In the post 9-11 climate in the frontline War on Terror state of Pakistan, the onus of proof has fallen to the defence. Accused men are apparently treated as guilty until proven innocent.

Pakistan's military government was and is willing to sacrifice innocents to win the approval of the West and the billions of dollars that have flowed its way since signing up to join the US in its War on Terror.

The prosecution case unravels under scrutiny.

Even the chief state prosecutor has boasted privately to me that he would have had the case thrown out and got all 14 accused acquitted, had he been leading the defence team.

Q: WHAT WAS THE MEDICAL PROOF OF RAPE?

The doctor who examined Mukhtar Mai eight days after the alleged gang-rape took nine vaginal swabs to test for semen: three internal swabs, three external (genital region) swabs, and three from the posterior fornix. They were dispatched to the city of Multan for testing by the Chemical Examiner, in the government health department.

The Chemical Examiner reported one week later that all swabs were stained with semen.

As medical science tells us that it's possible for non-motile sperm to remain inside the vaginal cavity for 17 to 21 days, it is entirely plausible that internal swabs would be stained with semen eight days after a rape.

But the possibility of semen remaining on the body externally, after eight days of toiletry and ablutions, is dim.

"The chemical report was an embarrassment to our case," one of the prosecutors admitted in a private interview in early 2006.

Mukhtar Mai conceded under cross-examination that she had, in the eight days between the alleged attack and the medical exam, used the toilet and washed herself afterwards.

A legitimate medical report would have noted that only the internal swabs were stained with non-motile semen.

"The report illustrates the pressure officials were under to manipulate evidence to get a conviction," said the prosecutor, who asked not to be identified.

Q: WHAT WAS THE MEDICAL PROOF OF GANG-RAPE?

None.

No semen group-analysis was performed, despite health officials claiming a full nine swabs were stained with semen.

No DNA testing was performed.

No semen serology was performed.

All such tests are available in Pakistan and are used in rape cases. Especially when capital punishment is sought, as it was sought in Mukhtar Mai's case.

DNA testing for rape cases is conducted in Islamabad at the Kahuta Research Laboratory hospital, in Lahore at the Institute of Microbiology, and in Karachi.

DNA testing is especially critical in cases of capital punishment.

If the prosecution is calling for death sentence, it wants no doubt hanging over the identity of a defendant.

The lady doctor who examined Mukhtar Mai admitted under cross-examination that the police did not request semen group-analysis.

The lady doctor concluded in her initial report, without waiting for the results of the swab tests, that rape had occurred. There was little other physical evidence to back the conclusion.

Normally a doctor waits for pathology results before giving a diagnosis; before reaching a conclusion of rape.

Q: WHAT MEDICAL TESTS WERE PERFORMED ON THE ACCUSED RAPISTS TO LINK THEM TO THE CRIME?

Prostatic massages.

The four accused men were all in handcuffs while a doctor stuck on a plastic glove, rubbed their prostate glands and watched their erections.

The effort proved: that they could 'get it up'.

It was never explained why, when the police had gone to the effort of bringing four accused men to the health clinic, they did not ask the doctor to collect semen samples for cross-matching with the semen swabs taken from Mukhtar Mai.

Instead, Doctor Fazl Hussain produced four formal medical reports on the so-called "Potency Tests" of the four accused. Each report concluded that they were "capable" at the time of the alleged incident.

Presumably, so was every adult male who does not suffer sexual dysfunction.

## Q: DID THE CLOTHES PROVIDE ANY PHYSICAL EVIDENCE?

When police came to Mukhtar Mai's house to gather evidence and interviews, she declined to hand over the clothes she wore at the time of the alleged gang-rape.

The police reported they received the clothes one or two days later.

*But* they were never tested for semen stains.

Nine vaginal swabs were sent to the Chemical Examiner in Multan for semen testing. But the clothes, which were eventually taken into police possession, were never sent for testing.

Mukhtar Mai testified that she was wearing her *kameez* (tunic) at the time of the alleged gang-rape, although her *shalwar* (trousers) had been removed. According to her own statement, she wrapped her *dopatta* (shawl) around her legs and private parts immediately after the alleged gang-rape.

Both items of clothing could have contained traces of semen, if rape or gang-rape had occurred, and could have provided stronger evidence of the claim of gang-rape.

She had told the court under cross-examination that her "private parts" were not wiped clean between each man's alleged forced intercourse with her. That means she would have had the semen of four men on her body when she wrapped her dopatta around her legs and waist, and traces of semen on her knee-length tunic.

## Q: WHY WERE KEY PROSECUTION WITNESSES DROPPED AT THE LAST MINUTE, WITHOUT EXPLANATION?

The star prosecution witness was supposed to be Mukhtar Mai's father, Ghulam Farid Tatla Gujjar.

He had brought his daughter to the gathering of the Mastoi men.

He allegedly had watched four men drag her into a compound.

He allegedly heard her pleas for help.

He allegedly saw her emerge about an hour later, in torn tunic, her trousers in her hand, and her dopatta wrapped around her legs.

He allegedly walked her home across the sugarcane field immediately afterwards.

But the day before he was to testify, prosecutors announced they had dropped him as "unnecessary." The meek woodcutter was saved from undergoing cross-examination.

A second key prosecution witness was Ghulam Nabi, a fellow villager.

According to the prosecution, he had accompanied Mukhtar and her father to the Mastois' gathering and there witnessed the same as her father: four men dragging Mukhtar into her house as she pleaded for for help, and her exit about an hour later, distraught and in torn clothes.

The day before Ghulam Nabi was to testify, he was dropped by prosecutors as "unnecessary."

Ghulam Nabi's statement to the investigating civil magistrate of Alipur on July 9, two weeks before the trial began, may offer an answer.

Mr Nabi told the magistrate that he was never at the scene of the alleged crime. He was not in Mirwala at the time of the alleged incident.

On June 22, the day of the alleged gang-rape of Mukhtar Mai, Mr Nabi was on a two-day visit to Dera Ghazi Khan, a city 3 hours drive from Mirwala.

Yet the prosecution persisted in its claim that he was one of the eyewitnesses to the presentation of Mukhtar Mai to the Mastoi gathering.

A third key prosecution witness was Mureed Abbas, a local do-gooder and wannabe journalist with a grudge against large landowners.

Mureed Abbas dabbled in freelance news articles, often without payment, for small-time rags in the nearby city of Multan.

He gathered evidence of honour crimes in the Jatoi area. He photographed rape victims as young as seven, and victims of heinous murders like the guy thrown into a crops-thresher, and showed his gruesome album to anyone who'd give him the time.

Abbas and two other aspiring freelancers were the first 'reporters' to hear of the alleged gang-rape case, after the vengeful preacher Maulvi Abdul Razzaq went public with his claims in a fiery Friday sermon on June 28.

Abbas seized on the tale. It fit his set view of the patterns of crimes in the area, but it had an extra sexy twist—the alleged gang-rape was a sentence decreed.

He saw huge bylines.

Abbas spent the next two days interviewing villagers, including Mukhtar Mai and her father.

He tried to coerce Mukhtar Mai's father into registering gang-rape charges, but Ghulam Farid Gujjar refused.

Giving up on the father, Abbas went himself to the police on July 30.

Waving the recorded interviews in his hand, he demanded police register gang-rape charges.

When they refused, Abbas threatened to go to their seniors in the district capital.

The officers told the righteous Abbas that they needed the victim to register the case.

Mureed Abbas led the police out to Mukhtar Mai's house 13 kilometres away on the afternoon of June 30, leading the way on his motor scooter. The police took Mukhtar from her house, packed her into their van, and transported her like a criminal into the Jatoi police station. They already had a charge statement drafted for her to sign—with her thumbprint. The preacher turned up at the police station.

The statement had already been drafted before Mukhtar Mai even was brought into the police station. As an illiterate, she could not read it, nor could she sign it.

Mukhtar's father and older brother tried to talk her out of it, but the preacher persuaded her to go ahead. She thumb-printed it.

The police needed a medical report, but as it was after 8pm on a Sunday night by the time they had the "victim's" attestation of the charge statement, the health clinic was closed.

Mureed Abbas was undeterred in his determination to see gang-rape charges registered.

He drove eight kilometres out to the village where the lady doctor lived and brought her from her house back into Jatoi township to the health clinic.

According to Abbas, Dr Shahida Safdar performed the medical test around 10pm on Sunday night. Mureed Abbas had already filed his reports to his stable of newspaper clients in Multan.

As a key player in the registration of the gang-rape charges with police, Mureed Abbas was summonsed by the court to testify as a prosecution witness.

But on the day he was to appear in court, police came to his residence in Jatoi and detained him.

They told the court that Abbas had absconded to the mountains of northern Pakistan.

Abbas believes he was detained because he planned to tell the court that police had got the wrong rape suspect in their arrest of Fayyaz Mastoi. He merely had the same name as the real suspect, who had fled the area to evade arrest. Abbas says he had the documentation to prove the wrong identity and wrongful arrest of Fayyaz Mastoi. Abbas was also going to reveal his role in reporting the case to the police. But his testimony would have directly contradicted the police version.

The police version was that Mukhtar Mai, her menfolk and the preacher had come independently to the police to file charges on the morning of Sunday June 30, in fact as early as 7.30 am – almost 12 hours earlier than the actual time Abbas had her brought by police van into the Jatoi police station.

Q: WAS THERE EVER A TRIBAL COUNCIL OR PANCHAYAT WHICH ALLEGEDLY ORDERED A GANG-RAPE?

Police, villagers, and the defence say there was no panchayat or any tribal council.

There was a gathering of one tribe, the Mastois, who had gathered earlier in the day for a funeral.

A panchayat is a council of elders representing all tribes in the area.

An akath is the gathering of one tribe. Scores of men belonging to the Mastoi tribe had gathered in an akath. An akath does not issue verdicts like a panchayat. An akath does not have the role of mediating on disputes and coming up with rulings, as a panchayat has. In an akath a tribe will discuss how to deal with issues affecting it, such as land, honour and women. But it is not a tribal council or jury.

Q: WHY WERE SO MANY MASTOI MEN PRESENT?

For funeral prayers.

They had gathered earlier in the day at the nearby home of another Mastoi family to mourn the recent death of a fellow tribesman.

Salma Mastoi's brothers were attending the funeral prayers when she was seen in the sugarcane field with Shakoor, Mukhtar Mai's teenage brother.

Salma's older brothers were called back from the funeral prayers to deal with Shakoor, whom the Mastois believed had molested their girl Salma.

Other Mastoi relatives followed over the next few hours as a crisis evolved over how to deal with Shakoor's violation of their girl's honour.

They were not called to form a panchayat. The only other tribe among them were some men from the Pachaars, including Ramzan Pachaar.

Q: WERE THE MASTOIS REALLY RICHER, MORE POWERFUL AND MORE INFLUENTIAL THAN MUKHTAR MAI'S FAMILY? WERE MUKHTAR MAI'S FAMILY A DOWNTRODDEN INFERIOR MINORITY?

The Mastois were and are one of the poorest families in the village. They were significantly poorer than Mukhtar Mai's family.

The family of the main accused rapist, Abdul Khaliq Mastoi, had one to 1.25 acres to its name. For a family of six brothers, five sisters, seven grandchildren, and a widowed grandmother, it's a paltry holding of land.

Mukhtar Mai's immediate family owned 2 acres of land at the time.

Police investigators conceded in the trial that Mukhtar Mai's family were financially better off than the Mastois.

The most powerful, wealthiest, and largest tribe in Mirwala are the Jatois. Two of the key prosecution witnesses supporting Mukhtar Mai's family were Jatois. The preacher who first went public with the claims and took them to the police is a Jatoi.

Contrary to reports of her family being a downtrodden minority, Mukhtar Mai's family had the backing of the most important tribe in Mirwala: Jatois – and one of the most powerful figures in the local community: the preacher of Mirwala, Maulvi Abdul Razzaq.

### Q: WHO REPORTED THE ALLEGED GANG-RAPE TO POLICE?

Neither Mukhtar Mai nor her family.

Two other men with separate personal agendas took the claims to police: the preacher, Maulvi Razzaq, and the wannabe reporter-cum-do-gooder Mureed Abbas.

Both belong to the Jatoi tribe.

Both had separate personal agendas.

Maulvi Razzaq, the mullah of Mirwala, had a history of enmity with Mastoi families. Their feuds were over land and his membership of an outlawed gang of violent Muslim extremists.

In this case, the mullah's efforts to broker a compromise between the Mastois and Mukhtar Mai's family was thwarted by the Mastois when they reneged on their promise to give their girl Salma in marriage to Mukhtar Mai's brother.

The Mastois instead married Salma to a Mastoi relative, Khalil Ahmed, five days after the feud erupted over the alleged rape of Salma by Mukhtar Mai's brother.

Mureed Abbas was a small-time campaigner against large landowners and tribal justice systems embodied by panchayats.

### Q: WHO WERE THE EIGHT MEN ACCUSED OF BEING MEMBERS OF THE SO-CALLED PANCHAYAT AND CHARGED ACCORDINGLY WITH ABETMENT?

They included Salma Mastoi's new husband Khalil Ahmed, his father, and three of his uncles.

They were acquitted of all charges in the first trial in August 2002, as the judge and police said there was no evidence against them. Six others were sent to death row: four for gang-rape, two for abetment.

Mukhtar Mai's appeal against their acquittal was thrown out by the High Court in March 2005. In the same finding, the High Court acquitted five of the six convicted men.

But three days after the High Court decision, these eight men were re-arrested and thrown back into a jail under a draconian law normally reserved for terror suspects: the Maintenance of Public Order act, which allows the government to lock people up for three months without charge.

When that expired, the Supreme Court weighed in and ordered their detention until the hearing of the next appeal.

Almost two years on, as I write, they are still incarcerated. Despite two acquittals.

The defence believes Khalil and his relatives were named by Maulvi Razzaq because of Khalil's marriage to Salma Mastoi, in defiance of the pact to marry her to Mukhtar's brother Shakoor in exchange for Abdul Khaliq's alleged on-the-spot marriage to Mukhtar.

## Q: WHY WAS THE MAN WHO ORDERED FORGIVENESS OF MUKTHAR MAI'S FAMILY SENTENCED TO BE HUNG?

Faiz Muhammad Mastoi, a 35-year-old landowner, was accused of ordering the gang-rape of Mukhtar Mai in his capacity as alleged head of the alleged panchayat.

But according to Mukhtar Mai's own testimony, Faiz Mastoi ordered that Mukhtar's family be forgiven and declared a compromise, after she was brought before the Mastoi gathering.

All prosecution witnesses testified that Faiz Mastoi declared: "The Gujjar family have brought their woman. In the name of God the Almighty, forgive her family and let compromise be effected."

Yet he was convicted and sentenced to death.

Mukhtar Mai improved on her statement when she appeared in court with four words:

"duniavi-siasi taurper." *It means literally* "in an insincere and superficial manner."

She had never used these words before the trial, either in her statements to police investigators or the civil magistrate.

On the basis of these words, the judge ruled that Faiz Mastoi's declaration of compromise and pronouncement of forgiveness were insincere, convicted him of abetting the alleged gang-rape, and sentenced him to death.

Faiz Mastoi spent two years and seven months on death row before the High Court acquitted him in March 2005. He was released on acquittal.

But, like the other acquitted men, Faiz Mastoi was thrown back into jail pending the Supreme Court appeal and remains there almost two years on, despite being declared innocent by the High Court.

Mukhtar Mai's appeal to the Supreme Court seeks the death sentence for all 14 men.

## Q: WHY WAS MUKHTAR MAI'S PRIVATE COUNSEL DROPPED FROM THE TRIAL?

At one point in the trial Mukhtar Mai tried to tell her story independently.

Not trusting the prosecutors appointed by the government to represent her, her family sought out an independent lawyer.

They privately engaged one of the top criminal lawyers in Dera Ghazi Khan, the town where the trial was being conducted.

They gave him a 12,000 rupee (200USD) advance on his 80,000 rupee (1,300 USD) fee.

That lawyer met Mukhtar Mai in private, in a sideroom of the courthouse where she was being kept under police guard. He asked her to tell him in full honesty what actually happened. In the account she gave to her private counsel, Mukhtar Mai described being assaulted, but she didn't mention rape.

When the police and state-appointed prosecutors discovered Mukhtar Mai had engaged a private counsel, they pressured her to dismiss him.

When the private counsel told the prosecution team that Mukhtar Mai had told him a different story to the version prepared by police and pushed by prosecutors, the official prosecutors accused him of trying to "destroy" their case.

The next day the private counsel was denied permission by the court to represent Mukhtar Mai, as he had not been approved by the government.

In disgust, the private counsel withdrew his power of attorney, walked out of the courthouse, and returned to his regular clients.

Q: WHAT WAS THE ROLE OF THE PREACHER MAULVI ABDUL RAZZAQ?

The bearded mullah of Mirwala, Maulvi Razzaq, belonged to Pakistan's most violent gang of Muslim extremists, the Sipah-e-Sahaba: Army of the Companions of the Prophet.

The gang was outlawed in 2001 for its links to the murders of thousands of Shias.

He had a murky past.

Razzaq was linked to violent protests against the US-led hunt for Osama bin Laden and rumours of militant training in Afghanistan.

The Mastois call him the "architect" of the gang-rape charges.

He was the negotiator who tried to solve the feud between Mukhtar Mai's family and their Mastoi neighbours after Mukhtar's teenage brother was caught in the sugarcane with the Mastoi teenager Salma.

Razzaq brokered the exchange marriage (*watta-satta*) deal which was to see Mukhtar given as a compensatory bride to Salma's 21 year old brother Abdul Khaliq, and in return Salma would be married to Mukhtar's brother.

He exploded in fury when the Mastois reneged on their part of the deal, by marrying Salma off to a relative on the other side of the Indus River.

The mullah threatened to take the Mastois to court.

He denounced them in a fiery Friday sermon on June 28, the day after Salma's marriage to her relative.

The next day he went to the police, and without the approval of Mukhtar Mai's family drew up gang-rape charges against the Mastois. It was June 29.

Razzaq already loathed the Mastois for taking him to the High Court seven years earlier on charges of corruptly conspiring to grab land from a Mastoi man.

*He also had it in for them after they tried to oust him from the Mirwala mosque for harbouring outlawed* Sipah-e-Sahaba *extremists.*

Q: WHY WAS THERE AN EIGHT-DAY DELAY IN REPORTING THREE SEPARATE ALLEGATIONS OF RAPE AND GANG-RAPE?

The first cry of rape came not from Mukhtar Mai's family. It came from the Mastoi family.

They accused Mukhtar Mai's teenage brother Shakoor of raping their teenage daughter Salma. Shakoor and Salma had been seen in the sugarcane field together.

The next morning, Mukhtar Mai's family accused three Mastoi relatives of gang-raping Shakoor.

According to the prosecution case, Mukhtar Mai informed her family of the alleged gang-rape on the night of June 22.

But neither side went to the police with their respective claims of rape, until June 29, when the preacher Maulvi Razzaq first approached the police.

A possibility is that in the days following the June 22 feud over Abdul Shakoor's coupling with Salma, Mukhtar Mai's family and Razzaq were trying to revive the compromise exchange-marriage deal. The prosecution also says this proposal had been discussed – in fact put forward by them.

Razzaq has never satisfactorily explained what he was doing between June 23 and 29, to the period in which he claims to have known nothing of the outcome of the feud of June 22, despite his pivotal involvement in negotiating a compromise.

Defence lawyers believe he was busy trying to rescue the compromise deal.

He suddenly went public with the gang-rape claims in his June 28 sermon.

Salma was married to her relative Khalil Ahmed Mastoi on June 27, the day before the sermon. That marriage destroyed any hopes of rescuing the compromise exchange-marriage deal.

On hearing of Salma's sudden marriage to another, the defence says Maulvi Razzaq burst into rage and threatened to take the Mastois to the police.

The next day he went public with the tale of alleged gang-rape.

The following day he took his claims to the police.

The cleric tried twice to persuade Mukhtar Mai's father to go to the police with gang-rape claims, but the father refused. The preacher went to the police regardless.

## Q: WHAT WERE THE GROUNDS FOR SODOMY CHARGES AGAINST THREE OTHER MASTOIS?

Three Mastoi relatives, including Salma's oldest brother, were charged with gang-raping Mukhtar's teenage brother Shakoor, convicted and sent to jail. In March 2006 they walked out of the ghastly Multan jail after doing three years inside.

The doctor who examined Abdul Shakoor for signs of sodomy found no evidence. Yet his report concluded sodomy, even before the Chemical Examiner looked at the anal swabs.

The Chemical Examiner's report, a week later, found no semen on the swabs.

Shakoor's clothes, also, were never submitted for testing.

The same absurd rituals were performed as in Mukhtar's gang-rape investigation: the accused men were given prostatic massages to prove they could achieve erection.

There were no witnesses to Shakoor's claim that he was dragged into the sugarcane by the three accused.

There is no evidence that the three were present in Mirwala on the day.

The claim of sodomy, according to the defence, is a concoction to justify Shakoor's capture by the Mastoi family, and to stave off a potential rape charge against him for being caught in the field with Salma.

## Q: WERE THERE WITNESSES TO THE ALLEGED GANG-RAPE OF MUKHTAR MAI?

None.

However, witnesses are not required for a rape conviction. There are several precedents in Pakistani case law where rapists have been convicted without witnesses.

## Q: WHAT IS THE MAIN WEAKNESS OF THE DEFENCE CASE?

*Razzaq denied performing a* sharai nikah *oral marriage, as the defence claim.*

There is no certificate to prove an oral marriage.

## Q: DID THE DEFENCE PRODUCE ANY WITNESSES TO THE ALLEGED ORAL MARRIAGE OF MUKHTAR MAI TO ABDUL KHALIQ?

Yes.

*Ghulam Hussain, maternal cousin of two accused rapists, testified in court that he was present at the* sharai nikah *oral marriage.*

Q: CAN AN ORAL MARRIAGE BE A DEFENCE AGAINST RAPE?

*No. An oral marriage, or* sharai nikah, *has no legal standing and cannot be a defence against rape.*

Q: WHERE DO THE TWO SIDES AGREE?

Both sides agree that Mukhtar Mai was delivered to the gathering of Mastois by her menfolk.

Q: WHERE DO THE TWO SIDES DIVERGE?

On the context in which she was brought by her menfolk to the Mastoi gathering.

The Mastois believed this met their demand for immediate 'rukhsti', delivery of the compensatory bride by her menfolk to the groom's family. The Gujjars, Mukhtar Mai's family, deny this.

The Gujjars say she was brought by them to seek vicarious pardon on behalf of her brother for allegedly raping Salma Mastoi. The Mastois deny this.

# 25

# The Poor in Spirit

**MARCH 2006, DERA GHAZI KHAN**

"I've been waiting to meet you!" exclaimed a pretty-faced man in black suit and tie, with diamond blue eyes.

He hadn't seen me at first, in his peripheral vision, when he burst into the crowded and tiny concrete cell of a room wearing a serious expression.

I had been ushered into the room, deep in a labyrinthine bazaar, by an unknown smiling gentleman summonsing me to meet the "lady lawyer."

"Madam, come with me. The lady lawyer is waiting to meet you." I heard him before I saw him. My eyes were shut to savour the bursting nectar of ruby-fleshed oranges. A moustached juice-wallah had just squeezed out the blushing fluid with   weeps up from the fertile plains of the wild right bank of the Indus, deep in Pakistan's dark south.

Next to them are pyramids of carrots the colour of tomatoes. I'd always marveled at the reds of the oranges and carrots in Pakistan, as testament to the river-fed fertility of the Punjab—"the land of five rivers."

I was telling myself to ignore fears the orange wheel might have mixed hepatitis into my fresh Indus-birthed juice, when the smiling be-smocked clerk tapped me on the arm.

"Madam, come with me. The lady lawyer is waiting to meet you."

He spoke as though I was expected. But this was only my second day ever on the right bank of the Indus, let alone in Dera Ghazi Khan. Foreigners are prohibited here.

I had another appointment in another part of the bazaar, but the gentleman was insistent. So, warning him I had only a few minutes, I followed.

We wound through the lanes of the open air marketplace. This wasn't a normal bazaar. This was the "chambers" of the barristers who do battle daily in the bougainvillea-draped British-era district courts across the road.

The people referred to the open air bazaar as "chambers" with deadpan expressions. Arched facades bordered twisting laneways, breezy sunshine-bathed passages ran between shop-front stalls, where paralegals and clerks sat by stenographer's boards advertising legal services in Urdu script.

Each lawyer's "chamber" was delineated by arrangements of rattan tables and chairs, around a small rickety table just big enough to hold a tray of *chai*, the sweet spicy tea of the subcontinent.

I couldn't see where they might store their files. These "chambers" looked more like places to sit and drink tea. They looked like the village plaza, where the men gather to smoke and chat.

But a snap of the fingers, and a be-smocked clerk disappears to reapper in moments with ribbon-tied bundles in hand.

I had entered this bustling barristers' bazaar for the first time the day before, looking for one Saleem Malik: eminent criminal barrister-at-law, member of the Punjab Bar Council, advocate to the Supreme Court.

Qamar led me through an oncoming sea of slow-striding turbanned men, ancient squashed faces, eyes with far distances in them. Smocks billowed, the creams and whites of their cloth warmed by mid-morning sun-rays catching their flutterings. These men swayed, as they strode into the bazaar from the sandy tribal territories beyond the city, looking for an advocate to hear their tales of brutality in the name of honour.

Horse-pulled carts jerked in between the human traffic, loaded with black-masked and veiled women.

A sign in Urdu script above a circle of rattan chairs announced the chambers of Saleem Malik. His advocates were waiting. The man himself was in court. Malik's chambers were shaded by arched portico. Tea-men with white-peppered beards bobbed between the arches, bearing thimble-sized cups of milky *chai*.

When Malik-sahib swept in, two hours later, an entourage of junior advocates and attorneys flanked him, respectfully a few steps behind. They cut the air with their importance.

"Mr Saleem Malik was reluctant to come and meet you," a particularly debonair hanger-on, in pin-stripe suit and crossed legs, announced with a smile.

He introduced himself as the District Attorney.

"Before we came over here Malik-sahib said: 'What is the point? The media has never wanted to listen. Why should it be any different now?' You see, no one wants to hear the other side of this case," the dapper District Attorney said.

"But I encouraged him to come and see you. I said 'why not? Let's give it a try.'"

I could hardly blame Mr Malik for his skepticism. I had been exploring, in-depth, this case for over six months, had reported on it for quick-fire news stories three-and-a half-years earlier, and had written a feature on Mukhtar Mai 18 months before. But this was the first time I had sought him out.

Why had it taken so long to seek out the chief of the defence case? This man had represented the accused men from the first trial in August 2002, to the High Court appeal of March 2005, to the Supreme Court appeal hearing of June 2005, and is still trying to get justice for his clients.

Partly because I was looking in the wrong place. Until now I had only been searching and exploring along the left bank of the Indus. They call the east bank 'left' and the west bank 'right'.

"Look south down the river," a tribesman once explained, to help me stop mixing up my right and left banks.

"As you look south, the west bank is on your right-hand side, and the east bank is on your left-hand side."

Mukhtar's village sits astride the left bank of the Indus.

The preacher who filed the gang-rape charges lives on the left bank. The four men accused of gang-raping her live on the left bank. The police who investigated the case are from the town of Jatoi and the larger district city of Muzaffargarh, also on the left bank.

But the trial was held across the Indus, on the right bank...here in Dera Ghazi Khan. Lawyers who participated in the trial—for prosecution and defence—are based here.

Six of the eight men accused of sitting on the mythical *panchayat* (tribal court) that allegedly sentenced Mukhtar to gang-rape are from the right bank.

Dera Ghazi Khan lies between the Suleiman mountain range and the Indus River. It slopes from desert hills in its west to lush crop-bearing plains in its east. It's one of the remotest parts of Pakistan. It is a classified "tribal area", zoned as a Provincially Administered Tribal Area or PATA. On the map, it falls under the Punjab provincial government.

But its laws and enforcers are its own. Dera Ghazi Khan is a heartland of Baloch and Pathan tribes. It is the seat of several Baloch feudal dynasties.

Foreigners are banned from entering Dera Ghazi Khan. There were never many here before anyway—a few mining outfits, as the land is swimming in mineral resources: gypsum, uranium, gas. And a few North American missionaries.

All were expelled three years ago, after one too many foreigners tried to photograph the uranium enrichment plant on the city outskirts.

It was the first settlement of the Baloch tribes when they began coming north to the Suleiman ranges from the southern Makran deserts and down from the hills 500 years ago, searching eastwards for fresh grazing lands. Ghazi Khan established a town within a mile of the pounding muddy river.

When the 14 Mastoi Baloch men accused of gang-rape or abetment faced trial, they did so in the heartland of their Baloch forefathers.

Muhammad Saleem Malik held court with me, my fixer Qamar, and his dapper entourage in the barristers' 'bar room.' It's a high-ceilinged spacious salon off the barristers' open-air bazaar. Low, decaying couches line the walls. Lawyers consort here, sinking deep into the worn sofas, lighting cigarettes.

Saleem Malik laid out the facts and the evidence on record, with a logic that was almost mathematical. They came in layers, building to a case that seemed to prove the innocence of 13 of his 14 clients. It certainly established more than reasonable doubt as to their guilt.

It was easy to see why the original trial court acquitted 8 of the 14 men.

It was easy to see why it convicted one of the six men.

But it was not easy to see how it convicted the other five. More alarmingly, how it ordered the men be sent to the gallows.

"I believe Mukhtar Mai did not grasp what was going on," Malik said. "She was like a blind woman. So many other people and forces were playing with this case. Each person had their own different agenda."

"So you're not saying that she was lying?" I asked.

"On the contrary. I believe Mukhtar Mai made an attempt to tell the true story," the learned barrister replied.

"How? When?" I asked.

"She tried to hire her own private counsel. She told him a different story to what was said in the trial," he replied.

"Did the private counsel reveal it?" I asked.

"No. He was never allowed to."

The room went silent. Malik-sahib's crowd of suited followers watched my expression.

Malik broke the silence: "The name of the counsel was Qazi Sodr-Udin."

The name hit a note of recognition, somewhere in my memory's recesses. Mentally I went back in my notes.

Then I saw it in front of my eyes—typed in small font, faint. Bunched with a group of other names. In the hundreds of pages of trial testimony and cross-examination transcripts I had spent months poring through, his name appeared twice only. First, among a bunch of counsels' names representing the plaintiff, Mukhtar Mai.

Then my memory turned aural. I could hear the judge mentioning the private counsel's name. I heard the gavel bang three times.

"Would all counsels for the prosecution stand and produce their certificates of government permission to represent the plaintiff....

Mr Qazi Sodr-Udin, have you no government permit to represent Ms Mukhtar Mai? I cannot permit you to continue on the prosecution team."

"Your honour, I withdraw my power of attorney."

"That counsel is here." One of Malik-sahib's followers was speaking, drawing me back from the trial transcripts.

"He has his chambers in this bazaar. You can meet him—if you wish to, that is."

I had never given the name of the dismissed counsel another thought after seeing his name in the transcripts. From the transcript, it had seemed no more than a case of someone forgetting their paperwork.

"Try to meet him," the pin-striped District Attorney piped up. "Ask him why he withdrew his power of attorney."

It was already late in the afternoon and we had a two hour drive ahead of us, back across the Indus River to the more civilised left bank, the familiarity of Multan city, where my hotel was. We needed to beat the dark. The river's banks are favoured hideouts of kidnappers and armed bandits.

I thought about seeking out the mysterious private counsel the next day.

My mind, however, was more focused on the possible meeting the following day with Salma Mastoi, the girl with whom it all began. Mr Malik had promised to have her brought in from the hinterlands where she now lives with her parents-in-law.

On our return the next morning, my first stop was the orange juice wheel, just inside the sun-dappled laneways that leads into the warren-like barristers' bazaar.

"Madam, come with me. The lady lawyer is waiting to meet you."

I knew the invitation would mean long civilities over tea, then a heavy lunch, then more tea, so I was insistent that I could only stay for a minute to meet the "lady lawyer", as I had an important appointment elsewhere in the bazaar.

In Pakistan's conservative corners, it's a novelty to have a lady among the professional classes. Hence the insertion of "lady" before their profession. The rural health clinics are proud to have a "lady doctor".

We were ushered into the concrete room, four-foot square at the most, where sat many men in waistcoats and *shalwar kameez* (long white smocks over pantaloon trousers).

In the corner, protectively flanked, was a masked woman. A *naqab* hung from her eyes to her neck, covering her face. Huge kohl-ringed topaz tiger-eyes rolled out from the narrow slat. The face-gear always made me think of female pirates, from Sinbad's era. The rest of her was draped in volumes of shapeless cloth.

"It's a pleasure to meet you," came her deep and heavy-accented voice. Her head bobbed  sideways in that confusing South Asian nod-and-shake, where you can never tell whether they are agreeing or disagreeing. "I am the lady lawyer."

I smiled and groaned inside to think how long I would have to go through the expected civilities, marveling as a Westerner is expected to at the fact that here is a woman lawyer in this backwards backwater where women are neither seen nor heard. She was so curtained off by her gear and virtually hiding in the corner that I wasn't really that impressed.

I was saved by the black-suited baby-faced man who burst in, his diamond blue eyes searching but not catching me at first, until he looked sideways.

"I've been waiting to meet you!" His voice was high-pitched, almost effeminate. He looked mid-30s. Sharply dressed. In a Western city he'd be taken for gay.

At first I thought he was just another irrelevant stranger excited by the visit of a white lady. Then he quick-fired off his credentials.

"My name is Qazi Sodr-Udin, I am a criminal lawyer representing so many murder cases, so many honour crimes cases, every day, I want to be a journalist and write about the honour crimes I am dealing with day in and day out, just today I have 11 murder cases to handle, come with me I want to tell you all about my life, my studies, how I came into this profession, how I have devoted myself to my career, and... (dropping to a whisper) my faith."

By the time Sodr-Udin drew breath we were out of the masked "lady lawyer's" den and already winding through the labyrinthine maze of lanes towards his own "chambers".

"Then I will tell you about my brief involvement with the case of Mukhtar Mai, and what she told me in private."

With that, he managed to lure me away from my long-awaited meeting with the girl who started it all, and into his own dim concrete room, where a gallery of turbanned tribesmen – clients from the 11 murder cases he was handling that day—sat waiting for him.

*   *   *   *

Qazi Sodr-Udin Alvi found God when his heart stopped beating.

It was 1992 and he was studying law at the Islamia University in Bahawalpur, a city of azure-tiled shrines, golden domes and Nawabs (mini-princes from a bygone era) that rises from the Cholistan desert near Pakistan's arid border with India.

It skirts the favoured hunting ground palaces of Arab sheikhs, who bring their falcons by private jet and undercover convoys twice a year to hunt Hubara bustards migrating seasonally between the swamps of western India and central Asia. The Hubara, it is said, is a great aphrodisiac.

Sodr-Udin took his condition to the doctor.

"Your heart is beating like a hurtling train," the doctor declared after examining his slender, pretty-faced patient. "You are having an obsession."

"But doctor, I cannot feel my heart. How can it be beating at all?"

Sodr-Udin's trip to the doctor didn't alter his condition. The diagnosis made no sense to him. The law student began to believe he was dying.

"Pray to Jesus," advised his mother, a Muslim like the rest of the family. "Jesus used to cure dying people."

Sodr-Udin began praying night and day to Jesus, a prophet in the eyes of Islam.

He bought a carpet with Jesus' image woven into it, and hung it on his bedroom wall.

"I used to sit on my bed at 3 and 4 in the morning looking at Jesus and praying to him to save me," Sodr-Udin remembers.

"After three months I was cured. My heart came back. From that moment I believed in Jesus' healing powers."

Sodr-Udin graduated from law with dreams of becoming a journalist. He enrolled in two masters degrees - one in mass communications, the other in international relations, - in the city of Quetta, on the western frontier region where the badlands of Afghanistan melt into Pakistan.

"I wanted fervently to become a journalist, to meet new people, to encounter new ideas, to debate and analyse.

"But in this country we never become what we want," Sodr-Udin grins, the corner of his lips twitching with regret.

With two masters degrees and a law degree in hand, Sodr-Udin returned home to Dera Ghazi Khan, the sweeping 500 year old city of sardars (tribal chiefs) and feudal lords, on the right bank of the Indus.

The uranium enrichment plant on the city's outskirts, splitting the indigenous blue mineral into nuclear fissure material for Pakistan's atomic bombs, renders the whole district off-limits to foreigners.

Sodr-Udin began representing murder cases. They come thick and fast in Dera Ghazi Khan. Tribesmen pour in from the untamed hinterland to the "dera" (Arabic for city), with tales of barbarity and revenge, blood feuds spanning generations, feuds of "honour" over land and women that climax in beastly slayings.

Half of the tales are concoctions.

In D.G. Khan, the locals' shorthand for Dera Ghazi Khan, to take one's enemies to the "dera" and its row of British-era district courts, is a sport.

Sodr-Udin quickly built a reputation as one of the gun lawyers on D.G. Khan's barristers' row—the bazaar of breezy open-air lawyers' "chambers" across the road from the 90-year-old courthouses.

His journalistic aspirations were soon overtaken by the ceaseless waves of clients who clamoured in from the cotton-fields and tented tribal lands with their stories of bloody revenge killings, peppered with accounts of their hidden womenfolk raped.

Hundreds of lawyers sit in the open-air chambers, around their rattan chairs and tea-tables, waiting for potential clients to seek them out.

But tribesmen striding into the "dera" and through the sunlit lanes of the barristers' bazaar to 'fix' their foes like to seek out one of the two top lawyers: Saleem Malik, or Qazi Sodr-Udin Alvi.

Barrister Malik is senior to Sodr-Udin by two decades, but the two face each other before the learned judges of the district and high courts daily, alternating between prosecution and defence - whichever side approaches them first.

By his 30s, Sodr-Udin was juggling up to 12 murder cases a day: an 11-year-old deaf and dumb girl, gang-raped and throat slit; a 55-year-old woman, caught in the cotton field with her 65-year-old "paramour", murdered by her son, in the name of the family's "honour."

They are usually crimes - or alleged crimes - of honour. Taking one's foe to court in this tribal backwater is as much a sport as killing one's foe, or lifting neighbour's cattle, or grabbing land, or trading women as commodities in compensatory marriages to score land or avoid a jail sentence.

Sodr-Udin attributes his reputation and success to two elements: he never wavers from his flat fee, unlike other barristers who add hidden fees along the way; and he demands utter honesty from his clients. He gives them the same.

In 1999, Sodr-Udin befriended two foreigners residing in Dera Ghazi Khan, a couple of years before the government expelled non-Pakistanis to protect the ultra-sensitive uranium enrichment plant. Mr Rick from Canada and Andrew Paul from the USA.

They were from the Good News Centre—discreetly tucked away in an unmarked shopfront. It was there he heard a reading that captivated his soul. The reading validated his daily toils in the courts, the miserable, poverty-corrupted lives of his clients: the Beatitudes in the Book of Matthew Chapter 5.

*"Blessed are the poor in spirit, for theirs is the kingdom of heaven. Blessed are they that mourn, for they shall be comforted. Blessed are the meek, for they shall inherit the earth. Blessed are those who hunger and thirst for righteousness, for they will be satisfied. Blessed are the merciful for they will be shown mercy. Blessed are the pure in heart, for they shall see God. Blessed are the peacemakers, for they shall be called God's children. Blessed are those who are persecuted for righteousness, for the kingdom of heaven belongs to them." 5:3-10*

Sodr-Udin recited the verses to my translator and I, by rote in racing breathless whispers, his face and shoulders turned away from the turbanned, bearded tribesmen filling the rows of chairs crowding his tiny chamber.

"This, to me, is the concept of life," he said on completion of his recital, long-lashed eyes emitting an internal light.

Sodr-Udin is immersed day to day in hair-raising crimes of savagery and abuse, toe-curling tales.

"I have devoted myself to my career and to my clients. I've left no time to marry. Now it is too late," he smiled, declaring 39 too "unfair" an age to marry.

Honour crimes are his daily fare.

Like lawyers worldwide, he suspends personal judgement of his clients and fights for what they have paid him to. He represents men accused of slaughtering their cousins, men accused of slaying their mothers, men accused of rape.

He knows from bitter experience that a good portion of the cases brought to him are fake.

Sodr-Udin's growing dilemmas about his profession, his growing disillusionment with the process of justice, stems less from the monstrosity of the crimes that come before him, and more from the growing bias of the courts against the accused.

The alarming frequency with which judges convict, casually, and easily, regardless of evidence or the lack of it, makes it hard for Sodr-Udin to sleep at night.

"It's gotten worse since 9-11," he remarks.

"The onus is no longer on the prosecution to prove guilt; it's on the defence to prove innocence. The old principle of innocent until proven guilty has vanished. Everything is upside down."

A particular case some years back plagues his conscience.

A tribesman came, seeking to prosecute his cousins over the murder of his father and brother.

"We were in the fields one morning cutting grass for fodder of our animals," the client told Sodr-Udin.

"Six men came out of the crops carrying .12-bore rifles. They shot dead my father and brother, and injured my other brother. I have pardoned two of them, because they gave me 5 acres of land and half a million rupees (11,000 AUD) in compensation. I am prosecuting the other four, who have given me nothing for pardon."

The accused murderers were all his cousins.

Sodr-Udin conducted the prosecution case with flair and flamboyance, cunning and verve. He fought hard in the court. He won a definitive conviction: two accused were sentenced to death, one was given life in prison, the fourth was given seven years in prison.

The client rejoiced.

He threw his hands in the air.

He bought halwa, traditional sweets of thick almond paste, milk, syrup & sugar, and distributed them.

He garlanded Sodr-Udin with blooded rose petals.

And he whispered: "Those four were never present!"

Sodr-Udin, not easily astounded after a decade as a criminal lawyer in the wild Indus tribal lands, was astounded.

"For what have you accused them?!"

The client then related to his stunned lawyer the story of an old theft case between the cousins.

"The two real culprits were the two I have already pardoned. It was they who shot my father and brothers. The other four men whom I have accused have three sisters, and they refused to hand the sisters over to my three brothers in pursuit of pardon. Now I have fixed them. I can get choti (money)."

The judge had pronounced his verdict. The court had already decided. The court decision can only be reversed through the formal process of appeal. An appeal against the four innocent men's conviction has been in the High Court queue for four years. Two men languish on death row in cramped solitary confinement cells. The two others sit in squalid prison cells.

At 39, Sodr-Udin is at the peak of his profession. But more and more he dreams of throwing in his booming practice and devoting himself to full-time prayer.

"So many times I think to myself that I would rather be sitting praying. Sometimes I cannot sleep at night when I see the kind of decisions handed down."

\*   \*   \*   \*

## AUGUST 2002, DERA GHAZI KHAN BARRISTERS' CHAMBERS

The mercury was heading towards 50 on a late July morning and Sodr-Udin's tiny "chambers" was filling with the usual cast of turbanned litigants when two men, one with a long beard and one bewildered, stepped in from the sunlight.

They weren't clients. He had not seen them before. But bearded tribesmen daily appeared in his door and filled up the plastic seats scattered around his desk, waiting to catch the hot-shot young lawyer's attention.

"One was a mullah, a man of the beard," Sodr-Udin recalls. "The other man was the father of Mukhtar Mai."

Across the road, in the Anti-Terrorism Court of Dera Ghazi Khan, the trial of Mukhtar Mai's four alleged gang-rapists and eight alleged abettors was just beginning. It was August 2002.

"We have come to ask you to represent us," the mullah, Maulvi Razzaq, stated. "We do not trust the prosecutors deputed by the government. We wish to engage a private counsel."

Sodr-Udin had only ever turned down one case in his life. It was a mass-murder of such animality, the would-be clients' guilt was so indisputable, that Sodr-Udin declined to represent them.

"OK. But my fee is 80,000 rupees (2,000 AUD). It's the same flat fee for everyone. And I must request direct power of attorney. From Mukhtar Mai herself," Sodr-Udin told the mullah and the woodcutter.

They gave the lawyer 12,000 rupees (300 AUD) down payment and took him over the road to the courthouse.

"Where is Mukhtar Mai?" Sodr-Udin asked, unable to see her among the crowd of advocates, defendants and police officers in the courtroom. Three or four advocates were there for the prosecution; at least twice that were there for the 14 defendants. The defendants' feet were in shackles; their hands were manacled.

"She is being kept in an ante-chamber, under police guard," a court clerk informed him.

Sodr-Udin was led out of the courtroom, around to a locked side room, past the police guards, and into a dim ante-chamber.

Several chairs leaned against the wall. A blade of sunlight struck through the dusty air.

On the floor sat Mukhtar Mai.

Her back was against the wall. Her knees were against her chest, her arms wrapped around them. She wore *shalwar kameez*, long tunic over pantaloon trousers, black with tiny red flowers. A black *dupatta* (shawl) fell down her hair. Stale cigarette smoke hung around her. The heat had matted her black hair against her forehead and the sides of her neck.

"Please, madam, sit on a chair," the lawyer asked.

She gathered herself up and sat, awkwardly, on the chair's edge. She looked at the floor. There was a stillness about her.

"Do you grant me power of attorney? I must have this if I am to represent you. Do you wish me to represent you?"

"*Ji (yes).*"

"Well then. You must talk to me frankly, as you would talk to your doctor. You must tell me every single thing. Hide nothing."

She nodded docilely, her mouth slightly open, one eye looking at her nose, the other looking just past him. Whether she had a lazy eye, or was cross-eyed, was impossible to tell in the muted light.

"Mukhtaran Bibi, what happened on June 22?"

She began in a mumble. A few words at a time.

"I was sitting in my house. My father came. He said: 'Get up. You must come to the Mastois. Your brother is in the police cell. We have to get him out. You must come to the Mastois, so we can get him from the police cell'," Mukhtar recounted to the young lawyer.

"My father took me from our house to the Mastois. When I reached there, four men grabbed me. They dragged me inside a room. Two of them stood guard outside. The other two touched me. They touched my chest, my breasts. They tore my shirt, at the front and sides. They tore it off me, over my head. They touched me more, grabbing me. Then they threw me out of the room."

Silence.

"Is that all?" asked Sodr-Udin.

"Then my father and my uncle took me home. Later my brother came back from the police cell," Mukhtar concluded.

Silence.

Qazi Sodr-Udin Alvi was shocked.

He knew the case from the saturated media coverage of the previous weeks: a village woman gang-raped on the orders of a panchayat tribal council, in vicarious eye-for-an-eye punishment for her brother's alleged rape of the Mastoi men's sister earlier the same day.

Sodr-Udin approached the official state-appointed prosecutors.

"I said to them: 'There are two different statements by Mukhtar Mai. One recorded by police, and one recorded later by the civil magistrate. The statements are different. She told me something different again. Which statement are you going to tutor her in?'"

"I will tutor her in the police statement," the prosecutor replied, according to Sodr-Udin's recollection almost four years later.

"But it is not the same as what she has told me," Sodr-Udin protested.

"What do you want, to destroy our case?" the prosecutor retorted angrily.

On the next day of hearing Sodr-Udin took his place among the prosecutors. He led Maulvi Razzaq, through his evidence-in-chief. Then Mukhtar Mai, prosecutrix, took the witness stand.

One of the government prosecutors stood up and sought the learned judge's attention on a point of order. He beseeched his honour to clarify the rules of engagement for the prosecutors.

The judge struck his gavel.

"Only those prosecutors appointed by the government may represent the complainant party," Judge Zulfikar Ali Malik stated. "Those representing the complainant are to show their certificates of appointment."

Three or four prosecutors produced their certificates. Qazi Sodr-Udin had none. He had been engaged privately by Mukhtar Mai and her family, unlike the prosecutors appointed by the government to represent her.

"Ms Mukhtar Mai, do you give Mr Qazi Sodr-Udin power of attorney to represent you in this case?" one of the prosecutors asked.

"No. I do not wish him to represent me."

Qazi Sodr-Udin stood to his feet.

"Your honour, I withdraw my power of attorney. I wish to do nothing further with this case," he pronounced in disgust.

Sodr-Udin gathered his file and walked out of the courthouse. He weaved through the mid-morning traffic of bullock-drawn wagons, around the giant four-wheel drives of feudal lords reigning over massive tracts of land beyond the city, and behind the garishly coloured donkey-pulled trolleys laden with women cloaked in black, *naqabs* drawn across their noses and mouths leaving only kohl-eyed eyes exposed. The cloaked women here look like pirates, Sinbad's cohorts still with us in the 21st century.

The young lawyer strode indignantly through the middle laneway of court stenographers and legal clerks, swung left into brilliant sunshine beaming down the widest lane of the barristers' bazaar, and into his grey office.

Sodr-Udin returned to the familiarity of his turbanned litigants and bearded defendants. He submerged himself back into his own clients' dark tales from the cotton and sugarcane fields, and his private communion with the Christian God. He paid no more attention to the trial of Mukhtar Mai and the apparent games of the government prosecutors and police. He knew their games too well.

With Sodr-Udin's departure from the Anti–Terrorism Courthouse of Dera Ghazi Khan, Mukhtar Mai's brief chance to tell her story straight, without the pressure or direction of others, melted into the mercury of the Indus plains' high summer.

\* \* \* \*

The Maulvi came to Sodr-Udin's office a day or two later.

"We are sorry. We are under pressure. You see, we are all staying in a 'circuit' house," Razzaq said, using the local term for the police safe house in which Mukhtar, her family and all the prosecution witnesses were being kept for the duration of the trial.

Nothing left to say, the man of the beard turned and left Sodr-Udin's crowded office. They never saw each other again.

# 26

# The Minister, The Barrister and the Police Investigator

### THE MINISTER

Nilofer Bakhtiar shot to notoriety as Pakistan's women's affairs minister when Mukhtar Mai was incredulously banned from traveling overseas in June 2005. Just as she was preparing to fly to the US to address a seminar, the government slapped Mukhtar's name on the Exit Control List – a list normally peopled by embezzlers, land grabbers, loan defaulters and suspected terrrorists. In the blaze of outrage over the travel ban, Mukhtar and her secretary disappeared for two days, last seen climbing into cars with government officials outside her village home. Not even Mukhtar's lawyer or the US embassy could locate her. Activist supporters received teary midnight phone calls from Mukhtar and Naseem, saying they were being held in an unfamiliar house somewhere in Islamabad.

When Mukhtar finally reappeared, bizarrely at a luncheon of diplomats at the well-to-do Islamabad Club, she was on the arm of Nilofer Bakhtiar. The minister's ghoulish toothy smile, alongside Mukhtar's stony countenance, was splashed across newspapers. Nilofer brought Mukhtar out of her secret location again the following day, before a show press-conference. With the same ghoulish smile, Nilofer declared the government had not 'kidnapped' Mukhtar as was reported in the press, and announced that Mukhtar had voluntarily cancelled her own US visit. Mukhtar's grim-faced expression and refusal to give apparently scripted answers left few in doubt that she had been dragged before the press to counteract the shameful publicity over placing a travel ban on an alleged rape victim.

By the time Nilofer agreed to be interviewed about Mukhtar Mai, she had been transferred to the Tourism portfolio. She called it a promotion for the excellent work she'd done for the women of Pakistan from 2003 to 2006.

She welcomed me with a hug to her new office in the Tourism Ministry the day after she moved. She was warmer and more gracious than those newspaper photos had suggested.

Nilofer had played a large role in Mukhtar's 'fight for justice'. As the 'Special Assistant to the Prime Minister' for Women's Development, Nilofer was one of the people Mukhtar sought out for help after the Lahore High Court's March 2005 acquittal of five of the six men convicted over the alleged gang-rape. Nilofer received Mukhtar in her office within a few days of the acquittal and put her on a direct phone line to the Prime Minister Shaukat Aziz. Mukhtar asked Nilofer and the Prime Minister for extra security, terrified that she and her family were in danger of attack from the newly freed Mastois. She got more than just a reinforced police guard. The government threw the acquitted men straight back into jail. The Mastois had been welcomed home to Mirwala with celebrations and traditional distributions of sweets. Three days later they were carted back to jail.

After Mukhtar lodged her Supreme Court appeal against the High Court's March 2005 acquittal, Nilofer assembled a legal team to help ensure the Court ruled in Mukhtar's favour.

*"When we had the Supreme Court appeal case coming up, we put all our efforts into winning it,"* the minister told me.

The star of the special legal team to win Mukhtar's appeal was no less than the Attorney General of Pakistan. Also brought in was a top Harvard-educated lawyer who specialised in crimes against women. The team thrashed out strategies to ensure the Supreme Court would accept Mukhtar's appeal.

Mukhtar had already accepted the offer of high-profile private counsel Aitzaz Ahsan, a former minister, high profile opposition politician and one of Pakistan's top barristers, to represent her *pro bono*.

With the best legal brains and the federal Attorney General on her side, Mukhtar won the day in the Supreme Court preliminary hearing in the last week of June 2005.

The apex court granted leave to hear her appeal, at a date still to be determined, and imposed fresh arrest orders on the 13 acquitted men – not just the five acquitted by the High Court in March 2005, but also the eight acquitted by the original trial court in August 2002.

The Supreme Court issued a rarely-used non-bailable arrest warrant for the 13 acquitted men, to jail them until the hearing of the final appeal.

The Maintenance of Public Order Act, under which they had been thrown back in jail in March, only allowed authorities to hold them without charge for three months. The order expired in early June. Without the Supreme Court's non-bailable arrest warrant, authorities would have been compelled to release the men who had been acquitted of any involvement in the alleged gang-rape. As of the writing of this book, the 13 acquitted men have been behind bars for 16 months. Recalling the March 2005 acquittal, Nilofer expressed frustration at criticism of the government's re-arrest of men who had been acquitted.

*"President Musharraf gave orders from his plane to put the men behind bars. Then we were criticized by rights groups who said 'This is unfair, it's against their rights to lock them up again',"* she expounded.

*"If we set them free, it's 'unfair'. If we put them behind bars, it's 'unfair'."*

*"By then (March 2005) the whole thing had been highlighted internationally and became such a hot issue.If these men were released it would be such a big setback to the image of the country."*

Nilofer confirmed that a 'secret' report into the crime against Mukhtar Mai, its background and its impact on the local community, had been commissioned by government intelligence agencies.

Despite being a cabinet member, she was never shown the report.

She had heard of its contents and claims second and third-hand, but was dismissive of them.

"The (intelligence) agencies have a report, which apparently says she was not raped by four people, that the time she was inside the room was too short for four men to rape her. But I didn't want to listen to that. I told them not to tell me such things. There is no proof to prove that she was not raped either," Nilofer told me.

"The report was presented to the President. I was never allowed to see it.

"I have always believed her. For me she was a victim, a woman who was raped. For me to go back at that point was impossible. The civil society and the media would have killed me.

*"My honest opinion is this: her case is very weak. So you see why it is difficult for us."*

## The Barrister

An eminent barrister from the prosecution team loves to talk with visitors, but only in private where he can drink his whisky. He refused to meet in hotel lobbies or restaurants because his high-profile meant he would surely be recognised. It had to be either his home or my hotel room. We met once in his loungeroom, and the second time in my hotel room with my fixer Qamar.

The barrister poured his scotch into a tall glass and filled it with soft drinks. He knocked back four full scotch and soft drink in two hours. Relaxing, he boasted that he would have got all 14 accused men acquitted in the first trial because the prosecution's case was so weak.

Despite the weakness of the case he was directed to represent, the barrister waived his right to order a reinvestigation because he feared a more thorough investigation would end up in favour of the defence.

*"Under Pakistani law it is possible to reinvestigate the case. Although the original police investigation was weak, I chose not to suggest a reinvestigation, because I felt I could prosecute based on the first investigation. It was enough," the barrister said.*

"I feared that if the investigation was repeated, it would cause a loss to the prosecution in the Mukhtar Mai case. So I didn't suggest it.

"It was in my mind that if the case was reinvestigated, it would smash the case of the prosecution. That the evidence may turn the other way. That the defence may get the benefit for the accused. That it may injure the cause of the prosecution."

*"Just like Mukhtar Mai improved her case in the court, by adding the term 'duniavi siasi taurper' to describe the manner of Faiz Mastoi when he decreed that she and her family be pardoned, so I feared fresh things may come up in favour of the defence."*

The three words *'duniavi siasi taurper'* meaning 'in an insincere manner' were added to Mukhtar Mai's statement for the trial, the barrister said. They were not used in her first statement to police.

*"She improved on her case for the trial,"* he said. *"According to Mukhtar Mai in her first statement to police Faiz Mastoi pardoned her family. But later on it was revealed by Mukhtar Mai that in fact he said so 'duniavi'—hypocritically, i.e. that he just said it for show.*

*"Mukhtar Mai changed her statement later on. She has improved the evidence by later adding the circumstances, i.e. that the words 'forgive her' were spoken 'insincerely'."*

Without accusing Faiz Mastoi of insincerity in his manner of pardoning her family, it may have been difficult to convict Faiz Mastoi of ordering the alleged gang-rape. Both defence and prosecution testified that he ordered the forgiveness of Mukhtar Mai's family for her brother's alleged rape of Salma Mastoi.

The trial judge in his summary said the four convicted rapists would not have committed their alleged acts if Faiz had really commanded that Mukhtar Mai be forgiven. On that count Faiz Mastoi was convicted of abetment and was sentenced to death.

I asked the barrister what the evidence was for convicting Ramzan Pachaar of abetting the gang-rape. The judge had said in his conclusion that without Pachaar's abetment the alleged pack-rape would not have happened.

*"Ramzan Pachaar actively participated in deciding on the rape,"* the barrister replied.

*"The court concluded this, based on the circumstances. Pachaar was the one who went to the police station to get Shakoor released. He took money from Shakoor's family to pay the police to free him."*

In our first meeting, the barrister had promised to go through the trial transcripts with me and explain which parts were 'police padding' and the reasons for their padding. In the second meeting he denied any police padding in this trial.

*"Police padding is a usual custom throughout the country. It is always done by police. But not in this case,"* he said in our second meeting.

I asked him what was behind the sudden dismissal of the privately-hired prosecution counsel Qazi Sadr-Udin Alvi, the only one who wasn't appointed by the state.

*"According to our thinking, he was a man of the defence. He might've gathered some information from the prosecution side and given it to the defence,"* the barrister replied.

The glaring weakness in the defence case was its lack of proof of the *sharai nikah*.

One of the glaring flaws in the prosecution was the lack of any tests like DNA, semen serology or semen group testing to match the semen swabs with the accused men. As they were facing death sentences, wasn't it important to be vacuum-tight on the identities of the alleged attackers?

The barrister said DNA tests were unknown in remote Punjab in mid-2002.

*"Even the 'higher-ups' were unaware of semen group-testing,"* he insisted.

The defence lawyers maintain, however, that such tests were available.

The medical report on Mukhtar Mai's semen test was *"an embarrassment"*, the barrister said, because the chemical examiner certified that the external swabs were stained, eight days after the incident. Defence lawyers point to this test as proof that all investigators including the Chemical Examiner were under pressure to win a conviction.

*"The Chemical Examiner's report shows you how much pressure the government officials were under,"* the prosecution barrister said, concurring with the defence.

*"The weakness of the prosecution case was in the evidence collected by the police."*

## THE POLICE INVESTIGATOR

In May 2006 Qamar and I located one of the original chief police investigators in the case. He had been suspended in its wake, but resurfaced three years later in Dera Ghazi Khan.

He would only speak to us off the record.

The investigator said that he and his team had been forbidden to investigate the case:

*"After publication of this news, our higher-ups (seniors) did not let us investigate the case. Instead they put pressure on us to complete the challan (file) of the case and arrest all the people nominated by Mukhtar Mai's father and supporters like Maulvi Razzaq,"* the police officer said.

The officer, who was based in the local Jatoi police station at the time that the gang-rape claim was made, said that the first people to approach police with claims that Mukhtar Mai had been gang-raped were local journalists. The local journalists were also the ones who pressed for the filing of charges:

*"Local press reporters forced for institution of this case so that they could get their stories in the newspapers. Mr. Mureed Abbas was more active among them. Mureed Abbas did not register the case. However he was the first person to inform police about this incident."*

He said the police then summoned Maulvi Razzaq to persuade Mukhtar Mai's reluctant father Ghulam Farid Gujjar to press charges.

*"Maulvi Razzaq was called by police to convince Mukhtar Mai's father to register a case, because her father was not ready to do so."*

Police were not convinced that the eight Mastois arrested from the village next to Mirwala and from another village on the other side of the Indus River, accused of participating in the supposed panchayat, were guilty.

*"We were neither confident that they were actually culprits."*

The investigating officer confirmed that two of the arrested Mastois were locked up on mistaken identity because their names matched two of the accused. Ghulam Fareed Mastoi and Fayyaz Mastoi had the same names as two suspects but were easier to arrest within the government-imposed deadlines for arrests. They ended up on death row, convicted of gang-rape.

*"It is a fact that some innocent Mastois were held because their names were identical,"* the investigator said. He concluded with his personal view:

*"It is my personal opinion that this case was exploited by different quarters to take revenge against the Mastois for past insults."*

# 27

# You Go, Girl!!

A Californian woman sits erect at a dinner table, beaming over a glass of wine, raised in toast.

*"Mukhtaran – I raise my glass to you and your bravery and courage. This is a tradition in my country when someone is deserving of special honor. Love from across the ocean where women are free."*

Signed: Joan, the smiling woman in the photograph. From a pile of letters to Mukhtar Mai from North America.

An illiterate woman's fight against brutalisation of women and illiteracy shook a universal chord with ordinary people on the other side of the world.

Glimmering in donations and letters to Mukhtar Mai via *The New York Times* columnist Nicholas Krystof, following his September 2004 op-ed piece "Sentenced to be Raped", is the universality of Mukhtar's bid to change the conditions she knows to save women from brutalisation and commoditisation. Mukhtar's campaign to end rape and bondage of women through education tapped into a collective longing, unbound by borders or creed.

Salutes of solidarity poured in from across America: a Beverly Hills Jewess; Indian immigrants in Texas; ladies' book clubs; a rape counselor in Colorado; a women's cooking club; a Californian captain of industry; a tiny mid-western school; the mother of an adopted Romanian girl; a retirement village. From humble five dollar contributions to 3,500 dollar cheques, together they raised 135,000 dollars for Mukhtar Mai and her two schools.

Yet this hand-written symphony of accolades, empathy, and respect for a woman worlds away in space, time and experience, reveals more: a post 9/11 Western world struggling to understand Islam and bridge religious differences.

Mukhtar's applauders sent photos: of Texan spring flowers, family shots of a 3 year old girl about to start school, a woman on a beach, class photos, and Joan raising her glass to Mukhtar. The letters included offers of spare rooms from Chicago to Ohio to the desert near Death Valley. In Colorado, this woman saw a sister in Mukhtar. She had survived rape.

*"You are my hero. Giving of yourself in service to others is to emulate and honor the divine... this is true in all religions. Your courage to stand up for, What Is Just is a shining example for women and men around the world. I enclose a check to help you with your school. I wish that we could*

*speak more easily because I feel we are sisters. I wish that we could join our forces to fight ignorance and injustice,"* wrote Kailuni.

*"I also was raped. I use the strength from surviving that experience to help others now. I volunteer for a rape crisis and domestic violence telephone hotline and work to provide shelter for the abused, and to educate the abusers and society as a whole that there is a better way. How I wish I could work with you... to visit with you, to bring you here, to hold your hand and give you strength! I send you lots of love with this check....You go, girl!!!"*

Kailuni cursed the mother of Mukhtar's one convicted rapist, Abdul Khaliq. She is also the mother of one of the men acquitted of gang-rape charges but still in jail, Allah Ditta:

"To Taj Bibi: It is YOU that is disgraced....in the eyes of all gods of all religions and of all civilized people. You are a disgrace to the female sex, whose responsibility it is to teach love to the world. To restore your grace you must cultivate a love and respect for all human beings, especially women. You must rise above your primitive feeling of superiority because, with such evil in your heart, you can only be inferior."

From a man in San Francisco:

*"You are a woman of incredible spirit and mental toughness. Indeed, a hero and leader for all the peoples of the world to emulate."*

In Illinois, Laurie established the "Women Cooking for Women" club after reading Mukhtar's tale.

*"Your story brought tears to my eyes and a sense of urgency to my soul,"* she wrote.

*"I could send you $10 by myself, or more if I could spread your story. So, I started a women's group which now meets every month to raise money for different projects and causes that help women around the world.*

*"The enclosed check is the result of donations collected from our first gathering. About twenty women met, shared a meal and discussed your story. We are not wealthy women, but women that want to reach out to help others. This check is sent with our blessings for a brighter future for you and women of Pakistan. Thanks for making a difference."*

A Marin County mid-wife and sexual assault nurse who examines rape victims acknowledged difficulties in prosecuting rape persist in the West as well.

*"Our evidentiary exams help support cases against the perpetrator,"* Melanie wrote of her work.

*"We live in a society that has only just recently started to come to terms with bringing justice to the perpetrator instead of blaming the victim. The reality is that most cases never see the light of day. Yes, at least we have a criminal justice system. Yet our social climate still tends to cast*

*suspicion on the woman and her sexual history. Most women don't report the rape or fail to pursue their assailant out of fear."*

*"I am not saying that women in the United States are in the same boat as Ms Bibi or the millions living in other countries. That is why I am sending this check. She needs money to stay alive.*

*"Ms Bibi's courage is so inspiring to me."*

The Laughing Ladies Book Club of British Columbia, Canada hailed Mukhtar's choice to educate boys as well as girls.

*"As the mothers of girls and boys, we admire greatly her efforts to educate the children, regardless of gender. While it's absolutely important to educate girls and women, the same is true of boys and men. What good does it do to just educate females if their marriage choices are limited to close-minded men?"*

A man called Richard shuddered *"like an earthquake"* at what men did to Mukhtar:

"Dear Friend: Your story moved my spirit like an earthquake shakes the ground. I am sad that men would treat you as they did. I pray that you will continue your great work in the village, which will bring joy to the hearts of so many children. Some day, women will be equal with men. This begins with education, so that boys will learn to respect girls, and girls will insist upon receiving respect.

"Please use this money to provide books and materials to your schools or salary for the teachers. I pray that others will join you and protect you so that you may continue. Some day my wife and I would like to visit you and your schools, God willing."

'Home Hi', a girls' middle school in Urbana, Illinois held a fall home-bake at the local farmers' market for Mukhtar's school. They raised 100 dollars, and enclosed a school photo of all 43 students.

*"Home Hi is an all girls middle school from 5th through 8th grades. We have a total of 43 girls in our school,"* wrote executive director Brigitte.

*"In the fall we had a bake sale at our local farmer's market. At the sale we featured the article (Krystof) had written about Mukhtaran Bibi and her act of courage in Pakistan. When people made a donation we gave them a pin that the girls had made in art class. We are enclosing a check for $100 because we value what she has done and what she is doing."*

The home bake was featured in the local Champaigne-*Urbana News Gazette*.

A desert dweller near Las Vegas' Death Valley offered his spare room:

*"Seems boys need proper education as much as girls, for different reasons! We all need to learn about respecting others. Muhammad (the*

Prophet, PBUH) as I've read about him was very mindful and considerate of women—something very wrong appears to have happened with those who consider themselves his followers.

"Should Ms Mukhtaran ever need to get away to a safe haven – not of much usefulness to others, – I live in the desert between Death Valley & Las Vegas (good airport) & would be happy to help her – or maybe going to Belgium easier these days with current US strictures on visitors from Middle East – let me know- have also friends & family in Brussels to ask about haven."

"*Dear Lady, I read of your story in the paper, and cried,*" wrote Deborah of San Jose, California.

"*I am a mother of an 11 year old boy, a free woman, a strong wife, a happy 47 year old writer and activist. You are my hero as of today.*"

"*I cannot believe the strength and love of life that God has bestowed on you, and I wish I could be there to give you happy hugs, warm smiles, and to personally beat the daylights out of anyone who dared to hurt you.*"

Deborah and her husband sent a donation towards "*the protection you so rightly deserve, the schools you have built as proof that women are powerful, important beings, and to help you in what you seek.*"

"*I can never know the horror of living through gang–rape and the attempt to humiliate and shame you into killing yourself—but I am so very, very proud of you for not letting others determine your future, and for loving life more than keeping the pain. The example you show – the sheer power of staying alive and standing up as proof to all the little girls and boys of your world—I am most humbled.*"

"*Women like you will be the ones that change the world for the better, and I send my love and support.*"

Frederic, the chairman of a Californian IT company asked Mukhtar to use his donation "*for herself, to bring her joy, happiness, and comfort in a world that has treated her so badly.*"

"*It is very upsetting for me to realize that while we have sponsored extremely sophisticated and learned philosophers creating exceptional scientific knowledge about multiple subjects that equal or exceed the fantasies of science fiction writers, we haven't been able or willing to divert efforts or funds to bring a reasonable level of sanitation, education, health and safety to multitudes in the third world,*" Frederic wrote.

A masseuse sent a day's earnings:

"I admire that you started schools in your village. I want to help. I enclose a check for $300 (what I will earn today doing massages). Also I plan to send paper, chalk and picture books to your Pakistan address."

A lady of Tower Grove Drive Beverly Hills compared Mukhtar to Anne

Frank, the Holocaust diarist who defied her persecutors from her attic hideout by writing a journal.

"*Bibi may only have a fourth grade education at this point but, in my eyes, she is more of a hero and leaders than lots of Ivy Leaguers I know,*" Martha wrote.

"*As a Jew, I am always highly sensitised to persecution and injustice. Bibi reminds me of Anne Frank, who, like Bibi, resisted despair, refused to abandon hope and, in the face of spectacular cruelty and injustice, nevertheless persisted in believing that the world could be much improved if only more people were to give of themselves. By refusing to be vanquished by the deplorable gang–rape, by refusing to bow to cultural pressure to commit suicide, by testifying against the rapists, and by dedicating herself and her meager resources to educating others, Bibi is living Anne Frank's vision.*"

"*It is easy for women in the US to take our gender rights and equality for granted, but we must not forget that much of that equality – in education, athletics, career and even reproductive rights – has been achieved only in the last 40 years. I could not agree more with Bibi's belief that education is the answer. I am enclosing a check for $1,000 for Bibi's school and/or police protection so that she can continue her quest for women's rights and education.*"

A Kansas doctor called Mukhtar "*a person of greatness in the world.*"

"*Many people have learned of your suffering and your courage....You have answered cruelty with goodness. This is a wonderful thing. It means you are a person of greatness in the world... Please accept this donation to help with your school. May all blessings come to you and those you love. You have my deepest respect.*"

On an anonymous card, a hand-drawn flower. "*For a strong woman – Peace. A friend in the United States.*"

From Rafael, address not listed: "*I live in the United States of America and I read about you, your troubles and your schools in the newspaper 'The New York Times.' Your are doing something very important, and I would like to help you with this small amount of money. God bless you.*"

Mukhtar's life touched a nerve with the mother of a Romanian-born daughter.

"*I am a single mom with an 8 year old daughter. She was born in Romania. We have a very happy and secure life. Your article reminds me of the reality that her fate could have taken a different turn.*"

Indian immigrants from Calcutta, leading a new life in Texas, saw hope for women across the sub-continent:

"*We deeply respect your courage and wisdom. We wish you and your family well. We are sending a small donation for your school. We are very confident that your path is the right path. Your courage will give courage to many, many women in the Indian sub-continent. May God bless you."*

In Colorado, another sister:

*"Thank you for your courage. I think of you everyday with love. We are sisters."*

The 'Friends of Mukhtaran Bibi' was established by a group of teachers in Los Angeles:

*"We heard about your story and struggle for justice and restoration of humanity of women through the New York Times article. As fellow women and educators, we want to stand behind you for your noble cause. As a token we would like to make a financial commitment each month for one year. We start off from three, but hopefully more friends would join in the coming month. We hope you would be encouraged by our small gift to continue to fight against injustice against women in Pakistan."* Their first letter, signed October 28, carried a 25 dollar contribution.

By the next month, the "Friends of Mukhtaran Bibi" had grown to four. *"As educators, we truly understand the need for education. We are cognizant that not only do women need to be informed of their human rights, but men need to be made aware also."*

Another women's book group sent a cheque for 500 dollars: "It's hard to imagine how Mukhtaran Bibi found such fortitude in her suffering. I shared this story with my book group and we wanted to help support Ms Bibi's school."

From David of San Francisco: *"Please let me know if somebody takes on the job of seeing that the schools stay open. I am not rich enough to fund anything of such scale, but it does seem to me worthy of doing – both as a symbolic gesture in support of common decency (to say nothing of uncommon courage) and as a material act in support of education."*

In Bethlehem, New Hampshire a mountain school raised 1,271 dollars.

*"I read about your unfortunate situation in the news a few months ago and decided to share it with my fellow students at The White Mountain School,"* wrote Alex.

*"So many of them wanted to help you that they gave a total of $1,271. We hope you can pay teachers, buy materials, give scholarships or whatever else is needed to keep your school open.*

*"Community Service is an important part of the school program and your situation caught the interest and compassion of everyone. We hope you can continue to run your school for a long time and to keep yourself safe."*

Another teacher, Careen: *"I teach. I care. And I wish I could do more. Here at least is a little."*

Valerie shared Mukhtar's story with her adolescent daughter. *"I'm not naive, but I'm consistently shocked at the cruel injustices which thrive in our world. What was amazing about your story was how Ms Bibi's strength of spirit survived and surpassed the terror and torture. I shared the story with my 13 year old daughter because I wanted it to take hold of her now, while she is developing a global awareness, as I agree that only education and awareness can change the twisted traditions of an ancient culture's views with concern to woman.*

*"I don't want my daughter to turn her head, but to see. Perhaps one day, she will be able to institute a program, a policy, or a vote which can facilitate better treatment of women, universally. Still, I rue the generations lost to the long process called change."*

Fom Ellaha and Nazilah, an offer of a room in Ohio. *"You're welcome any time."*

A law student living on loans and occasional part-time work found enough cash to send a *"small check."*

So did a single mother and her child, who *"both love and believe in education."*

A woman minister of the First Congregational Church in Connecticut sent her name card with a quote:

"We have come not as scholars but as seekers, needing wholeness, compassion and a challenge. We have come ready to journey on together." Inscribed in her own hand, a simple "Thank you, Mukhtaran."

A retirement village resident collected 165 dollars from fellow retirees. *"Sorry it isn't a lot more,"* she lamented.

Phyllis empathised with the need for change in both Mukhtar's country and her own:

*"Dear Mrs Bibi: Please know how deeply concerned many of us are with your situation and are praying with you. How I wish I could change things in your nation and mine."*

From Linda of Minneapolis: *"Be assured that you have great honor and respect across the world. I have shared your story with friends and relatives; we are in awe of your great courage and generosity of spirit. I hope this small donation will help support your schools."*

*"You are not all alone,"* wrote Ursula.

*"God bless you and give you strength for the wonderful work you are doing. It must be very hard for you. I thank God that there are women like you in this world."*

A doctor in Chicago offered her room.

"I read of your bravery in The New York Times. I do not want you killed by village bullies. Please let me sponsor a trip to America and you can be my guest in Chicago and we can sit down and figure out what your next move should be! I think you have done your best in that little village. Perhaps now you should move to the world stage!

*"Just let me know if you want to come for a visit and I will wire you a ticket."*

On a card with a reprint of an old Afghan marriage contract, above a Jewish proverb from the Torah: (Ketubbah): *"I greatly rejoice in the Lord, My whole being exults in God. For He has clothed me with garments of triumph, Wrapped me in a robe of victory, Like a bridegroom adorned with a turban, Like a bride bedecked with her finery."* Isaiah 61:10

Sally sent the card to Mukhtar with a donation in honour, she wrote, of her friends' marriage.

*"I wish that I could send more money, but please know that I deeply admire and respect your remarkable courage, strength, generosity and dignity."*

From an anonymous sender:

*"For the woman bettering the lives of women around her, May Allah's blessings be upon you."*

Evelyn: *"The actions of women like you make the world better. I admire your courage and strength."*

A watercolour butterfly card from Linda: *"You are very brave. I very much admire your courage and determination. You are an inspiration to women all over the world. I hope this small gift will be of some help."*

A simple salute from Beverly: *"I respect you."*

A prayer pledged from Mary: *"I admire your courage, wisdom and strength. I hope your school is successful in changing young girls' lives. I will pray for you and for your village."*

Inside a simple "Thank You" card, hand-drawn hearts and flowers from Paula of Santa Cruz: *"Mukhtaran, You are an inspiration to the women of the world. God bless you! Thank you for your great courage!"*

Nevet smiles from under a beach umbrella, sitting by an ocean shore:

*"Hello Mukhtaran: Your courage is great. My husband and children support you. This is a picture of me at the ocean. We want to help."*

A photo of pink spring flowers in Texas: *"Dear Mukhtaran, I admire your strength and your courage."*

A family snap of a New Hampshire philosophy lecturer with her husband and three-year old daughter, about to enter school:

*"I am very happy to see that you are doing well in your school. You are very courageous and should be proud. Here is a photo of my family here in the US. My daughter is 3 years old and starting school already!"*

Scribbled across a lined sheaf of paper from Jai, a modern American salute:

*"You go, girl!"*

# 28

# Deliverance

### THE MASTOI BROTHER

Punnu Mastoi is racked with bitterness and loathing. He and two cousins spent more than three years behind bars for an apparently concocted, unproven claim of raping Mukhtar's brother Shakoor in the sugarcane. The bitterness stings even more when he considers that, in his family's eyes, Shakoor had raped his little sister in the sugarcane – and that's how the whole sordid tale began.

The last time I met Punnu was the end of April 2006. It was my last trip to Mirwala, Multan, Jatoi and Dera Ghazi Khan. The southern Punjab was no longer bearable. The scorching heatwave had prematurely shrouded the southern Punjab in walls of close heat. It was already 46 degrees and climbing in the furnace of Pakistan. In this heat, more than at any other time, the Multan region matches its moniker of *"Gard, Garma, Gada, Goristan"* - Persian for "City of Dust, Heat, Beggars and Graveyards."

The fruit carts in the roadside bazaars of towns stretching west from Multan towards the Indus backwaters nearly rolled over themselves with a thousand and one watermelons.

Wheat was being harvested and gathered into bundles. Family groups were in the fields. Women squatted, headscarves trailing down their backs, and whipped their sickles at the base of the long grass. Men brought out threshing machines to sift the chaff from the grain. Fountains of gold chaff dust blew out from the threshers.

Bullocks pulled wooden carts loaded high with sacks of grain. Canopied mule-drawn buggies passed camel trains of four to five ambling beasts, all bearing hessian bags of new wheat. Every means of transport - donkeys, camels, bullock-drays, motorbikes, carts on wheels - was engaged in carrying the harvested wheat to the mills or markets. Trucks bulging like bloated cow udders with loads of grains weaved among the animals.

Young sugarcane stalks were shooting up in a few fields already switched to the summer crop. But irrigation canals had dried up. Drought set in. Villages on the other side of the Indus were being abandoned by tribes facing starvation after months of no water and dying livestock. Residents said large landowners were stealing what little water remained by plumbing the canals with their own hastily-installed wells along the banks.

The heat intensified the rot and wretchedness seething beneath the hospitality and piousness.

"Our children often go for days without food. They hadn't eaten for three days when you visited my mother's house six months ago," Punnu railed.

"They were starving!" His rage was inconsolable.

I remembered noticing on that November morning visit that there was no cooking fire, no chai (tea) on the boil, no dough being kneaded for roti (leavened bread). The children were in rags and weeping boils showed through the girls' threadbare sleeves.

"The Maulvi Razzaq's brother met a fatal car crash in Karachi. His body was cut into pieces," Punnu recounts breathlessly, pitilessly, coldly.

A white prayer cap crowned Punnu's glossy black hair. Thick curls of black chest hair protruded from the low open neck of his blue-grey kameez tunic. Thick black eyebrows overlapped and knitted together.

"It was punishment by the Almighty for plotting against us."

Punnu is speaking of Maulvi Razzaq's brother Haji Altaf Hussain, a landowner from the largest tribe in Mirwala, the Jatois. Haji had testified as a key prosecution witness, claiming to have been present when Mukhtar Mai was allegedly dragged into the home of Abdul Khaliq Mastoi and gang-raped.

There are suggestions that the Mecca pilgrim was a fabricated witness. In his original statement to police, Haji said he had actually stayed in Mukhtar Mai's home while her father and uncle Sabir took her to the gathering of the Mastois.

"Now Maulvi Razzaq is crying at night. He says Mastoi children are disturbing his dreams," Punnu rants.

Punnu was jailed for three years on the conviction of sodomising Mukhtar Mai's teenage brother Abdul Shakoor. That was the judiciary's response to Salma Mastoi's cry of rape.

The police and courts listened to Shakoor's denial of molesting Salma and his counter-claim that Salma's oldest brother Punnu and two Mastoi cousins seized him from out of the blue in the middle of the day as he was napping under a tree, dragged him into the sugarcane, and sodomised him.

The medical exam of Shakoor found no proof of rape. The chemical examiner found no traces of semen. The doctor, Fazl Hussain, found induration of the anal region but no bruising or tear marks. The doctor concluded rape anyway. Under cross-examination at the sodomy trial in 2003, Dr Hussain was unable to explain why.

In Jatoi this hot April, Punnu seems shorter and hairier than our first meeting at the barristers' chambers in Dera Ghazi Khan, and he is less restrained in fury.

I found Punnu, after hours of seemingly futile searching in the suffocating sauna of Jatoi and Mirwala, at a crude shop-front flour mill. Since getting out of jail two months earlier, he has found work grinding wheatgrain here for 100 rupees ($1.60) a day. He is the breadwinner for 32 mouths.

With Punnu was six year old Kashif, a son of Punnu's brother Allah Ditta. Allah Ditta is in jail despite being acquitted more than a year back of gang-rape charges.

Kashif is working in the fields on the wheat harvest. Even the six-year-old has to pitch in with labour to supplement Punnu's daily 100 rupee wage.

Punnu was astonished that I found him, confused as to how anyone could locate him in the endless rows of crude shopfronts and Dickensian light industry beyond the outskirts of Jatoi.

It wasn't a 'pleased to see you again' kind of astonishment.

A crowd of 30 or 40 labourers, street kids, and onlookers pressed in on us as we tried to talk to Punnu. We led him to an empty shopfront so we could go inside and talk privately. The crowd followed us and grew larger and more intense.

Punnu was in no mood to accommodate us.

"Come back at 6 when I've finished my work," he snapped aggressively.

We suggested he join us in our air-conditioned car. He preferred to mount his rusty bicycle and lead our car away from the crowd. We followed him over a crumbling bridge until he suddenly nosed his bike into a roadside clearing under a tree. The shade made little difference to the heat. Freshly cut wheat was being tied into bundles in the field alongside us.

He refused to step out of the heat into our cool car. Instead he shouted down at us from his standing point by the front passenger door. He refused to accept our bottled water. He tossed back the remaining half-pack of cigarettes we offered, taking and lighting just one.

"We have never begged for help from anyone. We passed through three years of poverty.

We faced starvation, we faced hunger. But we never begged for a single pint of water," he snarled. Even the six-year-old nephew refused to take a bottle of water from us.

Saturdays are working days throughout Pakistan. Punnu neither lived nor worked in Mirwala. He lived in Jatoi town with his wife and three children, 13 kilometres from Mirwala. Like every other Saturday, Punnu was at work on June 22, 2002 in Jatoi in the tannery he was employed at, he says.

Working by his side on June 22, as on every working day, was his brother Allah Ditta, Punnu adds.

Punnu says neither he nor his brother were present at the gathering or *akath* of Mastois in the hours after Salma's alleged rape.

Word of the alleged rape of Salma by Mukhtar Mai's brother did not reach them until Sunday, the one day of rest in the Pakistani week. They rushed immediately to Mirwala on the Sunday.

Cousins Jamil and Manzoor lived six kilometres away.

The counter-claims that Shakoor was gang-raped by Punnu and cousins Jamil and Manzoor in the middle of the day on June 22 were first mentioned to the police on June 30, according to prosecution testimony. Charges were formally filed on July 3.

At the time Punnu and cousins were supposed to have assaulted Shakoor in the sugarcane between Mukhtar's home and Punnu's mother's home, Punnu was at work as usual on a Saturday, in Jatoi 13 kilometres away from the sugarcane field.

The sodomy trial was held nine months after the conviction of six men over the alleged gang-rape of Shakoor's sister Mukhtar.

There were no witnesses to the alleged sodomisation of Shakoor and no medical evidence. They were convicted nevertheless. The appeal against their near-groundless convicion of gang-sodomy was thrown out in February 2004.

## THE GUJJAR BROTHER

I met Shakoor several times in 2005 but he evaded most requests to interview him. He finally agreed on November 28. My translator and I took him into the office of the school run by Mukhtar and her secretary Naseem Akhtar adjoining the family home. Naseem joined us, saying Shakoor needed her support during the interview.

Shakoor was shy and awkward and gave short, unelaborative answers. He was understandably uncomfortable when we asked him to recount the alleged sodomisation.

Shifting in his seat and wringing his hands, he repeated his story that he was asleep under a Shareen tree next to the sugarcane field, when a hand was slapped across his mouth and he was dragged into the sugarcane.

A few times he moved to get up and leave the room.

He didn't reply to the question of what actually happened.

"*Did they beat you?*"

"*Yes.*"

"*What did they do then?*"

Shakoor looked at Naseem as if seeking permission to leave.

"*Did all three attack you?*", I persisted.

"*Yes.*"

"*Did they tear your clothes?*"

"*Yes.*"

*"Then what?"*

*"I shouted for help. Then they dragged me into the Mastoi house."*

I asked him earlier if he had met or spoken to Salma before June 22. He said 'never'.

I asked him what he did after leaving school at the end of fifth grade. He had attended the government boys' primary school in the centre of Mirwala, nine kilometres away.

Shakoor said he used to help his brother in the fields.

Naseem spoke up.

*"Shakoor used to check the fields, look for seeds in the bazaar, sow the seeds,"* she volunteered.

*"Is that right Shakoor, you used to sow the seeds?"* I asked.

*"No,"* he replied.

*"So what did you do in the fields? Did you pick the cotton?"*

*"No, in this village, girls and women pick the cotton. I just used to watch the girls in the field."*

In our interview, three and a half years after the alleged gang-rape of Mukhtar Mai, Shakoor gave his age as 18 or 19. That would put him, by his own estimates, at around 15 on the fateful day of June 22, 2002. The prosecution had always given his age at the time as 11. Consequently suggestions that an 11 year old had raped an older woman were scoffed at.

Salma, when I met her in March 2006, put her own age at 23 or 24 – although she appeared younger. That would make her around 20 in the middle of 2002, by her own estimate. Some reporters had been told she was 30. Reports that she was 30 added to the incredulity at suggestions that Shakoor had raped or molested her in any way.

Had it been clear at the time that it was a case of a 15 to 16 year old having relations with a 20 to 21 year old, the public may not have been so dismissive.

Within a year of the alleged gang-rapes of Mukhtar and her brother, Shakoor was married to his first cousin Amna, the daughter of his paternal uncle. Amna bore Shakoor a son after one year.

They now live with his parents, Mukhtar and his older brother's family, in the walled compound he and Mukhtar were born in. Shakoor has opened a small shop selling basic amenities in Mirwala centre.

Salma had two and a half years of married life with her husband Khalil before he was taken away in March 2005 and locked up - for a crime he was acquitted of twice. As of the writing of this book he was still a jailed acquitee 16 months on. His alleged crime: to have been present among the gathering of Mastois (numbering either 30 or over 200, according to the two sides' conflicting estimates) before which Mukhtar Mai was allegedly dragged several dozen metres into the Mastoi family compound.

The Mastois say they had never gone to the police to lodge charges over the alleged rape of their girl Salma because they had got a compromise from the Gujjar family in the form of Mukhtar Mai as a compensatory bride. The handover of a compensatory bride accords with village customs.

Then the Mastois married Salma off to a cousin within five days of June 22. Salma left the area to live over the other side of the Indus in Jampur, on the left bank, with her husband's family.

Punnu and his two cousins served out their time for the alleged sodomisation of Abdul Shakoor. They say Shakoor concocted the story to hide his episode in the sugarcane with Salma Mastoi. But no one was listening to the Mastois.

"Prison is a hell," Punnu cursed.

"The other inmates use bad language about us. Because they think we committed an ugly crime. Everybody was profaning us. Nobody was ready to listen to us."

"Fourteen members of our biraderi (clan) are still behind bars, all — bar one — without any conviction or sentence. So many injustices have been inflicted on our family. We are very disturbed, emotionally and physically."

## The Mullah

*On the day of our last search for Punnu we were supposed to meet the mullah of Mirwala, Maulvi Razzaq. He had proved elusive on earlier trips. It was the same again. We drove to his Farooqia mosque in the centre of Mirwala. Kohl-eyed religious students and teachers from the madrassa (Koranic school) attached to the mosque gathered round our car.*

"Ustad *(master) has gone to Muzaffargarh (the district capital, two hours drive away) to meet the Nazim (mayor)," they said.*

I asked the curious students and teachers to confirm the name of Abdul Razzaq's mosque. It had been referred to as both Farooqia and Imamia. The name etched above the entrance in Urdu calligraphy was Farooqia.

"Sipah-e-Sahaba (Army of the Companions of the Prophet) demanded Maulvi Razzaq change the name to one of their names. So it was re-named Farooqia," one of the teachers said.

"So this is a Sipah-e-Sahaba mosque?" I asked.

"Yes," the students and teacher answered in chorus.

My erstwhile local researcher Qamar finally caught the elusive mullah in the mosque after Maghreb evening prayers in May 2006.

I wanted to ask the mullah whether it was true, as the defence lawyer team alleged, that he had drafted Mukhtar Mai's statement to police when the allegation of rape was first reported.

"Yes," he answered without hesitation. "*I drafted the statement of Mukhtar Mai on her behalf.*"

"*Did you perform sharai nikah between Mukhtar Mai and Abdul Khaliq?*" Qamar asked.

"*No. There was no nikah between Mukhtar Mai and Abdul Khaliq. That story was fabricated by the Mastois,*" Razzaq replied.

"*What were your relations like with Mastois before this incident?*"

"*I have good relations with the Mastois then and now,*" Razzaq said.

"*Were you angry when Mastois married Salma to Khalil Mastoi, instead of Shakoor? Wasn't she supposed to marry Shakoor under a* watta-satta *agreement?*"

"*Salma was married to Khalil and I have no concern with this marriage,*" Razzaq replied.

"How many Mastois were present in the gathering?"

"*About 200 to 250 people were present,*" the cleric answered.

"*Was it an akath or panchayat?*" Qamar asked.

"*It was a formal panchayat,*" Razzaq replied.

"How many people sat on the *panchayat?*"

"Four people. Faiz Mastoi, Ramzan Pachaar, Manzoor Khan Jatoi and myself."

### THE LUMBERDAR

Each village in rural Pakistan has a curious figure called the 'lumberdar'.

He is supposed to hear and see everything and report to the relevant higher departments. He is supposed to keep the police informed of wayward happenings and crimes.

A 75-year-old named Mulazim Hussain Jatoi, son of Ali Raza Khan, was the lumberdar of Mirwala in June 2002.

He says he saw and heard nothing on the actual day.

"*Did you witness the gathering?*" Qamar asked.

"*No, I did not see it. However I was in the Friday prayer congregation when Maulvi Abdul Razzaq narrated the story in a very sensational manner,*" the lumberdar replied.

"*Was the Mastois gathering an akath or panchayat?*

"*I don't know. However I heard from other people that it was an akath of a large number of people.*"

"What did you see?"

"I did not see anything."

"Was a *sharai nikah* performed between Abdul Khaliq and Mukhtar Mai?"

"I don't know."

"How many Mastois were present in the gathering?"

"I don't know."

"Were they armed?"

"I don't know."

"What did the gathering decide?"

*"I don't know."*

Punnu Mastoi maintains the innocence of all his family.

"If you were a Muslim, I would swear on the Holy Koran before you that none of this happened," he said in our second and last meeting in April 2006.

"No one can change the destiny of anyone. Back then no one was ready to listen to us. Everybody was profaning us. Now the time has changed and some people are saying we are innocent."

"While we were in prison (Federal Information Minister) Sheikh Rashid visited. A prisoner asked him 'Why do you keep innocent people who are acquitted in prison?'

Sheikh Rashid replied: 'I spent five years in prison myself, but to this day I am not aware what crime I committed'," Punnu related.

"The state is like a river. It can flood and erode the land at any time. When the Almighty is angry, everything is destroyed. Allah tests the people by giving them difficulties, putting them through hardship," Punnu declared.

"The day is not far off when we will be free."

# 29

# Into the Mirror

It was four years almost to the day since the violation of Mukhtar Mai when 13 men gathered in the village of Waddowala, 10 kilometres east of Mirwala. Like June 22, 2002, the afternoon of June 21, 2006 was inhumanly suffocating.

Mostly of the Kharos clan, the men had gathered to come up with a 'sulah' for a shocking cry of rape.

Among them was Hazoor Bakhsh of the Tatla Gujjar clan: Mukhtar Mai's elder brother.

\* \* \* \*

Three days earlier a girl called Nasim, aged 11 according to a doctor, was at home with her blind grandmother when three teenagers from her village burst into the home.

Nazir Ahmed, around 14 years old, and his cousins Abid a.k.a 'Daddy' and Muhammad Ajmal, dragged Nasim from the house. In a field Nazir raped Nasim. The trio left her unconscious in the field. That is the story according to Nasim's father, Rasul Bakhsh, 65 years old.

The girl's grandfather Haji Khan summonsed 12 other men to gather and decide on how to compensate his family—village style.

The men of Waddowala had sought out Hazoor Bakhsh to join the gathering. As Mukhtar Mai's stature grew, so had her family's stature and their influence in local affairs.

"I was an observer. I was invited by the elders of the Kharos clan to help them," Hazoor Bakhsh confirmed.[1]

The 'sulah' settled on by the 13 men gathered for the June 21 meeting was familiar: the cruel and common custom of vani.

The men ordered the teenager accused of rape, Nazir Ahmed, to hand over his 17 year old sister Faizan as a compromise vani bride to Nasim's 65-year-old father, Rasul Bakhsh. Nazir and Faizan's father Abdul Majid was absent.

The nikah took place swiftly—before Abdul Majid even knew of the rape allegation against his son and the gathering of tribesmen to sort out the feud.

Local prayer leader or 'maulvi' Hafiz Rasul Bakhsh Chachar performed

---

1. Interview with Abdul Sattar Qamar, July 5, 2006

an on-the-spot *nikah*. This time a registrar was on hand to register a *nikah-nama*—marriage certificate.

Sixty-five year old Rasul Bakhsh took home his new 17 year old bride.

Abdul Majid returned to his village the next day to discover his daughter married to an old man. In fury he marched to Rasul Bakhsh's house and seized his daughter back.

"How can I express my rage at this happening in my absence? As soon as I heard what happened I went and took my daughter back," Abdul Majid said in an interview two weeks later.[2]

Rasul Bakhsh responded to the loss of his compensation bride by going to the police and lodging formal rape charges against Abdul Majid's son Nazir. Abdul Majid cried conspiracy.

"I don't believe my son committed any rape, he is only 14 or 15 years old. Rasul Bakhsh told police that his daughter is seven years old but she's actually closer to 9 years old, and the medical report put her age at 11," the father said.[3]

"It's my suspicion that this is all a conspiracy by my hostile relatives to get my daughter."

Men who took part in the gathering said it was not a '*panchayat*', but an '*akath*'.

"We cannot say this was a '*panchayat*', but an '*akath*'—a gathering of clan members to negotiate compensation for the family of the raped girl," said Haji Khan, the girl's grandfather.[4]

"We settle our disputes, even murder or rape cases, through negotiation and we compensate the victim's family."

Another member of the gathering, Karam Hussain, said they had made the appropriate decision:

"We took the right decision, with the consent of the elders of the clan. We even got the affirmation of the accused boy, who confessed before us to the crime. We tried our best to save the family from litigation."[5]

Abdul Majid also went to the police, charging that the forced marriage of his daughter Faizan was equivalent to rape.

Days later, Faizan spoke up – another cry of rape. She said her 65-year-old groom tried to rape her when he took her home.

Abdul Majid filed formal police charges against the 13 members of the gathering for violating the 2005 law against *vani*. Among those charged on

---

2. Interview with Abdul Sattar Qamar, July 5, 2006 pg. 423
3. Interview with Abdul Sattar Qamar, July 5, 2006 pg. 423
4. Interview with Abdul Sattar Qamar, July 5, 2006 pg. 423
5. Interview with Abdul Sattar Qamar, July 5, 2006 pg. 424

July 5 2006 under Section 310-A of the Pakistan Penal Code was Hazoor Bakhsh, Mukhtar Mai's brother.

Hazoor Bakhsh admitted his presence at the gathering. He defended the decision to settle the feud through vani. But he said he was not the only one responsible, and denied accusations by some that he was the head of the gathering.

"I settled this case in the best interests of the two families because they are related. I saved them from running from pillar to post with litigation and fees," Hazoor Bakhsh said.[6]

"I don't deny that I attended this '*akath*'. But I was not on a '*panchayat*'. I am not responsible for sending the girl with Rasul Bakhsh. Our opponents are exploiting the situation to defame us."

Mukhtar Mai cried persecution.

"My brother is innocent and had no concern with the *panchayat*. Some political opponents are maligning him. If he is guilty of this crime then he should be prosecuted," she said in a telephone interview.[7]

"My brother was supporting the Dummer clan in the recent by-election and they lost. Now our opponents are making baseless propaganda against us."

She seemed unaware that her brother had already admitted at least twice publicly to his presence at the gathering, and to his support of its decision.

Three of the 13 charged men were arrested. But not Mukhtar Mai's brother. When she finally broke her silence to speak to reporters, she claimed that the charge was in fact against another Hazoor Bakhsh of the Kharos clan.

\* \* \* \*

Punnu Jatoi was working at the shopfront flour mill on the edges of Jatoi township when he heard about the mirror-image case.

"Why don't the authorities arrest Mukhtar Mai's brother? Why are they reluctant to give justice to Faizan? Is Mukhtar Mai's family above the law?", he asked bitterly.[8]

"This story is to some extent identical to my sister Salma's case. We are waiting for the help of the Almighty. The Gujjar family have always been tyrants."

"Mukhtar Mai has been exposed by using her influence to save the skin of her brother."

\* \* \* \*

---

6.  Interview with Abdul Sattar Qamar, July 1, 2006 pg. 424
7.  Interview with Abdul Sattar Qamar, July 5, 2006 pg. 425
8.  Interview with Abdul Sattar Qamar, July 5, 2006 pg. 425

It was a mirror image of the gathering that met on June 22, 2002. A cry of rape; the menfolk gather to thrash out a compromise compensation; the agreed-upon compensation or 'sulah' takes the form of a compensatory bride from the alleged rapist's family; a prayer leader performs a rushed nikah; the woman, her will disregarded, is taken away by the man who has won her as compensation booty; the deal falls apart the next day when the 'bride's' family raises objection; one of the families then goes to the police and lodges rape charges.

This time, witnesses say, it was Mukhtar's own brother sanctioning the compensatory marriage to atone for an alleged rape. Some of those present say he was the head of the gathering.

Hazoor Bakhsh himself says he was just an observer.

Eight men who say they were just observers at the June 2002 gathering that saw Mukhtar handed over in compensation have been in jail since March 2005 – despite being acquitted in trial.

Perhaps Hazoor Bakhsh, his prestige burnished by his sister's high-profile stature over the intervening four years—had stepped into the mirror.

# Epilogue

Mukhtar Mai's endeavours to raise the conditions of under-privileged women in rural Pakistan are ceaseless. She is expanding her girls' primary school, establishing a high school, setting up a health centre and welfare centre for women. She gives succour to those abused, and shows them the way to fight. She has evolved into a quiet but powerful symbol of women's rights. The attention on her case made her a lightning rod for channeling world attention on under-privileged and abused women. She calls herself their *"beacon of light"*. She is hailed by international political and rights leaders, and is invited to address the US Senate and Congress.

From an illiterate peasant sharing her parents' humble hamlet home with goats and water buffaloes, to an internationally-lauded celebrity heroine sharing a table with Hollywood celebrities at international galas, Mukhtar Mai's elevation to icon of women's rights has been meteoric.

But the question that begs to be asked—and it should not be considered bold or daring or taboo—is whether, in the process of iconisation, one has lost sight of getting to the full truth and thus nearer to justice.

What happens when iconisation and our hunger for a heroine collide with a complex reality that is too hard to simplify in a few pithy lines for a magazine or television piece? What is our idea of justice? What is the price of iconisation?

Is it just that people who have been accused but not convicted should spend five years plus in jail, despite court acquittals, to set an example? When it has been pointed out that many of the 14 men in jail may be innocent of rape or abetment (of rape), some people respond that they should stay in jail nevertheless to serve as a high-profile warning to potential rapists. Does guilt by association justify prolonged incarceration without conviction? Perhaps they remain in jail so Pakistan's leaders can tell the world that they take crimes against women seriously. Perhaps, as blurred memories blur truths, they are unwittingly atoning for the sins of men before them.

While distinguished human rights activists and Western officials jostle to hail the soft-spoken woman from a Pakistani village, there has been little scrutiny of the events and claims that propelled her into the world spotlight and on to the circuit of US and European awards ceremonies.

Forgotten in the flurry of adulation are the 13 voiceless men who remain in prison despite the quashing of charges against them.

The real question that committed rights activists should be asking is whether some of these men are heads-on-platters served up to the West to prove Pakistan's leaders' proclaimed policy of 'enlightened moderation'.

Mukhtar Mai may never have set out to cry rape, and she may never have had any grasp of the significance of what was happening in her name. She may well have been swept along in a chain of events that was well out of her hands, manipulated by a gallery of characters with separate agendas and vendettas.

There is no question of the good wand she has waved over the affair by seizing on it as a catalyst to enlighten the illiterate cotton-picking girls of her village, using the government compensation money to set up a school and campaign for better conditions for women.

But let's not forget the voiceless men who have been on death-row and remain in miserable prison cells today, for crimes they have been acquitted of.

Mukhtar Mai is without doubt a victim of many injustices: the chattelisation of women by their families in rural areas; handed over by her family to the men of an enemy clan to atone for her brother's sin in a perpetuation of the old tribal traditions of 'vani' and 'watta-satta'; manipulated by others pushing their own agendas.

Let's examine carefully whether another injustice is being perpetuated against the men in prison, and against the wives, daughters and sons of those men.

Islamabad,
October 2007

# Glossary

| | |
|---|---|
| **Akath:** | gathering of one clan from *ikatha*: (Sanskrit) 'collected together in one place' |
| **Astanja:** | ablutions of genitals before prayer |
| **Badla:** | revenge |
| **Biraderi:** | clan; extended family within a tribe |
| **Diyat:** | compensation |
| **Ghairat:** | honour; respect |
| **Izzat:** | honour |
| **Nikah:** | solemnization of a marriage |
| **Nikahnama:** | marriage certificate |
| **Sharai Nikah:** | oral marriage, without written certificate |
| **Panchayat:** | an informal council of elders and senior figures representing several tribes in a village |
| **Rukhsti:** | the delivery of a bribe by her menfolk to the family of the groom. (*has come to denote consummation of a marriage*) |
| **Sulah:** | compromise agreement to end a quarrel |
| **Vani:** | the custom of giving away a girl as a drudge-bride to compensate for the crime of her father, uncle or brother and save the male relative from jail or death sentence |
| **Watta-Satta:** | exchange marriage (one family gives a bride away to another family, and receives a bride from that family in exchange) |
| **Zina:** | (Arabic) fornication |
| **Zina-bil-jabr:** | fornication by force |
| **Ziadti:** | variation of zina, implying either fornication, adultery, molestation or rape |

# Index